INSIDE THE MINDS

Navigating Fashion Law

Leading Lawyers on Exploring the Trends, Cases, and Strategies of Fashion Law

ASPATORE

Inside the Minds Project Manager, Tiffany Smith; edited by Melissa Silvanic; proofread by Melanie Zimmerman

For additional copies or customer service inquiries, please e-mail west.customer.service@thomson.com.

ISBN 978-0-314-28057-2

Mat #41255155

Praise for *Inside the Minds*

"This series provides a practical and focused discussion of the leading issues in law today." – John V. Biernacki, Partner, Jones Day

"*Inside the Minds* draws from the collective experience of the best professionals. The books are informative from an academic, and, more importantly, practical perspective. I highly recommend them." – Keith M. Aurzada, Partner, Bryan Cave LLP

"Aspatore's *Inside the Minds* series provides practical, cutting edge advice from those with insight into the real world challenges that confront businesses in the global economy." – Michael Bednarek, Partner, Shearman & Sterling LLP

"What to read when you want to be in the know—topical, current, practical, and useful information on areas of the law that everyone is talking about." – Erika L. Morabito, Partner, Patton Boggs LLP

"Some of the best insight around from sources in the know" – Donald R. Kirk, Shareholder, Fowler White Boggs PA

"The *Inside the Minds* series provides a unique window into the strategic thinking of key players in business and law." – John M. Sylvester, Partner, K&L Gates LLP

"Comprehensive analysis and strategies you won't find anywhere else." – Stephen C. Stapleton, Of Counsel, Dykema Gossett PLLC

"The *Inside the Minds* series is a real hands-on, practical resource for cutting edge issues." – Trey Monsour, Partner, Haynes and Boone LLP

"A tremendous resource, amalgamating commentary from leading professionals that is presented in a concise, easy to read format." – Alan H. Aronson, Shareholder, Akerman Senterfitt

"Unique and invaluable opportunity to gain insight into the minds of experienced professionals." – Jura C. Zibas, Partner, Lewis Brisbois Bisgaard & Smith LLP

"A refreshing collection of strategic insights, not dreary commonplaces, from some of the best of the profession." – Roger J. Magnuson, Partner, Dorsey & Whitney LLP

"Provides valuable insights by experienced practitioners into practical and theoretical developments in today's ever-changing legal world." – Elizabeth Gray, Partner, Willkie, Farr & Gallagher LLP

"This series provides invaluable insight into the practical experiences of lawyers in the trenches." – Thomas H. Christopher, Partner, Kilpatrick Stockton LLP

ASPATORE

Aspatore Books, a Thomson Reuters business, exclusively publishes C-Level executives and partners from the world's most respected companies and law firms. Each publication provides professionals of all levels with proven business and legal intelligence from industry insiders—direct and unfiltered insight from those who know it best. Aspatore Books is committed to publishing an innovative line of business and legal titles that lay forth principles and offer insights that can have a direct financial impact on the reader's business objectives.

Each chapter in the *Inside the Minds* series offers thought leadership and expert analysis on an industry, profession, or topic, providing a future-oriented perspective and proven strategies for success. Each author has been selected based on their experience and C-Level standing within the business and legal communities. *Inside the Minds* was conceived to give a first-hand look into the leading minds of top business executives and lawyers worldwide, presenting an unprecedented collection of views on various industries and professions.

CONTENTS

Fiat Fashion Law! The Launch of a Label—and a New Branch of Law

Susan Scafidi
Professor and Academic Director
Fashion Law Institute at
Fordham University School of Law

ASPATORE

Introduction

Fashion Law. As long as there have been fashion houses—and almost as long as there have been people making clothes—there have been occasions to consult lawyers. When I first imagined a legal field devoted to the fashion industry, schools did not teach fashion law courses, bar associations did not recognize the subject, and law firms did not specialize in it as an area of law. The words "fashion" and "law" were not linked, and fashion law was not a recognized area of legal expertise.

Today, a few short years later, there is a legal field made to measure for the business of fashion. This chapter is an opportunity to read the label of this growing legal field, from origin and content, to care instructions and even size, and to reflect on the law's new fit with fashion.

Origin: Imagining a Field of Fashion Law

You may already know the story of fashion law's origin and road to respectability, or at least its outlines. It is a history I have been asked to recount many times by individuals and by audiences of lawyers, designers, and students around the globe, and it goes back to a question that first occurred to me in law school. As an aspiring scholar and then a junior professor, I did not set out to launch a new field of law, to tap into deep family background in the fashion industry, or even to combine my interests in law and fashion on a professional level, but I could not resist exploring the intersection of the two.

As the story progressed, there entered the villains: the myopic senior academics who over a decade ago all but forbade research on the topic. In their minds, the subject was "too girly" and "too frivolous," and they insisted that "no one will take you seriously." (Never mind the fascinating theoretical issues involved and the fact that fashion is a trillion-dollar industry.) With the tenure system being what it is, it seemed the better part of wisdom to write on other subjects and quietly continue to expand the research file on fashion. One bright spot along the way was a book by Jeanne Belhumeur, *Droit International de la Mode* (2000), which translates as *The International Law of Fashion*, but this slender volume in French from a northern Italian publisher was so rare that I had to track down a copy in

Quebec. Unfortunately, this and other books covering specific aspects of what I had come to conceptualize as a single subject had no apparent impact on the academics who scoffed at the idea of combining law and fashion. Over time, my other research interests became a book of their own, and the fashion law file and related books and exhibits filled first a closet and then a room.

My post-tenure return to writing in the area of law and fashion initially took the form of a website, something that could be shared beyond the ivory tower and could reach readers immediately. *Counterfeit Chic* (www.counterfeitchic.com) was the first blog to connect the legal community with the fashion world, and it was welcomed with amazing warmth by both legal bloggers on one hand and fashion bloggers on the other, not to mention the traditional mainstream media. Fellow law professors were immersed in a debate over whether blogs could constitute scholarship, but even as they argued, they also read and borrowed—and assigned the website to their students.

Who knew that a field of law could be launched by a blog?

Entering Law School

Then it was on to the classroom and a law school that would risk adding a newly imagined course to its curriculum. It took a fair amount of convincing—and a place where students who had read the blog championed the course, faculty members supported it, and the administration was willing to approve it. I will never forget the wonderful colleague who insisted, "We have sports law. In fact, we have two sections of sports law. Why can we not have fashion law?" But to seal the deal, it took a dean whose spouse had spent years working at Saks Fifth Avenue.

Even then, there were voices of doubt regarding the first fashion law course, like the administrator who warned that the class would be canceled if it had less than three students, and the student who expressed interest but asked if we could call it something else. As it happened, enrollment did turn out to be a problem: the course was oversubscribed from the very first time it was offered, and we were flooded with requests from not only our own student body but also neighboring schools and community members seeking to audit. In an effort to dampen demand, the first lecture included the top ten reasons to drop the course, including the fact that "Fashion Law" would appear on student transcripts and might require some explanation. The warning had no effect, and we have now expanded the curriculum to half a dozen different fashion law-related courses.

Fashion's Cultural Moment

A combination of cultural trends and timing helped further the cause as well. Fashion is having a cultural moment. Once upon a time little kids wanted to grow up to be celebrities; now celebrities want to grow up to be fashion designers. Large screens and small ones bring us not only images of gowns on the red carpet but also aspiring designers sitting behind sewing machines. On the legal side, I learned shortly after I started speaking publicly on the then-obscure issue that had first captured my attention—the relative lack of intellectual property protection for fashion designs under US law—that the fashion industry had decided to revisit the question as well. Despite the many hours involved, it has been a privilege to share my original research with members of Congress and the proponents of reform, first the Council of Fashion Designers of America (CFDA) and more recently the American Apparel and Footwear Association, and also with so many of you. Whatever your position, it is an issue that was too long ignored—though far from the only one.

But the most persuasive force of all, the one that did the most to silence the skeptics, was you. That is, the millions of readers who have celebrated *Counterfeit Chic*, devoured news reports, and opened this book. Fashion law emerged as not only a field but also a community of designers and lawyers, students and scholars, creators and copyists, fashionisti and ultimately friends.

Fast forward to today, when fashion law has shed the question mark ("Fashion law? Really?") and added an exclamation point ("Fashion law—cool!"). One day soon, it will be like health law, entertainment law, banking law, and other industry-specific fields—simply "fashion law." Period. There are a growing number of forward-thinking bar association sections and blogs, lawyers and law firms that focus on the field. Additional schools have begun to follow suit, renaming and refocusing previous courses or creating new ones. And the Fashion Law Institute, a nonprofit and the world's first academic center devoted to the field, was established in 2010 with the help of the CFDA and its president, Diane von Furstenberg. The Institute is currently based at Fordham Law School, and it is a source of information, training, and assistance for members of both the legal and fashion communities. From blog to org in five years—talk about fast fashion!

Content: Defining a Field of Law

So what is fashion law, exactly?

It is a field that embraces the legal substance of style, including the issues that may arise throughout the life of a garment, starting with the designer's original idea and continuing all the way to the consumer's closet. As a course, we defined fashion law to include four basic pillars: intellectual property; business and finance, with subcategories ranging from employment law to real estate; international trade and government regulation, including questions of safety and sustainability; and consumer culture and civil rights. In addition to its central focus on apparel and accessories, fashion law includes related areas such as textile production, modeling, media, and the beauty and fragrance industries.

From a practice perspective, fashion law may include the representation of clients engaged in the design, manufacturing, distribution, or retail sectors, among others, or even of consumers. While many of these stakeholders are part of an elaborate global system and work closely together, requiring an emphasis on licensing and other transactional work, others are structurally at odds with one another. For example, the interests of domestic manufacturers and importers often differ, as do the perspectives of creative designers and fast-fashion copyists. This complicates the policymaking process for the fashion industry, which is far from monolithic. Of course, as with all legal fields, fashion law requires swords as well as plowshares, and the fashion industry sees its fair share of litigation.

Intellectual Property—and Much More

Among these many issues, the ones closest to my heart (and at the core of my original expertise) involve intellectual property. This accounts for the trademark-inflected title of *Counterfeit Chic*, a deliberately multivalent concept that invites exploration of the tension between innovation and imitation. Unfortunately, my own emphasis on intellectual property and public engagement with the debate over IP and fashion design requires me to accept at least partial responsibility for the most prominent misconception regarding fashion law—at least apart from wry observations about the fashion police swooping in to issue citations for wearing white shoes after Labor Day or sheer stockings with sandals. (Actually, the latter probably calls for stiff sanctions.)

To set the record straight: not only are fashion lawyers distinct from the fashion police, but fashion law also includes more than intellectual property law. A great deal more. While side-by-side comparisons of handbag designs and their alleged knockoffs or bloody disputes over red-soled shoes are visually compelling and intellectually engaging, they do not begin to exhaust the range of issues important to the fashion industry or the attorneys who serve it. That said, included as Appendices A and B are the most recent iteration of the fashion design protection legislation pending before the US Congress, which I assisted in drafting, and my original testimony regarding the first introduction of the bill. Once some version of this narrowly tailored protection is officially declared a perfect fit, the US system will be in closer harmony with other IP-producing nations, and emerging designers in particular will have a long-awaited legal shield against copying. Consumers, too, will benefit from more varied choices from fast-fashion houses forced to interpret trends rather than slavishly copy individual garments. Perhaps best of all, fashion law will be able to move away from extended analogies regarding design pirates walking the plank or the extermination of design parasites and focus publicly on a broader range of issues.

Beyond a Reasonable Doubt

No modern discussion of a newly defined field of law would be complete without reference to Judge Frank Easterbrook's infamous dismissal of cyberlaw in the mid-1990s as akin to "law of the horse." Easterbrook urged instead the study of general rules, arguing that focus on a specialized field "is doomed to be shallow and to miss unifying principles." Frank H. Easterbrook, *Cyberspace and the Law of the Horse*, 1996 U. CH. L. FORUM 207,

207 (1996). Larry Lessig and other professors in the field begged to differ, and today cyberlaw is not only a regular fixture in the law school curriculum but also a recognized practice area. *See* Lawrence Lessig, *The Law of the Horse: What Cyberlaw Might Teach*, 113 HARV. L. REV. 501 (1999).

Fashion is an ancient industry whose legal concerns have long awaited systematic recognition, attention, clarification, and instruction. Fashion law is thus both older and younger than cyberlaw—and an equally valid endeavor. Rather than argue over the relative merits of general principles versus industry-specific foci, the legal profession is better served by remembering Frederic W. Maitland's observation that writing about any piece of history, including his own work in the history of law, requires tearing a "seamless web." F.W. Maitland, *A Prologue to a History of English Law*, 14 L. QTRLY REV. 13, 13 (1898). Similarly, studying or practicing in any one area of law, whether a black-letter course or a specialized industry, necessarily reveals certain connections and synergies while ignoring others. The fabric of fashion law is cut from the broader bolt of the law, but so is every other specific legal field.

Care Instructions: Becoming a Fashion Lawyer

While some aspects of the fashion industry are glamorous and/or mysterious from an outside perspective, others are extremely familiar. Most of us wear clothes most of the time, and as Mark Twain observed, "Naked people have little or no influence on society." Relatively few people have been backstage at Fashion Week or studied the details of apparel production and distribution, but we are more comfortable in our clothes than we are in our own skin. This combination of allure and intimacy with the subject matter no doubt accounts for some of the appeal of fashion law and its rapid growth as a newly defined field. Fashion is fun, particularly as it relates to self-fashioning, and it's no wonder that it attracts both practicing and aspiring attorneys.

Becoming an excellent fashion lawyer, however, requires a bit more than aggressive marketing, a "passion for fashion" (a phrase that should henceforth be banished from all cover letters), or a dedication to developing one's own wardrobe. Several years ago, I wrote a brief response to the many inquiries I received from aspiring fashion lawyers wondering how to enter the field. Susan Scafidi, *Fashion Law*, COUNTERFEIT CHIC, http://www.counterfeitchic.com/2008/09/fashion_law_1.php. It cautioned against trying to practice fashion law for the wrong reasons, like enjoying fashion but not particularly liking law. Fashion lawyers are lawyers first, and a contract is still a contract, whether the client is selling couture creations or widgets.

Since fashion law is such a recently defined field, very few lawyers who could currently claim to practice it actually started out doing so. In fact, quite a few still prefer to define themselves according to more established specialties like tax or consumer products law, even if many of their clients are in the fashion industry. This is already changing, as students and even prospective students learn of the field of fashion law and chart a course for the general counsel's office of their favorite label. I have received many e-mails from college and even high school students interested in the area. As any challenging and creative career, and indeed any other area related to the fashion industry, fashion law is quickly becoming competitive.

Still, there are a number of basic strategies to turn you into a legal asset to the fashion industry. The following are a few basic tips for entering the field:

Excel at Law

Potential employers will not hire you for your eagerness to chat about the latest season or trend. They may, however, hire you for your excellent grades, achievements, and references. While a degree of enthusiasm for a prospective job is fine, it's far easier to hire a star legal eaglet who can learn to apply her skills to the needs of a fashion client than it is to hire a starry-eyed fashionista and teach her how to read a case. As a colleague of mine says, "You cannot teach smart." And yes, dear follower of fashion, you are up against stereotype.

Think Laterally

As with other "cool" areas of law, you cannot expect fashion law jobs to come to you. Law firms typically do not visit campus in search of fashion lawyers. And, like other companies looking for in-house counsel, fashion houses rarely hire directly out of school, at least in the United States. Consider instead interning, if you are still in school, or joining a firm with fashion clients and requesting work on their issues as it arises. If you are connected within the fashion industry, let acquaintances know you are out there and engage in the fine art of rainmaking. Do not disdain pro bono opportunities that are within your skill set. And, if the opportunity arises, marry into a fashion family.

Do Your Homework

Read news stories, look at case documents, and troll websites for information on who is growing a legal practice in the fashion field. It is still extremely diffuse at this point—many attorneys have had a fashion client or two—but there are already significant nodes of experience in many cities. New York is, of course, the center of the American fashion industry, but do not overlook L.A., San Francisco, Chicago, your own hometown, or the myriad of international opportunities.

Do Not Cut Corners

If you are going to serve the fashion world well, you need to know as much about the industry and its legal issues as possible, and you need to stay current—for your clients' sake, as well as your own. I have personally offered many continuing legal education programs and courses, and as bar associations and other schools join the trend, there will be more opportunities out there. On a daily basis, read the latest news online, in industry papers, and in the business press.

And most importantly:

Make Yourself Uniquely Valuable

On an episode of the TV show *Mad Men*, a character summed up her career philosophy: "This is America. Pick a job, and then become the person that does it." Whether or not you are reading this stateside, it is brilliant advice for an emerging field. While I am flattered by those who tell me, "I want to do what you do," you must think about the possibilities for forging a path of your own. Intellectual property is a key area within fashion law, but it is also a crowded one. You could also develop a specialty in M&A, securities law, mediation, employment law, international trade, or any number of other areas that we have made part of the fashion law curriculum. Learn, think, practice, write, speak—and turn yourself into a genuine expert in your own niche.

Fashion law was launched not as a mere branding opportunity, but as a means of training lawyers and designers and of promoting research and legal services related to the business of fashion. If you turn initial interest into true expertise, think of your clients and not merely your closet or your wallet, and love the law, you will be mentally dressed for success.

Size: Tailoring Law to Fit Fashion

Fashion itself is one of the largest industries in the world, and the second-largest in New York City alone. So where have the fashion lawyers been all this time?

The relative neglect of the fashion industry by the legal profession and certainly by the legal academy over the years has less to do with the importance of fashion and more to do with what I have called its status as a pink-and-lavender discipline, one primarily associated with women and gay men, as well as men of color (and those willing to wear it). For a new generation of attorneys, this is an opportunity. It is the chance to develop a field outside of the influence of more traditional networks and hierarchies, and to form a legal community in support of a creative industry.

Fashion is a big business and an innovative one. For those on the cutting edge of a newly labeled and defined field, the possibilities are immeasurable.

Conclusion

Turning an idea and a group of issues into a defined field of law, a field into a course, and a course into a curriculum, an academic center, and a community has required many individuals to believe in this project and to add their own efforts to the cause of tailoring law to fit fashion. Going forward, the fashion industry will no longer have to settle for hand-me-down legislation and borrowed lawyers, but will have a body of law suited to any occasion.

Fiat fashion law!

Key Takeaways

- Yes, there is now a field of fashion law! It embraces the legal substance of style, including the issues that may arise throughout the life of a garment, starting with the designer's original idea and continuing all the way to the consumer's closet.
- Fashion law includes intellectual property issues, but also much more. Aspiring fashion lawyers can also develop specialties in fields like mergers and acquisitions, securities law, international trade, tax, mediation, employment law, or any number of fields that we have made part of the fashion law curriculum. Learn, think, practice, write, speak, and turn yourself into a genuine expert in your own niche.
- The best fashion lawyers are lawyers first—but also know a great deal about the business of fashion and can translate between the two worlds.
- Entering the field of fashion law often requires thinking laterally. Consider interning or joining a firm with fashion clients and requesting work on their issues as they arise. If you are connected within the fashion industry, let acquaintances know you are out there and engage in the fine art of rainmaking. Seek out pro bono opportunities that are within your skill set.
- Stay current on fashion law. Continuing legal education programs and courses provide excellent educational opportunities. On a daily basis, read the latest news online, in industry papers, and in the business press.
- Fashion law was launched not as a branding opportunity, but as a means of training lawyers and designers and of promoting research and legal services related to the business of fashion. Think of your clients, not just your closet or your wallet, and you will be mentally dressed for success.

Related Resources

- Counterfeit Chic, http://www.countefeitchic.com.
- Susan Scafidi, *Intellectual Property and Fashion Design*, 1 INTELLECTUAL PROPERTY AND INFORMATION WEALTH 115 (Peter K. Yu ed., 2006).

Susan Scafidi is a professor and the founder and academic director of the Fashion Law Institute*, a nonprofit based at the* Fordham *University School of Law and the world's first center dedicated to legal issues involving the fashion industry. She is also the first law professor ever to offer a course in fashion law and is internationally recognized for her expertise and her leadership in establishing the field. She has testified regarding the proposed extension of US legal protection to fashion designs and continues to work actively with members of Congress and the fashion industry on the proposed Innovative Design Protection and Piracy Prevention Act (formerly the Design Piracy Prohibition Act) and other issues. Professor Scafidi has spoken to legal, design, and academic audiences around the globe and has contributed commentary to hundreds of media reports on issues related to law and the fashion industry.*

Prior to establishing the Fashion *Law Institute, with the assistance of the Council of* Fashion *Designers of America and its president, Diane von Furstenberg, Professor Scafidi was a tenured member of both the law and history faculties at SMU and taught at a number of other law schools, including Yale and Georgetown. After attending Duke University and the Yale Law School, she pursued graduate study in legal history at Berkeley and the University of Chicago and clerked for Judge Morris S. Arnold of the Eighth Circuit Court of Appeals. Professor Scafidi is the author of the book* Who Owns Culture? Appropriation and Authenticity in American Law, *as well as numerous articles in the areas of intellectual property, cultural property, and of course, fashion law. In addition, she created and maintains the first website on fashion law,* Counterfeit Chic, *which has been recognized as one of the ABA's top 100 legal blogs.*

A Fashionable Career

Monica B. Richman

Partner

SNR Denton

ASPATORE

Introduction

Fashion law is not a traditional legal specialty, like tax or employment law. Rather, "fashion law" is a *nom de guerre* for the mélange of legal specialties that are needed by clients in the fashion industry. Over the course of a season, the many participants in the fashion world, including designers, manufacturers, importers/exporters, retailers, salvagers, test laboratories, and the lawyers who service them, confront a wide range of legal issues in disparate areas such as real estate, tax, intellectual property/licensing, customs, employment, privacy/and data security, and litigation. Fashion law is the combination of all of these and still more legal specialties that are necessary to support doing business in the modern fashion industry.

The best fashion lawyer is the one who truly "gets" the client's business. Given the complexity of the fashion business, it is essential to understand that clients want to operate their stores, sell their handbags, get their clothes to the market, or do whatever it is that they are in the business of doing because fashion is a business that must succeed to survive. Clients do not want long-winded legal theories. They do want you to take care of the problem and get the deal done, literally. That is your job as far as the client is concerned. The lawyer knows it must be done in compliance with the law and within certain other ethical and doctrinal principles as is true for business lawyers generally. The fashion lawyer also should understand the distinctive nature of the fashion industry and provide creative, cost-effective solutions that address the challenges of those distinctions, which often concern the fact that fashion, by its nature, changes quickly. Time, literally, is of the essence, for fashion clients. In order for the client to thrive in the fashion business, the fashion lawyer must provide top-notch counsel that is delivered with speed as well as accuracy. My best advice: know your client's business and understand that what is at stake requires you to appreciate the importance of timing for fashion.

I learned about timing before I became a fashion lawyer. I was supposed to be the CEO of a thriving retail and wholesale music company. My father opened my family's first record store (if you remember records!) when I was about three years old and our chain grew to twenty-five stores in the Northeast. We also were one of the largest regional wholesalers in the business, supplying independent music stores in six states. By the time I was fifteen years old, I knew and loved that business. By the time I was eighteen years old, I had worked as a cashier and as a bookkeeper and in our purchasing, returns, shipping, and fulfillment departments. I went to business school. I spent my summers in our warehouse (without air conditioning) to learn the business from the ground up. I learned how to run a retail store and how to manage a warehouse. I learned about employee conflicts and employee theft, cash flow, bank loans, inventory controls, and real estate. I learned that there is a causal relationship between selling a product and making a living. In brief, I learned how to run a business. If our stores did not do well, my family did not do well. If we went under, many people would lose their jobs. Then something happened in the late 1980s. The retail and wholesale world started changing.

When we could no longer renew our leases or obtain new ones because malls wanted national chain stores, our stores closed. Our wholesale business filed for bankruptcy. A big factor for our business was an inability to extend bank financing while the record companies demanded payment in ever-shorter timeframes. I learned a lot about life and business before turning twenty-five. Then I went to law school because I needed to earn a living. It seemed to me then that not only was law a profession, but it was also a business, and that I could combine my business background and legal training to create a unique business lawyer.

You do not have to have to operate a retail or wholesale business or go to business school or experience bankruptcy to be an effective fashion lawyer, although it probably does not hurt. But fashion lawyers should make a point of having some familiarity with bankruptcy law. You do need to get an understanding of the relevant legal principles and get into the minds of your clients. You need to appreciate what it is that keeps your clients up at night. Know their business. So, absent a decade in the retail trenches, think about the fashion business as a business and read about it. Read the trade magazines and the blogs. Learn about it. Learn how clothes are made, where beads are sourced, about factories, how merchants chose which brands to carry. Ask your client questions. Where do they see issues? What is their five-year plan? How can you be most helpful? Pay attention. Is your client selling online? If not, why not? Who will do the fulfillment? Is your client expanding into new markets, new countries? Is your client seeking new financial partners? What are the terms being considered? Can you help structure a better deal? Identify issues before your client sees them. Fashion is a highly competitive business, often with narrow profit margins. Many fashion companies will falter and go out of business. Your job is to help your clients stay in business and they will come to rely on you to compete in an incredibly competitive and often unpleasant environment. It is your job to make all that happen while remaining in compliance with the law.

Always support your clients and promote their businesses. When one jewelry designer client was running into cash flow problems, I organized a sample sale of her excess inventory. The sale garnered the right kind of attention, earned her badly needed cash, and moved inventory. When another client could not get needed fabric released from her supplier, I personally visited the supplier's office and negotiated a deal that resulted in the fabric being shipped to her factory that day. Without that fabric, the bridesmaid dresses that were on order would not have been ready for a wedding. For want of a nail, a kingdom would have been lost. For that client, in that situation, there would have been some very unhappy brides and quite a few bridal stores that never would have done business with my client again. I proudly wear my clients' shoes, clothes, and handbags. Every holiday season, I give gifts to my clients that were manufactured by other clients. They know I support them and they appreciate it. You walk the talk, every day, just as they do.

Who is a "Fashion Lawyer"?

In the last decade or so, the term "fashion lawyer" was coined. Fashion lawyers represent designers, retailers, wholesalers, manufacturers, and others in the chain from concept to consumer. Attorneys who work in-house for fashion companies focus 100 percent of their time on fashion and many, being in-house counsel, also are generalists who do get to practice in a variety of areas. Others, who work in larger law departments, often for major retailers, may be more specialized and may spend most of their time on real estate leasing (the stores), marketing/advertising (including the emerging issues involving social media, and online advertising versus traditional print), trademark/brand protection, and litigation. If the company is smaller, the in-house attorneys are more likely to be generalists and seek outside counsel for specialty areas. Some are start-ups or smaller entities that have no in-house counsel at all and rely on one attorney in private practice as an informal general counsel. Effectively then, for both in-house and outside counsel, a "fashion lawyer" really is an attorney who services clients in the fashion industry rather than an attorney bound to a specific section of the federal code or a particular historic collection of doctrines such as torts or contracts. Fashion lawyers counsel and represent people and companies who make, sell, and otherwise deal with fashion, in all aspects of the law.

Meeting with Clients

When you meet initially with a client, discuss what the client needs and try to understand what makes that client's company unique. Quite a few fashion businesses are family businesses. I represent one company that is in its third generation of family ownership and another company created by a husband and wife and now that brand is sold in the finest stores in the world. Understanding clients and what market niche they are serving and their short and long-term goals is what you need to be effective.

Small Companies versus Large Established Companies

Designers may be creative geniuses, but they are not necessarily good business people. They will look to you for help in raising money and running their business. They may not distinguish between an incipient crisis and a routine issue. You may get crazy phone calls at crazy hours. Many small companies do not have much cash flow, especially in the beginning. If they cannot pay you for a while, you may have to finance the legal work and hope you are paid someday. It may even turn out to be a good investment if the company grows. Ask yourself, do you want this role and for how long?

Established fashion businesses have different needs. They often have in-house legal counsel or a team of in-house lawyers, so that outside counsel generally is needed as a specialist in a certain area. Or, if an established business does not have in-house counsel, it generally relies on an astute executive who handles legal matters with the assistance of outside counsel that are consulted when necessary. If you serve in this role, it generally is as a trusted advisor to a smart and successful business in an exciting industry, which is a fate to be earned, and once earned, very much enjoyed.

What Else Do You Have to Know to Know Your Clients' Business?

The challenge in representing a variety of clients is ensuring that you know each of their various businesses and if that is not enough of a challenge, you have to keep learning as those businesses evolve. You also have to be knowledgeable in a variety of legal areas and stay up-to-date in each of those areas. Then you must take all of that and keep blending the business knowledge and the legal expertise. It is not enough, for example, to be an intellectual property attorney. You must know how intellectual property pertains to the fashion industry generally and to each of your clients particularly. Do you know when to seek copyright protection for a fabric design or patent protection for a handbag? When to register your client's trademarks with Customs? How to budget and manage a worldwide trademark program? Seize counterfeit goods?

As my specialty is IP, I address these issues every day in a fashion practice. I also need to keep my skills at the ready on contract and other issues and have associates at the ready to provide support in those areas in which I am not an expert, for example, the ever-changing tax code.

The key is managing both information about the general legal and business segments and understanding, in depth, each client's particular aspect of the fashion business. Each fashion segment has unique issues. Shoes are different from coats. I have visited my client's warehouses, their offices, and even some of their suppliers. I have toured client operations and met various employees, including those who make patterns, cut samples, do fittings, manage accounts, and process orders. I meet the creators of the designs and attend fashion shows, even on Sundays, in the pouring rain and "off the clock" because the client knows when the fashion lawyer is on the client's side.

One aspect of fashion law that differs from many other types of law is the emphasis on the seasonal nature of many of the fashion clients' needs. As a fashion lawyer, you have to get used to the cycles. The prestige shoe business presents four collections annually, with product that will not be in the market for at least nine months, while the clothing industry shows major, fall/spring collections twice a year for product that will be in the stores in less than six months. The bridal industry has a bi-annual market similar to the general clothing industry, but bridal is on a different schedule and, of course, there are other mini-seasons for cruise and other specialties. Something is always changing. Currently, the fine jewelry business is changing due to a shift in regulation and commodity pricing. There is no rest for the fashion lawyer, regardless of the segment.

Licensing in the Fashion World

Licensing plays a significant part in fashion law because it is often an effective way to create or expand a product line without a significant financial investment from the licensor and a quick way for the licensor to become a player in a new category. It allows growth without existing supplier relationships or the expertise to expand into a new category, for example, an expansion from clothing to handbags.

Licensing is a prime example why you need to understand how your client does business. There is a general structure to a license and most licenses will cover many of the same terms, such as a product, minimum sales, royalty rates, duration/renewal, and indemnification. However, there are many nuances to the fashion license and knowing the niche business for which you are doing a license is essential.

License Relationships

License relationships are delicate. In times of financial hardships, such as what we have termed the "new economy," you are often advising your clients on dealing with downside risk. In fact, a good lawyer always advises on downside risk, even in good economic times. You need to tailor your counsel to your client and its position in a transaction. How far do you want to push? If your licensee has not reached its minimum sales, does your client-licensor want to call a default? Do you want to force the licensee to pay minimum royalties in a bad year, when such action could force the licensee out of business? Is the licensor not cooperating with your licensee-client? Not providing useful feedback in a timely manner? Rejecting product without guidelines or explanation? How do you address an issue in a constructive manner? These are examples of the real world issues that should be considered when drafting a license.

I encourage you to investigate the potential licensor or licensee, as applicable, with whom your client is considering entering into a license. Particularly with small clients as the licensor, your client may not want to dig too deep or "rock the boat." Get that boat rocking while still securely tied to the dock and before your client is out in deep water. What other licenses has the licensee done? Can you speak to a current or past licensee? What is the licensee's distribution network? I have negotiated a few licenses in which the deal was a first license for the would-be licensee. I had a client who had a license in which the licensee had resisted investing in an advertising and marketing budget, rejected minimum sales obligations and minimum royalties, and did not commit to a marketing launch. That licensee did not have a design or sales staff dedicated to my client's product and did not even have a phone number or email account dedicated to the product. These are signs that the licensee is not sufficiently committed and, sure enough, the arrangement was short-lived. If you foresee such a situation, make sure your licensor can get out of the contract relatively pain-free or, at least, make the initial term quite modest. A little Internet research into a potential license party can be a surprisingly good investment before your client commits and takes what may be a ride on a very small boat out onto a very big and tempest-tossed sea.

When negotiating a license, know your audience, which would be the attorney on the other side of the table and that attorney's client. If you are representing or negotiating against a public company, the requirements are going to be stricter in the license. An average license with a public company can be well over fifty pages, whereas a license between two small private companies may be ten pages or less. For public companies, topics such as factory conditions are crucial. A public company will need inspection rights. Who will do the inspections, how often, and who will pay for them should be addressed in the license. What happens if an inspection is failed? The large company also will have very specific reporting mechanisms for product and sales—make sure your licensee can comply with the reporting requirements. A license between two small companies or a small company and an individual designer will be less formal. However, many of the same issues still remain and you should encourage your client to really spell out all key issues in the license. It will save a lot of aggravation later. The fashion lawyer also can share in the fashion industry's eternal optimism and anticipate a long-term success that results in the participants staying in the relationship and becoming bigger entities so make sure the documentation deals effectively with future restructurings and rights of assignments, among other boilerplate provisions.

Understand the Nuances of a Fashion License

Attorneys who are skilled lawyers but not experienced with fashion clients may decide to simply negotiate a license for a new fashion client, concluding that one can learn as one goes. This strategy might work or it might not. One of my favorite license debacle stories happened about four years ago. I represented the licensee and we were negotiating a license with a very famous brand to expand its product line. Counsel for the future licensor, who was a partner at a prestigious firm, sent over its proposed license to start the conversation. As I was reading the license, I noticed that it did not include minimum sales or minimum royalties for the renewal period. The license simply stated the figure that my client needed to reach in net sales to renew the license. I called an executive at my client's company and asked him to review—was I hallucinating? Apparently not. The client and I made a quick decision, let's not negotiate each point that may be more favorable to the licensor. Rather, we got the license signed because we could live with many terms favorable to the licensor given that, in exchange, we had no minimums for the whole renewal period! Sure enough, the famous licensor recently came to us to fix this "mutual mistake" and to "agree" to minimums in the renewal period. We said that in fact there was no mutual mistake, we had negotiated for and knowingly bargained for no minimums during the renewal period. The licensor was quite upset and we have since learned that the licensor has changed counsel. Ouch!

A new client hired me to address problems with one of her licensees that had resulted from her license agreement. The license required the designer to create original designs for fabric and the licensee, a prominent fabric manufacturer, would offer the designer's fabric collection. The arrangement worked fine for about two years. Then, the fabric manufacturer stopped fulfilling orders for the designer's collection and fabric customers contacted my client complaining that they could not get their orders filled. This lack of cooperation by the licensee hurt my client's reputation and her royalties. If you simply read the license, it appeared on its face to be reasonable. But you needed to dig deeper. What was the license missing? The license said nothing about who owned the designs or what recourse my client had in this situation. The license had no minimums and, in fact, had no obligation to produce the actual designs after a first run of the pattern, but the licensor had no right to take the design to a new manufacturer until the term expired. Such a license is not as uncommon as you may think. The fashion lawyer should advise clients against such an arrangement because as surely as the upside will take care of itself, the downside needs to be covered by the specific terms of the agreement.

Certain language may sound innocuous but, as a fashion lawyer, you need to tread carefully. What if a license provides that the licensee can renew the license on terms "substantially similar" to the current license provided the licensee meets a designated sales figure? If you are the licensor, this term is great, it gives you wiggle room. If you represent the licensee, this clause can be a death sentence. Your client has just spent two, three, four, or more years building up this business. You want the right to an automatic renewal on the exact terms you already negotiated—there should be no new negotiations and no arguments over "substantially similar" terms. The only requirement for the renewal should be meeting your sales and royalty obligations.

Some Basic Terms of a Fashion License

There are far too many nuances of a fashion license to discuss all such points in this chapter, but here are just a few highlights of a standard fashion license:

<u>Trademark</u>

What *trademark* is being licensed? If you are the licensor, you want to make it very narrow, for example, just the mark JANE SMITH. The licensor wants to maintain flexibility. If you are the licensee you will want the rights to the mark to be very broad, for example, the mark JANE SMITH and all derivative marks that include "JANE" or "SMITH" and any sub-brands marketed or developed in connection with the JANE SMITH mark. Why is it important to have such a large scope of rights as the licensee? Because unless the license clearly gives such expansive rights to the licensee, then the licensor may create a new sub-brand such as JANE BY JANE SMITH or FOR YOU BY JANE and compete in the same space or perhaps create a less expensive line that competes with your client's license, which can significantly damages licensee sales. Decreases in sales are never welcome, but it could be disastrous if your client can no longer reach the minimum sales figure stated in the license because the licensor has effectively cannibalized the license.

Product

What *products* are being licensed? Again, as the licensor, you want to be very narrow, very specific. Do not just say "bags" or "handbags." You need to list exactly what bags are covered, if you do not, there will be questions later.

Design Process and Product Approval

The design process often is a collaboration between the licensor and the licensee. The license should include a product development calendar and very clearly state the different stages of design and approval and the related timelines. Different parts of the fashion industry will have different product approval mechanisms, with different timelines. For example, the prestige she industry often has twenty-four hours for product approval of the final sample in order to get the shoes in the quarterly shows. The licensor must have a mechanism to review and approve/ reject within the twenty-four hour window. If you represent licensees in this situation, you often will be required to explain the product development calendar to licensor's counsel and why licensor must be required to respond within twenty-four hours or the product must be deemed approved.

Ownership of New Materials

Think carefully about which party is being credited with creating new designs and whether it is subject to intellectual property protection. If your client is a designer, s/he may create designs for use by the licensee of fine china. The designer would want to own the design and have the ability to use or interpret the design for products beyond a particular license, for example, the same design for china may translate well for tablecloths or placemats. Be careful that the license clearly identifies who owns the design and that the grant is of a limited license to use the design on fine china only. If you represent a licensee with multiple, unrelated licensors, be careful of language that a particular license agreement gives that licensor ownership of all product designs and that the licensee will not manufacture "confusingly similar" products for other parties. Such a standard for functional items may be too subjective. I often negotiate for a standard of "identical or nearly identical," which is more objective and better protects the licensee.

General Contracts in the Fashion World

Although licensing is a big issue in the fashion industry, a fashion lawyer may do many other kinds of contracts, including agreements covering manufacturing, distribution, sourcing, technology, real estate, sponsorship, advertising, general corporate matters, factoring, finance, employment, and other topics that cover just about every lawful business activity. As previously noted, no attorney has deep expertise in all of these areas but in-house generalists at fashion companies do tend to have a wide breadth of experience in many of these areas. As outside counsel, you tend to develop an expertise in some areas but seek specialists in others. For example, although my specialty is intellectual property, I have drafted quite a few employee separation agreements for clients, particularly for those I serve as an unofficial general counsel. That said, I have an excellent form agreement that I begin with and I always have an employment specialist bless the final document.

Trademarks and Branding at Home and Abroad

Selecting the Brand

Will the client consult with you before selecting the brand name? Unfortunately, often, no. There are many reasons why counsel was not consulted. The client may have started the brand out of a parental garage and simply picked a name that had meaning to the client who thought it unique. Or, the client may have started the brand under the then current family pet's name without giving it a second. In an ideal world, the client will come to you to before selecting a name to allow you to investigate the potential mark. I started my career as a trademark attorney, so this is one of my specialties. No client wants to adopt a mark, spend time and money building-up the goodwill in the brand, and then learn that there are conflicts with the mark or that it cannot be registered or protected. *See,* 15 U.S.C. §§ 1051-1141 (2006), which is the federal statute for trademark law. Most states also have trademark statutes and unfair competition and fraud laws that help protect trademarks.

Trademark Searching

As trademark counsel, you run various types of searches to determine the availability of the mark. You then present the client with the results of these searches and your opinion on the availability of the mark. This may sound simple but it is sophisticated, strategic work and the stakes are high. Before conducting searches of the mark, learn the client's plans for the brand, because that will influence how you search and evaluate the mark. Is the client interested in world domination or, will the mark only be used in one or two countries? This is a key issue. The client may have no intention of expanding outside the United States but you might want to cover North America when you do file and search internationally anyway because circumstances change and a good attorney needs to be prepared for product and geographic expansion.

There are methods to search online in over sixty trademark country-specific databases around the world. These databases are wonderful resources that provide a good idea of what marks are registered all over the world. You need to carefully structure your search to get the best search results. For example, searching clothing might be obvious if the client wants to select a new brand name for a t-shirt collection. But what about jewelry, bags, and other accessories? What if the mark is clear for clothing but not for jewelry or backpacks? Is that ok? You will not know or be able to counsel effectively unless you do the search.

To be truly effective, it helps to have a working knowledge of many local laws to identify if the hits revealed by the search outside of the United States are an issue. If your budget permits, recommend that local counsel review the search results or run their own searches and provide you with an opinion as most of us are not licensed outside of the United States. Sometimes I am shocked by what is considered a conflict in other countries. For example, BILLY for dresses easily can block SILLY for men's wear in China. Do not assume that United States trademark law is world law. It is not. Next, you will want to ask local counsel if the potential mark has a negative connotation in the local language. If you find out later that your client's mark means "smelly feet" in French or Russian, you may have a very annoyed client when the brand debuts in those countries.

In common law countries, including the United States, you would be prudent to conduct a more in-depth search, which can be obtained from a third party vendor. This search can reveal marks in use but not necessarily registered with the United States Patent & Trademark Office (USPTO). These "common law" marks give a prior user certain senior rights to the mark, so I always recommend such a search for an important new brand so that you can find what is out there that may cause a conflict.

Finally, let's talk budget. All these searches cost money, so recommend a workable scenario with a reasonable budget to your client. Then, discuss what your client's budget permits and do the broadest searches possible within the budget that is established. Make sure the client understands that the more limited the budget and the resulting search, the higher the odds of unexpected surprises down the road.

Trademark Registration

Once you have cleared the mark for the designated goods in the designated countries, it is time to start a trademark filing program. Again, formulate a strategy and a budget with your client. Your client, for example, swears to you that the brand only will be used for women's clothing that only will be sold in the United States. Hmmm.... So you file a USPTO trademark application to register the mark in connection with "women's clothing." A year later the same client calls and wants to expand the brand to men's clothing and cosmetics and start selling in Europe. What if a third party has filed applications that now block these other new categories in the USPTO. What if the mark is blocked in Europe for men's clothing? Hence, the need to carefully consider your strategy—do as much as you can within the budget provided. Ideally, ask the client annually or semi-annually where they plan to take the brand over the next twelve months—or five years. Get your filings in place or you may get blocked because your client's short-term success in an initial market can result in that blocking. Discuss that possibility with your client in a sensible way to make sure that the short and longer term are both considered at the outset of your registration program.

While counseling, remember to think internationally. The United States is part of the Paris Convention, which means that a USPTO filing gives you six months to file abroad claiming your USPTO filing date. So, you have six months reserved for no cost to see how the brand develops and to determine any issues with the USPTO. It is a good tool to use. The United States also is a member of the World Intellectual Property Association (WIPO). Through WIPO, you can file an international application to designated member countries based upon your USPTO application. There are certain advantages and disadvantages to using WIPO, but it can be a cost effective method to protect your client's mark internationally. A final thought on international protection—select local counsel carefully. Often, an application may receive a refusal to register. There are many ways to get the local examiner to withdraw the refusal but you need creative counsel to work with you to fight for the mark. Many foreign counsel simply report the refusal without suggestions on how to overcome it. As with many problems involving foreign jurisdictions, there often is a solution, you just need to figure it out.

Why Trademark Registration Matters

Here are just a few reasons why your client should seek trademark registration for its brand.

1. Registration provides nationwide rights in the United States in and to the brand for the goods listed in the registration (subject to prior senior rights that may be in use in a geographic region);
2. Registration gives certain desired presumptions in a trademark infringement lawsuit;
3. Registration entitles your client to statutory damages in counterfeiting cases;
4. Registration in the USPTO will block other marks that the trademark examiner considers confusingly similar;
5. Licensees, distributors and even manufacturers, often require proof of registration in the countries of interest;

6. Licensees often require representations and warranties that the licensor owns the mark and has the right to license the mark - the trademark registration is the best proof of that right and you can draft the language accordingly;
7. A potential investor or purchaser of the brand will require the requisite trademark registrations;
8. US Customs requires a trademark registration to protect the mark with Customs;
9. In most countries outside the United States, the only way to create trademark rights is via a trademark registration; and
10. Registration provides actual and constructive notice to third parties of your client's rights in and to the mark.

Beyond Trademark Protection

Ideally, your client has selected and protected its fashion brand with your able assistance. Below is a quick primer on other methods to protect your client's fashion products.

<u>Patents</u>

In the United States and in many countries internationally, you can register the ornamental features of a design, for example, select elements on a handbag or a shoe. Patent registration gives your client access to statutory damages and attorneys' fees. *See* 35 U.S.C. §§ 1-376 (2006) for specifics.

<u>Copyright</u>

You can register fabric designs that are considered "sufficiently creative" with the United States Copyright Office. If you register the design before a third party infringement or within ninety days of first publication of the design, the copyright owner is entitled to statutory damages and attorneys' fees. In the United States, you cannot protect the actual design of clothing under copyright, as clothing is considered functional. The European Community does offer some limited protection for clothing designs. *See,* 17 U.S.C. §§ 101-1332 (2006).

Nontraditional Trademarks / Trade Dress

- Secondary Marks: Think outside the brand box. Monograms and designs are increasingly popular and often can be placed on the physical product rather than simply inside the product. This strategy increases consumer recognition of the brand, for example, the Louis Vuitton "LV" is everywhere on its products. The Chanel "CC" also can be found on a variety of Chanel products, including its jewelry.
- Trade Dress—Product Packaging: An ornamental product package, for example, a distinct perfume bottle or lipstick case also can serve as a source identifier, subject to trademark protection.
- Trade Dress—Product Design: Through significant use and, therefore, the ability to show acquired distinctiveness, a fashion company may be able to protect non-functional, purely ornamental product design as well. While building-up "acquired distinctiveness," a design patent can protect the product. When a patent expires, trade dress protection still may be available, provided you protected the design from third party infringers and the design indicates a single source. The Hermes Birkin bag is a great example of a product design whose elements are subject to various federal trademark registrations and Hermes has been vigilant in protecting its design of the Birkin bag.

Contract

Before sending original designs to manufacturers, enter into a contract protecting the designs and perhaps even providing for liquidated damages if the manufacturer misuses designs. Obtain a nondisclosure agreement before sharing design ideas with any third party. If your client works with a factory when creating or finalizing designs, you want a contract that makes clear that your client owns the final designs and that the factory cannot use those designs except for your client's products. "Designs" can be fabric patterns, jewelry, packaging, handbags, and many other items if properly defined. Although contracts may not stop bad behavior, it is an additional weapon to discourage such behavior and to protect your client's interests when it occurs. Generally, a contract is better than no contract and a good contract is better than one that doesn't follow the best practices described here.

Cases of Interest

Here are a few representative cases that illustrate the topics discussed above.

Trademark Selection

- *Glow Industries Inc. v. Lopez*, 273 F. Supp. 2d 1095 (C.D.Cal. 2003); *see also*, Bo Burlingham, *The Sweet Smell of Settlement*, Inc. Magazine (Dec. 1, 2003). Dispute over the mark GLOW BY J.LO for perfume brought by Glow Industries, owner of the registered trademark GLOW for skin soaps, bubble bath, skin lotions, and skin moisturizes. Good example of the risks associated with selecting a mark.
- *Masters Software Inc. v. Discovery Communications Inc.*, 725 F. Supp. 2d 1294 (W.D.Wash. 2010). Although not a fashion law case, a good example of the risks of not conducting a trademark search. In this case, Masters Software had used CAKE BOSS for at least two years prior to the show launch in connection with her bakery website and bakery software. Court granted preliminary injunction against use of CAKE BOSS by the television show owned by Discovery Communications. Parties settled.

Licensing

- *The Levy Group Inc.* v. *L.C. Licensing Inc. and Liz Claiborne Inc.*, No. 650034/2010 (N.Y. Sup. Ct. Jan. 21, 2010), *available at* http://iapps.courts.state.ny.us/webcivil/FCASMain. The case demonstrates why defining the parameters of the license grant is so important. Plaintiff licensee sold "Liz Claiborne" outerwear in the "better zone" trade channels, such as Macy's. Defendant did a deal to bring the "Liz Claiborne" brand to JC Penney's. Plaintiff sued alleging that the license between the parties prevented licensor from "downgrading" the "Liz Claiborne" brand. Plaintiff licensee alleged that "better zone" stores would no longer carry plaintiff's licensed products and that JC Penney's could not match the volume of the lost "best zone" trade channel. The court found that the specific language of the license created no obligation by defendant to maintain the mark at the "better zone" level and that the contract language clearly permitted defendant to develop the brand at its discretion, except for the products clearly carved out and licensed to plaintiff.

- *The Snack Factory LLC v. Eizen, Fineburg & McCarthy P.C.*, No. 09-6483 (D. N.J. filed Dec. 24, 2009). Although not a fashion law case, this is an excellent example of the dangers of negotiating a sophisticated license without the proper licensing experience and experience in the relevant industry. In this case, Snack Factory sued its counsel for malpractice for allegedly botching a license with Pepperidge Farms. Case details the expertise needed to negotiate the license at issue.

Trademark Rights

- *JA Apparel Corp v. Abboud*, 682 F. Supp. 2d 294 (S.D.N.Y. 2010). This case is a hybrid between trademark ownership and licensing. Fascinating case that exemplifies the absolute importance that a fashion contract addressing trademark rights (license, purchase agreement, distribution agreement) clearly spell out the exact rights in the trademark and, when applicable, the rights of the designer to use his or her own name after selling the name as a trademark. After spending $65.5 million for the exclusive right to the JOSEPH ABBOUD name and mark, the court found that under the contract terms Mr. Abboud still had limited rights to use his name commercially.
- *L.A. Triumph, Inc. v. Madonna Louise Veronica Ciccone*, No. 10-6195 (C.D. Cal. filed Aug. 19, 2010). Plaintiff owned a trademark registration for the mark MATERIAL GIRL for clothing and alleged use of the mark since 1997. Madonna claimed rights to the mark via her 1985 hit song and the alleged sale of $85 million worth of "Material Girl" merchandise throughout the 1980s. Judge S. James Otero, however, disagreed, stating that "singing of a song does not create a trademark" and that selling concert-related goods is not the same as selling a clothing line. Case pending.

Protection of Fashion Designs

- *Hermes International v. Thursday Friday Inc.*, No. 11-580, (S.D.N.Y. June 6, 2011). Defendant created a canvas tote bag with pictures of the iconic Birkin Bag on each side of the tote. Hermes sued for trademark infringement, unfair competition, and dilution. Hermes provided significant proof of secondary meaning of the design of the bag, including federal trademark registration of the design. Defendant agreed to a permanent injunction.
- *Bernardo Footwear LLP v. Brown Shoe Company Inc.*, No. 06-1613 (S.D. Tex. filed May 11, 2006). Plaintiff owned design patents for ornamental designs for two sandal styles. Sued a host of third parties alleging that each party infringed the design patents and demanded royalties, permanent injunction, attorney's fees and costs.

Success as a Fashion Lawyer

What makes for a successful fashion lawyer? Loving the business and being willing to learn and understand how it works. Empathy and respect for your clients is a necessity. As for lawyers practicing fashion law? If you are working with small businesses, realize that you may need to get other clients to pay your bills because you may not be able to make a living from small fashion clients alone given the economics of fashion start-ups.

Be flexible with your practice. While I began as a traditional IP attorney, my skill-set now is far more wide-ranging. I draft and negotiate all types of contracts for my clients, who include fashion companies and other clients, including online store agreements between suppliers and the brand owner, website terms and conditions, manufacturing and distribution agreements, licenses, non-disclosure agreements, and financing agreements that include a variety of promissory notes and instruments. I litigate when necessary, although I always make sure I have an expert litigator at my side. There are many areas, in which I seek counsel for my fashion clients early in the process. If you want to be a fashion lawyer generally, you will need a strong network of specialists to assist you. For example, issues beyond the relatively mundane that concern immigration, tax and now privacy/data security are increasingly besetting fashion lawyers' clients, for which I would consult a specialist to assure that my client is well served.

Joining a Fashion Network

Fashion is a multibillion dollar business and many of the fashion leaders have their headquarters in New York City, making it a world leader of fashion and the related businesses that support fashion. Fashion Week in New York is nearly a sacred event for those in the business. Fashion is definitely part of the pulse of New York and the New York City Bar Association (City Bar) wants to be the place for fashion lawyers.

I have chaired the City Bar Trademark and Unfair Competition committee for the last three years and have found that there is a significant overlap between IP generally and fashion. Because I have represented many clients in the fashion industry, I know that fashion is something more and somehow different. When the City Bar decided to create the Committee on Fashion Law, they invited me to serve as the inaugural chair. The Committee is comprised of thirty members from all aspects of the legal spectrum. We have solo practitioners who work with developing designers and small fashion houses. We have attorneys who practice in some of the country's largest law firms and represent fashion conglomerates and big box retailers. We have in-house counsel from a variety of retailers, including large department stores, national and regional discount clothing chains, prestige fashion houses, and beauty/cosmetic companies. The specialties of our committee members are just as diverse as their employers. Our committee's mission is to be a place where those who practice law in the fashion industry and thereby legitimately have created the "fashion law" category, can share ideas and concerns, debate new judicial decisions, discuss new laws, explore different viewpoints, and network. As to networking, I would quote an attorney on the committee who is the general counsel for one of the largest discount clothing retail chains. He confided that he "used to think networking was a waste of time and then I joined a few committees and attended a few conferences. Slowly I started building up a network of people with whom I could ask questions, seek ideas, and suggestions, discuss common concerns. I found it to be very useful. That is why I joined this committee."

If you want to be a fashion lawyer, go to places where you will interact with fashion lawyers and people in the fashion industry generally. Develop a network of those who make a living in fashion. Live what you love and follow my advice by learning the business of fashion generally and then your clients' businesses specifically. By joining committees, attending conferences, and engaging in similar activities, you literally are "in the fashion world," exposed to trends and concerns that are confronting your fashion clients. Not to mention that you will be building a network that will be a source of information and perhaps referrals for your practice.

As part of the committee's first year activities, we are presenting two programs that are open to the public. The first program is "The Business of Beauty," featuring in-house counsel from four leading cosmetic and fragrance companies headquartered in New York City. Early in 2012, we will conduct a parallel program, "The Business of Fashion," which will feature leading in-house counsel from various fashion houses and retailers located in New York. Both programs will focus on what makes these businesses unique, what the attorneys who serve them often confront, what trends they are seeing, and what career paths they followed to become "fashion lawyers." We also will offer a CLE program on licensing and intellectual property focused the fashion industry. These programs are essential for a fashion lawyer, first as a point of entry and then to stay current. You owe the first to yourself and the second to both yourself and your clients, most especially your clients. Fashion is tough and having a good lawyer is a necessity. For the fashion lawyer, a little networking, as well as the right CLE program, helps to provide the client with a good fashion lawyer. That is one of the goals of the Fashion Law committee, which is shared by each of its members. Hopefully, that goal has also been served by this discussion.

Conclusion

Be passionate about the fashion industry and driven to work with your clients to help them succeed in this hyper-competitive industry. Develop a legal expertise needed in the fashion industry and stay current in this area. Understand the limitations of your clients' budgets and advise them on various strategies, offering different options and different cost structures. Develop and expand your network of industry insiders, both on the business and the legal sides.

Key Takeaways

- Learn the fashion business. Fashion law, as with fashion itself, is ever-changing and you must stay current to succeed.
- Know when to hire some outside smarts. You cannot be an expert in every aspect of fashion law, so do not be shy about bringing in some help.
- Do not skimp on branding and the registration of trademarks. International protection often is worth it in the long term.
- Always consider "non-traditional" types of protection for your client's fashion designs. Work with your client to develop a reputation for aggressively protecting its designs.
- Understand the unique nature of the client's business before advising and negotiating on a fashion contract or license.

Related Resources

- Women's Wear Daily, www.wwd.com.
- Guillermo C. Jimenez and Barbara Kolsun, *Fashion Law: A Guide for Designers, Fashion Executives, and Attorneys* (Fairchild Books 2010).
- Law of Fashion Blog, http://lawoffashion.com (last visited Oct. 5, 2011).
- New York City Bar Association, Fashion Law Committee webpage, http://www.abcny.org/fashion-law (coming November 2011).

Monica Richman is a partner of SNR Denton's Intellectual Property and Technology practice and co-chair of the Fashion Law industry sector. She has broad experience in the areas of trademark and copyright law, including counseling, brand development and protection, licensing, trademark portfolio management, international aspects of IP, and intellectual property issues related to secured transactions, mergers and acquisitions, and litigations. Ms. Richman has a special focus on the fashion industry, representing a wide-range of clients from high-profile designers to international fashion houses covering diverse areas such as intellectual property, marketing, manufacturing and distribution, online store development and management, and litigation. She currently serves as the inaugural chair of the Fashion Law Committee for the Bar Association for the City of New York.

In Fashion Law, Timing is Everything

Alan Behr

Partner and Head, Fashion & Luxury Goods Practice

Alston & Bird LLP

ASPATORE

Introduction

The fashion business creates an ongoing paradox for a commercial lawyer: you cannot be useful to your client unless you understand its business, but fashion never stands still long enough for an attorney to get to know it all. You can blunt the effect of that paradox by mixing in the lawyer's time-honored brew of preparation and diligence, but that will only partly suffice in a business that, by definition, is all about setting trends.

For my fashion and accessories practice, I had the good luck of a head start; members of my family had been in the fashion business, in one capacity or another, since the nineteenth century. Family lore has it that a great-grandmother sent sons, one after the other, from their village in Germany to seek their fortune in the United States. In 1903, four of the brothers opened a department store in New Orleans called Krauss Company. It closed in the last years of the twentieth century—one of the three native New Orleans department stores that once lined Canal Street, all of which have disappeared.

My father went to work for his uncles at an early age and, like many German-born men of his generation, he was all business, even at home. Dinnertime conversation drifted toward department store management theory, and practice. As a boy, I accompanied him on his buying trips through the showrooms of the garment district in New York, observing how he negotiated and learning from him how the trade functioned. After my father's death, I went to work at Krauss part-time, selling youth-oriented menswear.

The Fashion Business

Overview

When I started in the business, there were some basic rules that had been true for a long time. To determine the retail price for clothing, the retailer would typically "keystone" from wholesale, which means that the retail price would be double the wholesale cost. The price tags on clothing at Krauss had the retail price, but they also bore, in a simple alphabetical cipher, the wholesale cost. It was therefore easy for managers to see that, for example, a pair of Levi's 501 jeans selling for $7.50 had cost the store $3.75. Today, retail markup, using the manufacturer's suggested retail price or otherwise, is typically much higher, ranging from 1.4 to as much as 3.1 times wholesale, and sometimes more.

The word *import* used to be synonymous with a rare and expensive item sold at a higher-end store. To get articles of clothing made in the US today, you increasingly have to go to specialty shops and expect to pay a premium. As everyone knows, most clothing sold in this country is made in lower-cost territories, such as China. As for what used to be called imports, the luxury end of the market is made in traditional premium sources such as Britain, Italy, and France.

What that means for a fashion lawyer is that many of the contracts involved in the business now are international in scope, with all the choice-of-law and importation issues and the enforcement concerns that international deals for merchandise involve. Today's fashion lawyer working on the manufacturing side should therefore keep a network of reliable lawyers available to help in the countries where clients are likely to have their goods made.

Putting aside resort wear, formal wear, and other special items, there remain two seasons in fashion, fall/winter and spring/summer. What that means in practice is that on the huge sales floors of a typical department store, almost everything there has to be gone and replaced by something else within no more than six months. That is the origin of the seasonal sale.

Today the word *sale* is almost seems to be part of a typical retailer's name, so often is the sign announcing one hung in the window. At first glance, it may look as if all retailers have become discount stores, but remember the premium over keystone that a typical first markup contains. A retailer can easily discount more than once and still make a good profit as long as the average sale price for all units of a single stock-keeping unit (SKU) sold at everything from full retail to final markdown ultimately gives the retailer the necessary revenue.

One model to achieve the necessary revenue is to have generally fixed points at which markdowns occur, beginning as early as the first weeks after delivery to the sales floor and continuing to the day that, depending on the deal, unsold remainders are shipped back to the manufacturer or carted off to a captive or third-party outlet store. By that model, pricing can be as simple as a strict movement from full retail to 40 percent off to 60 percent off to out the back door.

Another model is to discount and rediscount and mark up again, and to send out coupons to so-called "friends and family," the holders of store credit cards, or anybody else on the store's mailing list, and otherwise to vary the price so often during the period on which the item will be on the floor that any consumer who tries to catch the best deal for a particular item will find it about as difficult as trying to snag the lowest price for an airline ticket.

As with the airlines, much of it depends on what the seller's computer says about quantity remaining in relation to time left to sell on the day that the customer makes the purchase. For consumers, that model can provide engagement with the retailer, since it forces them to keep watch if they want a good deal. The challenge for counsel, however, is to be sure that the retailer obeys all applicable laws and regulations concerning consumer advertising, that the retailer does not inadvertently discount items contrary to its arrangements with vendors, and that those arrangements themselves do not violate the antitrust laws.

Another change in department stores is the "leased department." That is a trade term. The vendor does not literally become a tenant of the store, as if renting office space; the arrangement is in the form of a license, albeit an intricate and specific one for activities in a defined space. In many stores, vendors actually lease the space that they are occupying, and they either directly employ sales staff dedicated to the department or enter into an arrangement with the retailer to help subsidize the salaries of those staff members. That is often (but not always) why you may find that a section of a department store dedicated to one vendor carries the look, the trade dress, and the sales staff knowledge of the vendor's own boutiques.

Because of the licensing, labor, trademark, and liability issues involved, counsel should be aware that these in-store deals can be complex and may involve attorneys from several areas of concentration. Consider those boutiques. It used to be rare for a manufacturer to compete against the stores that sold its goods at retail. That it happens regularly today is the result in large part of two fairly recent developments. The first was the rise of luxury designer and other brand-name clothing. The second was the internationalization of the marketplace.

A Business of Brand Names

Brand names have always meant something in the business. When I sold Levi's, I also sold shirts by Van Heusen and both names were known to our customers. Much else of what we sold came from reputable manufacturers whose names were known mostly in the trade. For example, there were two basic kinds of dresses, budget dresses and better dresses, each to be found in a department named as such. In those cases, the names of the vendors were secondary to the store's own designations for quality. Brand-name departments would come later. In my time, the brand was Krauss, and customers expected the store to stand behind what it sold, whatever the source.

The retailer's brand is still significant; a designer label's market position, and relative level of success within that position, can be measured by which retailers sell its goods. The big shift in the past decades has been the movement of public perception regarding vendors' brands. Once thought of as being indicators of quality in manufacture, product brands are now seen as indicators; indeed, in the most successful cases, they are free-standing monuments of style. Luxury designers have led the way, but all market segments are now deeply affected.

In the unending struggle between vendor and retailer as to dominance in their dealings with each other, that perceptual change, along with the rise of vendor-branded retailing, has helped give vendors extra leverage. On the other hand, there can be few acts in commerce as humbling as when a major retailer "throws out" a vendor—that is, stops carrying its lines. The relationship can get touchy regarding discounting. How can the vendor not annoy its retailers if its own boutiques get an unfair priority on shipments of new styles or if they start discounting the goods earlier or deeper in the season than its retail accounts feel comfortable doing? And how can those retailers in turn not fail to annoy their vendors if they became more aggressive with discounts, a common occurrence after the financial crisis in 2008, than reputation-sensitive vendors like?

The cult of the designer has created some interesting side effects as well. Independent boutiques and department stores rarely carry all of a line, opting instead to carry just those items that the buyers think will sell, that fit the expectations of that store's customers, and that integrate well with items bought from other sources. A designer's own retail stores are showcases for the brand; such stores therefore carry as much of the designer's lines as space and context permit, and they are not necessarily expected to make a profit, giving them another advantage over the designer's own retail accounts.

In many ways, the relationship between vendor and retailer has never been more complex and symbiotic, and lawyers on both sides of the deal should remain sensitive to the potentially far-ranging business implications of what they do.

The internationalization of the fashion business has made even small players go global. During my father's time, it was expected in the trade for New Orleans to buy styles one year behind Atlanta, and for Atlanta to buy them one year behind New York. That meant that something that was new in New York would take two years to get to New Orleans before it reached a level of consumer acceptance high enough to warrant placing it inside a department store.

Today, a style seen on a catwalk in Paris is copied and rushed into production by an inexpensive maker, such as Zara, and sent to stores worldwide to appear in the same season as the copied original. A new look becomes global within the space of months.

Mall Clothes

Shopping malls, with their capacious anchor stores and the chain stores rowed in between, have moved downtowns to the suburbs and harmonized what people around the country are offered to buy. That has helped raise general taste levels, but it comes at a price, especially for those with greater stylistic ambitions. When a fashionable lawyer says that her adversary came to court in "mall clothes," she does not mean it as a compliment. At about the same time, the modern big-box discounters appeared, led by Wal-Mart where price rules, taste will step back, but as Target and others have shown, it need not exit altogether. Big wallets and good taste have never entirely gone hand in hand.

Old-time discounters had followed a pattern: start strong, grow fast, and then go bust. Their model was to sell cheap and make it up on volume. Add a touch of overexpansion plus a dash of economic downturn, and they were out of business. Walmart and the newer generation follow a different model. These mass merchants operate as little more than warehouses open to the public. Everything in stock is on the sales floor.

One of the biggest legal challenges with malls is the leases, which dictate everything from hours of operation to the appearance of store frontage. For a lawyer dealing with a vendor seeking to get into a mass merchant's doors, the initial challenge will probably be what looks like the biggest, toughest, one-sided warranty and indemnity on planet Earth. (You think you're good? Try negotiating away key parts of that one.)

Always with a Sense of Style

Despite the many changes over the years, the core values that make fashion what it is have remained constant. At nearly all price points, fashion is about aspiration, beauty, acceptance, and belonging. It is true that vanity has always been a part of it ("Don't I look the best, darling?") and so has fear ("Oh, darling, is everybody here dressed better than I am?"). If that were the whole story, museums such as the Metropolitan Museum of Art and the Guggenheim Museum would not be showing designer clothes as decorative art.

Fashion as museum art? Fashion as a social statement? Giorgio Armani rocked the Guggenheim's flagship museum with a show of his designs; just over ten years later, a brilliantly mounted retrospective of the work of Alexander McQueen became the eighth most popular exhibition since the museum was established in 1870. Art makes you pause, look, and think beyond the mere surface of the object in front of you. As the display at the

Met demonstrated, no one who ever wore McQueen ever thought she was first throwing on a dress.

Fashions come and go, but style is for life. My wife, a fashion stylist for a major luxury department store, can spot a well-dressed woman from twenty yards away and tell who made her clothes, what season they appeared in, and what they cost. That comes from an understanding of fashion. What moves her, however, is seeing a woman who knows how to wear her clothes well, displaying taste, confidence, and poise. That is style.

For the people in the business and their lawyers, style is what makes all the hard work, the financial risks, and the licensing and endorsement deals, to say nothing of the drama of dealing with fashion editors, fashion photographers, fashion models, and self-appointed fashion police, all worth it in the end. Fashion is a business and it is also one of the applied arts. It is fun, it is aggravating, it is unpredictable, and were it not in our lives, we would all be so much more the poorer.

Artists own the products of their creation; fashion and accessories designers take their chances. Fashion and accessories designers employ many of the same talents and techniques used in a number of the fine arts, but their creations are given more limited legal protection due to their inherently functional nature and the strongly commercial practicalities of making new things intended to be worn and not merely displayed.

As with all intellectual property, however, fashion and accessories designs are protectable under four broad-ranging categories: trade secrets, trademarks (including service marks and trade dress), patents, and copyrights.

Trade Secrets

The law of trade secrets applies, in context, only to commercially used formulae, processes, methods, systems, and techniques that are held as a secret by the organization that developed or otherwise owns them. As an overly simple illustration, a formula for a soft drink is a trade secret if people who are not in the limited circle of those in the know would possibly be aware that the formula exists and is a secret but would not readily know its ingredients or their proportions. The classic example of that is the formula for Coca-Cola. Everybody drinks it, but the recipe is known only to a few employees at the Coca-Cola Company. Although fashion companies have developed secrets, such as manufacturing techniques and special dyes, as a practical matter, in a highly public business such as fashion, where much is spoken and little is held back and where the success of the end product can be wholly independent from the complexity or proprietary nature of its making, trade secrets are not a major factor.

Trademarks

The most important form of protection for fashions and accessories is the most commercially oriented one: trademark law. At its simplest, a trademark identifies the source of goods. For many companies in the business, however, especially those in the luxury sector, their trademarks are the most effective communication devices for the most enduring property that the brand has, which is its story.

As an example, think of the Ralph Lauren trademark, and the story of the brand comes quickly to mind, helped along by the trademarks of the individual product lines. It is a tale of an idealized vision of the Anglo-American life, from the country clubs of the American East Coast to the ranches that carry on the cowboy spirit to the playing fields and campus life of elite schools and universities of the English-speaking world, on safari and in the boardroom, and wherever Anglo-American style may rule.

Think of the trademark Giorgio Armani, in contrast, and visions arise of Italian elegance, of self-restraint and a desire to bring style and good design to all facets of life, from one's formal wear down to one's teacups and the tea poured into them.

Those are two different stories, but the branding message in each is distinct, clear, and, perhaps most important, evocative of an aspirational way of life.

Since the rise to almost cult-like status of some designer brands, the name on the product has never counted for more. But it still matters enormously where a customer shops and service marks for retail operations therefore remain of great consequence. In no small part due to the uniformity that chain stores and malls bring to the business, that is perhaps particularly true for retail brands that call to mind not only quality but a sense of a place, such as Gump's San Francisco, Barneys New York, and Saks Fifth Avenue, because great places tell unique stories, too. When choosing trademarks and service marks that incorporate geographic terms, however, beware of the pitfall of geographic descriptiveness.

Into the mix comes a hybrid: a private label is a brand for one or more lines that are both owned and exclusively sold by a retailer. As a brand, the private label has to stay associated in the minds of consumers with the retailer, but will extend that association to the products themselves, even though a different name is used on their labels than the name over the door.

Because of the importance of trademarks to the business, attorneys counseling fashion and accessories companies should be particularly proactive. The attorneys should be brought in when new brands are in the planning stages so that they will have enough time to search for the availability of the proposed marks and leave sufficient time remaining to give any bad news to marketers, who typically do not take bad news from trademark lawyers at all well, so they can come up with a workable alternative. Then the attorneys should register any of the trademarks, service marks, and trade dress that are going to be important for the business in the future, and do so in all major jurisdictions where the business operates or expects to operate within the next handful of years.

Rules vary around the world as to what can be registered, for which goods and services, and for how long and whether use is required to obtain and maintain a registration. Having that good network of international counsel is useful. There is much international harmony in trademark laws, but national and territorial laws vary as to the registration of marks not yet in use and the description of the goods and services for which an application may be filed, among other key variables.

Because of online shopping, almost any business of any size has a global reach of some kind. For fashion, where a brand name can mean so much more than in most other lines of business, neglecting to register a mark in key territories can prove a serious and expensive mistake.

Just as businesses balk at taking those proactive legal steps, whether because of concerns about cost, a lack of awareness, or simple procrastination, lawyers and even some business people may sometimes overdo it. Not everything needs to be registered. If a mark is to be used for a particular style or model that will likely be around for only a season or two, it is likely that the registration will not be issued until after use of the mark has ceased, which, under United States law, makes the registration effectively useless.

The Protection of Designs

When Imitation May Be More Than Just Flattery

Over the past ten years, there has been an increased interest in the protection of designs of fashion and accessories by trade dress, copyright, and design patent law, even as traditionally protectable properties such as news articles, books, audio recordings, and movies have become increasingly difficult to protect. It sometimes seems as if physical goods are moving into the empty spaces abandoned by the intangibles when digital copying tools were placed into almost everyone's hands.

It can be all too easy to forget, in the excitement to stake a proprietary claim in what is new, that the very word *fashion*, that is, to be in fashion or out of fashion, carries with it the promise of perpetual change. Why seek to protect something that is made for now and not for tomorrow? Perhaps people in the applied arts simply like to see their creations recognized. There is also that natural commercial desire to block competitors from using the fruits of a creative person's inspiration; that kind of thinking may prove narrow minded, and it may backfire.

As noted earlier, companies like Zara make copies of luxury designs and sell them inexpensively. The Zara customer is not buying luxury quality and knows it, but she is getting something of the aura of the copied designer. The purchase of a copy from Zara is aspirational, but without the benefit of brand. Of course, the customer would prefer the original from Prada, for example, but the Prada original may be too expensive for her right now.

Let us say the customer is a young woman at the start of her career. By shopping at Zara for a copy, she keeps Prada on her mind. As she moves on in life, perhaps one day she will fulfill her aspiration by wearing Prada originals. Deprive her of her starting point, and Prada may lose that kind of bankable attention from her.

That is not true for all markets. Someone who is able to buy a copy of designer eyeglass frames, home and bath accessories, and handbags and luggage, for example, will probably be less likely to move on to the original if that customer can be satisfied with the copy. Outright counterfeiting, by which not merely the style is copied but the trademark of the original is falsely placed upon the copy, is just plain illegal in all major territories and rightly so, given the importance of branding in the fashion business.

Trade Dress

Trade dress law is easiest to consider when viewed as a subset of trademark law. Like a trademark, trade dress can provide protection for products for as long as they are on the market and as long as the owner follows commercially prudent measures to defend the trade dress against infringement.

Trade dress encompasses "the total image of a product and may include features such as size, shape, color or color combinations, texture, graphics, or even particular sales techniques." *See John H. Harland Co. v. Clarke Checks, Inc.,* 711 F.2d 966, 980 (11th Cir. 1983).

The traditional rule was that trade dress applied to packaging: it was about the box that the item came in, not the item itself. Examples of strong packaging trade dress can be seen in the beverage industry, from the Coca-Cola bottle to the Perrier bottle and beyond. Distinctive packaging is protected as unregistered trade dress without the need to show secondary meaning. *See Two Pesos Inc. v. Taco Cabana* Inc., 505 U.S. 763 (1992). In *Two Pesos,* a case in which the "packaging" was the distinctive design common to the restaurants in a chain, the US Supreme Court defined secondary meaning:

> Secondary meaning is used generally to indicate that a mark or dress "has come through use to be uniquely associated with a specific source." Restatement (Third) of Unfair

> Competition § 13, Comment *e* (Tent. Draft No. 2, Mar. 23, 1990). "To establish secondary meaning, a manufacturer must show that, in the minds of the public, the primary significance of a product feature or term is to identify the source of the product rather than the product itself."

Inwood Laboratories Inc. v. Ives Laboratories Inc., 456 U.S. 844, 851, n.11 (1982); 505 U.S. at 766. As the law has evolved, trade dress can extend to the goods themselves but with an important additional burden. For the goods, independent of the packaging, secondary meaning must be proven to establish the necessary distinctiveness for protection as unregistered trade dress. *See Wal-Mart Stores Inc. v. Sanara Bros. Inc.*, 529 U.S. 205 (2000).

The difference is that packaging can be inherently distinctive for protection as unregistered trade dress, but for the product, distinctiveness must be acquired through the development of secondary meaning. In *Wal-Mart Stores*, the trade dress at issue was for a line of children's clothing. That the leading case in point should be a fashion case is a clear warning: if you think you have unique trade dress in a clothing line, make sure to build consumer and trade awareness of your equally unique role as the sole source of that trade dress.

Whether it is the product, with secondary meaning, or its packaging, with or without secondary meaning, trade dress protection is limited to nonfunctional design elements that are source designating. The owner must show that the design is nonfunctional and distinctive and that the alleged infringer's design is likely to cause consumer confusion as to its source. *See* Jerome Gilson & Anne Gilson Lalonde, *1 Gilson on Trademark Protection and Practice § 2A.01[1]* (2006 ed.). In offering proof, the burden is on the owner of unregistered trade dress to prove that it is not functional. *See First Brands Corp. v. Fred Meyer, Inc.*, 809 F.2d 1378 (9th Cir. 1987).

The obvious conclusion is to register trade dress, but a lawyer attempting to do so must be prepared for something of a tough go of it. The biggest hurdle for many trade dress applications is the question of functionality. If the product configuration is found to be functional, and the user has no reasonable expectation of overcoming that, the user will not get a registration. States the Patent and Trademark Office (PTO) in its manual for trademark examiners:

> Functional matter cannot be protected as a trademark. 15 U.S.C. §§ 1052(e)(5) and (f), 1091(c), 1064(3), and 1115(b). A feature is functional as a matter of law if it is "essential to the use or purpose of the product or if it affects the cost or quality of the device." *TrafFix Devices Inc. v. Marketing Displays, Inc.*, 532 U.S. 23, 33, 58 USPQ2d 1001, 1006 (2001); *Qualitex Co. v. Jacobson Products Co. Inc.*, 514 U.S. 159, 165, 34 USPQ2d 1161, 1163-64 (1995); *Inwood Laboratories Inc. v. Ives Laboratories Inc.*, 456 U.S. 844, 850 n.10, 214 USPQ 1, 4 n.10 (1982).... The determination that a proposed mark is functional constitutes, for public policy reasons, an absolute bar to registration on either the Principal Register or the Supplemental Register, regardless of evidence showing that the proposed mark has acquired distinctiveness.

TrafFix, 532 U.S. at 29-33, 58 USPQ2d at 1005-1007. *See also In re Controls Corp. of America,* 46 USPQ2d 1308, 1311 (TTAB 1998). TMEP § 1202.02(a)(iii)(A).

Trade dress is often three-dimensional, and the famously precise and exacting PTO can be quite strict about what is an acceptable drawing that represents a three-dimensional design. It is always best practice, therefore, to use a professional trademark artist in the preparation of the required drawings. Each of them must depict a single rendition of the trade dress in a manner that demonstrates its three-dimensionality.

At the PTO, it is the burden of the applicant to prove distinctiveness. Useful tools, depending on the circumstances, can be proof that the trade dress has been registered or otherwise protected as trade dress anywhere else in the world, a showing of substantial sales of the designs in the United States, by unit and dollar sales volume by year for each of the last five years, if at all possible, and evidence of substantial advertising and promotional efforts in the United States during the last five years, if at all possible.

In using the last tool, a lawyer should take care that the advertisements chosen are those that state the source and show the trade dress as a source identifier. For example, suppose the trade dress is a question mark shaped bottle for a perfume called Avocado. To prove distinctiveness, use the advertisements that say, "Look for the question-mark-shaped bottle the next time you yearn for that scent of Avocado." Gather up and submit copies of those advertising materials, information regarding the media outlets through which the advertisements were distributed, information on the amounts spent by year to advertise and promote the trade dress in the United States as a source identifier, and other information on efforts to obtain distinctiveness, such as the use of outside advertising agencies, design firms, and others.

In the end, trade dress is one of those protections that both lawyer and client have to work for; it is hard to prove, and it can be expensive to enforce, and when it is enforced, it is often without expectation of recovery of damages, even if the enforcement action was successful. As with trademarks, the traditional reward for victory against infringement is an injunction rather than damages.

Although almost every designer swears that his work is distinctive, the law is tough when it comes to both originality and distinctiveness, at least by the commercial measure of marketplace acceptance applied by trademark and trade dress law. None of that, however, should deter anyone from protecting valuable trade dress in a unique design, in packaging, or a setting, such as the look of a retail space that signifies a single source in the marketplace.

Design Patents

Utility patents can be used to protect items of fashion that serve a purpose, which is the fashion version of inventing the better mousetrap. The use of utility patents is somewhat rare; recent breakthrough inventions include the power loom (utility patent, 1785) and the sewing machine (utility patent, 1791). If you invent something that can replace the zipper, or you are ready to market the next Velcro (utility patent, 1955), the opportunity is yours. Of more widespread use, however, is the design patent.

The statute protecting design patents, 35 U.S.C. § 171, has its origins in legislation first enacted in 1842. In contrast to the theoretically perpetual protection given to trade dress that remains continuously in use, design patents are for a limited duration, fourteen years, but the potential for obtaining damages as a remedy is much better.

Proof of infringement is straightforward and fact-specific. A plaintiff must demonstrate that the accused design and the claimed design are substantially the same in view of the prior art (pre-existing, publicly available information). More specifically, the test is whether the accused product and the patented design are substantially the same such that a person who is familiar with the type of product and the prior art, giving the product the level of attention a purchaser would usually give it, would be induced to purchase the accused product, supposing it to be the patented design. See *Egyptian Goddess v. Swisa*, 543 F.3d 665 (Fed. Cir. 2008). Although a successful plaintiff can seek as damages either an infringer's total profits or an amount equal to no less than a reasonable royalty (*see* 35 U.S.C. §§ 289, 284), in nearly all design patent cases, the patent holder goes after the infringer's total profits.

A design patent protects a new and original design for an article of manufacture: the shape or surface decoration of an article or a combination of both. *See* 35 U.S.C. § 171; U.S. Patent and Trademark Office, *A Guide to Filing a Patent Application 1* (2003), *available at* http://www.uspto.gov/web/offices/com/iip/pdf/brochure_05.pdf. As with utility patents, which have to be for inventions capable of being reproduced in order to be protected by a design patent, designs must be preconceived and capable of reproduction. *See* M.P.E.P. § 1502.

For a design patent to be granted, the design must be "novel," "nonobvious," and "ornamental." *See OddzOn Prods. Inc. v. Just Toys Inc.*, 122 F.3d 1396 (Fed. Cir. 1997); *Lee v. Dayton Hudson Corp.*, 666 F. Supp. 1072 (E.D. Tenn. 1987). Nonobviousness is analyzed from the perspective of "a designer of ordinary skill or capability" in the same line of trade. *See In Re Sung Nam Cho*, 813 F.2d 378, 381 (Fed. Cir. 1987). What that means, in practice, is that the design cannot be something that a craftsman or designer skilled in the trade would consider a natural progression from ordinary expectations of what the design would include. Instead, the design must display enough originality to give that craftsman or designer something of an "ah-hah" moment.

Note that, here again, the protection is for the appearance of the article, not its function. If the particular design of the article is essential to its use, it will not qualify for a design patent. "If the particular design is essential to the use of the article, it can not [sic] be the subject of a design patent." *See L.A. Gear Inc. v. Thom McAn Shoe Co.*, 988 F.2d 1117, 1123 (Fed. Cir. 1993). In practice, that means a design patent can only protect the nonfunctional aspects of a design. *See* U.S. Patent and Trademark Office, Manual of Patent Examining Procedure (M.P.E.P.) §1502.01, Revision 5 (Aug. 2006).

Functional elements of a design are at least discounted in considering the design as a whole. *See Good Sportsman v. Li & Fung Ltd.*, No. 6:07-cv-395, 2010 WL 2640385, *2-4 (E.D. Tex. June 29, 2010, *applying Richardson v. Stanley Works Inc.*, 597 F.3d 1288 (Fed. Cir. 2010). If form indeed follows function, that is, if the form is primarily dictated by the function of the article, a design patent will not be issued. *See L.A. Gear*, 988 F.2d at 1123. It is also important to keep in mind that the claim is for the design and not the specific product for which it is intended to be used. Elizabeth Ferrill & Tina Tanhehco, *Protecting the Material World: The Role of Design Patents in the Fashion Industry*, 12 N.C. J. L. & Tech. 251 (2011).

A designer must apply for a design patent within one year following the first publication of the design, the first offer to sell the design, or the first public use of a product embodying the design. 35 U.S.C. § 102(b). Otherwise, the designer loses the right to patent the design. *Id.* It usually is not difficult to obtain a design patent, as long as the correct formalities are observed. As an application to register trade dress, key to the success of a design patent application are the graphics; for design patents, that means the drawings submitted with the application. *Id.* at 280. For the form and content of supporting graphics, nothing beats clear, professionally rendered black-and-white drawings. *Id.* at 283.

None of the forms of protection offered by the law is exclusive over the other. It is possible to have a utility patent on the same article as a design patent, and it is possible to have trademark or trade dress protection for it. *See Catalina Lighting Inc. v. Lamps Plus*, 295 F.3d 1277 (Fed. Cir. 2002).

The key difference between design patent and trade dress protection is that for the latter the operative test is source identification. Trade dress protection identifies elements of design that identify the origin of the design; it does not, strictly speaking, protect the design in and of itself from use by others. Unless a particular item of trade dress creates a mark that is distinctive and famous, its use in connection with the goods in one category may not necessarily permit the owner to block the use of the same or similar trade dress by another user in connection with goods in a different and unrelated category.

In theory, a distinctive design that is protected by a design patent for use on a shower curtain may also protect against similar uses on bed sheets, curtains, candles, trash cans, and toothbrushes.

One area of overlap that is quite useful is that the presence of a design patent can help support the claim of secondary meaning in trade dress, which, as noted above, is critical for obtaining registration of trade dress for products. A design patent can initially and relatively quickly be obtained to protect against similar uses of a design by third parties. During the fourteen-year term of the design patent, the design may obtain secondary meaning to support a claim for trade dress protection. The owner can then register the design as trade dress before the term of the design patent expires, thereby leveraging the design patent to obtain continuous, if somewhat mutated, protection for the design. *See* Tracy-Gene G. Durkin and Julie D. Shirk, *Design Patents and Trade Dress Protection: Are the Two Mutually Exclusive?*, 87 J. of Patent & Trademark Office Society 770 (Oct. 2005).

There is overlap with copyright law as well, but as discussed below, copyrights protect against the reproduction, dissemination, and display of creative expression. The copyright holder has to prove that the alleged infringer actually saw his creation in order for him to sustain a claim of infringement.

A design patent protects against even independent invention. If two designers came up with basically the same ornamental feature but one of them did it first and applied to register the design patent within the allowed grace periods or before the other designer conceived of the same design, in theory, the first designer wins, even if the later designer had never heard of him or saw what he had patented.

An attorney and client have to consider the costs and the time commitment of registering. Registering a copyright is inexpensive and easy to do; simply log onto www.copyright.gov and follow the instructions. The process is about as simple as getting a driver's license. For a design patent, the designer needs a lawyer who understands design patent protection and should be prepared to spend a good bit more time and money, not only for the lawyer and for the complexities of PTO examination and response, but for such extras as having those drawings of the design done in the specific way required by the PTO.

Because it typically takes between twelve to fifteen months to get a design patent registered, as with the other forms of protection discussed here, seeking a design patent for a style that will be around for a season or two is likely not cost-effective. Although slightly expedited review is technically possible for an additional fee and effort, there is usually little to gain in starting lawsuits over designs that are nothing but memories by the time that the parties go to trial. For an enduring "signature" piece, however, given the winner-takes-all ability of a successful plaintiff to obtain all the profits of the infringer, a design patent can be a powerful weapon.

Copyright

A copyright protects original expression by providing a monopoly in the reproduction, dissemination, display, and other uses of that expression. *See* 17 U.S.C. § 101, *et seq.* Conceived as a method to protect literature, copyright remains, in general terms, most comfortable with the written word, but the concept has broadened to take in all of the arts, or at least those that can be fixed in a form of expression.

A performance artist who does a piece for a quarter minute consisting mostly of standing in place, trying to decide what to do with his fifteen seconds of self-appointed fame, will not get a copyright for it. He has to fix an original work of authorship in a tangible medium of expression. 17 U.S.C. § 102(a).

If the performance artist records a video of his performance, copies the video onto a disc, and has done something sufficiently unique, such as add a shrug, say a few words about the perils of fame, and throw a softball over the head of an unsuspecting museum guard, he can send the disc to Washington, and obtain a copyright, at least for whatever constitutes the unique parts.

In all, copyright should therefore be seen as generous and forgiving in what it protects, with the one bell-ringing exception applicable to fashions and accessories, which is the first of two leitmotifs of this chapter. Copyright does not protect utilitarian function. *See Fabrica Inc. v. El Dorado Corp.*, 697 F.2d 890 (9th Cir. 1983).

Function, in the case of clothing, essentially means its use in covering and protecting the body. What that means for fashion is that the shape of a garment, being deemed functional in nearly all respects, is not protectable by copyright. Pattern, however, is protectable. *See* Ferrill & Tanhehco, *supra*, at 272.

Suppose a designer wants to design a little black dress. If the design is copied, he must accept imitation as the highest form of flattery. If the designer embroiders onto the dress the image of an odalisque as an original vision only, since copies of Velasquez, Ingres, or Manet would at best have a thin copyright in whatever protectable differences the designer creates, that image can be protected separately by copyright, just as if the designer had embroidered it onto a cloth, framed the cloth, and sold it as a work as art. For jewelry, as long as the shape of the piece is not related to function, it is protectable. For example, the unique design of a pendant on an ordinary chain, not the chain itself or the unadorned clasp, is protectable.

Key to the analysis is the severability of the design from the functional elements. At times, that can be a subtle process. In *Animal Fair v. AMFESCO Indus. Inc.*, 620 F. Supp. 175, 187-88 (D. Minn. 1985), *aff'd.*, 794 F.2d 678 (8th Cir. 1986), copyright was upheld in a slipper that was shaped like a bear paw because the protectable elements of the design were conceptually separate from the utilitarian aspects of the slipper. That conceptual partition between the utilitarian and the protectable elements was sufficient; it was not necessary to show that they were physically separable.

What does that mean in practice? It is probably simplest to say that protectable and functional elements can all be literally stitched together to make a salable product, but it should be reasonably easy to spot what is new and unique. Care should be taken that the elements to be protected by copyright do not contribute to the function of the piece.

What is the reason behind the law? Like much of American intellectual property law, copyright law is largely framed in support of commercial expediency, but copyright, alone among the forms of intellectual property protection, also supports and defends originality and creativity in the arts by helping insulate the incomes of artists, writers, and other creative people from the economic consequences of infringement. It is therefore perceived by many as the law's goalie in the defense of the arts and those who make them.

The tension in that comes from the fact that commercial expediency says that it is best to keep the fashion and accessories businesses going, keep people employed, and reduce expensive controversy to a minimum. Let the marketplace sort out who profits from the work of whoever started the next trend in dresses or shoes. In countries in which the arts, even the applied arts, are held in what we might gently call greater esteem than in the pragmatic and practical United States, the rule is quite different; designers can indeed protect fashion designs, to a point.

The European Perspective

An Overview

The European Directive on the Legal Protection of Designs (1998 Directive) was passed in 1998 and created a design right. *See* Council Directive 98/71, art. 1, 1998 O.J. (L 289) 28, 30 (EC), *available at* http://www.ipjur.com/data/981013DIR987EC.pdf. To qualify for protection, a design must be new and have individual character. *Id.* at art. 3 (2). A design is "new" if no identical design has previously been made available to the public. *Id.* at art. 4. A design has individual character if the "overall impression" on the "informed user" is different from that made from the designs that came before it. *Id.* at art. 5. Articles that qualify will receive protection for five years from the filing date. *Id.* at art. 10.

The European Regulation on Community designs (2002 Regulation) was passed in 2002 and protects both registered and unregistered works. *See* Council Regulation 6/2002, 2002 O.J. (L 3) 2 (EC), *available at* http://oami.europa.eu/en/design/pdf/reg2002_6.pdf. Registered designs are protected for five years under the 2002 Regulation; unregistered designs are given protection for three years. *Id.* at art. 11-12.

The key difference between an EU directive and an EU regulation is that a regulation directly applies to member states and EU residents in the manner of a statute. A directive only obliges all or selected member states to incorporate its provisions into national law.

France

France, the Western nation that has perhaps best balanced the needs of culture and commerce, has protected fashion designs as applied art in one form or another since 1793. *See* Emma Yao Xiao, Note and Recent Development, *The New Trend: Protecting American Fashion Designs Through National Copyright Measures*, 28 CARDOZO ARTS & ENT. L.J. 417, 413 (2010). In 1909, copyright protection was expanded to include nonfunctional designs and patterns. *Id.* at 413. Original fashion designs are granted protection, without registration on the date of creation. Infringement can result in civil liability, with fines up to €300,000, as well as criminal liability, with a maximum sentence of three years in prison. *Id.* at 414.

In perhaps the most famous case, in 1994, Yves St. Laurent was awarded an injunction and the equivalent of about $383,000 in damages against Ralph Lauren for copying a tuxedo dress. How important was that legal victory, over a question that would not have survived a motion for summary judgment in the United States? *The New York Times* listed it among Saint Laurent's successes in the designer's obituary, published on June 1, 2008.

Germany

German copyright law does not explicitly protect designs in fashion, but they can be protected as works of art. *See* § 2 I Nr. 4 UrhG. *(Gesetz über Urheberrecht und Verwandte Schutzrechte).* A work is only given copyright protection if the artistic value of the work and the skills necessary for its realization are significantly above those required by conventional fashion design, an intriguing limitation that opens up interesting questions about proof.

Germany also offers protection for fashion works under design patent law for up to twenty-five years. Indeed, design patent protection is generally preferred over copyright because it is usually easier to meet the requirements for enforcement. Protection can also be offered by competition law, via § 4 Nr. 9 UWG *(Gesetz gegen den unlauteren Wettbewerb).* Commentary indicates that fashion designs are covered by that provision. *See* Nordemann, Wettbewerbs- und Markenrecht, *9. Auflage* 2003, S. 227. The statute grants protection against unfair competitive business activities; one such practice would be the sale of a product of substantially similar design to a protected design. § 3 I UWG. The provision provides the opportunity to seek an injunction. § 9 UWG.

<u>The Application of the European System</u>

Into the European spirit of protection for the creative mind and soul should be added a cautionary note of American pragmatism. For all its presumed benefits, the European system has not been nearly as widely used as one might think. As of 2006, there were a total of 1,631 European registrations. Of those, hundreds are for simple T-shirts, jerseys, and sweatshirts. Of the total number, 409 were not from one of the great fashion houses but a German company, Street One, known for fun and youthful items such as €9.95 tank tops. Two other companies, neither of them major fashion houses, together held nearly an equal number of the total registrations.

Why was that so? Carrying through the other leitmotif of this chapter, perhaps the transitory nature of high fashion calls for an unsentimental and pragmatic approach to protection; you guard what will most likely matter in the near or long term and leave undefended what is here now but not for long.

Multiple attempts at bringing, perhaps dragging, kicking, and screaming, European principles into United States law over the years have not met with success. Much of the resistance is indeed practical, but there are cultural issues as well and, to use a loan word from the French, we cannot overlook the influence of chauvinism. At a gathering of copyright lawyers a few years back, a speaker tried addressing skepticism about enforcement difficulties of the proposals that would become part of some of the legislation described below. Unfortunately, his only response was a form of, "The new version of the bill will fix all that; I can't tell you how but just trust us," rendered with a pronounced French accent, causing suspicious snickering and mutterings to arise from those assembled.

Recent Legislative Efforts

The Design Piracy Prohibition Act (DPPA) was introduced in 2007 and would have amended the Copyright Act to give three years of protection to fashion designs registered with the US Copyright Office within three months following public disclosure. *See* Design Piracy Prohibition Act, H.R. 2033, 110th Cong. (2007). Making, importing, selling, or distributing any article embodying a registered design would be an act of infringement. *Id.* § 2(d). Lack of knowledge of the registration would be a defense, as would independent creation or the proof that the registered design reflects a trend. *Id.* at § 2(e).

The bill ran into trouble, in part because two influential trade groups, the Council of Fashion Designers in America (CFDA) and the American Apparel and Footwear Association (AAFA), took opposing positions. The AAFA feared that the proposed law, if enacted, would hamper creativity and lead to frivolous lawsuits. The CFDA favored adoption of the act as necessary for the protection of up-and-coming fashion designers, a number of whom felt that they were powerless to prevent their entry cards into the business, that is, their novel designs, from being taken and used by others. *See* Ferrill & Tanhehco, *supra*, at 274.

Next came the Innovative Design Protection and Piracy Prevention Act (IDPPA). Introduced in 2010, it would have removed the registration requirement for protection of designs. *See* Innovative Design Protection and Piracy Prevention Act, S. 3728 § 2(f), 111th Cong (2010). A designer would have to plead and prove, however, that an allegedly infringed design embodied a nontrivial variation of what had come before, that it was indeed an original work. *Id.* at § 2(g). Protection would again last for three years. *Id.* § 2(d).

Perhaps to show that it is the result of compromise and not hostile to consumers, the IDPPA includes a new fashion-world form of the home taping exception for audio and audio-visual content, the "home sewing exception." It would allow an amateur seamstress the chance to make a single copy for personal use. *Id.* at § 2(e)(i). This time, both the CFDA and the AAFA supported the legislation. *See* Ferrill & Tanhehco, *supra*, at 275. Although the IDPPA made it through the Senate Judiciary Committee during the 111th Congress, the legislation was not passed. It was, however, reintroduced in the House of Representatives on July 13, 2011. *See* Innovative Design Protection and Piracy Prevention Act, H.R. 2511, 112th Cong. (2011). The journey continues.

Is enacting such legislation a good idea? For a lawyer, especially a litigator, the answer is, of course, yes. New laws and new rights nearly always mean more work for lawyers. Aside from massaging the bruised egos of those designers for whom copying is not flattery, it probably will not make that much of a difference in how business is conducted. With stacks of European statutes seemingly piled against it, the Spanish company Zara became quite rich copying the designs of the famous. It recently paid a grand sum to open a store on New York's Fifth Avenue, surrounded by the boutiques of those brand names that "inspire," to use the preferred word of copyists, its budget-priced renditions.

Despite several well-publicized lawsuits by designers claiming that their works were wrongly copied, the Los Angeles-based Forever 21, now also on Fifth Avenue in space vacated by a Japanese luxury department store, appears able to build brand loyalty around the world. The likely reason is that, although there are exceptions, suing over a design that may be a hit for a season or two and that is not being copied at the same price point for sale to the same customers may just not be something that a well-run business lightly undertakes. In fashion, litigation is generally not seen, to paraphrase Frederick the Great, as negotiation by another means; it is more commonly seen as a weapon used only with care and deliberation. The fashion business moves too fast for most people in it eager to take the time to sue, especially considering that the object of a lawsuit today may be old and half forgotten by tomorrow.

Conclusion

For all of the competitiveness, the ego trips, and bouts of blazing hysteria, fashion is a rather collegial business. After all, fashionistas do not dress up to impress people who do not understand fashion. They do it to impress each other.

That is the fun part. For those of us providing professional services, fashion remains a business in which commerce and art complement and clash, one in which our primary job is to watch the backs of those working on both sides of the house. The best defense in a business that defines quickness in business is to be quicker than all the rest: the more you do the protect your work *before* the trouble starts, the more likely it is that you will be able to bring the troublemakers to bay without spending too much money and time. The key for lawyers and their clients in the business is to get in and get protection going early and do it in a broad enough way so that, later on, when it is time to reap the rewards, the business gets the benefit and not someone whose primary talent lies in knowing what to copy.

Key Takeaways

- Know your client's business, from the styles it handles to the economics of its operations.
- Every brand has a story. Know the story of your client's brands and those of its competitors. Be proactive in the protection of key trademarks associated with each brand but consider carefully whether and to what extent branding devices with a limited projected lifecycle need protection.
- Not all copying of fashion and accessories designs is infringement, and not all copying in the fashion and accessories world is necessarily bad. It depends on circumstances, context and business objectives.
- Dress like a lawyer with a fashion sense. Just because your client wears jeans to work does not mean he wants to see his lawyer show up that way. Fashion clients know the grammar of dress and will respect you all the more if you do as well.

Alan Behr, a partner in the New York office of Alston & Bird LLP, is a member of the firm's IP & Technology Transactions and Trademarks Groups and the head of the firm's Fashion & Luxury Goods Practice. Mr. Behr counsels many of the world's leaders in the field and is regularly invited to write for legal and general-interest journals and to speak at international legal and business conferences on fashion and design related topics. Mr. Behr also maintains an arbitration and mediation practice, handling ADR cases both as an advocate and as a neutral. He is recognized as one of the leading intellectual property lawyers in Best Lawyers in America *and* Super Lawyers.

Acknowledgment *I would like to thanks the following attorneys and law students for their kind assistance in the preparation of this chapter. Their thoughtfulness, insight, and diligence is greatly appreciated: Meredith D. Fogel, VP and associate general counsel, Saks Incorporated; Sunny S. Park, assistant general counsel, Saks Incorporated; Edward M. Prince, of counsel, Alston & Bird LLP; Christopher J. Gegg, partner, Alston & Bird LLP; summer associates: Leah Feinman, Fordham University, and Bethany Eroh-Simmons, Hofstra University; Referendare: Markus Morgenroth, Ludwig Maximilian University, Munich, and Malte Dingwort, Bucerius Law School, Hamburg.*

Negotiating a Successful Licensing Deal

Lois Herzeca

Partner and Co-Chair,

Fashion, Apparel and Consumer Products Practice Group

Gibson, Dunn & Crutcher LLP

ASPATORE

Introduction

The fashion industry has experienced unprecedented changes in recent years. The global financial crisis fueled economic uncertainty and negatively impacted consumer demand. Yet, at the same time, new geographic markets (in Asia and elsewhere) opened for the sale of luxury goods. Moreover, the rise of e-commerce and social media has fundamentally altered the way in which the fashion industry advertises and sells its products. As a consequence of these significant developments, fashion companies are continuing to re-evaluate their global business strategies, including the use of strategic licensing arrangements.

A company can use a license arrangement to cost-effectively extend its product range and its geographic reach, without the significant capital investment required to build new manufacturing facilities and distribution and sales forces. Licenses can be used to introduce brand extensions under existing trademarks, to create new product lines at a different price point under new trademarks, or to expand existing brands into new territories.

Typically, a license arrangement provides that the company will continue to own its intellectual property, but will grant a limited right to the licensee to use certain of its intellectual property for a specific purpose in a given geographic area over a limited time period. The licensee manufactures, distributes and sells the licensed products—subject to the quality standards and approval rights of the company—and retains the proceeds of sale while paying a royalty to the company. Since license agreements can be strategically important, and since they involve a company's brands, an arrangement that does not produce the desired results can potentially damage the reputation of the brand as well as the future financial success of the company. Accordingly, it is critical to approach a license arrangement with sufficient advance planning, an experienced team and a critical eye.

The key to negotiating a financially successful licensing agreement is to identify the specific strategic objectives of the company and to craft a payment formula that achieves those objectives but also properly incentivizes the licensee. Of course, the company also needs to establish quality control and approval mechanisms to ensure that the final licensed product will be appropriate for, and enhance the value of, the brand.

Structuring the License

Determining Objectives

The first step in considering a license arrangement is to determine the short term and long term qualitative and quantitative objectives of the license. Is it a trial run or one step in a multi-faceted business plan? Does it require the introduction of an entirely new brand with attendant marketing risks? Is it fundamental to the financial success of the company or is it a means to generate some ancillary revenues? What are the risks of entering into the license arrangement and how can they be minimized? What would be the best outcome of the license arrangement? A company should not enter into a license arrangement unless and until it can adequately address these issues.

Selecting a Licensee

Once the company's objectives have been determined, the company should consider which potential licensee has the best ability to achieve those objectives. In evaluating potential licensees, attention should be directed to the licensee's particular experience and expertise in the product lines and geographic areas of the proposed license—an experienced licensee for shoes may not have the right design staff and facilities to produce jewelry and a strong licensee in Europe may not have the right network for Asia. Moreover, all proposed licensees should submit their views as to the potential size of the market for the licensed product. Similarly, proposed licensees should be vetted for their financial stability, commercial reputation, and longevity in the business, as well as their roster of other licensors. In certain circumstances, it may not be advisable for the licensee to be working with a direct competitor or a company with similar products that have a different quality and price point.

Defining the Scope of the License

Once an appropriate licensee has been selected, it is important to carefully circumscribe the scope of the license to match the company's objectives. The initial issue to focus on is the company's intellectual property rights—i.e., the protective rights granted by the government relating to certain scientific and creative matters principally patents, trademarks, and copyrights. Which intellectual property rights will be licensed under the agreement? Will they be existing rights or newly created ones? Since the licensee will likely ask the company for representations and warranties on the intellectual property rights being licensed, the company should carefully review with counsel the status of such rights in each jurisdiction relevant to the license, and take appropriate actions to register the rights as needed. Moreover, the company should be certain that the corporate entity signing the license agreement owns or has adequate rights to the licensed intellectual property.

Next, the company should determine which product lines will be covered by the license. The description of the product lines should be drafted as narrowly as possible so as to avoid an unintended expansion of the license—e.g., rather than simply saying "jewelry," consider specifying "women's gold and silver necklaces, bracelets and rings." It may also be useful to explicitly exclude certain product lines—e.g., women's gold and silver rings, but not rings with gemstones.

Similarly, the geographic scope of the license should be carefully considered and narrowly defined. Instead of specifying geographic regions, it may be preferable in some circumstances to identify the particular countries in which the goods may be sold. To strengthen the territorial limitations, the licensee should be specifically prohibited from exporting the licensed products outside the countries included in the license and from selling to third parties who intend to sell the products outside such countries. The license agreement should also clearly specify the intended channels of distribution for the licensed products—such as certain department stores, specialty retailers, mass market stores, or the internet—and whether, and in what quantities, they can be sold to off price or discount retailers. Importantly, the company should consider whether the license should be exclusive as to certain product lines, geographic areas, or channels of distribution. For example, the company may want to retain the right to have additional licensees under certain circumstances, such as where the territory is particularly large.

The company should also consider imposing certain restrictions on the licensee that will advance the company's larger strategic objectives. For example, the company may want approval rights over the granting of sublicenses and inspection rights over both manufacturing facilities and sublicensees, to enable the company to ensure quality control and maintenance of appropriate workplace and labor standards. In addition, the company may believe that it is critical to prohibit the licensee from entering into similar license agreements with certain key competitors of the company in the same geographic territories or for the same types of products at the same price points. And, the company may want to prohibit, or impose restrictions on, the ability of the licensee to sell the licensed products to certain types of retailers.

Finally, the company should limit the term of the license to a period which is long enough to obtain the intended benefits of the license but short enough that it does not unduly commit the company to an ineffective or unproductive licensee (who may be meeting its minimum obligations under the license agreement but not growing the brand sufficiently). Typically, license agreements have an initial term of three to six years.

The Licensee's Concerns

If the company is successful in narrowing the scope of the license, the licensee may seek additional rights to protect its investment. The licensee may argue that it is investing significant capital and resources in developing the brand, and so should have first rights in connection with extensions of the brand into additional products or territories. A right of first offer, for example, would require the company to offer a subsequent license deal for specified products or territories first to the licensee—rather than third parties—and agree to negotiate in good faith for a specified time period to reach agreement on the terms and conditions of the new license. The licensee also might have the right to propose a new license to the company for specified products or territories, with a similar obligation to negotiate in good faith for a specified period of time.

Alternatively, the licensee might seek a right of first refusal, or right to match, any third party's offer of a license deal for specified products or territories. In either case, these first rights should be granted sparingly because they could hamper a company's ability to timely enter into new licenses with the best licensee for that product or territory. If first rights are granted, the negotiation period should be as short as possible—ideally no more than thirty days—and the license agreement should specifically provide that after the end of the negotiation period, if the parties have not reached full agreement on terms and conditions, the company is free to enter into a license agreement with a third party for those products or territories.

Similarly, the licensee may also seek one or more automatic renewal rights after the expiration of the initial term of the license. If the company is willing to grant renewal rights, it should be careful to tie any renewals to achievement of certain milestones—perhaps in excess of any guaranteed minimums. In any event, renewal rights should not be granted if the licensee is in material breach of the license agreement.

Structuring the Payment Formula

The Planning Process

At the beginning of the negotiation process, the parties should agree on a business plan for the initial term of the license. The business plan should specify in detail when each product will be introduced in each territory and what the projected revenues are expected to be for each product and territory. An agreed business plan will avoid miscommunication on the financial goals of the license and, more importantly, will serve as the foundation for the payment structure of the license agreement.

Next, the parties need to agree on a payment structure for the license. License agreements have several different types of payment provisions that function interdependently: up-front or signing payments, royalties, advertising payments, and creative fees. The company should consider at the outset what is most important—a large up-front fee, a steady income stream from a creative fee, a large upside if the business is successful, or a high advertising budget to increase the brand's presence in the marketplace—and negotiate accordingly.

Up-Front Payments

A company with a valuable brand may want, and be able to obtain, a large up-front payment in order to compensate it for the brand value and opportunity cost of choosing that particular licensee, and to help ensure that the licensee is sufficiently motivated to exploit the license. An up-front payment may be particularly desirable if there will be a long lead time before introduction of the licensed product into commerce, and therefore a long time before the company will receive any royalties. The up-front payment may, in whole or part, be treated as an advance against future royalty payments, and be offset against the licensee's obligation to make such payments. In such event, the licensee may insist that the unearned part of the up-front payment be returned if the company materially breaches the license agreement before the up-front payment is fully offset against earned royalties.

Royalties

Royalty payments are generally the predominant financial provisions of a license agreement. They are typically calculated based on a percentage of "net wholesale sales" of the licensed product. The definition of "net wholesale sales" is almost as important as the percentage in determining the amount of royalties that will actually be paid. Typically, the term "net wholesale sales" is defined to mean the gross invoiced price to retailers of the products sold under the license agreement, subject to certain negotiated exclusions. The licensee may try to exclude as many items as possible to lower the amount of the royalty. The most common exclusions are: sales tax, trade discounts, freight costs, merchandise returns, markdowns, chargebacks, and allowances. The company should try to limit markdowns and chargebacks to those that are, in accordance with GAAP, treated as deductions from gross sales. The company should also limit deductions for chargebacks for advertising, fixtures, or retail shop costs. The company should also try to avoid any additional deductions—such as for uncollectible accounts—and try to set a cap on the total amount of deductions in any given year—i.e., they cannot exceed a specified percentage of "net wholesale sales" for such year.

The size of the royalties can be fixed or can vary within a single license agreement, depending upon the volume of sales or the type of distribution channel. If certain channels carry lower royalty rates, the company may want to cap the amount of annual sales through that particular channel. The amount of royalties for licensed products typically ranges from 3 percent to

16 percent of "net wholesale sales," depending on a number of factors including the strength of the brand, the type of products being produced, and the intended distribution channels.

In order to both ensure a guaranteed income stream and growth of a brand, a company should try to negotiate for both annual guaranteed minimum royalty payments and annual guaranteed minimum sales volumes. These would be calculated based on an agreed upon discount to the annual sales projections contained in the agreed upon business plan. It might be inappropriate to use the actual annual sales projections as the minimum, to the extent that they are aspirational. It is useful to have minimum sales requirements, in addition to minimum royalties, to ensure that the licensed products are actually being produced and getting to market, and that the licensee is not simply paying the minimum royalties to maintain the license in hopes of achieving future profits. If the licensee fails to satisfy the guaranteed minimum royalty or sales requirements, it may be in breach of the license agreement and may lose its renewal rights.

Advertising Minimums

Similarly, the license agreement should contain minimum annual amounts that the licensee must spend on advertising. These are usually expressed as a percentage of "net wholesale sales," and the percentage may be greater in the initial years when advertising expenses need to be higher and sales may be lower. Advertising minimums are important because marketing may be the key to the successful introduction of a new product or an existing product into a new territory. The parties should also agree on a detailed annual advertising budget, specifying where and how the licensed products will be advertised—i.e., in what media and territories—and the type and number of personnel who will be involved. The company may want to have final approval rights over all advertising, press, and promotion, in order to control the brand image.

Annual Creative Fees

Finally, if employees of the company, principally key designers or celebrities, are expected to take an active role in the design, implementation, or publicity for the licensed product, the company should be appropriately compensated. This often takes the form of an annual creative fee. The creative fee may operate on a sliding scale, depending on the extent of the commitment. The license agreement should set forth, in detail, any required obligations to grant interviews, attend the product launch and subsequent publicity events, or maintain a social media presence—such as a Twitter account—for the licensed products and the brand.

Payment Mechanisms

The license agreement should detail the mechanism for payment and audit rights of the company. All royalty and creative fee payments should be made at specified periodic intervals, together with a detailed breakdown of the payment—in the case of royalties—by product and country. It is helpful if the form of payment report is agreed in advance and attached as an exhibit to the license agreement. If sales are made in foreign currencies, the license agreement should also contain the mechanism for determining the exchange rate—i.e., using an average exchange rate for the applicable period. The company must have the right to audit the licensee's books and records to confirm that the payment calculations conform to the terms of the agreement. Generally, audits are at the expense of the company, unless a material deficiency is found, in which case it should be reimbursed by the licensee.

Puts and Calls

In some circumstances, it may be advantageous to have a mechanism in the license agreement to allow the company to eventually cash in on a successful brand and to allow the licensee to take full ownership of the brand. Such a mechanism might incentivize the licensee to more aggressively fund and launch a new product or brand and to hire additional staff to handle the design, manufacture, and distribution of the products. One mechanism to achieve this goal is a put/call feature. The parties agree that, after a specified period of time or after the achievement of specified sales volumes, the company can "put" the license agreement to the licensee or the licensee can "call" the license agreement from the company. The put/call feature may be exercisable only once, for a specified period, or may be exercisable periodically after the initial target has been achieved. In each case, upon the exercise of the put or call, the license agreement would terminate and full ownership of the trademarks and associated rights and goodwill relating to the licensed products would be transferred to the licensee. These provisions typically provide either a formula or a mechanism for determining the put/call price. A formula might be based on a multiple of net sales or royalties over a specified period prior to the exercise of the put or call.

Alternatively, a mechanism might provide for an independent third party arbiter to make a binding determination of the value of the license agreement. A provision which utilizes a third party arbiter may be problematical because it commits the parties to a future price determination that they cannot predict with certainty in advance and may be materially different than their expectations at the time of entering into a licensing agreement. The put/call feature clearly has risks—at the time of exercise, one party may find that it is economically disadvantaged because of either the timing or pricing. However, it can be a useful mechanism for achieving certain strategic objectives and generating increased value.

Conclusion

Licensing deals can be a cost-efficient way to increase brand exposure and generate additional revenues. On the other hand, if a license deal is poorly designed or executed it can inflict significant damage on a company's brand image and reputation. The company may have to delay reintroduction of the licensed product or new products under the same brand for a significant period of time, or abandon the product line altogether. Therefore, it is critical to make sure that every license agreement is designed properly.

A successful licensing deal requires the right strategy, the right licensing partner, and an economic structure designed to deliver the expected value.

Key Takeaways

- Licensing deals can be used to introduce brand extensions, create new product lines, and to expand brands into new territories.
- Identify the strategic objectives of the company and craft a formula that achieves the objectives while also incentivizing the licensee.

- Evaluate potential licensees by reviewing their experience and expertise in the product lines within the geographic areas of the proposed license, reviewing their financial stability, commercial reputation, longevity in the business, and the other licensors they are working with.
- Structure payment provisions based on what is most important to the licensor—a large up-front fee, a steady income stream, a large upside, or a high advertising budget—and negotiate accordingly.

Lois Herzeca is a corporate partner in the New York office of Gibson, Dunn & Crutcher LLP and Co-Chair of its Fashion, Apparel and Consumer Products Practice Group. Ms. Herzeca's broad corporate practice includes client counseling, joint ventures, equity investments, mergers and acquisitions, licensing agreements, and other commercial transactions. She represents a wide spectrum of luxury goods companies, retail companies, and manufacturing companies, and numerous fashion designers and celebrities.

She has written many articles for legal and financial publications and has spoken at conferences for the Practising Law Institute, the Strategic Research Institute and the Conference Board. She has been quoted widely in such publications as the Wall Street Journal, Law 360, *the* AmLaw Daily, *and* the New York Law Journal.

The Opportunities of Fashion Law

Vicki Dallas

Partner and Chair, Apparel Industry Practice Group

Rutan & Tucker LLP

ASPATORE

Introduction

As a corporate partner in a regional law firm, I have had extensive experience working with start-ups and emerging growth companies in various industry sectors, taking them from their formation to their exit strategy, which is typically an acquisition, licensing transaction, or initial public offering.

I have always been interested in the fashion industry, having followed the local Southern California action sports and apparel companies for many years. In the last five years, I have noticed the uptick in M&A and IPO activity involving our local apparel and action sports companies. I also became aware of the local talent that was joining forces with veteran apparel entrepreneurs to start new brands.

What Fashion Law Encompasses

My skill set was ideal for a fashion law practice, a rapidly growing specialty that requires thorough knowledge of several different legal practice areas, such as, business and corporate law, financing, commercial sale transactions, licensing and distribution arrangements, intellectual property, including copyright and trademark law, and employment law.

Having worked with many technology companies, I was familiar with these practice areas, and I easily adapted to the fashion industry. Lawyers need to understand that the fashion law business is different in that there are ever-changing product cycles and trade arrangements, so adaptability to change and understanding an apparel company's basic business strategy is essential to being an effective legal advisor in this practice area.

In recent years, fashion law has become a quickly growing legal specialty. More and more fashion law courses and programs are springing up in American law schools and design schools. Fashion is now an international business. Small to midsized companies are being acquired by large international apparel and lifestyle companies, and private equity firms have also entered into the playing field, making this a dynamic and growing practice area.

The Trends of Fashion Law

Copyright infringement cases have been on the rise. In an effort to stem the tide, Congress is addressing the Innovative Design Protection and Piracy Prevention Act, a bill to amend the Copyright Act to add fashion designs as a protected type of design. To fit within the definition of fashion design and gain protection under the Act, the article of apparel must include original elements or the original arrangement or placement of original or non-original elements, resulting from the designer's own creative efforts, and must provide a unique and non-utilitarian variation over prior designs for similar types of articles. To receive protection under the Act, registration is not required. Instead, a design notice is utilized, and the protection under the Act extends for a period of three years from the date the design was first made public. This Act has generated much controversy, with proponents on both sides of the issue. How this issue will be resolved remains to be seen.

Fashion Law as a Distinct Practice Area

With the globalization of the fashion industry, fashion conglomerates are looking for new small to midsized brands with strong growth prospects. For example, the sports and lifestyle segments are huge and still growing, particularly internationally in emerging markets. These international conglomerates can pay higher premiums for newer brands, since they have the business structures in place to maximize profits by capitalizing on their international market knowledge, sourcing capabilities, and operational expertise in product development, distribution, and retailing. Although many of these companies have in-house counsel, the in-house legal departments generate sufficient legal work to justify employing outside lawyers and experts who are specialists in the fashion industry.

Licensing

Licensing has traditionally been an important way for a brand to increase profit and revenue streams by expanding into new product categories. This trend is continuing and expanding.

Strategic licensing enables a company to form an alliance with a third-party licensee with expertise in a particular brand category, thereby off-loading the manufacture and marketing costs of product categories that are not part of the company's core business. One facet of this is celebrities creating new brands and entering into licensing arrangements to promote their celebrity status.

The Lawyer's Role

For a lawyer involved in a licensing transaction, it is important to make sure that the arrangement makes sense to the client and that it will enhance and improve the client's brand. It is also important to understand and limit the time commitments that will be involved from a creative and management point of view for the client.

Performance metrics need to be incorporated into the agreement to ensure performance goals and objectives are met. Other key terms include which products and trademarks are covered, the royalty arrangements and design fees, whether the arrangement is exclusive or nonexclusive, the definition of the design and approval relationships relating to the products and product promotion, and the term and termination of the license agreement.

Working with Fashion Law Clients

Working with fashion clients presents challenges that are unique to the particular company. Much depends on the maturity and size of the company. I represent start-ups and early stage apparel companies as well as mature companies. Generally, the start-ups and early stage clients have unique issues and challenges.

Challenges of New Companies

One of the first challenges faced by young companies is finding the money to hire an attorney and other professionals. Although it sounds like a cliché, every small business needs to assemble a team that includes a lawyer, a banker, and an accountant. This is particularly true for an apparel company interested in developing a brand.

A more mature company typically has a management structure in place, with a general strategic plan for developing the business. This is usually not the case with start-ups and early stage companies. They typically have a designer, and perhaps a few other people who are multitasking in various positions.

Determining Objectives

At the first meeting with a new client, the lawyer must ascertain the long-term objectives of the client. For example, is the client interested in building the brand and operating it as a stand-alone business? Is the client interested in developing the brand and then licensing the brand? Is the client interested in going public? Is the client interested in selling the company after developing the brand? In each of these scenarios, there are certain critical issues that need to be addressed up front to avoid problems later.

Laying the Foundation

Larger companies need new brands to grow their businesses internationally. Rather than developing the new brands in-house, these companies are paying premiums for proven brands. If a small to midsized company is planning to capitalize on an acquisition down the road, it is important that the early formation steps are done properly to attract a suitor and to maximize value. There are several issues that need to be addressed at a fashion company's beginning; these issues must be structured properly as they may affect the feasibility and value of a future deal.

<u>Agreements</u>

First, founder's agreements and option grants need to be formalized so that the ownership of the company is clearly reflected in the corporate records.

<u>Freelance Contracts</u>

Employment and consulting relationships need to be carefully documented. Many small companies use freelance designers, which requires the use of carefully drafted work-for-hire contracts that specify that any IP created by the designer is the property of the company. These contracts are critical going into an acquisition setting, as the buyer will conduct substantial due diligence to ensure that the company owns the rights that the buyer is purchasing in the deal.

Real Estate Issues

Real estate contracts and leases need to be properly drafted so that a company can grow or contract its real estate requirements as needed. In an acquisition setting, for example, a buyer may need to consolidate facilities, so it is important to understand the termination options in a lease. If a lease is favorable, it is important to negotiate and understand renewal options in the lease.

Import Considerations

If a company is involved in the importation of products or materials, there are a number of issues to be addressed, such as human rights compliance issues, monitoring import duties, inspection certificates, and letters of credit and bank guarantees.

Marketing, Licensing, and Sales

Marketing and advertising issues are also critical. If the company has been using photos of celebrities using or wearing their products, a buyer will want to be sure the company has the rights to exploit the celebrity's image on the website and in the marketing materials. Copyright permissions and releases need to be included in the company files.

If there are any licensing arrangements in place, the scope of the license, the royalty rates, and the termination provisions need to be addressed to determine the impact of the license on a future acquisition opportunity.

Sales arrangements, such as the use of distributors, sales representatives, dealers, consignment, and leased departments, need to be reviewed and the impact of those arrangements on a potential deal needs to be assessed.

Labor Concerns

Labor and employment issues, including antidiscrimination and sweatshop issues, need to be addressed on an ongoing basis. A purchaser of a company will almost always require representations and warranties regarding labor and employment issues.

Making sure the company is ready for the intense due diligence process from the onset makes getting the deal done so much easier in the end.

Licensing and Compliance in Fashion Law

Licensing has become an important tool for a company to grow a brand. For example, licensing may facilitate the expansion of a brand's awareness by increasing market opportunities in new niches, opening up new distribution channels, creating new markets in new geographic areas, and extending core products into complementary products that might not otherwise be available to a company.

Before embarking on a licensing opportunity, a licensor should have a design philosophy and creative vision in place in order to keep the brand identity intact. A licensor may also need a compliance group in place to monitor production and marketing, as well as an accounting team to ensure that proper accounting for royalties is in place.

Selecting a Licensee

In selecting a licensee, it is important to determine if the licensee has the financial strength to perform its obligations under the license agreement and to ensure that no conflicting obligations exist to which that licensee is a party and that might interfere with the licensee performing its obligations under the license agreement. There are several key issues to address and alternatives to consider in a licensing agreement.

<u>License Grant</u>

Defining the products to be covered and the rights granted in the license agreement is the first step and it is a critical one. A licensor can control the scope of the license by carving out specific provisions. For example, exclusivity and territorial restrictions are key factors for consideration by the parties.

Specifying the trademarks that are the subject of the license also need to be set forth in writing. The broader the license grant, the higher the royalty rate. The ability to sublicense or assign the license is also a key factor, and in many cases will depend on whether the licensor intends to compete with its licensees.

If the licensor does not intend to compete, then permitting sublicensing or assignment may allow the licensor to increase its potential revenue stream by expanding its sales base through sublicensing or assignment. If authorized, the licensor should retain approval rights over the assignment or sublicensing parties, and they should be subject to any restrictions contained in the underlying license agreement.

Initial Payments, Royalty Rates, and Advertising and Promotion Minimums

Initial payments are generally nonrefundable license fees, used to compensate the licensor for the costs of investigating the licensee and covering documentation costs, and they may or may not be creditable to future royalties. The royalty fee is the main source of revenue for the licensor, and may be fixed, or varied based on a percentage of sales, or other factors.

Royalties are often structured with minimum payments to ensure that the licensor will have a reliable royalty stream. In negotiating the royalty rate, gross sales and net sales are generally favored by both licensors and licensees. From the licensor's point of view, gross sales and net sales are harder to manipulate, and from the licensee's point of view, the licensee can avoid disclosing profit information to the licensor.

Another method of calculating royalties is to use gross profit. This method subtracts from gross sales the cost of goods sold, which generally includes directly allocable expenses, such as manufacturing expenses, raw material costs, and direct labor costs. An advantage of this method for the licensor is that the licensor can take advantage of increasing profit margins. On the other hand, from the licensee's perspective, the licensee is forced to open up its books to the licensor, disclosing more financial information than the licensee may desire to disclose.

A third royalty option is to use a per unit royalty rate on product sold. This method does not require the licensee to disclose financial information. Like the sales method, this method does not take profitability into account, and therefore this method is useful if the licensee wants to limit disclosure of financial information.

The license agreement may contain advertising and promotion minimums, in addition to the initial payments and royalty payments. In all cases, the licensor needs to retain audit rights to verify the accuracy of the licensee's accounting for royalties and other financial obligations. The licensor will also need to retain rights to police the quality control of any licensed products to ensure brand integrity. The licensor may want to retain approvals over manufacturing quality, distribution channels, and advertising and promotion programs, and to incorporate a compliance program requiring samples, or rights to inspection.

<u>Term and Renewal Options</u>

The term of the license agreement needs to be set forth in the agreement, with clearly specified instructions on what occurs upon termination. Any proprietary materials belonging to the licensor should be returned immediately. As is the case in other agreements, the parties should be able to terminate the license agreement upon the occurrence of a material breach.

A licensee will generally want a longer term if a substantial start-up investment is involved. That must be balanced by the licensor with a minimum sales requirement to ensure that the licensee will be actively marketing the licensed products. The licensor will want to reserve the right to terminate the license if the licensee is not performing to the minimum performance thresholds.

Managing Fashion Law Complications

Designers are by nature creative people, and continually on the move. It is important to stay on top of them and to encourage them to identify the people and resources in their company who have the authority to assist you in tying up the loose ends. For example, making sure all the trademarks are filed with correct descriptions and in the right classes can be challenging, as well as documenting a transaction or relationship that is in flux. If getting access to the designer or owner is problematic, it is critical to explain to your client why it is important to have access to the people you need so that you can do your job and be an effective attorney and advocate.

Conclusion: The Future of Fashion Law

There are always challenges in any economic environment. Despite these challenges, the Internet and other digital technologies have made the world a smaller place and have allowed the fashion and apparel industry to become a large and dynamic force in the global economy. The image of a celebrity in a beautiful gown at the Oscars or a famous actor wearing designer denim at a sporting event is immediately transmitted by digital technology and new trends can become instant mega hits in a fast fashion environment. This creates enormous opportunities for the fashion industry, and in turn for the legal professionals who support the industry.

Key Takeaways

- Because the fashion law business is different, with its ever-changing product cycles and trade arrangements, adaptability to change and understanding an apparel company's basic business strategy is essential to being an effective legal advisor.
- When forming an apparel company, formalizing founder's agreements, option grants, and freelance contracts are important, as well as addressing marketing, sales, and employment concerns.
- Licensing is an important way for a brand to increase profit and revenue streams by expanding into new product categories. Strategic licensing enables a company to form an alliance with a third-party licensee and allows it to offload the manufacture and marketing costs of product categories that are not part of its core business.
- In drawing up a licensing agreement, defining the products to be covered and the rights granted is the critical first step. A licensor can control the scope of the license by carving out specific provisions, such as exclusivity and territory.

- If a small to midsized company wants to capitalize on an acquisition in the future, it is important that the early formation steps are done properly to attract a buyer and to maximize value. Making sure the company is ready for the intense due diligence process from the onset makes getting the deal done easier in the end.

Related Resources

- The California Fashion Association (CFA) is a non-profit organization established to provide information for business expansion and growth to the apparel and textile industry of California.
- The Fashion Business Inc., a 501(c)(3) non-profit organization, provides the fashion industry with entrepreneurial development, resources and training, to support its growth and profitability. The Fashion Business Inc. (FBI) offers targeted business education, sourcing, networking opportunities, marketing and consulting services through its resource center and business partnerships.

Vicki Dallas is a partner in the law firm of Rutan & Tucker LLP, and is the chair of the firm's Apparel Practice Group. She has a JD and an LLM from the University of Florida College of Law. Ms. Dallas specializes in mergers and acquisitions, emerging growth company representation, corporate finance, venture capital, licensing, distribution, and marketing arrangements. She counsels fashion companies of all sizes in all aspects of their business law requirements, including structure and formation of business entities, capital raising and financing arrangements, mergers and acquisitions, strategic partnerships, joint ventures, and other growth and exit strategies.

An Exploration into the Practice of Fashion Law

Richard Reinis

Senior Partner

Steptoe & Johnson LLP

ASPATORE

Introduction

Fashion law is a relatively new area of legal practice. At the beginning of the twentieth century, the fashion industry was predominately a highly fragmented, East Coast concern. Few clients employed general counsel, and few budgeted significant legal expense to protect their rights. The business was very competitive, marked by relatively low margins of profit, with precious little allocated to professional services. The fashion market was easily accessible with very low capital requirements, but frustratingly difficult to penetrate. Investment was confined to very tangible needs, rarely available to support legal work other than basic organizational formation, including the choice of business organization and location, compliance with basic and very limited regulatory issues, occasional labor or union problems, minor intellectual property work, and the legal necessities occasioned by exiting from the business.

Much has changed in the fashion industry since the end of World War II to require more highly developed legal skills, and, happily, to demand a much greater allocation to legal expense. The industry is hardly confined to one region; it is entirely global, and the gritty nature of fashion commerce is now somewhat obscured by unremitting glamour depicted in every type of media. While still fragmented, a surprisingly large number of members of the fashion industry have grown into mega multi-nationals, with large in-house legal departments and brand name law firms to match the power of their own brand names. These companies have become enormously powerful and media savvy, and they are capable of penetrating any market directly, through print, and via the Internet. To be sure, the vast number of fashion businesses only aspire to reach the heights of the numerous public and private fashion giants, with stables of trademarks, worldwide licenses, branded retail locations, and close working relationships with the great retailers of the world, but in that aspiration, fashion industry members have to resort to legal assistance to build a proper aspirational foundation.

This chapter will review the skill sets necessitated by these demands. Within the sphere of a typical transactional practice, we review the corporate and securities, real estate, and mergers and acquisitions legal needs of fashion industry members. Also included are discussions of the IP and trade secret demands and the employment/wage and hour problems that need to be addressed. Union related issues are also reviewed. Transactional problems related to the geographic scope of the work of the client are described. The litigation problems confronted by fashion lawyers include those inherent in protecting IP, licensing and trade secrets, recovering money from recalcitrant debtors, and those problems typical of any unraveling business. We review the skills necessary to solve the occasional dispute with institutional lenders, or the frequent disputes with retailers. Related to the litigation issues that need legal attention are the increasing administrative and regulatory demands imposed by the US and other sovereign nations' customs and tariff agencies, safety regulations, import and export controls, immigration regulations, state and federal labor issues, labeling regulations, and a growing number of regulations imposed on internet sales and advertising sites.

Developing expertise in fashion law will require a broad knowledge of various areas of the law, and an understanding of the material in the following chapters should be invaluable to that end.

Defining Fashion Law

Fashion law involves representation of members in the fashion industry—a diverse group. When I first started my practice as a solo in 1981, I located in the California Mart, the center of the California apparel industry for the purpose of marketing my skills as a fashion lawyer. By 1986, the firm had grown to ten lawyers, representing more members of the apparel community than any other firm of which we were aware. Our malpractice carrier told us we were the only firm that reported apparel law as the dominant area of its practice.

Fashion Law Clientele

Fashion industry lawyers represent diverse clients, including individuals, those whose names are unknown and celebrities; corporations or LLCs, private, and public companies; vertical organizations whose employees perform all tasks from conception to sale; horizontal companies that provide a business-to-business function; apparel and other fashion companies themselves and companies that service the industry; importers, exporters, wholesalers, and retailers. Each type of client presents different challenges.

My clients have included manufacturers, cutting and sewing contractors, designers, sales representatives, artists, knitters, spongers, embroiderers, finishers, retailers, freight forwarders, importers, exporters, factors, financial institutions with apparel clients, media, marketing and advertising specialists, fashion colleges, fashion photographers, and others who make a living in this extraordinary, vibrant business.

Thirty years ago, fashion industry executives were viewed by the legal community as idiosyncratic, non-professional, unsophisticated, and somewhat unsavory. Very little of this professional snobbery exists today, as so many major international law firms realize the benefits of a fashion law practice, and the extraordinary talents of those who manage fashion businesses.

The Emergence of Fashion Law

Fashion law has become more popular as apparel companies have grown in size and scope. According to the Los Angeles Country Economic Development Corporation, the apparel and textile industry manufacturing in Los Angeles County employs 76,000 people, and with that size come legal issues of sufficient economic impact to warrant lawyers' attention and marketing efforts. Los Angeles Country Economic Development Corporation, Calif. App. News, July 22, 2011 at 2. Annual fashion and accessory retail sales in America amount to $150 billion (according to Hoovers.com) from more than 100,000 outlets, and fifty companies account for 65 percent of that revenue. These companies are major targets for lawyers, and with good reason.

The vast size of many apparel companies necessitates vast legal undertakings. However, a fashion law practice rarely commences with representation of one of the largest companies. Generally, the larger fashion businesses are public, requiring securities practitioners. The size of the companies is often attained through acquisition, requiring M&A practitioners. The industry is known for its ability to leverage its assets, either borrowing from factors or more traditional asset based lenders. These arrangements provide easy access to markets, and require legal expertise in financing arrangements and a knowledge of the Uniform Commercial Code (UCC). Manufacturing is inevitably performed non-domestically, requiring Customs and logistics practitioners. Fashion industry companies survive, in part, because they acquire government sponsored monopolies, trademarks, and copyrights; some even acquire patents. These companies require international IP practitioners. The brands that are owned by these companies are frequently licensed, requiring licensing specialists. Larger companies are targets for class action lawsuits initiated by lawyers for consumers or employees. These companies require the services of specialized litigators. Labor issues arise constantly, complicated often by the seasonal use by fashion industry manufacturers of independent and specialized contractors on an as needed basis. The United States Department of Labor and state counterparts have differing views on just which company is responsible for payment of a particular wage to a particular worker. This requires knowledgeable labor counsel. Talent is critical to the success of fashion industry companies, and securing unfettered rights in designs requires trade secrets legal expertise. Active and passive, international sources of revenue of fashion industry clients requires tax counseling and planning. The list of legal demands is as immense as the industry.

However, the newcomer to the legal world of fashion is not frequently blessed with a mega client. What differentiates a fashion law practice from other industry-centric practices is that vast size may be attained by newcomers at any time and within a relatively short period of time. This promise of breathtaking success is the essence of the fashion industry. The lure keeps attracting new entrants, most of which will fail, and usually in a brief period of time. No matter; these new entrants should be part of any fashion law practice. The point is that by representing enough newcomers, a fashion law practitioner will, sooner or later, find him or herself representing a "hot" new label.

Current Fashion Law Trends and Developments

The most important legal trend in the fashion industry has occurred at the top, as Wall Street has assisted large fashion clients to become even larger. The M&A practice in the fashion industry is booming. Another growth area is labor law, as federal and state labor agencies grapple with the industry's particular problems of seasonality and the use of independent contractors. A swimsuit manufacturer does not manufacture products in equal amounts each month. As summer approaches, manufacturing output increases, and as fall approaches, manufacturing decreases. Thus, the swimsuit manufacturer cannot afford to maintain manufacturing employees year round. Independent contractors are retained for that purpose. These independent contractors manufacture swimsuits as seasonally required, and jackets or other apparel at other times. Labor agencies claim that the independent contractors pay piece rates to their employees, and those less capable do not earn minimum wage or overtime. Labor violations during the manufacture of goods intended for interstate commerce render the products "hot goods," or not shippable across state lines. Thus, the labor practitioner is called upon—and promptly. A solution at once is the only solution. Copyright trolling has propelled infringement defense work significantly in recent years. Wage and hour claims are popular in California, so class action work has increased as companies have grown larger or are suddenly contracted on account of the turmoil in the economy. Immigration issues tend to by cyclical, often responding to the political climate. Problems with overseas manufacture and transportation of goods and intellectual property have grown steadily. Over the last thirty years, much of the labor function has moved to Asia from the United States and Mexico. This presents cultural issues that often metastasize as legal problems. As financial institutions, upon which the fashion industry relies as much as an asthmatic may rely on an iron lung, have been challenged by the great recession, their fashion industry clients have also been impacted. A shortage of factoring capital threatens the emergence of new companies and growth of older companies.

Suddenly, Congress has taken an interest in the fashion industry. Senator Charles Schumer (D, NY) and Rep. Robert Goodlatte (R, Va.) have each proposed an amendment to Article 13 of U.S. Codes to provide the first ever protection of an original design of apparel, purses, footwear, eyeglasses, belts, and other utilitarian items. If passed, this new statute, known as the Innovative Design Protection and Piracy Prevention Act, may well become the "hottest" new item in fashion law.

The Joys and Challenges of Practicing Fashion Law

What is so inviting about such a practice? The people; the speed from conception to market; the "glitz"; the fragmentation; the sources of influence, inspiration, and production; the global nature of the business; the short cycle from start-up to failure or success; and the ever-present possibility that your start-up client may get "hot." The litmus test of talent in the fashion industry is demonstrable skill as measured *today*. Recognition comes to those who offer the public something that sells, and "no questions asked." The clientele may drive you nuts, but will never be boring.

But what does it mean to have a practice dedicated to an industry? It means you learn a new language, you know the players, you connect people, and you develop an institutional history that comforts clients and entices potential clients. Done well, your representation should develop into a means by which clients enhance their own credibility. The goal of such a practice for some may be developing a reputation that is of such character as to draw clients who seek the imprimatur of the attorney's representation.

The challenges are numerous: is your firm willing to accept start-ups? Does your firm accept the inevitable bad debts accruing from such business? Have you the patience to deal with off-beat clients, many of whom have no interest in the legal predicates to success? How much time are you willing to devote to teaching clients the basics of record keeping, employer-employee relationships, compliance with lengthy, complex financing relationships, conformity with retailer purchase contracts and shipping requirements, and other basics, some of which will never be billable? As a practitioner with current demands to keep the lights on, how much of your resources are you willing to invest in the future of a fashion law practice?

The breadth of expertise required for proficiency in this area is daunting. A fashion law practitioner must understand basic corporate law, along with employment agreements, designer agreements, trademark and copyright applications, business licenses and permits, and, very much a function of a fashion practice, assistance with securing contracting licenses, factoring agreements, sales representation agreements, and letters of credit or overseas credit lines. As noted above, the ultimate goal of many fashion industry clients is a sale or acquisition, so M&A capability is a prerequisite. That is just the beginning! A "hot" label will require not only an ability to draft license agreements for everything from perfume to pillows, but also how to "slice the pie" to maximize brand value. Licensing in the fashion industry is a major part of the practice, so an understanding of the business dynamics is necessary.

The task is no less challenging for litigators. This business invites "knock offs." A lawyer must help police this and work with the client to judiciously pick targets. Protecting the brand is essential to the ultimate outcome of the business plan, and when the transactional protections are insufficient, the litigator must react. That may require federal or state court litigation, but almost certainly will involve arbitration and administrative and regulatory work, frequently in international settings. In this connection, the practitioner may find it quite difficult to navigate the need to protect the client's interests with a sensitivity to the client's bargaining position. The fashion industry practitioner often faces a choice between recovering what is due and "biting the hand that feeds."

Preparing the Necessary Skills

Any lawyer about to commence representation of a fashion industry client would be well-served by a review of the Worth Street Rules. (See www.ncto.org/links/worthstreet.pdf). These basic rules of commerce have been a reference source since 1926. Textile purchase agreements may refer to these for dispute resolution purposes, and when an issue is best resolved before a third party by reference to custom and practice, the Worth Street Rules may be offered in evidence.

California, New York, and other states have enacted statutes specifically applicable to the fashion industry. Industry associations in respective states may provide a summary for the new practitioner. Generally, the fashion industry is subject to the same statutory framework as any business organization.

Corporate lawyers need no special skills in representation of a fashion industry client. In forming the business organization, however, much attention must be paid to a potential divorce, since the typical pairings of an administrative type with a creative type often results in a fatal rupture. Rare is the individual capable of meeting the aesthetic demands of the industry, on the one hand, and the administrative and organizational requirements of a truly competitive business, on the other. These pairings are more often dysfunctional than productive. Operationally, an administrator or "inside" person, rarely shares the limelight attracted to the business by the creative, or "outside" partner. This may lead to complications best resolved with employment agreements.

Termination of the existence of these business organizations is a major part of the practice. Litigation is becoming more common, as the stakes in the wake of a split are increasing. In view of this, buy-sell agreements are essential. Spousal or significant other waivers must be included. In creating these documents, the fashion industry practitioner must be certain as to whom he or she represents. If one of the principals is the designer, must there be an employment agreement that protects trade secrets? Consider the ramifications of identifying the designer with the corporate client. The loss of use of one's own name is not uncommon in the fashion industry. Is the name an asset of the corporate client or of the individual? Is equity for the business provided in cash by one owner and sweat by another? How is that to be documented?

Start-up costs of a new fashion industry business are relatively small; hence the great number of new businesses each year. When the lucky few succeed, they frequently are presented with a very serious challenge: how to finance growth. Too often, the cash and credit demands outstrip the financial resources of the founders. What are the alternatives? Here, the fashion industry lawyer plays a key role.

The unlucky many face the challenges of dissolution without personal exposure. The fashion lawyer must be sure of a termination that results in a clear demarcation between the business organization and its principals, to protect against creditors' claims. The typical factoring agreement requires the principals of the business to personally guaranty obligations to the factor. Care must be taken to avoid unnecessary risk incident to any such guaranty. The intellectual property must be fairly and equitably distributed. Personal obligations of the principals to their landlord, factor or other lending institution must be resolved. This requires an understanding of the Uniform Commercial Code (UCC) and of creditors' rights. Informal work-outs following a bleak ending are not uncommon.

The arc of an apparel business from inception to termination occupies the bulk of the practice. The practitioner is involved in structuring the capitalization of the business, reviewing the lease of the business premises, providing guidance as to insurance requirements, employment counseling, product safety—especially as relates to children's apparel and toys—and labeling, international intellectual property right perfection and good practices, assisting in issues related to export of designs for non-US fabrication, import and tariff issues, sales representation agreements, manufacturing agreements, confidentiality agreements, and relations with retailers, to identify some of the more obvious areas of legal endeavor.

Retailers have a love/hate relationship with apparel manufacturers. This presents the fashion lawyer with many issues, but central to them all is the constant battle over risk sharing. In this realm, the fashion lawyer must be conversant with purchase order forms, confirmations, bills of lading, return authorizations, and the myriad of chargebacks inventive retailers utilize to shift the cost of markdowns to the suppliers.

The ordinary and necessary skills of M&A specialists are required of the fashion lawyer. However, the focus is typically on "soft" assets, largely intellectual property and the continued employment of those essential to preservation of value. International trademark expertise has become increasingly important. Real estate, plants, equipment, and receivables are assets not commonly subject to much controversy, if any, in fashion industry M&A transactions. However, real estate expertise has become more important in a fashion industry practice, as more and more fashion industry companies explore their own retail opportunities. Those fashion industry companies that also rely on Internet sales and advertising require legal practitioners knowledgeable in the field.

With the growth of publicly held fashion industry clients, securities litigation has become more prevalent, giving rise to the importance of shareholder lawsuit defense experience. Federal court litigation is quite common in trademark and copyright disputes, as well as FLSA, and Corrupt Practices Act matters. As the apparel industry has been global for many years, issues arise that require adjudication, including US Customs duties, freight handling issues, and international contract disputes. Immigration specialists and tax lawyers may be included in the stable of lawyers in a fashion practice. Considerable expertise in regulatory matters is helpful. This has increasingly become a specialty for fashion lawyers.

Effective Client Marketing Strategies

How does one effectively market legal services to the fashion industry? The principal method I used in a pre-internet world was geographic. Locating offices convenient to the industry was a strong statement of commitment to the industry. Advertising in industry press was useful, and inexpensive. Speaking on pertinent issues at industry association meetings builds awareness, but should not be undertaken without some working knowledge of the topic. Trying to "wing-it" on most topics is dangerous, and you may well find an experienced fashion lawyer in the audience with no other aim than embarrassing the speaker. Diligently studying a factoring agreement will not make a lawyer an expert, whose presentation will enlighten and demonstrate special skills, so one must take care not to promise too much.

The fashion industry prides itself on charitable work. This is a genuine commitment of the time and resources of many members of the industry. It is imperative that an industry practitioner join industry associations and attend industry functions. Making donations to industry charities may help, but not nearly as much as volunteering time to the industry. This will not generate results at once, unless networking at such events develops a relationship. Over time, however, working with industry members for a charitable purpose should provide the desired outcome.

Attending industry trade shows is a common method of attracting clients. So many lawyers walk the aisles, however, each tends to dilute the presence of the other, and some industry attendees object. After all, the shows are intended primarily for the sale of merchandise, and a lawyer is not a buyer. However, there are judicious methods that will not offend. Use industry trade shows to meet clients from other parts of the country, and do this by appointment. Meet with factors, with whom lawyers are aligned in the search for new clients. The real business to be done at trade shows is during the evenings. After hour events offer a far superior opportunity to network. There may be speaking opportunities organized by industry associations, and these should be exploited.

Fashion Law Complications and Challenges

Like every other practice that is industry specific, fashion lawyers encounter conflicts. There are many areas where these may arise. A fashion lawyer who represents a factor or industry lender may find it difficult to represent a manufacturer/borrower from that same lender. If a fashion lawyer represents a major retailer, conflicts may arise when representing manufacturers who are vendors to the retailer client. Representation of a copyright troll may create conflicts. Conflicts arise amidst trade secret disputes between two clients.

A different type of complication arises when a government agency threatens to delay delivery of a client's goods. Apparel products are perishables! Right or wrong, if a government agency has the power to hold up delivery, prudence dictates a focus on getting goods to market. This arises in connection with US Customs issues as well as labor issues and questions raised by the US Department of Labor.

Similarly, retailers' claims must be handled delicately. The long term relationship may be of greater importance to an apparel client than which party is right. In connection with these issues, when the retailer assesses chargebacks against the client, the choice is unenviable: accept the wrongful credit claim or challenge it and potentially lose the account. The fashion client realizes not only this dilemma, but also that the simple retention of counsel to raise the issue may have a negative impact on the relationship. To be truly productive for fashion clients, assist in advance. This can be done by counseling the client as to how to win the battle of the forms.

How can one succeed in this with a generally uneven playing field between seller/manufacturer and buyer/retailer? Be certain your client's purchase order forms permit your client all lawful advantages. Consider how to contractually limit the retailer's rights to the many credits it will claim post-shipment. There will be electronic transfer of offer and acceptance, and the terms proposed by buyer and seller will vary widely. Thus, the battle lines are drawn. A good practice for the seller is to notify the retailer in writing that the seller does not accept the modification of the terms proposed by the retailer in its confirmation. This creates a potential conflict, but it arises pre-shipment.

Importers in the fashion industry face a similar, uneven playing field issue with respect to overseas production of goods. How does a practitioner assist an importer fashion industry client with respect to late or defective delivery from an overseas supplier? The best practice is to address this issue in advance of placing an order with the supplier, rather than to try to solve the problem when customer delivery dates alter the equation and deprive your client of bargaining room. Anticipate these problems in documentation. Provide for bonuses, sanctions, or penalties, but be fair. The goal is not to collect a sanction but to provide incentives for compliance. However, it is inevitable that delays and defects will occur. The parties must agree in advance as to how to resolve issues, and where. International arbitration is a popular mechanism used to resolve disputes. However, it is not inexpensive. What is saved in the litigation is the cost of the constant uncertainty as to when adjudication will be administered in a courtroom. However, filing fees and other costs of international arbitration may reduce or nullify any such savings. Trying to bring an overseas supplier within the jurisdiction of American courts is not often achieved. For this reason, many importers place orders with domestic companies that, in effect, play the role of distributor of goods manufactured by the overseas supplier. Recourse for the manufacturer is then against the domestic entity.

If a fashion industry lawyer is willing to accept start-up clients, the lawyer must also accept a high rate of failure. One of the many challenges is how to liquidate the business at a reasonable cost. Informal work-outs are commonly undertaken by the lawyer, working closely with the defunct company's accounting firm. The company notifies all creditors of its decision to cease business operations, of the amount of assets and liabilities, and the decision to liquidate and pay each creditor pro-rata. The notification presents alternatives to an informal work-out, including a bankruptcy filing and/or a receivership or assignment for benefit of creditors or other alternative. A cost/benefit analysis should be presented that results in the recommendation of the informal approach. Some creditors will balk at this, and the proposal may have to be abandoned in favor of a bankruptcy filing. The key is to mirror bankruptcy code priorities. Another frequently encountered complication is the potential existence of personal guarantees to lenders, landlords or others. These present significant challenges to the practitioner. Again, the best advice to the client is in advance of the problem: avoid personal guarantees or insure them, if at all possible. Lastly, the sale of the intangible assets can raise creditors' ire, unless handled transparently. Valuation issues must be anticipated. If the individual principal of the debtor or a substantial creditor purchases the IP, for instance, there will almost certainly be a challenge that the amounts paid (or credit bid) are not reflective of the fair market value of the asset. The fashion industry lawyer should be alert to these issues and recommend a process that is fair to all creditors.

Conclusion

After thirty years of fashion law practice, I can say without reservation that the field is very exciting. A lawyer need know nothing about what is fashionable, but he or she must learn who is responsible for making fashionable goods. That imperative requires an inquisitive mind and someone with great energy. It requires fearlessness. A fashion layer transacts, litigates, negotiates with regulators, corresponds with international counterparts, and coddles designers. It is fascinating and never staid. The fashion industry demands talent of its members—and its lawyers.

Keep in mind that the fashion industry is subject to massive changes that affect fashion lawyers. The good news is that the industry is not shrinking. It is global and supplying fashion merchandise to ever-increasing members of the middle class. Many industry-specific practices have been affected by the analog to digital changes, which, if nothing else, have created great uncertainty in such fields as print media and music. The people of the world insist on fashion merchandise and demography will out: the species is enlarging daily. To be sure, those who supply the merchandise must be nimble to meet growing demand, must be resilient to resist the pressures of giant retailers, must be efficient in purchasing labor and transporting products, and must be adept at modifying processes to the digital arena. However, these abilities are demonstrated daily, and the challenges are being met. The lawyer must find and market to those most able to overcome these day-to-day obstacles, but the targets are not dwindling.

Persistence is the key. Maintain a presence by marketing constantly and do not take for granted that the huge fashion industry client (HFIC) you presently represent has made for you an indelible reputation as a fashion industry practitioner. Constantly search for the new "hot" commodity and be willing to take on newcomers as clients. If the HFIC passes through the common arc of meteoric rise and fall, it will take you with it. The phone or e-mail should be active even when your time is absorbed by one or two demanding clients and it is wise to invest the time, no matter how scarce, to bring in new clients, even start-ups. For this, delegation and training is essential. It should be obvious that The HFIC requires the talents of many lawyers, so a fashion industry practitioner must bring on talented associates and partners. One lawyer cannot be all things—corporate lawyer, IP lawyer, labor/wage and hour lawyer, regulatory and administrative lawyer, litigator, bankruptcy lawyer—to all clients. And while you are realizing the importance of deepening your bench, remember that the fashion industry is energized and managed by about as diverse a group of executives as any industry in the world. A law firm's bench should reflect that diversity.

The fashion industry is a "what have you done for me lately" business. Yesterday's success is no guarantee of tomorrow's. This applies to fashion lawyers as well. Clients will depart, often without reason. Be prepared. Reflect on what might have been done better, internalize it, but do not dwell on speculation. Move on. In that sense, a fashion industry practice is not much different from any other.

What is unique is the combination of innumerable participants and the ever-changing landscape of leaders. Entry costs are low enough to attract people with what they consider to be marketable ideas to have their day. Fashion lawyers share in this.

Key Takeaways

- Dedicate yourself to the industry by learning the values of the people who drive it.
- Learn the process from inception to consumption.
- Understand terms of art and the language of the industry.
- Gain an understanding of the significant players and institutions, including the major providers of education, training, capital, raw goods, labor, freight forwarding, media, and retail.
- Recognize that so many different skills are required, that delegation of responsibility is inevitable.
- Be prepared to be affected by the rise and fall of fashion industry favorites.

- Never take for granted your reputation as a fashion industry lawyer; market constantly.
- Accept newcomers as clients and nurture them.
- Protect principals as you form new entities and dissemble them.

Richard Reinis is a senior partner in the Century City office of Steptoe & Johnson LLP, where he practices in the Business Solutions and Litigation departments. From 1981 until 2000, he was the managing partner of Reinis & Reinis, a Los Angeles law firm located in the California Mart, the center of the California apparel industry, from which the firm serviced fashion industry clients from all over the world. Since joining Steptoe & Johnson, he has been involved as lead counsel in mergers and acquisitions of middle market companies and significant commercial litigation. Transactions that have concluded under his leadership include the sale of an LED company, an apparel company, a blanket company, an energy company, and a large California ranch. He has represented buyers in connection with the acquisition of an apparel company, a wind energy generation company, and other businesses. He was lead counsel in the sale of certain assets of a large apparel manufacturer and the recapitalization of an apparel manufacturer. He has served as lead counsel in trade secrets litigation, probate matters, and licensing disputes.

Mr. Reinis commenced his law practice in 1969. Over the years, he has gained extensive fashion industry experience, working in the industry as an officer of an apparel manufacturer and general counsel to a fashion industry service provider, along with extensive experience in franchising, licensing, branding, and assisting companies in workouts. He founded a licensing company of a surf brand with many global licensees. He has lectured on various topics including factoring agreements, trademarks and copyrights, and other fashion industry topics. He has taught business law at the Fashion Institute of Design and Merchandising. His current speaking topics include matters pertaining to corporate governance and ethical management, trademarks and copyrights, and brand management. From 1998 until 2006, Mr. Reinis performed services for the Krispy Kreme franchise in Southern California, and he has spoken nationally of his experiences about that company's meteoric rise to prominence and subsequent challenges.

Mr. Reinis has served as an expert witness on apparel-related litigation matters and is a court-appointed special master. He previously served as lead counsel in several state court jury trials and has experience with the American Arbitration Association, the ICC, and Federal Court litigation. Mr. Reinis is a founding board member of the California Fashion Association. He is trustee and secretary of the Maxwell H. Gluck Foundation, a Trustee of the University of California at Riverside Foundation, and is a former Board member of LAFLA, LA Children's Museum, and the State Bar Fund. He was the founder of the Compliance Alliance, the nation's largest volunteer organization dedicated to FLSA compliance. His work in this arena earned him national recognition as a labor reformer. On behalf of the USDOL, he lectured national retailers on FLSA issues.

Mr. Reinis married his wife Lois in 1964, and they have five children and nine grandchildren.

Acknowledgment: *I am indebted to Rosenthal & Rosenthal Inc., a veteran factor in the fashion industry, and its employees for assistance in connection with this chapter.*

An Overview of Intellectual Property Issues Relevant to the Fashion Industry

Charles E. Colman

Founder

Charles Colman Law PLLC

ASPATORE

Introduction

Many law students, and even some practicing attorneys, equate fashion law with intellectual property law, and specifically, trademark law. The many other chapters of this book illustrate that fashion law is much more than that. However, one might reasonably consider intellectual property (IP) to be the core of fashion law, since the value of fashion—as opposed to *clothing*—rests in large part on the allure of a brand, and that allure is protected primarily by intellectual property law.

The term "intellectual property," conventionally understood, includes, on a federal level, utility and design patents and copyrights[1]; on a federal and state level, trademark and trade dress protection; and on a state level, trade secret protection, the right of publicity, the right against misappropriation, and other causes of action that vary by state. Some would define IP even more broadly than this, but the above definition suffices for our purposes.

Intellectual property, especially in the form of trademark protection, is often the most valuable asset owned by a fashion enterprise; indeed, in today's fashion world, many companies are little more than vendors of licenses to use well-known brand names in connection with particular categories of apparel and accessories.[2] This central emphasis on trademark protection is arguably the result of

- fashion's function as an indicator of social status,[3] with the corollary quality of being an "aspirational" good
- the newly widespread availability of affordable clothing following the Industrial Revolution, and the displacement of *actual* scarcity of clothing by *perceived* scarcity in form of "luxury" brands
- the lack of robust copyright protection for fashion design which largely shifts the emphasis from *what* is being sold to *who* is selling it.
- a combination of any or all of these factors

---

[1] *But see* footnote 4, infra.

[2] See, e.g., *JA Apparel Said to Favor Licensing Model*, Women's Wear Daily (July 21, 2011), *available by subscription at* http://www.wwd.com/business-news/ja-apparel-said-to-favor-licensing-model-3728944 (reporting that parent company of JA Apparel "has decided not to sell the company and instead will pursue a licensing business model").

[3] *See generally* Barton Beebe, *Intellectual Property and the Sumptuary Code*, 123 HARV. L. REV. 809 (2010).

Whatever the explanation, trademark protection tends to eclipse other forms of intellectual property protection in the fashion world. However, it is important to have at least a basic understanding of all of the remaining categories of IP, particularly copyright, in order to be an effective fashion lawyer. Thus, this chapter will begin by examining copyright law and its highly delineated protection for fashion design, then proceed to discuss utility and design patents (lingering briefly on trade secret protection), delve into trademark law next, and conclude by touching on the remaining forms of IP mentioned above. Due to space constraints, certain topics and nuances have necessarily been omitted; this chapter should be considered only an introduction to intellectual property.

Navigating Copyright Law

Introduction to Copyright Protection

Copyright, almost exclusively a creature of federal law in the United States,[4] is often described as a "bundle of rights" granted to the creator of an original work of authorship that is fixed in a tangible form. *Feist Pubs. v. Rural Telephone Service Co.*, 499 U.S. 340, 355 (1991). The United States Supreme Court has explained that the word "original" has a special meaning in the context of copyright: a work may be "original," even if it is *not* entirely novel, provided that it was "independently created by the author—as opposed to copied from other works—and that it possesses at least some minimal degree of creativity." *Id.* at 345. As the Second Circuit has since elaborated, "the level of originality and creativity that must be shown is minimal, only an 'unmistakable dash of originality need be demonstrated, [and] high standards of uniqueness in creativity are dispensed with.'" *Folio Impressions Inc. v. Byer California*, 937 F.2d 759, 764-65 (2d Cir. 1991) (internal citations omitted).

[4] There is a limited "common-law copyright" arising under state law, see discussion at *Capitol Records v. Naxos of America*, 4 N.Y.2d 540, 552-55 (2005), but it is of limited importance for our purposes. While the New York Court of Appeals has not definitively addressed the issue, and lower court opinions are somewhat contradictory, prevailing authority—at least in New York—seems to indicate that apparel designs "are not protected by so-called common-law copyright, for design copyrights do not exist at common law." *A.J. Sandy Inc. v. Junior City Inc.*, 17 A.D.2d 407, 409, 234 N.Y.S.2d 508, 511 (1st Dep't 1962). A review of all fifty states' case law on the subject of common-law copyright is not feasible here; in any event, most states' law on the subject is far less developed than that of New York, and often non-existent.

This is a low threshold, and "[t]he vast majority of works make the grade quite easily[.]" *Feist*, 499 U.S. at 355. However, as discussed below, the case law evaluating protection for the copyright-eligible categories of fashion design suggests that the otherwise lax originality requirement may have more "teeth" when it comes to clothing and jewelry. Further, satisfying the threshold requirements for copyright is just the first step toward enforcing one's rights; as discussed below, there are several statutory bars that withhold protection from otherwise copyrightable works, various tests for determining whether a later worked has infringed an earlier one, and certain statutory and judge-crafted limitations on the enforceability of otherwise protected works.

The rights in a copyright owner's "bundle" are listed in 17 U.S.C. § 106, and can be summed up for present purposes as the exclusive right to:

- reproduce the work
- prepare derivative works based on it
- publicly distribute the work
- where applicable, perform the work
- where applicable display the work

Many of these terms are defined in 17 U.S.C. § 101, the first section of the US Copyright Act,[5] and have been further elaborated upon in a substantial body of case law.

In determining whether a party has infringed on one's copyright, one must first assess the validity of the copyright (see discussion below); then evaluate whether "substantial similarity" exists between the plaintiff's work and the defendant's—the threshold requirement for a finding of copyright infringement; and finally determine whether conduct that would otherwise constitute infringement is insulated by any of a number of defenses, codified at 17 U.S.C. *et seq.* and in federal case law (see discussion below).

[5] This chapter summarizes important provisions of the 1976 Copyright Act. Works pre-dating the 1976 Act, but not yet in the public domain, are governed by the 1909 Copyright Act, which differs in many respects from the newer law. Unfortunately, an exploration of the 1909 Act is beyond the scope of this chapter.

The validity of one's copyright in a fashion article hinges on a number of factors, including the "idea/expression dichotomy" (see discussion below) and, particularly important for fashion design, the "separability" test discussed in the following section.

In determining whether "substantial similarity" exists between a plaintiff's and defendant's works that could potentially give rise to copyright infringement, federal courts ask typically whether 1) a non-trivial amount of the original work was used, *Ringgold v. Black Entertainment TV*, 126 F.3d 70 (2d Cir. 1997), and, if the amount used was more than "*de minimis*," whether 2) "the ordinary observer, unless he set out to detect the disparities [between the works at issue], would be disposed to overlook them, and regard their aesthetic appeal as the same." *Peter Pan Fabrics Inc. v. Martin Weiner Corp.*, 274 F.2d 487, 489 (2d Cir. 1960). Evidence of actual copying is technically required to prevail on an infringement claim, but this rarely proves to be a major obstacle, since "[i]t is well settled that copying *may be inferred* where a plaintiff establishes that the defendant had access to the copyrighted work and that the two works are substantially similar." *ABKCO Music Inc. v. Harrisongs Music Ltd.*, 722 F.2d 988, 997 (2d Cir. 1983). Further, as the *ABKCO* case illustrates, "access" is construed very liberally. On occasion, however, the so-called "independent creation" defense (whose definition is essentially self-explanatory) does get a defendant off the hook for a work that would otherwise infringe on another's copyright.

Importantly, "substantial similarity" may exist even when the copyrighted work is copied from one medium into another. *See Walco Products Inc. v. Kittay & Blitz Inc.*, 354 F. Supp. 121 (S.D.N.Y. 1972) (imposing liability for reproducing three-dimensional work of art in two-dimensional format). Further, copying need not be intentional to be actionable. *See Sheldon v. Metro-Goldwyn Pictures Corp.*, 81 F.2d 49, 54 (2d Cir. 1936) ("unconscious plagiarism is actionable quite as much as deliberate"). For this reason, it is sometimes said that civil copyright is a "strict liability" offense—though that term is arguably misleading in various ways, and should probably be avoided, if possible.

Scope of Protection: The "Useful Article" Bar and "Separability"

The Rule: No Copyright Protection for Fashion

Under the US Copyright Act, "pictorial, graphic, and sculptural works" are generally eligible for protection, and in fact, receive copyright protection immediately upon fixation in a tangible medium.[6] Thus, the moment one creates an illustration of a garment, for example, that *illustration* is protected by copyright.

However, once the illustration is turned into a three-dimensional garment, the legal analysis becomes far more complicated. Even where drawings or photographs of garments are protected by copyright, the garments themselves have long been considered "useful articles" by the US federal courts. *See* 17 U.S.C. § 101; *Chosun Int'l v. Chrisha Creations, Ltd.*, 413 F.3d 324, 328 (2d Cir. 2005). Because the Copyright Act excludes "useful articles" from federally copyrightable subject matter, 17 U.S.C. § 101, clothing—"useful" insofar as it covers the body for reasons of warmth or social norms—generally receives no protection under copyright law.

Newcomers to fashion law, and even designers themselves, are often surprised (and dismayed) by this state of affairs. Many have argued, with some force, that the "useful article" bar to protection makes little sense in an age when much of fashion is more ornamental than functional.[7] But the

---

[6] However, registration, or at least "preregistration," of one's works with the US Copyright Office is necessary to file suit for infringement, 17 U.S.C. § 411, and registration within three months of publication or one month of the owner's knowledge of infringement is required in order to obtain an award of attorneys' fees or so-called "statutory damages" of up to $150,000 per infringed work. *See* 17 U.S.C. §§ 412, 505, 505.

[7] Some countries' intellectual property regimes are more generous to fashion designers. *See* Amy M. Spindler, *COMPANY NEWS; A Ruling by French Court Finds Copyright in a Design*, N.Y. TIMES (May 19, 1994), *available at* http://www.nytimes.com/1994/05/19/business/company-news-a-ruling-by-french-court-finds-copyright-in-a-design.html (noting French court's award of nearly $400,000 in damages to Yves Saint Laurent, for Ralph Lauren's sale of garment similar to YSL's "tuxedo dress"). An examination of foreign law is beyond the scope of this chapter; further, note that such law will typically be unavailing to all but the most high-powered, internationally distributed labels, as "[c]opyright protection is territorial" — *i.e.*, the rights granted under one country's copyright laws generally cannot be enforced abroad. *See Quality King Distribs. v. L'Anza Research Int'l*, 523 U.S. 135, 154 (1998) (Ginsburg, J., concurring).

fact remains that until federal law is changed by legislation (see discussion above) or by court decree (which is unlikely, given that the "useful article" issue is widely considered settled as a matter of statutory interpretation) only limited aspects of fashion design are entitled copyright protection. This has arguably left a void that trademark law—in particular, a component of trademark law known as *trade dress* protection—has attempted to fill (see discussion above), with mixed results.

The Exception: Separability

Fashion is not left entirely out in the cold under federal copyright law, however. Garments, along with other types of fashion accessories, *are* eligible for copyright protection to the extent that their design "incorporates pictorial, graphic, or sculptural features that can be identified separately from, and are capable of existing independently of, the utilitarian aspects of the article." 17 U.S.C. § 101. (As explained below, jewelry is generally exempt from the "useful article" bar to protection, though jewelry designers sometimes face other legal obstacles.)

In interpreting this portion of 17 U.S.C. § 101, most federal circuits have adopted a two-pronged, disjunctive test for copyright protection of useful articles: "if a useful article incorporates a design element that is *physically* ***or*** *conceptually separable* from the underlying product, the element is eligible for copyright protection." *Chosun Int'l*, 413 F.3d at 328 (emphasis added); *cf. OddzOn Prods. Inc. v. Oman*, 924 F.2d 346, 350 (D.C. Cir. 1991) (declining to fully "enter the 'conceptual separability' fray"). Unfortunately, this test—especially its "conceptual separability" prong—has proven difficult to apply in a consistent and coherent manner. *See Masquerade Novelty v. Unique Industries*, 912 F.2d 663, 670 (3d Cir. 1990) ("Courts have twisted themselves into knots trying to create a test to effectively ascertain whether the artistic aspects of a useful article can be identified separately from and exist independently of the article's utilitarian function."). In fact, courts and commentators have proposed no fewer than six different definitions of conceptual separability alone. *Jovani Fashion v. Cinderella Divine Inc.*, 10 Civ. 7085, 2011 WL 2671584 (S.D.N.Y. Jul. 6, 2011) (citing *Galiano v. Harrah's Operating Co.*, 416 F.3d 411, 417 n.13 (5th Cir. 2005)).

In any event, for the day-to-day practice of fashion law, the current legal landscape provides copyright protection for only certain categories or characteristics of fashion design, which can be summed up as follows: fabric patterns of sufficient originality; images affixed to garments; some embroidery, beading, and lace; some sculptural components of fashion; original jewelry; and certain elements of "fanciful" costumes.

The Typical Case: No Protection for Fashion Design

A recent case involving dresses illustrates the "no copyright protection" *status quo* for fashion designs. In *Jovani Fashion v. Cinderella Divine Inc.*, 10 Civ. 7085, 2011 WL 2671584 (S.D.N.Y. Jul. 6, 2011), plaintiff Jovani Fashion had obtained copyright registrations for its catalogs, which contained photographs of the dresses it designed and sold. Jovani sued nearly a dozen competing designers over garments that allegedly infringed its copyrights, basing its claims on both the registrations in Jovani's two-dimensional catalogs and the artistic, ornamental components of the dresses themselves.

One of the dozen defendants, Fiesta, moved to dismiss, arguing that Jovani's copyright registrations accorded it protection only in two-dimensional images of its dresses, rather than any three-dimensional objects depicted therein. *Id.* The court rejected this argument out of hand, noting that "[t]he registration of a catalog as a single work is commonly used to register three-dimensional copyrightable items pictured in the catalog[.]" *Id.* The court nevertheless granted defendant Fiesta's motion based on the "useful article" bar to protection (while denying another defendant's motion for failing to make its "useful article" argument with enough specificity.) *Id.*

The plaintiff had urged the court to reject Fiesta's motion to dismiss, which concerned one particular dress, on the basis of the following artistic design elements: "the size of the sequins, a ruched-satin waistband across the midriff of the dress, and the multi-layered tulle portion that covers the wearer's upper legs, along with 'the compilation, selection, coordination, and arrangement' of all these components." *Id.*.

The court began its analysis by noting that it is "well settled that dress designs are useful articles for purposes of the Copyright Act and thus 'are not typically copyrightable.'" *Id.* The first exception to the "useful article" bar, physical separability, was inapplicable in this case, because it required that "a design element 'can actually be removed from the original item and separately sold, without adversely impacting the article's functionality." *Id.* (*citing Chosun*, 413 F.3d at 329). Since the plaintiff had not alleged, and the court could not discern, any "value in [the design elements'] freestanding form (above, of course, the value of [their] constituent material)," the physical separability test could not be satisfied here.

The court found that Jovani's conceptual separability argument likewise failed, because the allegedly copyrighted elements did not "invoke in the viewer a concept separate from that of the [dress's] 'clothing' function," "reflect[] the designer's artistic judgment exercised independently of functional influences," evidence that "ornamental aspects" were "'primary' over the elements' 'subsidiary utilitarian function,'" or have any "likelihood of marketability" on their own. *Id.*

In short, Jovani's dress was merely a "useful article," and it could not "be reasonably found [to be] protected by a valid copyright"; accordingly, the court granted Fiesta's motion to dismiss. *Id.*

Exceptions to the No-Copyright Status Quo

<u>Fabric Patterns</u>

Fabric designs, unlike fashion design in general, "are considered 'writings' for purposes of copyright law and are accordingly protectable." *Knitwaves Inc. v. Lollytogs Ltd.*, 71 F.3d 996, 1002 (2d Cir. 1995).

Thus, for example, in *Folio Impressions Inc. v. Byer California*, 937 F.2d 759 (2d Cir. 1991), the court accorded "limited" protection to a fabric design of "slight originality" consisting of "roses [that] were placed in straight lines and turned so that the roses faced on various directions." The court noted that if the design of this particular pattern had been determined by ease of manufacturing, no copyright protection would be available. (As we will see later, the so-called "functionality" bar to protection is a common theme in many IP cases outside the realm of utility patents.) In *Folio*, however, the available evidence indicated that the designer's placement of the roses in a straight line was "an artistic decision" rather than a manufacturing-based one, so copyright protection was available. The Second Circuit nevertheless concluded with a caveat: "what is protected in this case is the Folio Rose itself and the way in which that rose is arranged; the copyright umbrella does not cover the idea of arranging roses generally in a straight line pattern." (This touches on another crucial theme in copyright: the so-called "idea/expression dichotomy," a legal doctrine that seeks to ensure that an idea, by itself, cannot receive federal copyright protection; under this doctrine, copyright attaches — if at all — only to the original *expression* of an idea, once embodied in a fixed form. (See discussion below.)

Fabric designs' eligibility for copyright protection means, among other things, that designers must be careful where they buy their fabric. Some attorneys have observed that lawsuits by "copyright trolls"—entities that purchase copyrights solely for the purpose of suing and collecting money from others who have infringed on those copyrights—seem to be on the rise. Because a finding of copyright infringement in a civil proceeding requires no showing of intent, this is a ripe area for lawsuits against the unwary. Fortunately, many fabric distributors will agree to an "indemnification" provision that makes the distributor, and not the designer, liable, if the fabric does turn out to infringe on a third party's intellectual property rights. An indemnification provision is especially important when dealing with an overseas manufacturer or distributor, though of course such a provision is only as good as the party backing it up.[8]

When buying from domestic fabric companies, a designer can take some comfort in a widely enacted statutory provision, Uniform Commercial Code § 2-312, that (at least absent an agreement to the contrary) imposes a warranty on merchant sellers as to their goods' non-infringement on third-party rights. Note, however, that not all sellers are "merchants" for purposes of the UCC, and that even "merchants" will not be the hook unless they "regularly deal[] in goods of the kind" at issue. Also, it must be reiterated that any warranty is only as strong as the party making it.

---

[8] Though discussed in passing at various points in this chapter, IP licensing is a topic unto itself, to which entire volumes can (and have) been devoted.

Images Affixed to Garments

As one might expect, given the protection available for fabric patterns, images affixed to garments are also eligible for copyright protection. In *Knitwaves Inc. v. Lollytogs Ltd.*, 71 F.3d 996, 999 (2d Cir. 1995), for example, the Second Circuit upheld a finding of copyright infringement based on one children's sweater with "puffy leaf appliqués" and another with "a squirrel and leaves appliquéd onto its multi-paneled front."

Likewise, in *Samara Bros. v. Wal-Mart Stores*, 165 F.3d 120, 132 (2d. Cir. 1998), *abrogated on other grounds*, 529 U.S. 205 (2000), the Second Circuit found that copyright protection was appropriate for appliqués of strawberries, daisies, hearts, and tulips. The court supported its ruling in part by noting that a certificate of registration from the Copyright Office, which had been issued to this plaintiff, was *prima facie* evidence of the validity of a copyright. *Id.* at 132 (citing 17 U.S.C. § 410(c)). However, the court went on to caution that "copyrights depicting familiar objects, such as the hearts, daisies, and strawberries in Samara's copyrights, are entitled to narrow protection [as against the] virtually identical copying" present in the instant case. *Id.* (citing *Folio Impressions*, 937 F.2d at 765). This narrow protection is sometimes described by practitioners as "thin" copyright.

Some Embroidery, Beading, and Lace

One step away from images affixed to garments are *other* materials affixed to garments, such as embroidery, beading, and lace. Courts have reached different results in cases involving these materials, in large part based on the originality of the work in question. However, in the proper case, copyright can be a useful tool for a designer whose embroidery, beading, or lace work has been copied by another.

In *Mon Cheri Bridal Inc. v. Wu*, 09 Civ. 1239, 09 Civ. 1321, 2010 WL 2222497 (3d Cir. Jun. 4, 2010) (non-precedential), for example, wedding dress designer Mon Cheri sued Wu and others, alleging that the defendants "had conspired to copy an entire line of Mon Cheri dresses[.]" At the district court level, some defendants settled, but not the Wu defendants, who went to trial, lost before a jury, and appealed the ruling to the Third Circuit. The Wu defendants argued to the Third Circuit that Mon Cheri was not entitled to copyright protection for its embroidery and bead patterns, but the appellate court disagreed:

> The jury properly concluded that the works for which Mon Cheri sought copyrights were sufficiently original. According to [the designer], she found inspiration from many sources and in the case of dress number 21917, she was inspired by a particular flower and vine drawing. She used these two common elements, but rearranged them, changed their size, color, and frequency, and created an embroidery and bead pattern that she considered to be her original work. This work is sufficiently original under copyright law.

Id. at *4.

Mon Cheri notwithstanding, cases based on the embroidery and beading components of dresses have led to divergent outcomes; often, these cases (like litigation in general) are settled before a judge can determine whether the design(s) at issue is copyrightable or not. *Compare Mon Cheri*, *supra*; *Jovani Fashion v. Cinderella Divine Inc.*, 10 Civ. 7085, 2011 WL 2671584 (S.D.N.Y. Jul. 6, 2011) (motion to dismiss for lack of copyrightability granted as to one defendant, but denied as to another); *Hill v. Let's Fashion Inc.*, 10 Civ. 2682 (C.D. Cal. filed Apr. 13, 2010) (reportedly settled on terms favorable to plaintiff designer); and *Hill v. Nox Anabel Inc.*, 10 Civ. 5871 (C.D. Cal. filed Aug. 6, 2010) (reportedly settled on terms favorable to designer).

As for lace designs, district courts in both the Second and Ninth Circuits have found they are copyrightable, at least where they are irrelevant to the utilitarian functions of a garment. *See Eve of Milady v. Impression Bridal*, 957 F. Supp. 484, 489 (S.D.N.Y. 1997); and *Express, LLC v. Fetish Group Inc.*, 424 F. Supp. 2d 1211, 1224-25 (C.D. Cal. 2006) (citing *Eve of Milady*, 957 F. Supp. at 489). But even when a lace design is deemed eligible for copyright protection, courts and/or juries will closely scrutinize the plaintiffs' and defendants' products to determine if they are, in fact, "substantially similar." *See, e.g.*, *Imperial Laces v. Westchester Lace*, 95 Civ. 5353, 1998 WL 830630 (S.D.N.Y. Nov. 30, 1998) (lace pattern was sufficiently original for copyright protection, but defendant's pattern was not substantially similar to plaintiff's).

Some Sculptural Components of Fashion

The seminal case of *Kieselstein-Cord v. Accessories by Pearl*, 632 F.2d 989 (2d Cir. 1980) established that a predominantly ornamental component of an otherwise useful article may be entitled to copyright protection under a "conceptual separability" theory. At the time, the Second Circuit felt compelled to start its opinion by declaring that "[t]his case is on a razor's edge of copyright law." *Id.* at 990. However, the principle established by *Kieselstein-Cord* is now widely accepted, both in the Second Circuit, and in many other circuits. *See Chosun Int'l, Inc. v. Chrisha Creations, Ltd.*, 413 F.3d 324, 328 (2d Cir. 2005).

At issue in *Kieselstein-Cord* were two unusual belt buckles that the court described as "solid sculptured designs . . . 'with rounded corners, a sculpted surface, a rectangular cut-out at one end for the belt attachment,' and 'several surface levels.'" *Id.* at 990. Of potentially dispositive significance to the court was the fact that "[a] shortened version of the belt with the small Winchester buckle is sometimes worn around the neck or elsewhere on the body rather than around the waist" and that "[s]ales of both buckles were made primarily in high fashion stores and jewelry stores[.]" *Id.* at 991. (As explained in the following section, jewelry designs are eligible for copyright protection.)

Over a vigorous dissent by District Judge Weinstein, sitting by designation, the Second Circuit ruled that the buckles were entitled to copyright protection:

> We see in appellant's belt buckles conceptually separable sculptural elements, as apparently have the buckles' wearers who have used them as ornamentation for parts of the body other than the waist. The primary ornamental aspect of the Vaquero and Winchester buckles is conceptually separable from their subsidiary utilitarian function. This conclusion is not at variance with the expressed congressional intent to distinguish copyrightable applied art and uncopyrightable industrial design[.]

Id. at 993. While *Kieselstein-Cord* presented an idiosyncratic set of facts, its holding may nevertheless prove useful for vendors of certain items of apparel or accessories whose appeal stems from what it, in essence, a sculptural work incorporated into an otherwise "useful article."

<u>Original Jewelry Designs</u>

If the belt buckles in *Kieselstein-Cord* were entitled to copyright protection, it should come as no surprise that jewelry designs are likewise copyrightable. *See, e.g., Yurman Studio v. Castaneda*, 591 F. Supp. 2d 471 (S.D.N.Y. 2008). As one judge explained in *Trifari, Krussman & Fishel Inc. v. Charel Co.*, 134 F. Supp. 551, 553 (S.D.N.Y. 1955):

> Unlike an automobile, a refrigerator, or a gas range, the design of a necklace or of a bracelet, may take as many forms as the ingenuity of the artist may conceive. There is neither basis in the Copyright Act nor judicial precedent for excluding . . . jewelry from works of art to which copyright protection may attach. Simply because it is a commonplace fashion accessory, not an expression of 'pure' or 'fine' art does not preclude a finding that plaintiff's copyrighted article is a 'work of art' within the meaning and intendment of the Act.

In *Davis v. Gap Inc.*, 246 F.3d 152, 156 (2d Cir. 2001) (Leval, J.), the Second Circuit ruled that copyright protection was available to "nonfunctional jewelry worn over the eyes in the manner of eyeglasses," which had been used in a Gap ad without the designer's consent (and which the court deemed was not a "fair use"; (see discussion below). While one cannot be sure, it seems that if one placed lenses into the eyewear such that they could function as glasses, the reasoning of *Kieselstein-Cord* would apply, and copyright protection would still attach to the eyewear's sculptural components.

But while jewelry designers are entitled to copyright protection for their original creations, they have not always had great luck in the courts. In *Mag Jewelry Co. v. Cherokee Inc.*, 496 F.3d 108 (1st Cir. 2007), for example, one jewelry designer lost at the summary judgment stage after failing to produce any evidence from which a jury could reasonably conclude that defendant had copied its design.

Further, it appears that some courts have held jewelry designers to a higher standard of "originality" than that applicable to other copyright owners. To illustrate, it is a general principle of copyright law that works consisting solely of elements in the public domain are only entitled to protection for their authors' original contributions and arrangements, regardless of medium. *See Yurman Design Inc. v. PAJ Inc.*, 262 F.3d 101, 109-10 (2d Cir. 2001), questioned on other grounds, *Coach Inc. v. We Care Trading Co.*, 67 Fed. Appx. 626 (2d Cir. 2002). But this rule has sometimes had a disparate impact on jewelry designers. In *Todd v. Mont. Silversmiths Inc.*, 379 F. Supp. 2d 1110, 1114 (D. Colo. 2005), for example, a court denied copyright protection to the creator of bracelets and earrings made in the style of barbed-wire, because the works' "arrangement [was] visually but not conceptually distinguishable from barbed-wire." Additionally, because barbed-wire had long been in the public domain, the court found that the works were "not truly 'original' in the ordinary meaning of the word."

Some Elements of Fanciful Costumes

In the words of the US Copyright Office, "'[f]anciful' costumes, as opposed to 'garment designs,' are 'useful articles,' and therefore copyright-ineligible taken as a whole, but . . . *elements of fanciful costumes may themselves be copyrighted*, so long as those elements meet the requirements of 'physical or conceptual separability.'" United States Copyright Office Policy Decision: Registrability of Costume Designs, 56 Fed.Reg. 56530, 56532 (1991) (emphasis added).

While it is probably fair to say that costume knock-offs are not litigated with great frequency, some disputes have resulted in judicial decisions providing guidance on the copyrightability of costumes. For instance, the primary issue in *Chosun Int'l Inc. v. Chrisha Creations Ltd.*, 413 F.3d 324, 325 (2d Cir. 2005) (Calabresi, J.) was the copyrightability of "animal-themed children's costumes, including a line of 'plush sculpture' costumes, each of which consist[ed] of a bodysuit and a sculpted hood." Applying the conceptual separability test developed in *Kieselstein-Cord*, the Second Circuit found it inappropriate to allow dismissal of a complaint for copyright infringement over the costumes at issue—at least, at such an early stage of the case:

> It is at least possible that elements of Chosun's plush sculpted animal costumes are separable from the overall design of the costume, and hence eligible for protection under the Copyright Act. It might, for example, be the case that the sculpted "heads" of these designs are physically separable from the overall costume, in that they could be removed from the costume without adversely impacting the wearer's ability to cover his or her body. Similarly, it could be that the sculpted "heads" (and perhaps "hands") are conceptually separable. That is, Chosun may be able to show that they invoke in the viewer a concept separate from that of the costume's "clothing" function, and that their addition to the costume was not motivated by a desire to enhance the costume's functionality *qua* clothing. It is, of course, possible that at any of several later stages Chosun will have failed, as a matter of law, to prove that such separability exists. But that possibility cannot justify dismissal of Chosun's complaint now on a Rule 12(b)(6) motion.

Id. at 329-30.

This except illustrates that when it comes to costumes, as is true in the realm of "conceptual separability" more generally, there is surefire way to predict what will or will not be held protectable under copyright. The outcome in a given case may hinge on the plaintiff's ability to produce evidence of separability, on a judge's intuitive sense of whether the protected material is more akin to a true costume or to "regular clothing," and on the equities of the case at hand.

In one recent, interesting costume-related copyright saga, George Lucas's production company, Lucasfilm, sued one of the British designers of the iconic "Imperial Stormtrooper" helmet made for the *Star Wars* films. The co-designer, who had apparently assigned his rights to the helmet to Lucasfilm, had begun selling replicas of the helmet through his website, based in the United Kingdom, some twenty-five years after the helmets were first created for *Star Wars: A New Hope* (1977). Lucasfilm sued in California federal court in 2005, where it obtained a default judgment—suggesting that the Central District of California deemed the helmets "separable" and thus copyrightable under US law. However, when Lucasfilm sought to enforce the judgment in the United Kingdom, the British court refused to oblige, on the ground that there had been no basis for the U.S. court to exercise personal jurisdiction over the helmet's co-designer. Thus, the courts analyzed Lucasfilm's copyright infringement claims under British law, and determined that liability was inappropriate due to certain quirks of the UK's copyright regime. *See Lucasfilm Ltd. v. Ainsworth*, [2011] UKSC 39, at ¶¶ 10-13, 25 (Jul. 27, 2011).

Other Limitations on Copyright Protection and Enforceability

Idea/Expression Dichotomy

A fashion lawyer will frequently encounter the question, "How can I keep other people from stealing my idea?" A helpful answer generally cannot be found in copyright law. As Section 102(b) of the US Copyright Act states:

> In no case does copyright protection for an original work of authorship extend to *any idea*, procedure, process, system, method of operation, *concept*, *principle*, or discovery, regardless of the form in which it is described, explained, illustrated, or embodied in such work.

(Emphasis added.) The Second Circuit has paraphrased this principle by stating that "[i]t is an axiom of copyright law that the protection granted to a copyrightable work extends only to the particular expression of an idea and never to the idea itself." *Reyher v. Children's Television Workshop*, 533 F.2d 87, 90 (2d Cir. 1976).

N.B. Some of the items in the § 102 list ("methods of operation," "discoveries," etc.) may be protectable under *patent* law. See Navigating Patent Law section, below.

Though this "idea/expression dichotomy," as it is often called, may sound simple, it can prove difficult to apply in theory, especially in the realm of the visual arts. It is relatively straightforward, for example, to state that "[s]tockpiling vegetable purees for covert use in children's food is an idea that cannot be copyrighted." *Lapine v. Seinfeld*, 375 Fed. Appx. 81 (2d Cir. Apr. 28, 2010) (affirming district court ruling that similarities between two cookbooks about sneaking vegetables into children's food could not give rise to liability under copyright law). But in the visual arts, including fashion, "it is not clear that there is any real distinction between the idea in a work of art and its expression [because an] artist's idea, among other things, is to depict a particular subject in a particular way." *Mannion v. Coors Brewing Co.*, 377 F. Supp. 2d 444, 458 (S.D.N.Y. 2005).

Thus, it may come as no surprise that (here again) the courts have reached different results in different cases. In *Bill Diodato Photography v. Kate Spade LLC*, 388 F. Supp. 2d 382 (S.D.N.Y. 2005) (Chin, J.), for example, a Kate Spade advertisement showing "a woman's feet, astride a toilet, in stylish, colorful shoes, with a handbag on the floor" merely embodied "an idea that has been used often in popular culture," and thus, as a matter of law, could not constitute copyright infringement in a photograph that had likely served as the ad's inspiration.

A more recent case, also in the Southern District of New York, went quite differently. In *LaChapelle v. Fenty*, 11 Civ. 945, 2011 WL 2947007 (S.D.N.Y. Jul. 20, 2011) (Scheindlin, J.), fashion photographer David LaChapelle sued singer Rihanna and others for visual similarities between the music video for her song "S&M" and his successful S&M-themed photo series. On a motion to dismiss, the court found that LaChapelle had stated a plausible claim for infringement of his artistic expression. Rihanna and the other defendants had gone beyond merely copying unprotecable *ideas*; in particular, they had duplicated "specific choices concerning staging and color" that "contribute[d] significantly to the overall feel of the image." *Id.* at 24. After this ruling, the parties promptly settled.

It seems fairly obvious in both the Kate Spade and the Rihanna cases that the second work had indeed been derived from the first; however, where the only material copied has been an *idea*, the derivation of that idea is irrelevant under federal copyright law.[9]

Fair Use

"Fair use" is a legal doctrine, codified at 17 U.S.C. § 107, which allows one to use another's copyrighted material without permission or compensation, but only under certain circumstances. The U.S. Supreme Court has explained that fair use, along with the idea/expression dichotomy explained above, are crucial safeguards ensuring that federal copyright law (which, by its nature, imposes restrictions on speech) remains in harmony with the First Amendment. *See Eldred v. Ashcroft*, 537 U.S. 186, 219 (2003).

Entire volumes have been written about fair use, but due to space constraints and topicality, only the basics can be addressed here. The doctrine, at its essence, reflects the recognition that certain uses of copyrighted material—such as use of another's copyright work in order to criticize or parody it, certain uses for educational and other non-commercial purposes, fleeting uses for which no economic market exists, and/or certain uses that incorporate some portion of the original work into a new creation—*should* not, as a matter of public policy, require a user to seek the permission of the copyright owner.

It can be difficult to predict the outcome of fair use disputes, in part because the US Supreme Court has only ruled on the doctrine a handful of times (and perhaps *never* in the context of fashion, since most fashion designs are not eligible for copyright to begin with.) When deciding whether

[9] Under state law, the picture is more complicated. For example, state-law "theft of idea" cases are sometimes premised on a theory of implied contract—namely, "I'll share my idea with you under the mutual understanding that, if you like it, you will pay me in order to use it." Naturally, the federal courts have considered whether these state-law "theft of idea" claims are preempted by the federal Copyright Act. It appears that at present, the New York and California federal courts have reached a stalemate on the issue, with the former typically finding preemption and the latter not. *See* Robert W. Clarida & Robert J. Bernstein, *New York and California Courts Split on Preemption of Idea Claims*, NEW YORK LAW JOURNAL 3 (July 15, 2011). The entertainment industry has solicited a ruling from the U.S. Supreme Court on the preemption question (*see Pilgrim Films & Television v. Montz*, Petition For a Writ of Certiorari, 11-143 (U.S. Aug. 2, 2011)), but the high court has not ruled on the issue as of this writing.

a proposed use is "fair," one should in the first instance examine the four factors listed in 17 U.S.C. § 107:

1. the purpose and character of the use, including whether such use is of a commercial nature or is for nonprofit educational purposes
2. the nature of the copyrighted work
3. the amount and substantiality of the portion used in relation to the copyrighted work as a whole
4. the effect of the use upon the potential market for or value of the copyrighted work

In practice, some factors—and even factors not explicitly mentioned in § 107—carry far more weight than others. *See generally* Barton Beebe, *An Empirical Study of U.S. Copyright Fair Use Opinions, 1978-2005*, 156 U. PA. L. REV. 549 (2008).

If one had to select a single criterion to guide fair use inquiries—a crude and both over- and under-inclusive endeavor—that criterion would likely be whether the new use of the original copyrighted work is "transformative." *See Campbell v. Acuff-Rose Music*, 510 U.S. 569, 579 (1994). With that said, the absence of "transformativeness" is not necessarily fatal to a fair use claim, just as its presence does not necessarily guarantee a finding of fair use. This area of law is fact-intensive and requires a deep familiarity with both the case law on the subject and the realities of litigation.

Special Considerations in Copyright Law

Joint Authorship and Works Made for Hire

Under the US Copyright Act, "[a] 'joint work' is a work prepared by two or more authors with the intention that their contributions be merged into inseparable or interdependent parts of a unitary whole." 17 U.S.C. § 101. The question of joint authorship is of considerable interest to (actual or alleged) creative collaborators, including fashion designers working on copyrightable components of apparel and accessories. The reason this question carries such importance is that, as the Second Circuit explained in

Thomson v. Larson, 147 F.3d 195, 199 (2d Cir. 1998), "[j]oint authorship entitles the co-authors to equal undivided interests in the whole work—in other words, each joint author has the right to use or to license the work as he or she wishes, subject only to the obligation to account to the other joint owner for any profits that are made."

The central inquiry in determinations of joint authorship, as recited by the Thomson court, is whether multiple creators "intend[ed] their contributions to be merged into inseparable parts of a unitary whole." *Id.* at 200 (quoting *Childress v. Taylor*, 945 F.2d 500, 507 (2d Cir. 1991)). Because joint authorship hinges in intent, it is always wise for parties to commit that intent to writing at the outset of a collaborative project, no matter how insignificant one party's contribution may seem. Putting the arrangement in writing may avoid long, expensive trials—of the variety that occurred in Thomson over the authorship of the musical *Rent*—that require a fact finder to determine intent based on primarily circumstantial evidence.

However, concerns about copyright ownership do not begin and end with joint authorship. Any party who relies on the creativity of another to produce copyrightable works should be familiar with the rules governing "works made for hire" and copyright assignments. (The rules in this area apply not just to fashion, but to all industries as well.)

The best arrangement for a hiring party, at least insofar as copyright is concerned, is usually to arrange for a hired party's contributions to qualify as "works made for hire"—which has a special meaning in copyright law. If a work is deemed "made for hire," then the hiring party is considered the author for purposes of US copyright law. It is generally better to be the *author* of a copyrighted work than to be an *assignee* or *licensee* of another's copyright (discussed below), in part because assignors and licensors of copyrights—or their heirs—can eventually "terminate" a third party's ownership rights through the mechanism provided in 17 U.S.C. § 203.

However, there are only two ways to get a creation into the "work made for hire" category. The first is if the work is "prepared by an employee within the scope of his or her employment"; the second is if the work is "specially ordered or commissioned for use as a contribution to a collective work [or] compilation"—or certain other, narrow categories of works—*provided that* the hiring and hired parties "expressly agree in a written instrument signed by them that the work shall be considered a work made for hire." 17 U.S.C. § 101.

In other words, if a hiring party either does not have a written instrument from the creator—which can simply be a clause in a contract—or the created work does not fall within one of the qualifying categories of "specially ordered or commissioned" works, the hiring party must be prepared to show ***both*** that the contested work was created a) by an employee—rather than an independent contractor—and b) that the work was created within the scope of employment.

The difficulty is that no bright-line test exists to determine if someone is an employee or an independent contractor, for copyright purposes. But in *Community for Creative Non-Violence v. Reid*, 490 U.S. 730 (1989), the Supreme Court ruled that the employee/contractor determination should be guided by principles of the "common law of agency," with courts looking to numerous factors, none dispositive. Per Justice Marshall, writing for a unanimous Court, those factors include:

> the skill required [to create the copyrighted work]; the source of the instrumentalities and tools [used in its creation]; the location of the work; the duration of the relationship between the parties; whether the hiring party has the right to assign additional projects to the hired party; the extent of the hired party's discretion over when and how long to work; the method of payment; the hired party's role in hiring and paying assistants; whether the work is part of the regular business of the hiring party; whether the hiring party is in business; the provision of employee benefits; and the tax treatment of the hired party.

(Internal citations omitted.) In other words, tax treatment or classification in internal records will not ultimately control the outcome of the employee/independent contractor inquiry for copyright purposes. To complicate matters further, many circuit courts have arrived at a shorter list of factors that they consider especially important, and these differ from one circuit to another.

Assignments, Licenses, and Equitable Doctrines

When it is simply impossible to get a creative contribution into the "work made for hire" box, there are other ways to manage copyrights initially owned by hired parties. For example, if a party—*any* party, not just one who hired the original copyright owner—can get "a note or memorandum of . . . transfer," he can become the "assignee" of the copyright(s) at issue. The status achieved via an assignment of rights is similar to that enjoyed by a work's original author, with the notable exceptions of the possibility of copyright termination (mentioned above) and the duration of copyright protection for the work.

After an assignment, the next-best option for an aspiring rights-consolidator will often be a *license* to use a copyrighted work. Copyright licenses may be exclusive, royalty-free, and even irrevocable—at least, subject to the termination provision in 17 U.S.C. § 203. Licenses may be either express or implied; implied licenses are frequently alleged between parties with informal working relationships. Note, however, that licenses may be revoked in circumstances, which is why it is sometimes important to obtain an assignment or an irrevocable license.[10]

Finally, there are various doctrines, most equitable in nature, for an aspiring rights-consolidator who simply cannot make a colorable argument based on the rules governing "works made for hire," assignments, or licenses. These doctrines, including estoppel and laches, are typically considered options of last resort; due to their equitable nature, they will be applied only where a judge deems their application "just."

---

[10] In practice, contracts drafted for rights-consolidators frequently run through the entire litany of rights-management mechanisms discussed here, from most desirable to least, just to make sure all bases are covered. Such contracts also typically address "moral rights"—a creator's right to attribution for and the integrity of his work—because such rights are important in many countries besides the United States. Foreign law often provides that moral rights may be waived, but *not* assigned; rights-consolidators should keep this in mind when drafting legal documents. The US Copyright Act grants only limited moral rights to certain authors, through the provisions of the "Visual Artists' Rights Act," codified at 17 U.S.C. § 106A.

An Overview of Secondary Liability

Courts presiding over copyright cases have long recognized a doctrine known as "secondary liability," which, as its name suggests, is a tool for imposing liability on a party other than a "direct infringer." Secondary liability was traditionally divided into two types. The first, "vicarious liability," is typically imposed when a defendant had the right to control the direct infringer's activities and derived a profit therefrom, but stood idly by and collected his money rather than intervening. The other traditional type of secondary liability is for "contributory infringement," most often found where a third party knowingly facilitated the infringement at issue. Since a 2005 Supreme Court ruling in a case involving peer-to-peer file-sharing software, *Metro-Goldwyn-Mayer Studios Inc. v. Grokster Ltd.*, 545 U.S. 913, 919 (2005), there is arguably a new, third type of secondary liability—"inducement infringement"—appropriate for situations in which one "distributes a device with the object of promoting its use to infringe copyright [and thereby becomes] liable for the resulting acts of infringement by third parties."

Secondary liability principles in copyright law, which had developed almost exclusively through the case-by-case judicial decision-making process, received a major statutory overhaul in the form of the 1998 Digital Millennium Copyright Act (DMCA). The DMCA, which added new provisions throughout Title 17 of the U.S. Code, accomplished a number of objectives, including the creation of certain "safe harbors" for Internet intermediaries—like search engines, website hosts, and Internet service providers—that may inadvertently facilitate copyright infringement, but take prescribed measures to avoid such facilitation and promptly address infringement brought to their attention. Please consult other reference guides for more information on these issues.

The Innovative Design Protection and Piracy Prevention Act (IDPPPA)

Perhaps surprisingly, the DMCA provision of the greatest relevance to fashion designers at the moment has nothing to do with new technology. A rather obscure component of the DMCA was its creation of a new chapter to Title 17 that created copyright-like protection for original boat hulls. *See* 17 U.S.C. § 1301 *et seq.* Chapter 13, also known as the "Vessel Hull Design

Protection Act," is important to the fashion industry because of legislation currently pending on Congress would grant copyright-like protection to unique fashion designs *by modifying the Vessel Hull Act*. While this might seem nonsensical at first, it turns out that there is, in fact, a method to the madness: the Vessel Hull Act grants "*sui generis*," copyright-like protection to items that would otherwise be categorized—like most fashion design under the current copyright regime—as "useful articles," and thus be largely deprived of the benefits of copyright law.

As of this writing, Congress is considering the latest iteration of a bill titled the Innovative Design Protection and Piracy Prevention Act (IDPPPA), which would confer copyright-like protection on fashion apparel and accessory designs displaying "a unique, distinguishable, non-trivial, and non-utilitarian variation over prior designs." This current version of the bill represents a compromise between the Council of Fashion Designers of America (CFDA) and the American Apparel and Footwear Association (AAFA)—the former having proposed additional IP protection for fashion for years, and the latter wary of such proposals until very recently.

Legislation like the IDPPPA has repeatedly been introduced in Congress over the years to correct what some see as copyright law's general (and erroneous) exclusion of fashion design from copyright protection. But the IDPPPA, in particular, has made headlines, perhaps because of certain prominent supporters and because the bill made more progress in late 2010 than most, if not all, previous bills of its kind. The IDPPPA started life in 2007 as the Design Piracy Prohibition Act (DPPA), but was renamed after it received drastic revisions in an effort to gain the support of the AAFA. One of the most significant changes made was the ratcheting-up of the required showing for liability—from the usual copyright-law standard of "substantial similarity" to a more stringent requirement that a fashion design plaintiff prove his work and that of the defendant are "substantially identical." The current threshold requirement for protection (that a plaintiff's design display "a unique, distinguishable, non-trivial, and non-utilitarian variation over prior designs") is quite daunting on its face, in part because it would appear to make the entire history of fashion fair game for defendants to locate an earlier design that would invalidate protection for an allegedly "new" creation.

Although the IDPPPA is often informally referred to as the "fashion copyright bill," the proposed law would not, in fact, be part of the US Copyright Act, which concludes at Chapter 12 of Title 17 of the US Code. Instead, as mentioned above, Chapter 13, which currently covers only boats, would be expanded to cover unique fashion designs as well. It is thus unclear what, if any, provisions of the Copyright Act will apply to cases brought under the proposed law. If the IDPPPA is enacted, it will undoubtedly take years of litigation, with the guidance provided by the resulting case law, to adequately delineate the contours of this new intellectual property protection for fashion. This is especially true because very few cases have been brought under the Vessel Hull Act, so there is little precedent illuminating the meaning of Chapter 13's existing provisions.

Equally unclear is whether the bill has any real chance of becoming law, at least in its current form. Although the CFDA and the AAFA are now aligned in their support of the IDPPPA, the influential California Fashion Association (CFA) remains vehemently opposed to the bill. The President of the CFA (which, incidentally, counts frequent knockoff defendant Forever 21 among its members) has questioned whether anything in fashion is truly "new" and whether the proposed "substantially identical" standard is workable.

Furthermore, many retailers who do not design, but merely sell apparel, remain staunchly opposed to the bill. This is undoubtedly due, in part, to the possibility of secondary (or even direct) liability for selling products they do not realize is infringing. These concerns are not entirely unfounded. The IDPPPA clearly contemplates secondary liability for intermediaries in some circumstances, noting, for example, that a piracy plaintiff would be required to allege specific facts establishing that "the protected design or an image thereof was available in such location … and for such duration that it can be reasonably inferred from the totality of the … circumstances *that the defendant saw or otherwise had knowledge of the protected design*." (Emphasis added.) Further, the Vessel Hull Act to which the IDPPPA would be appended likewise envisions secondary liability in certain circumstances, as evidenced by the VHDPA's safe harbor for retailers and distributors that have dealt in infringing goods, but have not 1) "induced" or "colluded" to make or import the infringing article, 2) withheld the source of the infringing article, or 3) reordered the infringing article after having been notified of its illegality. 17 U.S.C. § 1309.

The bill remains controversial, and its likelihood of passage and potential for real-world impact are uncertain, at best. Perhaps the most one can state with confidence about the IDPPPA is that it would carry out a massive doctrinal shift that would require a radical reassessment of IP protection for fashion design.

Navigating Patent Law

Because copyright protection is often unavailing for designers and vendors of apparel, it is worthwhile to consider the alternative forms of intellectual property protection known as patents and trade secrets. Patents, exclusively a creature of federal law, come in two varieties that are relevant for present purposes: utility patents, which protect previously undiscovered utilitarian processes and devices; and design patents, which protect non-functional, original, ornamental designs for manufactured articles.

Patent protection is powerful, but lasts for a far shorter time than copyright protection (generally, the life of the author plus seventy years) or trademark protection (which theoretically exist in perpetuity.) Further, the process to obtain a utility or design patent is expensive and time-consuming, so fashion companies often look to other types of IP protection for their creations. Patent protection does have its place in fashion, however, as explained below.

In addition, trade secret protection is available in certain instances to protect (as its name suggests) processes, techniques, and/or information that a company has made reasonable efforts to keep secret. Unlike patent protection, trade secret protection is primarily a creature of *state* law, and its term of protection is not fixed, but rather dictated by the actions (or omissions) of the trade secret's owner.

Utility Patents

Utility patents, which are likely what first comes to mind when most people think of patents, provide a temporary right to exclude[11] others from one's *utilitarian inventions.* 35 U.S.C. § 101 provides that:

---

[11] Note that patent law's "right to exclude" is *not* synonymous with a "right to use." *See* discussion at Janice M. Mueller, *Patent Law* (3d ed. Wolters Kluwer), at 15.

> Whoever invents or discovers any new and useful process, machine, manufacture, or composition of matter, or any new and useful improvement thereof, may obtain a patent thereof, subject to the conditions and requirements of this title [35 USCS §§ 1 *et seq.*].

Some of the more important conditions and requirements for utility patent protection are described below.

<u>Scope of Protection</u>

Utility patents are granted to new, non-obvious inventions that qualify as a useful process, machine, manufacture, composition of matter, or new and useful improvement on existing technology. Once the United States Patent and Trademark Office grants a patent—after what can be a long and arduous process—protection generally lasts for twenty years from the date on which the application was filed. 35 U.S.C. § 154(a)(1)(2).

Until now, the United States has always been a so-called "first to invent" country; in fact, until landmark legislation[12] changing this state of affairs was enacted into law in September 2011, the US was the *only* such country. This traditionally meant that a patent would issue to the inventor who conceived of and reduced an invention to practice. The required "reduction to practice" could be *actual*—such as the construction of a working prototype—or *constructive*—i.e., "sufficient disclosure in the specification to enable any person skilled in the art to take advantage of that utility where it would not be obvious how this is done." *Kawai v. Werner Metlestics*, 480 F.2d 880, 886 (C.C.P.A. 1973), cited approvingly, *Frazer v. Schlegel*, 498 F.3d 1283, 1287 (Fed. Cir. 2007). When an inventor applies for a patent based on constructive reduction to practice, the USPTO examiner has the burden to

[12] The Leahy-Smith "America Invents Act," the first major statutory overhaul of US patent law in sixty years, was enacted into law in September 2011. The new law will affect many dramatic changes to the American patent landscape, including bringing the US into harmony with the rest of the international community by making it a "first to file" (instead of a "first to invent") country. The bill also amends the rules and/or definitions regarding prior art, novelty, and non-obviousness, and provides a mechanism for the initiation of post-grant, *inter partes* review of patents. These are just a few of the changes executed by this landmark bill, which cannot be analyzed in depth here due to space constraints and topicality.

establish a reasonable basis for believing that the invention would not work. *In re Wright*, 999 F.2d 1557, 1562 (Fed. Cir. 1993).

Despite the massive changes effected by 2011 America Invents Act, most basic principles of patent law should remain unchanged. (Naturally, one should consult qualified patent counsel to understand the full ramifications of the new law.) It is a bedrock principle of patent law that in order to be eligible for patent protection, an invention must be *useful*, *novel*, and *non-obvious*. 35 U.S.C. §§ 101, 102, 103. In deciding whether an invention is non-obvious, courts use a *hypothetical skilled practitioner test*, which seeks to determine whether the differences between the claimed invention and the existing body of scientific knowledge at the time of invention—referred to as "prior art"—would be "obvious to a person reasonably skilled in [the field]." *Graham v. John Deere*, 383 U.S. 1, 37 (1966).

Traditionally, patent protection has not been available if "the invention was patented or described in a printed publication in this or a foreign country, in public use or on sale in this country, or more than one year prior to the date of [the US] application." 35 U.S.C. § 102(b). This policy seeks to avoid the situation in which an invention seems to be freely available, only to be suddenly removed from the market. The policy also protects the public from any attempt by inventors to use a late-filing strategy to extend their exclusive rights on a patent longer than the statutory period.

There are various ways that a party granted patent rights might lose them. One may challenge the patent on the ground of invalidity, though in doing so, one faces the obstacle that an issued patent "shall be presumed valid," 35 U.S.C. § 282, unless shown otherwise by "clear and convincing evidence." *Microsoft Corp. v. i4i Ltd. P'ship*, 131 S. Ct. 2238, 2242 (2011).

Even if a patent was validly issued, however, the "exhaustion doctrine" provides that "[t]he unrestricted [i.e., non-contractually controlled] sale of a patented article, by or with the authority of the patentee, 'exhausts' the patentee's right to control further sale and use of that article by enforcing the patent under which it was first sold." *Jazz Photo Corp. v. ITC*, 264 F.3d 1094, 1105 (Fed. Cir. 2001). This rule has an obvious analogue in trademark law's "naked licensing" doctrine, discussed in the discussion below.

One type of utility patent less well-known than "scientific" patents is the so-called "business method" patent, which—though not as broad as its name suggests—can sometimes fill the void left by the Copyright Act's refusal to protect "systems" and "methods of operation." *See* 17 U.S.C. § 102(b). The Supreme Court recently addressed such patents in the closely watched case of *Bilski v. Kappos*, 130 S. Ct. 3128 (2010). Though many onlookers expected the *Bilski* Court to narrow the category of eligible business method patents into oblivion, the Court did not oblige.

Justice Kennedy, writing for the Court, recognized that "business method patents were rarely issued until modern times," and noted that "some business method patents raise special problems in terms of vagueness and suspect validity." *Id.* at 3229. But while some business method patents, like the one at issue in *Bilski*, should be "rejected under [the Court's] precedents on the unpatentability of abstract ideas," not all business method patents would meet with the same fate. *Id.* at 3231. However, the Court stopped short of announcing an all-encompassing test for a valid business method patent, saying only what could *not* serve as the exclusive test: the Federal Circuit's so-called "machine-or-transformation" standard, which had required that "(1) [the business system be] tied to a particular machine or apparatus, or (2) [the system] transform[] a particular article into a different state or thing." *Id.* at 3226-27.

In instructing the Federal Circuit that some business method patents should be deemed valid notwithstanding their inability to satisfy the appellate court's longtime "machine-or-transformation" test, but failing to specify what criteria should take that test's place, the Supreme Court left "system" patents in something of a state of limbo. As of this writing, the Federal Circuit has deftly worked around the vagueness of *Bilski*—for example, recently affirming the invalidity of a system patent for identity theft prevention in *CyberSource Corp. v. Retail Decisions Inc.*, 654 F.3d 1366 (Fed. Cir. Aug. 16, 2011), on the basis that the patent's claims represented unpatentable "abstract ideas" and "mental processes"—but more definitive guidance on business method patents is likely forthcoming, from either the Federal Circuit or the Supreme Court.

Utility Patents in Fashion

- Scientific and engineering patents

  Fashion-related utility patents, though discussed and considered less often than trademarks and copyright protection, do exist. Such patents tend to be clustered in areas of the fashion industry that are slower to change, such as footwear, undergarments, and component parts, such as fasteners. The modern zipper, patented in 1917 by Gideon Sundback (Patent Number 1,219,881) is a well-known example of a utility patent in the apparel context. While Sundback's patent has been in the public domain for decades, it is interesting to note that at least four different zipper-related patents have been granted in the last ten years, including "Multiple pitch zipper [1]" (No. 6,453,521; Sep. 24, 2002); "Multiple pitch zipper [2]" (No. 6,604,263; Aug. 12, 2003); "Zipper stringer having coupling elements with variable properties" (No. 6,681,456; Jan. 27, 2004); and "Display device with electrical zipper interconnect" (No. 7479940; Jan. 20, 2009).

  Additional examples of fashion-related utility patents include those covering newly developed textiles, novel chemical formulas for cosmetics, and even certain biotechnology, such as a 2003 patent on a gene that boosts the number of sheep born in a flock (secured abroad by a New Zealand company.)

- "Business Method" Patents in Fashion

  It must be noted that despite the Supreme Court's opinion affirmation of the continued viability of business method patents in *Bilski*, the vast majority of business methods are not novel. Further, the time it takes to obtain such a patent is reportedly even longer than that required to obtain a more conventional patent. With that said, some novel business methods in the fashion industry could conceivably be eligible for utility patent protection, particularly as technology plays an increasingly significant role in the industry.

Indeed, one fashion-related business method patent was granted to Andrea Rose (Patent Number 5,930,769) for her "System and Method for Fashion Shopping," described in the patent's abstract as follows:

> The present invention provides a method of manual fashion shopping and method for electronic fashion shopping by a customer using a programmed computer, CD-ROM, television, Internet, or other electronic medium such as video. The method comprises of receiving personal information from the customers; selecting a body type and fashion category based on the personal information; selecting fashions from a plurality of clothing items based on the body type and fashion category; outputting a plurality of fashion data based on the selected fashions; and receiving selection information from the customer.

One cannot predict with complete accuracy whether this particular patent, or any other, would be upheld if challenged in court. However, in the wake of *i4i*, 131 S. Ct. at 2242, in which the Supreme Court held that issued patents may not be judicially invalidated absent "clear and convincing evidence," the hurdle to challenge patent validity post-grant is decidedly higher than before. Please consult outside reference guides for an explanation of the likely effect, if any, of the 2011 "America Invents Act" on the principles recounted in this section.

Design Patents

Design patents are sometimes available to step in—if imperfectly—to fill the void where copyright and trademark law currently fail to thoroughly protect unique fashion designs. Indeed, one commentator states that "[d]esign patent protection is an increasingly important form of intellectual property protection because judicial decisions have made it more difficult to attain trademark protection for product design." *Mueller*, *supra* at 289, n.13. Currently, the industry that makes the greatest use of design patents is the furniture industry, which is somewhat similarly situated to the fashion industry it its inability to rely on robust copyright protection due to the Copyright Act's "useful article" bar. *Id.* at 289 n.168.

Scope of Protection

Under 35 U.S.C. § 171, "[w]hoever invents any new, original, and ornamental design for an article of manufacture may obtain a patent thereof, subject to the conditions and requirements of this title." The protection accorded by a design patent lasts for fourteen years from the date of the patent is issued. 35 U.S.C. § 173. *(Note the difference in the "start date" between utility and design patents.)*

Design patent protection is only available for an "article that is ornamental, a product of aesthetic skill, and artistic conception." *Warbern Packaging Industries Inc. v. Cut Rate Plastic Hangers Inc.*, 652 F.2d 987, 988 n.1 (2d Cir. 1981). While the article may be useful in nature,[13] design patent protection is unavailable where "functional features dominate the design" of the article. *Tough Traveler v. Outbound Prods.*, 60 F.3d 964, 971, 35 U.S.P.Q.2d 1617 (2d Cir. 1995) (Jacobs, J., concurring in the result), abrogated on other grounds as stated in *Marks Org. Inc. v. Joles*, 784 F. Supp. 2d 322 (S.D.N.Y. Mar. 18, 2001). Similarly, if the design is dictated by the function of the object, design patent protection will be unavailable. In these circumstances, a utility patent (assuming all relevant criteria are satisfied) is the proper method of protecting the inventor's right to exclude others from his creation.

Design patents are not a viable avenue for protecting most articles of apparel because of the cost and time to prosecute a patent before the US Patent and Trademark Office. In a typical scenario, by the time a patent is issued, a particular article of clothing will have become obsolete, from the brand or the marketer's point of view.

[13] In reasoning reminiscent of copyright law's "conceptual separability" doctrine, the Federal Circuit has recognized that "a distinction exists between the functionality of an article or features thereof and the functionality of the particular design of such article or features thereof that perform a function." *Avia Group Int'l Inc. v. L.A. Gear Cal. Inc.*, 853 F.2d 1557, 1563 (Fed. Cir. 1988).

Further, as with utility patents, only "nonobvious" designs are eligible for patent protection. *See, e.g.*, *Avia Group Int'l Inc. v. L.A. Gear Cal. Inc.*, 853 F.2d 1557, 1563 (Fed. Cir. 1988) ("obviousness is determined from the vantage of 'the designer of ordinary capability who designs articles of the type presented in the application'"). Some, and perhaps many, design patent applications could present legitimate questions—similar to those raised in the debate surrounding proposed copyright-like protection for "unique" fashion designs—about whether the designs at issue are, in fact, truly *new*.

Design Patents in Fashion

For these reasons, design patents tend to be clustered in areas of the fashion industry where products change relatively slowly, such in the footwear, sportswear, and accessory segments of the market. Arguably, this results in something of a paradox: the "staples" of fashion for which design protection will typically be sought may be far less "novel" than "runway fashion" that may reveal greater innovation and wield greater influence over the direction of fashion design, but whose shelf life is too fleeting to justify the time and expense of patent prosecution.

Although one might argue that there are "only so many variations on shoes and bags," fashion companies regularly obtain design patents for these products, and have sued over them—sometimes successfully—in court. In *Avia Group*, 853 F.2d at 1559, for example, shoe manufacturer Avia Group sued rival L.A. Gear for allegedly infringing its patents in an "ornamental design for an athletic shoe outer sole" and "an ornamental design for an athletic shoe upper." L.A. Gear lost before the district court and appealed to the Federal Circuit, which has exclusive jurisdiction over most patent appeals (see discussion below.)

The appellate court affirmed the district court's ruling that the designs at issue were, in fact, ornamental rather than functional. *Id.* at 1563. The Federal Circuit also rejected L.A. Gear's argument that the designs at issue were "obvious," as the defendant had failed to produce "clear and convincing evidence" to this effect (a test for invalidating patents not adopted by the Supreme Court for another twenty-three years, in *i4i*, discussed above.) *Id.* at 1562.

The Federal Circuit next recounted the test for determining infringement in the design patent context: "if, in the eye of an ordinary observer, giving such attention as a purchaser usually gives, two designs are substantially the same, if the resemblance is such as to deceive such an observer, inducing him to purchase one supposing it to be the other, the first one patented is infringed by the other." *Id.* at 1565 (quoting *Gorham Co. v. White*, 81 U.S. 511, 528 (1871)).[14]

The Federal Circuit found that the district court had correctly ruled that L.A. Gear's shoes had infringed on Avia's patents by virtue of their "overall similarity to the patented designs and incorporat[ion of] the novel features thereof," including a "swirl effect" and "pivot point" (on the outer sole) and "the combination of saddle, eyestay, and perforations" (on the shoe upper.) *Id.* at 1565. The court went on to find that the infringement had been "willful," and that the district court had not abused its discretion in awarding attorneys' fees to Avia. *Id.* at 1567.[15]

Clearly, design patent protection can serve as a powerful tool for IP protection, *when it can be timely and economically obtained.* Thus, the decisive question for IP owners in the fashion industry is less whether a patent will be useful once issued, but rather whether an accessory or item of apparel is truly novel and sufficiently worthy of investment to pursue patent protection in the first place. Naturally, this decision should be made with the assistance of qualified patent counsel.

A Word About Design Protection in Other Countries

Design protection is a fairly common feature of other countries' legal systems, where such protection often resembles copyright in the ease of

[14] Interestingly, this test is something of a hybrid between copyright law's "substantial similarity" test, discussed *supra*, and trademark law's "likelihood of confusion" test, discussed *infra*. The *Avia Group* court went on to recount another requirement for a finding of infringement, a separate inquiry into novelty, which was decisively abandoned in *Egyptian Goddess Inc. v. Swisa Inc.*, 543 F.3d 665 (Fed. Cir. 2008) (*en banc*).

[15] For readers interested in following a more recent patent infringement case involving competing athletic shoes, see *Vibram S.P.A. v. Fila U.S.A Inc.*, 11 Civ. 11192 (D. Mass. Jul. 6, 2011). In *Vibram*, shoemaker Vibram sued competitor Fila over shoes that allegedly infringed three of its patents—one utility and two design patents—associated with Vibram's "FiveFingers®" running shoes—or as they are described in the plaintiff's utility patent, "Footwear Having Independently Articulable Toe Portions." *Id.* Complaint at 3.

registration and nature of protection. However, even where such protection is available, whether under the rubric of copyright, patent, or a separate IP regime, the term is typically far shorter than for traditional copyrighted works. *See, e.g.*, *Lucasfilm Ltd. v. Ainsworth*, [2011] UKSC 39, at ¶¶ 10-13, 25 (Jul. 27, 2011), in which the court explained that depending on the date of creation, UK law grants only fifteen or twenty-five years of IP protection to two-dimensional artistic works from which three-dimensional articles are produced.

To date, the US does not have a design protection regime that resembles that of most Western European countries in cost-effectiveness, speed, and ease of use.

Jurisdictional Idiosyncrasies

In 1983, Congress established the United States Court of Appeals for Federal Circuit, which has exclusive jurisdiction over appeals in cases in which the district court's subject-matter jurisdiction is based, in whole or in part, on a legal question hinging on US patent law. 28 U.S.C. §§ 1295, 1338. Since 1983, the Supreme Court has considered utility patent issues relatively infrequently. (The high court *virtually never* addresses questions about design patent protection.) Thus, from 1983 until recent years, Federal Circuit decisions were considered gospel among patent practitioners. However, beginning roughly three years ago, the US Supreme Court has shown a renewed interest in patents, granting *certiorari* in patent cases at higher rate than before, then modifying or even reversing certain longstanding rules crafted by the Federal Circuit (while affirming others.) *Compare i4i Ltd. P'ship*, 131 S. Ct. 2238 *with Bilski v. Kappos*, 130 S. Ct. 3128, both discussed *supra*.

The Federal Circuit's jurisdiction is not limited to *inter partes* proceedings. If/when the US Patent and Trademark Office issues a final denial of a patent application, the spurned applicant is entitled to appeal the denial to the Federal Circuit, or may initiate a civil action against the Director of the Patent Office in the United States District Court for the District of Columbia. 35 U.S.C. § 145. The record developed before the Patent Office may be admitted into evidence during these proceedings. If the court rules in favor of the applicant's right to the patent, then that functions as authorization for the Director to issue it. *Id.* (This procedure may be used for *inter partes* proceedings as well, in which case the appearance of adverse parties will be procured by summons.)

Trade Secrets

Unlike patent protection, trade secret protection arises under *state* law (with the minor caveat that some federal protection is also available under the Economic Espionage Act.) In contrast to the relatively short terms of protection granted under patent law, protection for trade secrets can theoretically last forever—or at least, for as long as a business entity takes the necessary protective measures for the protection to endure.

As trade secret law varies by state, the advice of local counsel is indispensable in this area. To generalize, however, in order for information to be considered a trade secret, it cannot be known outside of the business entity that owns the secret; employees, vendors, and others directly involved in the business may have limited access to the secret on a need-to-know basis. The secret must have economic value, and must be guarded using reasonable measures, which will vary with the circumstances. It is possible for a trade secret to be held concurrently with a patent application up until eighteen months after a patent is filed, at which point all patent applications are made public and the trade secret will necessarily be exposed.

Trade secret protection can be extremely useful in certain circumstances. If the information fails to qualify for patent protection, trade secret protection can confer a similar benefit. Further, trade secret protection is generally less complicated and less expensive to obtain than patent protection. And if a company wants some form of IP protection, but does not want sensitive information revealed to the public, it can avoid patent law's eighteen-month publication requirement altogether by instead opting for trade secret protection.

Individuals and companies in the fashion industry might find trade secret protection useful, in appropriate circumstances, to protect design and manufacturing processes, to help defend against certain types of counterfeiting, and to protect business practices. However, trade secret protection is something of a "niche" area within intellectual property law, so the advice of counsel with *trade secret-specific* expertise is critical if a company wishes to make use of this unique type of protection.

Navigating Trademark Law

The Nature of Trademark Protection

At a fundamental level, trademarks serve to indicate the source of goods and services.[16] Conventionally understood, trademark law emphasizing the reliability of source designation in furtherance of two ends:

1. to provide entrepreneurs with an incentive to invest in their ventures and sell a high-quality product, secure in the knowledge that the law will keep others from poaching their consumer goodwill; and
2. to prevent confusion among consumers about the true source of goods or services, enabling them to make informed decisions based on meaningful indicators of quality and origin.

Various limitations imposed by law, including the denial of protection for functional components of trademarks and the requirement that "merely descriptive" trademarks attain "secondary meaning" among consumers in order to receive protection (each discussed below), attempt to prevent trademark law from conferring a broader monopoly on language and imagery than is necessary to achieve the law's policy objectives.

Trademark protection is especially important in the US fashion industry, because most of the products sold by that industry are not independently protectable under the copyright and patent regimes described above. In the absence of copyright or patent protection, it is generally the case that anyone can duplicate a particular accessory or item of apparel. What makes *this purse* or *that jacket* valuable, then, is often the source of the good rather than its intrinsic value. As such, fashion companies put on runway shows and spend millions of dollars on advertising to create a certain "magic" or "exclusivity" surrounding their brand name, to which consumers are drawn for reasons of fantasy, status, and/or quality. Trademark law attempts to ensure that no third party "free-rides" on that magic, which can only be cultivated through hard work, often at great expense.

---

[16] The term "trademark" technically refers to a mark used in connection with *goods*, while the term "service mark" applies to a mark used in connection with *services*. But in this chapter, as in common parlance, "trademarks" (or sometimes simply "marks") will be used as a catchall term.

Of course, counterfeiting, the most serious variety of trademark infringement, is specifically calculated to "free-ride" on another's brand, which is one reason why the phenomenon is a serious concern for the fashion industry. But many acts of trademark infringement are not deliberate. Like civil copyright infringement, civil trademark infringement is often described, perhaps not entirely accurately, as a "strict liability" offense; however, as we will see, the intent of the "junior user" of an allegedly confusing mark is an important factor for courts deciding the outcome of trademark infringement cases. Yet many new marks and novel uses of existing marks belonging to others sit uncomfortably on the border between lawful competitive activity and actionable "unfair competition" (a common-law cause of action from which modern trademark law evolved.)

In addition to trademark infringement, which is actionable under both federal law (the 1946 Lanham Act) and state law, federal and state legislatures and courts have created remedies for trademark dilution, cybersquatting, broader acts of unfair competition, and invasions of individuals' "right of publicity." Trademark counterfeiting, although falling under the umbrella of trademark infringement, is addressed by a number of provisions at the federal and state level that provide for enhanced penalties and additional remedial tools for aggrieved trademark owners. Unlike in the copyright and patent contexts, the doctrine of federal preemption plays little to no role in trademark law.

The Central Inquiry: Likelihood of Confusion

Traditional trademark disputes frequently came down to the question of "how close is too close?" In order to provide some guideposts for judges to answer that question, each federal circuit adopted a variation of the so-called "likelihood of confusion" test.[17] This test, as its name suggests, asks not only whether consumers actually are confused about the source of a good or service (an inquiry that is often difficult or impossible to make.) Rather, the test seeks to determine whether, if a defendant is permitted to continue using his or her mark in a certain way, an appreciable number of

[17] As discussed below, a trademark *dilution* plaintiff need not prove a likelihood of confusion to prevail. The Federal Trademark Dilution Act of 1995, as modified by the Trademark Dilution Revision Act of 2006, imposes different requirements for a defendant to be held liable on a trademark dilution theory.

ordinarily prudent purchasers are "likely to be confused" about the source, sponsorship, or affiliation of the goods or services at issue. *See Western Pub. Co. v. Rose Art Indus.*, 910 F.2d 57, 59 (2d Cir. 1990).

Each federal circuit has developed its own "likelihood of confusion" factors, which are then conventionally referred to by the name of the case in which the circuit's factors were first articulated. For example, in the Second Circuit, the determination is made using the "*Polaroid*" factors, first developed in *Polaroid Corp. v. Polarad Electronics Corp.*, 287 F.2d 492 (2d Cir.), *cert. denied*, 368 U.S. 820 (1961). Because the Second Circuit was the first federal appellate court to develop a set of factors to guide the likelihood of confusion inquiry, the phrase "*Polaroid* test" or "*Polaroid* factors" is sometimes used generically to refer to all variations of the test, regardless of circuit.

The likelihood of confusion test is one of "equitable balancing," and not all factors will be given equal weight in each case. *See Arrow Fastener Co. v. Stanley Works*, 59 F.3d 384, 400 (2d Cir. 1995). Further, the enumerated factors are non-exhaustive, so a court may consider circumstances outside the purview of the listed factors in its circuit. *See Elvis Presley Ent. V. Capece*, 141 F.3d 188, 194 (5th Cir. 1998). With that said, the following factors are applied in most circuits, plus or minus a factor here or there:

1. the similarity of the marks at issue
2. the similarity of the products or services associated with each mark
3. the likelihood that one party will bridge the gap between its products or services and those of the other party
4. the strength of the plaintiff's mark (see discussion above)
5. the degree of overlap in marketing, distribution, and sales channels
6. consumer sophistication and care exercised in making the purchases at issue
7. evidence of actual confusion, if any, among relevant consumers
8. defendant's intent in adopting the mark at issue

See, e.g., The Wella Corporation v. Wella Graphics, 37 F.3d 46, 48 (2d Cir. 1994) (citing *Polaroid*); *AMF Inc. v. Sleekcraft Boats*, 599 F.2d 341, 348-49 (9th Cir. 1979) (announcing what is now known as "the *Sleekcraft* test").

The version of the likelihood of confusion test that deviates most from the norm is the thirteen-factor "*du Pont* test," applied by the Court of Appeals for the Federal Circuit. *See In re E.I. du Pont de Nemours & Co.*, 476 F.2d 1357 (C.C.P.A. 1973). The Federal Circuit—whose predecessor, the United States Court of Customs and Patent Appeals, first developed the *du Pont* test—applies the *du Pont* factors when presiding over appeals from a final denial of registration (one of the Federal Circuit's several areas of subject matter-specific jurisdiction. *See* 28 U.S.C. § 1295.) Perhaps more importantly for a typical trademark applicant, the *du Pont* factors are applied by the Trademark Trial and Appeal Board, the highest decision-making body within the US Patent and Trademark Office and thus exert significant influence over trademark examiners' day-to-day processing of trademark application. *See, e.g., Citigroup Inc. v. Capital City Bank Group Inc.*, 94 U.S.P.Q.2d 1645 (T.T.A.B. 2010).

The Concept of "First-to-Use"

Both federal and state trademark law place great emphasis on *priority* in the use of a given mark—that is, the chronology of competing claimants' use of a mark in connection with similar goods or services. The party with priority is referred to as the "senior user"; a party that began using a similar mark on a later date is known as the "junior user."

This all-important "first-to-use" principle can lead to surprising results, as illustrated by a recent case involving Polo Ralph Lauren (PRL). In *United States Polo Association v. PRL USA Holdings*, 09 Civ. 9476, 2011 WL 1842980 (S.D.N.Y. May 13, 2011), the US Polo Association, founded in 1890, brought suit for a judicial declaration that it was entitled to use the phrase "US POLO ASSN." and a particular "Double Horseman" image in connection with men's fragrances. Judge Sweet of the Southern District of New York ruled that the Association was forbidden from doing so, because fashion company Polo Ralph Lauren had entered the fragrance market twenty years earlier, affixing its name and now famous horseman logo to products that included men's fragrances. Following a trial, Judge Sweet applied the *Polaroid* factors and concluded: "The marks are so similar it is likely that consumers would be confused, whether by believing that PRL had authorized a down market product or by confusing the products outright." *Id.* at *18. Interestingly, in 2006, a jury had found that "the solid

Double Horsemen mark with [the accompanying text] 'USPA' [was] not infringing [on Polo Ralph Lauren's trademark] in the context of the *apparel* market." *Id.* at *7 (emphasis added). However, for Judge Sweet, the fact that the present dispute involved fragrances, rather than apparel, and that the text accompanying the "Double Horsemen mark" differed in the two cases, meant that the earlier outcome had no bearing here. *Id.*

In short, *PRL* shows that for trademark law purposes, what matters is not which entity has been in existence the longest, but rather which entity was the first to use the mark *in connection with the goods or services at issue.* Although Polo Ralph Lauren had a far less substantial connection to the sport of polo than did the official association dedicated to the sport, the "first-to-use" principle dictated that PRL owned the exclusive right to use the word "Polo" or the image of a polo horseman in the fragrance arena.

Federal Registration

Copyright protection exists from the moment an original work is embodied in a fixed, tangible form. Patent protection, at the opposite end of the spectrum, arises only after a lengthy registration process. Trademark protection falls somewhere in the middle.

Trademark protection is somewhat akin to copyright in that, even if one does not register a mark with a state or federal agency, he accrues so-called "common-law trademark rights" by virtue of using the mark in commerce. But trademark law diverges from copyright in that these common-law rights do not exist from the moment one fixes a trademark in a tangible form; it is *use in commerce* that gives rise to their existence. In general, as is true in patent law, nationwide rights can be achieved only through a formal registration process. Further, unlike the copyright registration process, which is inexpensive and so permissive as to be something of a formality, the trademark registration process often requires back-and-forth with the US Patent and Trademark Office (USPTO) to arrive at an acceptable version and/or scope of the claimed mark. The cost of obtaining a federal trademark registration is far greater than that of a copyright registration, but still substantially less than that of a patent registration.

Although federal registration of trademarks is, in a certain sense, "optional," it is almost always advisable for a company to register its primary brand name (along with secondary brand names, any important, non-functional product features, and other imagery centrally connected with the brand) as early as possible. Reliance on common-law rights in lieu of federal registration is problematic for a variety of reasons — perhaps most notably, because such rights are limited to the geographic region of actual commercial penetration by the mark. *Allard Enterprises Inc. v. Advanced Programming Resources Inc.*, 249 F.3d 564, 572 (6th Cir. 2001). Countless business owners have used their marks without seeking a federal registration, only to learn sometime later that they are "frozen" to their existing geographic market because of a federal registration subsequently filed by a third party. *See, e.g.*, *Thrifty Rent-A-Car System v. Thrift Cars Inc.*, 831 F.2d 1177 (1st Cir. 1987).

In order to allow entrepreneurs some degree of certainty in their business ventures, Congress has authorized the USPTO to accept "intent-to-use" (ITU) applications, which are essentially a means of temporarily reserving a mark that one has a "*bona fide*" intention to use, but has not yet employed in commerce. *See* 15 U.S.C. § 1051(b). It is wise to complete *at least* the ITU application process before devoting significant resources to the development and marketing of a new brand. This process is fairly simple, and can be accomplished largely, or even entirely, over the Internet, using the USPTO's "TEAS" system.

The process of obtaining a trademark registration can be smooth and simple, or fraught with difficulties; the precise contours of the "trademark prosecution" process are beyond the scope of this chapter. Although it is far easier to register a trademark without the assistance of an attorney than, say, a patent, it is always prudent to consult a trademark attorney early in the process, both to minimize the likelihood of objections from the USPTO or third parties, and to do preemptive "damage control" in the event one is later sued for infringement despite having been granted a registration.

In any event, once a federal registration is issued, it provides "constructive notice" of the registrant's trademark rights throughout the United States, even where the registrant has not yet engaged in any commercial activity. 15

U.S.C. § 1072. (The law is somewhat unsettled as to the precise effect of this notice on *junior* users in remote geographic areas. *See Rebel Debutante LLC v. Forsythe Cosmetic Group Ltd.*, 1:11cv00113, 2011 WL 2620450 (M.D.N.C. Jul. 1, 2011)). These rights are retroactive to the date of the registrant's application; however, as noted above, any third-party use of a similar mark pre-dating the filing of the federal application are "grandfathered in." In other words, the user of the unregistered mark can generally continue to use that mark in the same manner and region as before, unless the registrant had penetrated the relevant market prior to its application date. See 15 U.S.C. § 1115(b)(5); *Thrifty Rent-A-Car System*, 831 F.2d 1177; *National Association for Healthcare Communications v. Central Arkansas Area Agency on Aging*, 257 F.3d 732, 735 (8th Cir. 2001). If, at some point thereafter, the third party ceases to use the unregistered mark in commerce, even for a relatively limited period, he may lose his common-law rights altogether. *Thrifty*, 831 F.2d at 1183.

Federal registration confers other benefits besides nationwide constructive notice, including:

- a legal presumption of one's ownership of the mark, and of one's exclusive right to use that mark in connection with the goods or services identified in the registration
- the right to use the ® system as opposed to the ™ designation—or ℠, for service marks—which one may use at any time, whether one has filed an application or not
- the ability to use the registration as a basis to extend one's protection to other countries which is necessary because trademark rights, like copyrights and patents, are territorial in nature

US Patent and Trademark Office, *What are the benefits of federal trademark registration?*, http://www.uspto.gov/faq/trademarks.jsp#_Toc275426681 (last visited Sept. 18, 2011). One benefit of registration particularly useful to the fashion industry is the ability to record the registration with US Customs and Border Protection, in order to prevent the importation of infringing goods. *Id.* Put differently, the federal government will not stop infringing goods at the border *unless* the allegedly infringed trademark has been registered with the USPTO and recorded with Customs.

State trademark registrations are less logistically complicated and significantly less expensive than their federal counterparts, but they also confer far fewer benefits, and thus are usually recommended only where one simply cannot afford to register a mark with the USPTO. *Compare* New York State, Department of State, Division of Corporations, State Records & UCC, *Trademark Registration, http://www.dos.ny.gov/forms/corporations/0241-f-l-a.pdf (last visited Sept. 18, 2011) ($50 per class of goods/services claimed), with* USPTO Fee Schedule, *Trademark Processing Fees, http://www.uspto.gov/web/* offices/ac/qs/ope/fee2009september15.htm#tm (last visited Sept. 18, 2011) ($325 or more per class of goods/services claimed, depending on manner of registration).

Types of Trademarks and Requirements for Protection

Word Marks

The "strength" of a trademark will determine whether it is protectable at all, and if so, whether the "strength of the plaintiff's mark" factor in the *Polaroid* test (see discussion above) will favor one party or another in litigation. Under the rubric developed by the respected jurist Judge Friendly, in *Abercrombie & Fitch Co. v. Hunting World, Inc.*, 537 F.2d 4, 9 (2d Cir. 1976), marks fall into one of the following categories: generic, descriptive, suggestive, arbitrary, or fanciful. Generic and descriptive marks are each treated in a unique way; suggestive, arbitrary, and fanciful marks are treated in largely the same manner under trademark law.

- Generic

  Generic trademarks are those that describe the category of good or service at issue—i.e., terms which are "the common descriptive name of an article or substance." *Id.* at 9. The phrase "generic mark" is actually an oxymoron, since generic terms may *never* function as trademarks. *Id.* The rationale for this absolute prohibition is that it would be unfair to "deprive competing manufacturers of the product of the right to call an article by its name." *Id.*

Determining genericism is more difficult than it might appear at first glance; to do so, one must closely examine the connection between the name and the goods or services with which it is associated. For instance, "Canada Goose" would likely be "generic" if used to sell geese from Canada, but it is not generic when applied to, say, outerwear. (The Canadian apparel company "Canada Goose" has used the term in this manner since 1957.) A more nuanced example is the term "Jean Shop," which would likely be generic if associated with a shop selling jeans. The brand "Jean Shop," however, managed to convince the USPTO to allow the registration of its mark in connection with "retail store services featuring clothing," and later on, in connection with "shirts, t-shirts, jeans, sweatshirts, belts, [and] scarves." In each instance, the registration includes a disclaimer: "NO CLAIM IS MADE TO THE EXCLUSIVE RIGHT TO USE "JEAN" [first registration] [or] "JEAN SHOP" [second registration] APART FROM THE MARK AS SHOWN." Such disclaimers sometimes enable one to get around the genericism bar to registration. *See* 15 U.S.C. § 1056(a). The trademark protection enjoyed by the owner, then, is limited to the non-disclaimed portion of the mark, such as the remaining words, the stylized font used for an otherwise generic phrase, or an image accompanying the text.

(The "Jean Shop" example provides an opportunity highlight an important rule in trademark law: the USPTO's issuance of a registration, although granted some deference by the courts, does not by any means guarantee the registration will be upheld if challenged in court. *See, e.g., Louboutin S.A. v. Yves Saint Laurent America*, 11 Civ. 2381 (S.D.N.Y. Apr. 7, 2011) (discussed at length below.)

One common concern for brand owners is so-called "genericide," which can occur when a trademark is so successful that it becomes the commonly used term for an entire category of goods. *See, e.g., Dupont Cellophane Co. Inc. v. Waxed Products Co. Inc.*, 85 F.2d 75 (2d Cir. 1936) ("Cellophane" had likely become generic, even if certain consumers still associated it with the product's original manufacturer.) The disastrous effect of this outcome for a brand owner is obvious. For this reason, one sometimes sees advertisements urging the public not to use trademarks in a generic sense, such as the full back-page ad that appeared in *Women's Wear Daily* on September 20, 2010, featuring the following excerpt:

> "Chanel is our registered trademark for fragrance, cosmetics, clothing, accessories, and other lovely things. Although our style is justly famous, a jacket is not a 'Chanel jacket' unless it is ours, and somebody else's cardigans are not 'Chanel for now.' And even if we are flattered by such tributes to our fame as 'Chanel-issime, Chanel-ed, Chanels, and Chanel-ized', PLEASE DON'T."

Interestingly, *Women's Wear Daily* itself routinely contacts other publications to request that writers refer to the magazine by its full name before using the abbreviation "*WWD*," presumably to avoid the genericide of its primary mark.

- Descriptive

A descriptive mark (sometimes called a "merely descriptive" mark) is one that literally describes the goods or services at issue, but is not the generic term for such goods or services. In the words of one judge: "A term is descriptive if it forthwith conveys an immediate idea of the ingredients, qualities, or characteristics of the goods." *Abercrombie*, 537 F.2d at 11 (quoting *Stix Products Inc. v. United Merchants & Manufacturers Inc.*, 295 F. Supp. 479, 488 (S.D.N.Y. 1968)). One example of a fashion-related descriptive mark is "American Apparel," as the mark is used in connection with apparel made in the United States. Another example, arguably, is "*Women's Wear Daily*," for a publication that comes out daily and reports on women's wear. Marks qualifying as "descriptive" may only be registered or enforced in court *if* they have become "distinctive of the applicant's goods in commerce." *Abercrombie*, 537 F.2d at 10; 15 U.S.C. § 1052(e). (The acceptability of descriptive marks helps to illustrate that there is no originality requirement in trademarks comparable to that found in copyright. See discussion *supra.*)

One possible method of showing acquired distinctiveness at the registration stage is by providing the USPTO with "proof of substantially exclusive and continuous use [of the] mark by the applicant in commerce for the five years before the date on which the claim of distinctiveness is made." 15 U.S.C. § 1052(f).

Often, however, the question of distinctiveness arises during enforcement proceedings. In this situation, courts inquire whether the plaintiff's descriptive mark enjoys "acquired distinctiveness," perhaps more commonly referred to as "secondary meaning." *Secondary* meaning is something of a misnomer, as it will be found "when the *primary* meaning attributed to a term"—such as 'American Apparel' when used to describe domestically-made clothing, or *Women's Wear Daily* when used to describe a daily publication about women's apparel—"is supplanted in the perception of the consuming public to one of source identification." *Inwood Laboratories v. Ives Laboratories*, 456 U.S. 844, 851 n.11 (1982). Apart from the above-mentioned presumption of secondary meaning that may arise after five years, a plaintiff attempting to prove secondary meaning is generally required to produce evidence of the following types:

1. The period of time the mark has been in use. *See, e.g., Int'l Kennel Club of Chicago v. Mighty Star*, 846 F.2d 1079 (7th Cir. 1988) (fifty years of use strongly suggested secondary meaning).
2. Volume of sales, with greater volumes increasing the likelihood that secondary meaning exists. *See, e.g., E. & J. Gallo Winery v. Consorzio Del Gallo Nero*, 782 F. Supp. 457 (N.D. Cal. 1991).
3. The amount—or according to some courts, the *effectiveness*—of advertising. *Compare Japan Telecom v. Japan Telecom America*, 287 F.3d 866, 875 (9th Cir. 2002), *with Paramount Pictures Corp. v. Worldwide Ent. Corp.*, 195 U.S.P.Q. 539, 542 (S.D.N.Y. 1977).

4. Perhaps most powerfully, methodologically-sound surveys indicating that a sufficient percentage of consumers understand the primary meaning of the alleged mark as an indication of the product's source. *See Levi Strauss & Co. v. Blue Bell, Inc.*, 778 F.2d 1352, 1358 (9th Cir. 1984). The testimony of individual consumers, by contrast, will usually be given little, if any, weight. *See, e.g.*, *Heirs of the Estate of Jenkins v. Paramount Pictures Corp.*, 90 F. Supp. 2d. 706, 714 (E.D. Va. 2000), *aff'd*, 7 Fed. Appx. 270 (4th Cir. 2001).
5. Defendant's intent in copying the mark, which may in some instances constitute evidence of secondary meaning. *See, e.g.*, *Laureyssens v. Idea Group Inc.*, 964 F.2d 131 (2d Cir. 1992).

Under these criteria, "American Apparel" and *Women's Wear Daily* would almost certainly be found to carry the requisite secondary meaning for enforcement. Further, once a mark has been registered on the USPTO's Principal Register—though not on the less significant "Supplemental Register"—for five years, the mark *may no longer be challenged* based on mere descriptiveness. Such a mark has achieved the status of "incontestability." 15 U.S.C. § 1115(b). However, this term, too, is somewhat misleading, as an "incontestable" mark may still be challenged and potentially invalidated on a variety of other bases, including genericism and functionality.

- Suggestive, Arbitrary, and Fanciful

The remaining categories of word marks are, in increasing order of strength, suggestive, arbitrary, and fanciful marks. Though the categories are theoretically "ranked" in this order, there is no difference among these categories for registration purposes; all are deemed "inherently distinctive," requiring no evidence of secondary meaning to obtain a registration. *Abercrombie*, 537 F.2d at 11. While the hierarchy among the three could theoretically go to the "strength of the mark" factor in the *Polaroid* test, in practice it will rarely be dispositive.

A "suggestive" mark is one that does not directly describe, but rather, *suggests* the product or service with which it is associated. The Second Circuit explained that a mark is suggestive if it "requires imagination, thought, and perception to reach a conclusion as to the nature of goods." *Abercrombie*, 537 F.2d at 11 (quoting *Stix Products*, 295 F. Supp. at 488). "The North Face" is commonly used example of a suggestive mark, because its name evokes the cold weather that its outerwear protects against, but a conceptual leap is required for a consumer to get from the name to the product. Another mark, which toes the line between suggestive and arbitrary, is "Comme des Garçons." The phrase is French for "like some boys", and thus arguably evokes the gender-neutralizing quality of the label's clothes.[18]

An "arbitrary" mark is one in which a "common word . . . is applied in an unfamiliar way." *Abercrombie*, 537 F.2d at 11 n.12. Two examples in fashion are "Acne" and "Theory," because these words are common English words whose meaning has no apparent connection with the clothing sold by each company.

Finally, the term "fanciful" is "usually applied to words invented solely for their use as trademarks." *Id.* An example of a fanciful mark in fashion is "Akris," a completely new word created by mashing up the founder's name: Alice Kriemler Schoch. *See* Official Akris Website, History at 4, http://www.akris.ch/html/english/index.html (last visited Aug. 6, 2011).

---

[18] Rather than dwelling on Comme des Garçons to debate the suggestive/arbitrary distinction—as explained above, that distinction is of little legal consequence—we should pause to consider Comme des Garçons' illustration of the prevailing, though not unanimous rule, that in determining whether a mark is generic, descriptive, suggestive, etc., the English translation of the mark must be considered. *See, e.g.*, *Otokoyama Co. Ltd. v. Wine of Japan Import Inc.*, 175 F.3d 266, 270-71 (2d Cir. 1999) (because term was generic in Japan for variety of sake, it was not entitled to U.S. trademark protection, despite most American consumers' ignorance of the term's meaning). *But see Anheuser-Busch Inc. v. Stroh Brewery Co.*, 750 F.2d 631, 642 (8th Cir. 1984) (only meaning to U.S. consumers should be considered to determine protection.)

When choosing a name for a new venture or line of clothing, it is wise to select as strong a trademark as possible on the generic-to-fanciful spectrum. Selection of a strong mark will:

1. facilitate the registration process,
2. increase one's chances of success in litigation to enforce the mark, and
3. lessen—though not eliminate—the likelihood that one's mark will be invalidated in adversarial proceedings.

<u>Names and Personas</u>

Of particular importance to the fashion industry is the principle that proper names may, subject to certain caveats explained herein, serve as trademarks. Indeed, the list of proper-name marks in the apparel industry is virtually limitless: Marc Jacobs, Jil Sander, Marni, Gucci, Chanel, and countless others. These names have been chosen on purpose, however, to illustrate certain concepts below. Of less importance to fashion designers specifically, but great importance to celebrities in general, individuals' images, and even their *personas*, may be protected under federal trademark law (and/or related state law.)

- Surnames

  A mark that consists solely of a surname—i.e., a last name—may receive trademark protection, but only upon a showing of secondary meaning. 15 U.S.C. § 1052(e)(4) & (f).

  The threshold test that determines whether one must surmount this additional hurdle to registration is whether the primary significance of the word to the average member of the American public is that of a surname; thus, even a rare name will be held to the secondary meaning requirement if it is likely to be perceived as a surname by purchasers. *See In re Cazes*, 21 U.S.P.Q.2d 1796 (T.T.A.B. 1991). The label "Marni," for example, actually borrowed its name from the *first* name of the founder's sister. However, if the relevant purchasing public in the United States perceived "Marni" as a last name and the company was registering its mark for the first time, it would be required to produce proof of secondary meaning, using, *inter alia*, the types of evidence listed above.

Few would dispute that "Gucci" and "Chanel," though primarily perceived as surnames, enjoy secondary meaning among the purchasing public. What is notable about these marks is that the original namesake of each house has passed away. It will come as no surprise that, provided trademark rights are properly structured from the outset and/or assigned later on, a company is legally entitled to continue using the name of its deceased namesake designer as its trademark. (As fashion acolytes are no doubt aware, companies may even be entitled to use the names of living designers *no longer affiliated with the company*, depending on contractual and other considerations. *See JA Apparel v. Abboud*, discussed below.

Sometimes, there may be close calls: when a mark is primarily recognized as an ordinary word—even if the word is also a common surname—no proof of secondary meaning will be required to obtain a federal trademark registration. *See Fisher Radio Corp. v. Bird Electronic Corp.*, 162 U.S.P.Q. 265 (T.T.A.B. 1969) (proposed mark "BIRD" deemed protectable without evidence of acquired distinctiveness). One example from today's fashion industry would be "Hunter," the manufacturer of rain boots and other accessories.

Interestingly, where a historical figure's name is first chosen as a trademark, that mark may be protected *without* any showing of secondary meaning. *See Lucien Piccard Watch Corp v. Since 1868 Crescent Corp.*, 165 U.S.P.Q. 459 (S.D.N.Y. 1970) ("DA VINCI" is primarily understood as an historical figure, not surname).

- Full Names

Some trademarks in the form of full proper names, such as "Jack Spade," are invented, rather than derived from real-life individuals. *See* Jon Caramanica, *At Jack Spade, Carefully Appearing Not to Care*, N.Y. TIMES (Sept. 1, 2010), *available at* http://www.nytimes.com/

2010/09/02/fashion/02CRITIC.html. Other marks are based on the names of real individuals who have legally changed their names for business or other reasons. *Ralph Lauren, Formerly Ralph Lifshitz, Dislikes His First Name Too*, HUFFINGTON POST (Sept. 23, 2009), *available at* http://www.huffingtonpost.com/2009/09/23/ralph-lauren-formerly-ral_n_295986.html. Some marks are based on the full names of living individuals still affiliated with the company (like Marc Jacobs), while others are based on designers who have since left the company. *See* Lisa March, *Devi Kroell Leaves Her Own Company*, STYLELIST (May 21, 2010), *available at* http://www.stylelist.com/2010/05/21/devi-kroell-leaves-company/(also noting that "[t]he most famous label without its living namesake is Jil Sander.")

Despite the differences described, all of the foregoing categories of full-name marks are generally treated in the same manner under trademark law: no secondary meaning is required for trademark protection. The most notable exception to the "all full names are treated the same" rule is the phenomenon of federal courts displaying some hesitance to entirely enjoin an individual from using his or her birth name in commerce. Nevertheless, federal judges have strayed quite far from the once widely accepted principle that each person possessed a "natural right" to use her given name, despite the existence of similarly-named competitors. The current approach is more measured: courts will attempt to allow the individual whose given name is "taken" to make *some* use of it, but also impose safeguards to minimize confusion arising from the dual use.

This approach was employed by the district court in the relatively well-known case of *JA Apparel v. Abboud*. The dispute arose after designer Joseph Abboud had sold his eponymous trademark to JA Apparel for a hefty sum, but later began independently marketing a new line under the brand name "jaz"—often accompanied by a tagline that included the name "Joseph Abboud." JA Apparel sued Abboud, claiming that it had been denied the "benefit of the bargain" for which it had paid so handsomely. After a district court ruling and a Second Circuit reversal and remand, 568 F.3d 390 (2d Cir. 2009), the district court crafted a nuanced injunction:

- Abboud was not entitled to use his name *as a trademark*.
- Abboud was not entitled to use his name on "jaz" clothes, labels, or product packaging.
- Abboud *was* entitled to use his name in promotional and advertising materials, but only "in the context of a complete sentence or descriptive phrase," and only if the name was printed in the same size and font as the surrounding words. In any such materials, the "jaz" trademark would have to be the most prominent text.
- Anytime Abboud used his name in this manner, he was required to include "a disclaimer of any affiliation with JA Apparel and products sold under the Joseph Abboud trademarks." This disclaimer would also need to appear in the same size and font as his name.

JA Apparel Corp. v. Abboud, 682 F. Supp. 2d 294, 322 (S.D.N.Y. 2010).

The *Abboud* court was guided by an injunction issued in a similar case two decades earlier. In that case, one Paolo Gucci wished to continue plying his craft after a falling-out with his family's renowned apparel company. The court ruled that Paolo could make only limited use of his name in connection with clothing:

> [T]o protect the interests of [the Gucci company] in the "Gucci" name, Paolo is enjoined from using "Paolo Gucci" as a trademark or trade name. To enable Paolo to exploit his own talents and identity, however, he is entitled to use his name to identify himself as the designer of products sold under a separate trademark which does not include the name "Gucci." To avoid confusion, the name Paolo Gucci must always appear after the trademark in advertisements and on labels, and must be no more prominent than the

> trademark. Moreover, plaintiff must use a disclaimer, similar to the one he now employs, which notifies consumers that he is no longer affiliated with any of the Gucci entities.

Gucci v. Gucci Shops, Inc., 688 F.Supp. 916, 928 (1988).

However, where there is a suggestion of bad faith, courts will be far less inclined to bend over backwards in order to allow an individual to use his name in some capacity. In a more recent trademark infringement lawsuit involving the Gucci mark, Paolo's widow and daughter, Jennifer and Gemma Gucci, were penalized for litigation-related misconduct with sanctions that virtually guaranteed they would never again dare to use the Gucci name in commerce. *See Gucci America v. Gucci*, 07 Civ. 6820, 2010 WL 5490905 (S.D.N.Y. Dec. 30, 2010).

- Tributes and "False Endorsement" Claims

Because the Lanham Act provides for trademark liability not only when there is a likelihood of consumer confusion about the source of goods or services, but also regarding the "affiliation, connection . . . sponsorship, or approval" of the products, 15 U.S.C. § 1125(a)(1)(A), questions sometimes arise about whether self-proclaimed "tributes" making use of a famous individual's name are infringing—in other words, whether the consuming public is likely to be confused about the celebrity's sponsorship of the goods or services in question.

For example, in April 2011, the company that administers the rights of deceased designer Tony Duquette sued J. Crew for an item the latter had marketed as the "J. Crew Duquette Factory Leopard Print Sweater." Alexandra Steigrad, *Tony Duquette Sues J. Crew Over Cardigan Print*, WOMEN'S WEAR DAILY (Apr. 25, 2011), *available at* http://www.wwd.com/business-news/legal/tony-duquette-sues-j-crew-3591529. The Duquette plaintiffs alleged that J. Crew had "knowingly and willfully used the Duquette trademark without permission or license in connection with a leopard print product because of Tony Duquette's unique association with leopard print in the company's designs and products."

The outcome of tribute cases brought under the Lanham Act will hinge, at least doctrinally, on the many prongs of the above-mentioned *Polaroid* likelihood of confusion test. But in practice, the single most influential factor in these cases may be the court's intuitive sense of whether a putative tribute was, in reality, a "marketing scheme based on the tremendous drawing power of [a celebrity's] name and its ability to attract consumer interest and attention." *Elvis Presley Enterprises Inc. v. Capece*, 141 F.3d 188, 196 (5th Cir. 1998) (nightclub lacking affiliation with the Elvis Presley Estate enjoined from continuing to do business as "The Velvet Elvis").

Courts presiding over cases involving tributes also consider the number of products on the market bearing the name or likeness of the celebrity in question. Thus, in *Cairns v. Franklin Mint*, 292 F.3d 1139 (9th Cir. 2002), Princess Diana's trustees and executors sued a collectibles company for its sale of jewelry, plates, and dolls bearing the deceased's name and likeness. The Ninth Circuit Court of Appeals had little trouble concluding that there could be no likelihood of confusion about any "official endorsement" of the products at issue where:

> Between 1981 and 1997, many products, including some that were largely indistinguishable from Franklin Mint products, bore the name and likeness of Princess Diana, who neither endorsed nor objected to any of these products. Consumers, therefore, had no reason to believe Franklin Mint's Diana-related products were endorsed by the Princess. This did not change when, following Princess Diana's death in 1997, the Fund endorsed approximately 20 products—but not Franklin Mint's—amidst a flood of un-endorsed Diana-related memorabilia.

Id. at 1149-50. This passage illustrates one reason why trademark attorneys frequently tout the importance of "policing the unauthorized use of one's mark."

Interestingly, a celebrity's actual name or image need not be used for a claim based on a likelihood of confusion regarding a company's or individual's "affiliation, connection . . . sponsorship, or approval" of the products, 15 U.S.C. § 1125(a)(1)(A). (Such claims are often described as "false endorsement" claims.)

Thus, in the well-known case of *Allen v. National Video*, 610 F. Supp. 612, 628 (S.D.N.Y. 1985), a video rental chain was held liable for using a Woody Allen look-alike in an ad, without the actor's permission, finding that "defendants' use of [the look-alike's] photograph in their advertisement creates a likelihood of consumer confusion over plaintiff's endorsement or involvement."

Much more recently, celebrity Kim Kardashian brought a similar "lookalike" claim against Gap, Inc., the parent company of Old Navy, which had run an ad featuring a woman bearing an uncanny resemblance to Kardashian, allegedly in an attempt to deceive viewers into believing that Kardashian had endorsed the Old Navy brand. *See* Eriq Gardner, *Can Kim Kardashian Win Her Multi-Million Dollar Lawsuit Against Old Navy? (Analysis)*, THE HOLLYWOOD REPORTER (Jul. 20, 2011), *available at* http://www.hollywoodreporter.com/thr-esq/can-kim-kardashian-win-her-213481.

Pictorial or Design Marks

Like marks based on designer names, fashion trademarks consisting of images are too numerous to count. To cite just a few examples, however, there is the famous Nike swoosh, the Polo Ralph Lauren horseman logo (see discussion above), and the Lacoste alligator. Sometimes, the pictorial mark is a stylized version of the full name or initials of the brand, such as the distinctive lettering in the Prada logo or the interlocking "YSL" often used by the Yves Saint Laurent company. Pictorial and design marks are generally protectable without secondary meaning, provided that:

1. the imagery is not merely ornamental, and
2. the image creates a commercial impression unrelated to the claimed mark's aesthetic impact.

See In re Paramount Pictures Corp., 213 U.S.P.Q. 1111, 1113 (T.T.A.B. 1982); *In re E.J. Brach & Sons*, 256 F.2d 325, 327 (C.C.P.A. 1958).

One particularly contentious pictorial mark is the 133-year-old "Arcuate" stitch design found on the rear pocket of Levi's jeans. Levi's has sued Abercrombie, Polo Ralph Lauren, and Dolce & Gabbana, among many other apparel companies, for allegedly coming too close to the plaintiff's venerable curved "V" stitch design. *See* Michael Barbaro & Julie Creswell, *Levi's Turns to Suing Its Rivals*, N.Y. TIMES (Jan. 28, 2007), *available at* http://www.nytimes.com/2007/01/29/business/29jeans.html?pagewanted=all (calling the Arcuate design "the biggest legal battleground in American fashion").

Occasionally, it is unclear whether a purported mark is merely ornamental, a source-designating component of the product's design, or a graphic mark like any other. A merely ornamental design cannot serve as a trademark because of the so-called aesthetic functionality bar to protection, discussed below. At the opposite end of the spectrum, a graphic mark such as the Lacoste alligator, consistently applied regardless of the product to which it is affixed, is almost certainly serving a source-designation function rather than a design function (in large part because the selection of an alligator is so arbitrary in the relevant context.) A graphic mark like the Lacoste alligator, if properly presented to the USPTO/court, will receive protection just like any other inherently distinctive mark.

The difficulty arises in the space in between, where a certain component of a product is arguably ornamental, but also arguably source designating. One potentially borderline scenario is Adidas's longtime litigation campaign against other companies—recently, Land's End, in *Adidas America Inc. v. Land's End, Inc.*, 11 Civ. 552 HU (D. Or. May 15, 2011)—that have used diagonal stripe patterns on the side of their sneakers. Adidas possesses a federal registration in its "Three-Stripe Mark" (see Figure 1, from Adidas's USPTO registration), but one might reasonably question whether the pattern is actually a component of the product design rather than a traditional pictorial trademark. As explained in greater detail below, the difference is significant, as product designs cannot be protected without a showing of secondary meaning. Further, although the relevant case law is currently in an extreme state of flux, certain visual components fashion articles may be ineligible for trademark protection altogether based on "aesthetic functionality," also discussed below.

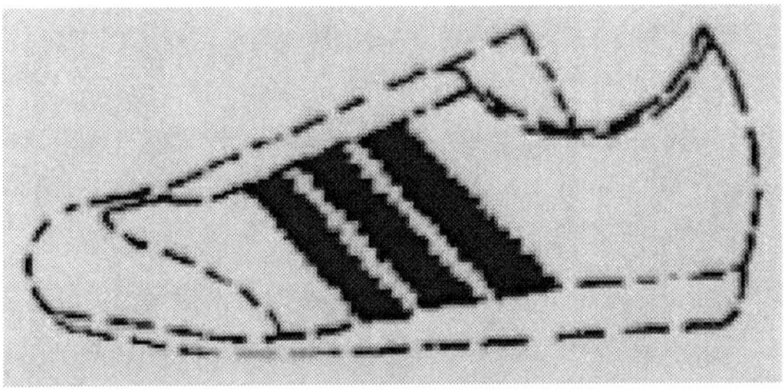

Finally, it is worth noting that a design mark need not be created from sheer imagination: images of pre-existing objects, including those that exist in nature (like an alligator) may function as trademarks. *See Prudential Ins. Co. v. Gibraltar Financial Corp. of California*, 694 F.2d 1150 (9th Cir. 1982) (Rock of Gibraltar protectable). By contrast, ordinary geometric shapes are protected only with evidence of secondary meaning. *Wiley v. American Greetings Corp.*, 762 F.2d 139, 141-42 (red heart); *Brooks Shoe Mfg. Co. v. Suave Shoe Corp.*, 716 F.2d 854, 857-58 (11th Cir. 1983) ("V" design on sneakers). And where the alleged shape mark serves a function, even an aesthetic one, it may be wholly ineligible for trademark protection. *See Franco & Sons v. Franek*, 615 F.3d 855 (7th Cir. 2010) (trademark protection unavailable for round shape of towel, due to functionality).

Sound and Smell

There is relatively little to say about sound and smell marks, both of which are eligible for trademark protection in the United States (though not in all countries.) *See, e.g., Oliveira v. Frito-Lay Inc.*, 251 F.3d 56, 61-62 (2d Cir. 2001) (NBC's three chimes); *In re Clarke*, 17 U.S.P.Q.2d 1238 (T.T.A.B. 1990) (embroidery yarn with particular scent). However, two important caveats are necessary: 1) commonplace sounds must acquire secondary meaning before they may function as trademarks, *In re General Electric Broadcasting Co.*, 199 U.S.P.Q. 560 (T.T.A.B. 1978); and 2) scents used specifically for their sensory appeal, such as perfumes and colognes, cannot be protected, on the ground that such use is functional. *See In re Clarke*, 17 U.S.P.Q.2d at 1239 n.4.

- Functionality

As the "functionality" bar to trademark protection has now been mentioned several times, it is necessary to explain this bedrock principle of trademark law in some detail before proceeding.

As previously noted, trademark law attempts to serve two primary purposes:

1. to ensure that a brand owner will reap the benefit of the investment he makes into his brand; and
2. to prevent consumer confusion.

US policymakers have determined that awarding monopolies on certain words, phrases, images, etc., at least in connection with certain classes of goods and services, is justified by the importance of trademark law's policy objectives, and that the public's resulting inability to use those words, phrases, and images in a potentially confusing manner provides little or no cause for concern. As such, policymakers have chosen *not to limit the duration of trademark rights* (provided the limitations on those rights are respected by owners and courts—a question hotly debated among intellectual property acolytes.)

Trademark law thus differs from copyright and patent law, where the balancing of interests between the rights of creators (or the parties that pay for their creations) and the rights of the public to make full use of those creations justifies a *time-limited term of protection.* (Indeed, the importance of balancing these rights is enshrined in nothing less than the US Constitution, which empowers Congress to grant copyright and patent rights to authors and inventors only for "limited Times." U.S. CONST. ART. I, Sec. 8, Cl. 8. Because trademark protection can exist in perpetuity, this is an area of law in which safeguards are particularly necessary to ensure that trademarks are used to promote—and not to hinder—competition in the marketplace. We have already seen multiple examples of such safeguards, including the denial of protection to generic phrases (which would prevent others from referring to their goods or services) and the requirement that "merely descriptive" marks have accrued secondary meaning among consumers in order to be protected (which ensures that descriptive words are not removed from one's commercial vocabulary unnecessarily.)

Another important safeguard that helps to keep trademark law from hindering competition is the long-established rule that trademark protection is unavailable for "functional" components of claimed marks. As explained by the US Supreme Court in *Qualitex Co. v. Jacobson Products Co. Inc.*, 514 U.S. 159, 164 (1995) (emphasis added):

> The functionality doctrine prevents trademark law, which seeks to promote competition by protecting a firm's reputation, from instead inhibiting legitimate competition by allowing a producer to control *a useful product feature.* It is the province of patent law, not trademark law, to encourage invention by granting inventors a monopoly over new product designs or functions for a limited time, 35 U.S.C. §§ 154, 173, after which competitors are free to use the innovation. *If a product's functional features could be used as trademarks*, however, a monopoly over such features could be obtained without regard to whether they qualify as patents and *could be extended forever* because trademarks may be renewed in perpetuity. [T]he functionality doctrine ensures that protection for utilitarian product features be properly sought through a limited-duration utility patent, and not through the potentially unlimited protection of a trademark registration.

A feature of a trademark—or in some instances, an *entire* trademark—will be deemed "functional" if a grant of exclusive rights over that feature would "put a competitor at a significant disadvantage because the feature is 'essential to the use or purpose of the article' or 'affects [its] cost or quality.'" *Id.* at 169 (emphasis added).

Functionality, in its most conventional form, is illustrated by *TrafFix Devices Inc. v. Marketing Displays Inc.*, 532 U.S. 23 (2001). In *TrafFix*, the Supreme Court ruled that trademark protection was unavailable for a product configuration that used two springs to keep highway signs from blowing away in the wind. The configuration was functional, the Court explained, in part because requiring competitors to use a different number of springs would either make their products less effective or more expensive to manufacture. (Further, the fact that the two-spring system was the subject of an expired patent was deemed strong evidence of functionality.)

A less conventional type of functionality, of particular concern to the fashion industry, is so-called "aesthetic functionality." This doctrine denies trademark protection "where an ornamental feature is claimed as a trademark and trademark protection would significantly hinder competition by limiting the range of adequate alternative designs[.]" *Knitwaves Inc. v. Lollytogs Ltd.*, 71 F.3d 996, 1006 (2d Cir. 1995). In *Franco & Sons v. Franek*, 615 F.3d 855 (7th Cir. 2010), for example, the Seventh Circuit withheld trademark protection claimed in the round shape of a towel, in part because some consumers would prefer a round towel because of its aesthetic appeal (without regard to the company that had made it.) As discussed in "*Color*," immediately below, the doctrine of aesthetic functionality is currently in an extreme state of flux insofar as it precludes protection for certain ornamental elements of fashion.

In any event, where either conventional or aesthetic functionality is present, it serves as an absolute defense to an action for trademark infringement, and likewise imposes an absolute bar to trademark registration for the functional feature. As with genericism, functionality precludes trademark protection *even if* consumers associate the generic/functional feature with a single source:

> The determination that a proposed mark is functional constitutes, for public policy reasons, an absolute bar to registration on either the Principal Register or the Supplemental Register—*regardless of evidence showing that the proposed mark has acquired distinctiveness.*

Trademark Manual of Examining Procedure (TMEP) § 1202.02(a)(iii)(A) (Fourth Ed. April 2005) (emphasis added).

Color

Partly due to the doctrine of functionality, *color* is its own animal in the trademark realm. Naturally, color trademarks are of particular interest to the fashion industry, where visual impact is of the utmost importance.

One might assume that no one can "own" a single color—and this indisputably correct as a matter of *copyright* law. However, one *can* "own" a color for trademark purposes, subject to two significant limitations imposed by the US Supreme Court in *Qualitex Co. v. Jacobson Prods. Co.*, 514 U.S. 159 (1995).

At issue in the *Qualitex* case was a special shade of green-gold that Qualitex had long used on its dry cleaning pads. After a competitor, Jacobson, began selling pads of the same color, Qualitex sued it for trademark infringement. The question of whether color alone can function as a trademark eventually reached the Supreme Court, which ruled that it could—in certain circumstances.

The Court observed that "over time, customers may come to treat a particular color on a product or its packaging—e.g., a color that in context seems unusual, such as pink on a firm's insulating material or red on the head of a large industrial bolt—as signifying a brand. And, if so, that color would have come to identify and distinguish the goods—i.e., to indicate their source—much in the way that descriptive words on a product—e.g.,

'Trim' on nail clippers or 'Car-Freshener' on deodorizer—can come to indicate a product's origin." *Id.* at 163.

But as the Court explained, such consumer association was not merely observable as a descriptive matter; as a normative matter, this association was *required* for trademark protection. Such protection would arise only "where [a] color has attained 'secondary meaning' and therefore identifies and distinguishes a particular brand and thus indicates its 'source.'" *Id.*

The defendant in *Qualitex* had also argued that there should be an absolute bar against trademark protection for color alone because, *inter alia*, "colors are in limited supply," and "to permit one or a few producers to use colors as trademarks will 'deplete' the supply of usable colors to the point where a competitor's inability to find a suitable color will put that competitor at a significant disadvantage." *Id.* at 168. The Court acknowledged that this was a valid concern, but was of the opinion that "the trademark doctrine of 'functionality' normally would seem available to prevent the anticompetitive consequences that [the defendant's] argument posits, thereby minimizing that argument's practical force." *Id.* at 169.

As such, it would be inappropriate to confer trademark protection for a color "where doing so will put a competitor at a significant disadvantage because the feature is 'essential to the use or purpose of the article' or 'affects [its] cost or quality.'" *Id.*

In short, colors are eligible for trademark protection where they are non-functional and have accrued secondary meaning. Determining "functionality" in the realm of color, however, can be a very tricky proposition, as shown by the following case.

- The Colorful Case of *Louboutin v. Yves Saint Laurent*

    In 2011, luxury shoemaker Christian Louboutin S.A. sued Yves Saint Laurent over several styles of shoes that included bright-red soles, Louboutin's self-proclaimed "signature" and the subject of a federally registered trademark. *See Christian Louboutin S.A. v. Yves Saint Laurent America Inc.*, 11 Civ. 2381 (S.D.N.Y. Apr. 7, 2011) (Marrero, J.). Yves Saint Laurent (YSL) had sold bright-red monochrome shoes in several styles; in each instance, the red shade extended from the "uppers" to the "outsoles," and it was this application of Louboutin's signature color to the soles that drew the its ire.

In response to Louboutin's motion for a preliminary injunction seeking to halt sales of the offending shoes and the creation of any new shoe styles with bright-red soles, YSL made several arguments, including the argument that its actions were protected under the doctrine of aesthetic functionality. In fact, YSL did not stop at asserting that its conduct alone was immunized, but rather went on to argue that "*[i]n the fashion industry, color is inherently functional* because the essence of fashion is using a few basic elements—color, texture, and material — to give life to a design concept." *Id.*, YSL Opposition Brief at 17, *Christian Louboutin S.A. v. Yves Saint Laurent America Inc.* (S.D.N.Y. Apr. 7, 2011) (No. 11 Civ. 2381) (emphasis added).

On August 10, 2011, Judge Marrero denied Louboutin's requested injunction, in an unusually flowery opinion that included the following sweeping language:

> Because *in the fashion industry color serves ornamental and aesthetic functions vital to robust competition*, the Court finds that Louboutin is unlikely to be able to prove that its red outsole brand is entitled to trademark protection even if it has gained enough public recognition in the market to have acquired secondary meaning.

Decision and Order at 8, *Christian Louboutin S.A. v. Yves Saint Laurent America Inc.* (S.D.N.Y. Apr. 7, 2011) (No. 11 Civ. 2381) (emphasis added).

The court further required Louboutin to show cause why the proceeding should not be converted into one over summary judgment on the cancellation of Louboutin's trademark registration. When Louboutin (unsurprisingly) indicated that it would appeal Judge Marrero's ruling on the preliminary injunction, Marrero agreed to hold off on the cancellation proceedings until the Second Circuit had addressed the issue. If the Second Circuit adopts Marrero's reasoning, the *Louboutin* case could conceivably mean that *a single color on an item of apparel can never qualify for trademark protection.* The importance of such a ruling for fashion design and branding—not to mention the viability, or at least, profitability of Christian Louboutin's enterprise—is clear. Thus, this case ultimately find its way to the US Supreme Court, and could dramatically alter the contours of trademark protection for colors, either in fashion or more broadly.

Trade Dress Protection

The US Lanham Act employs expansive language in its definition of protectable marks, covering "any word, term, name, symbol, or device, or any combination thereof . . . which . . . is likely to cause confusion" as to source, sponsorship, or affiliation. 15 U.S.C. § 1125(a)(1)(A). In essence, this means that *almost anything* can function as a trademark.

A large portion of this "almost anything" falls under the umbrella of so-called "trade dress," which "refers to 'the image and overall appearance of a product' [and] embodies 'that arrangement of identifying characteristics or decorations connected with a product, whether by packaging or otherwise, [that] make[s] the source of the product distinguishable from another and ... promote[s] its sale.'" *See Abercrombie & Fitch Stores Inc. v. American Eagle Outfitters Inc.*, 280 F.3d 619, 629 (6th Cir. 2002).

In fact, "recently, 'trade dress' has taken on a more expansive meaning and includes the design and appearance of the product as well as that of the container and all elements making up the total visual image by which the product is presented to customers." *Id.* at 630 (quoting *Jeffrey Milstein Inc. v. Greger, Lawlor, Roth Inc.*, 58 F.3d 27, 31 (2d Cir. 1995)).

According to the Second Circuit, when a plaintiff or registrant claims his product and the protected trade dress are one in the same, courts (or the USPTO) "do not ask whether [the trade dress] is 'generic,' 'descriptive,' 'suggestive,' or 'arbitrary or fanciful'—categorizations which we find inapplicable to product features. Rather, [they] ask whether it is 'likely to serve primarily as a designator of origin of the product.'" *Knitwaves Inc. v. Lollytogs Ltd.*, 71 F.3d 996, 1008 (2d. Cir. 1995); *see Abercrombie & Fitch*, 280 F.3d at 638 (discussing "generic product configurations").

Trade dress has been held to include such varied items as:

- cover designs of books and magazines
- the layout and appearance of a mail-order catalog
- the use of a lighthouse as part of the design of a golf hole
- a combination of features of a folding table
- a fish-shaped cracker
- the "Marlboro Man" western cowboy motif
- the "G" shape of a Gucci watch

Id. at 630.

Some of these items might well be protected by copyright, too, but *for different reasons.* Recall that copyright law rewards creators for their original works of authorship; trademark, by contrast, is primarily focused on the integrity of a mark's *source-designating function*, even when that mark is an unconventional one, such as those listed immediately above. Thus, it is not uncommon for plaintiffs to prevail on their copyright claims, while losing on their trade dress claims. *See, e.g., Knitwaves Inc. v. Lollytogs Ltd.*, 71 F.3d 996, 1002 (2d Cir. 1995) (images appliquéd to sweaters are protected by copyright, but not as trade dress); *Keystone Retaining Wall Systems Inc. v. Westrock Inc.*, 997 F.2d 1444, 1447 n.2 (Fed. Cir. 1993) (noting that jury had found for plaintiff on copyright claim, but for defendant on trade dress claim). Because of trademark law's emphasis on source-designation rather than creativity, it is often difficult, or even impossible, to determine in the abstract whether something constitutes "trade dress"; that determination can only be made by examining the context in which the claimed trade dress is used by vendors, and perceived by consumers.

The US Supreme Court's opinion in *Wal-Mart Stores v. Samara Bros.*, 529 U.S. 205 (2000) drew an important distinction between two categories of trade dress: *product packaging*, which the Court held *can* be "inherently distinctive"; and *product design*, which the Court held *cannot* be inherently distinctive. The latter, the Court ruled, is protectable only upon acquisition of "secondary meaning" among relevant consumers. The Court acknowledged that in certain instances, it might be difficult to place certain trade dress in one category or the other; however, as Justice Scalia wrote for a unanimous Court: "the frequency and the difficulty of having to distinguish between product design and product packaging will be much less than the frequency and the difficulty of having to decide when a product design is inherently distinctive." *Id.* at 215.

Naturally, then, the outcome of trade dress cases will sometimes hinge on the categorization of the substance at issue as either product packaging or product design. Because it is almost always the case that the appearance of a particular fashion article will fall on the product design side, the post-*Samara Bros.* landscape is decidedly hostile to designers who have been "knocked off." If such designers have not obtained a design patent (which is quite rare), and if their work does not qualify for copyright protection, (which, as this chapter explains, will often be the case), they can prevail in court only upon a showing that a sufficient portion of the public associates the design with a single source. Unless the design at issue is among the few iconic designs in fashion, a plaintiff seeking redress against "knockoff" artists under the Lanham Act will typically lose. (Note, however, that if the designer's *house mark*—like "Chanel" or "Gucci"—is replicated along with the design itself, a plaintiff can base a trademark infringement claim on that—and perhaps a counterfeiting claim as well.)

Trade Dress: Product Packaging

Traditional forms of trade dress, such as the boxes in which shoes are sold, or the bags in which undergarments are sold, clearly fall on the "product packaging" side of the line. As such, this type of packaging can be registered with the USPTO without any proof of secondary meaning among consumers.

Further, the Supreme Court made clear in a case called *Two Pesos Inc. v. Taco Cabana Inc.*, 505 U.S. 763 (1992), that the appearance of a commercial establishment is a form of product packaging that may be inherently distinctive. Again, this means store interiors may be registered with the

USPTO before secondary meaning is acquired—indeed, before the first store with the allegedly protected appearance is even built. As such, many retail chains attempt to register their stores' look and feel with the USPTO as early as possible.

Other marketing materials, however, have presented a closer case, as explained in the next section.

Trade Dress: Product Design

- Requirements

  As mentioned above, the Supreme Court has ruled that product *design*—e.g., color—can never be inherently distinctive. *Samara Bros.*, 529 U.S. at 212. The Court reasoned: "Consumers are aware of the reality that, almost invariably, even the most unusual of product designs—such as a cocktail shaker shaped like a penguin—is intended not to identify the source, but to render the product itself more useful or more appealing." *Id.*

  By granting a monopoly on a certain product design through trademark law, consumers are "deprived of the benefits of competition with regard to the utilitarian and aesthetic purposes that product design ordinarily serves[.]" *Id.* Thus, "in an action for [trade dress] infringement . . . , a product's design is distinctive, and therefore protectable, only upon a showing of secondary meaning." *Id.* at 216.

  Naturally, following *Samara Bros.*, plaintiffs want to get their trade dress into the "packaging" category, while defendants routinely argue that product *design* is at issue. In one high-profile fashion case, the Sixth Circuit ruled, perhaps unexpectedly, that certain marketing materials fell on the design side.

- Sample Case: *Abercrombie v. American Eagle*

  In the high-profile dispute *Abercrombie & Fitch v. American Eagle Outfitters*, 280 F.3d 619 (6th Cir. 2002), Abercrombie & Fitch

(A&F) alleged that American Eagle's clothing, in-store advertising displays, and catalogs infringed A&F's unregistered, but nevertheless protected, trade dress. The district court granted summary judgment in favor of American Eagle finding that the elements in which A&F claimed protection "did not constitute trade dress at all." *Id.* at 624. The Sixth Circuit affirmed the grant of summary judgment, but for different reasons. *Id.*

As an initial matter, the Sixth Circuit deemed it inappropriate to aggregate the items at issue and treat the resulting look and feel as product packaging; rather, it declared, a court must examine "the specific elements which comprise [the allegedly distinctive] trade dress." *Id.* at 634 (quoting *Landscape Forms Inc. v. Columbia Cascade Co.*, 113 F.3d 373, 381 (2d Cir. 1997)).

The appellate court thus parsed the elements of the claimed trade dress—in-store advertising, catalogs, and the clothing itself—and found that each qualified as product design rather than product packaging. However, the Court disagreed with the "severe" view of the district court that each element was "generic"; as such, "Abercrombie [could] meet the distinctiveness requirement by showing attachment of secondary meaning to its designs." *Id.* at 639-40 (citing *Samara Bros.*, 529 U.S. at 211). The Court found that "A&F successfully cleared the distinctiveness hurdle" through the following evidence of secondary meaning:

> American Eagle's limited admission of intentional copying constitutes evidence that Abercrombie's dress has acquired strong secondary meaning. A&F introduced other evidence confirming the existence of secondary meaning in its trade dress, including an affidavit from A&F's CFO accompanied by exhibits in the form of e-mails purportedly from consumers remarking on the similarity of designs and advertising methods, and inquiring about the relationship between A&F and American Eagle. A&F considers this as evidence

> of actual confusion by consumers and as further support for its claim of secondary meaning.

Id. at 639.

Nevertheless, A&F's claim failed because "the paucity of comparable alternative features that competitors could use to compete in the market for casual clothing would leave competitors at a significant non-reputational competitive disadvantage and would, therefore, prevent effective competition in the market." *Id.* at 643. Nor could any reasonable jury find that there was a likelihood of confusion between the two companies' trade dress. *Id.* at 646-48.

- Can Fashion Design, Alone, Serve as Protectable Trade Dress?

The short answer to this question is yes, but rarely. That does not mean that trademark cases premised on product design knockoffs are not regularly brought—they are—but such cases are very difficult to win, due to the *Samara Bros.*-imposed secondary meaning requirement. Further, as demonstrated by *Louboutin v. Yves Saint Laurent*, even if one can produce compelling evidence of the requisite secondary meaning, the doctrine of aesthetic functionality may serve as a bar to trade dress protection for articles of apparel.

With that said, there have been cases where fashion design, standing alone, has been protected as trade dress. For example, in *Dallas Cowboys Cheerleaders Inc. v. Pussycat Cinema Ltd.*, 604 F.2d 200, 203 (2d Cir. 1979), the Dallas Cowboy Cheerleaders obtained an order from the district court preliminarily enjoining the release of a pornographic movie called *Debbie Does Dallas*, which featured "approximately 12 minutes of film footage [with actors engaged] in various sex acts while clad or partially clad in [a] uniform" that was "strikingly similar to that worn by the Dallas Cowboys Cheerleaders." On appeal, the Second Circuit adopted the district court's finding that "the uniform worn in the movie and shown on the marquee closely resembled the plaintiff's uniform and that the public was likely to identify it as the plaintiff's uniform," and further agreed that "[t]he district court did not err in holding that plaintiff had established a likelihood of confusion within the meaning of the Lanham Act sufficient to entitle it to a preliminary injunction[.]" *Id.* at 205.

The vintage and idiosyncratic fact pattern of *Pussycat Cinema* means it cannot be relied upon with any certainty. Other cases in which clothing design alone has made significant head as protectable trade dress are few and far between, but one notable trade dress lawsuit captured the public's attention in 2008 and 2009: *Trovata Inc. v. Forever 21*, 07 Civ. 1196 (C.D. Cal. Oct. 8, 2007) (Selna, J.).

In *Trovata*, fast-fashion retailer Forever 21—which has reportedly been sued more than fifty times for various forms of intellectual property infringement—came out with virtually identical versions of Trovata garments. Unlike several plaintiffs that had taken action against Forever 21 in the past, Trovata grounded its case in alleged trade dress protection, rather than copyright. David Lipke, *Trovata, Forever 21 Case Set for Trial*, WOMEN'S WEAR DAILY (Apr. 13, 2009), *available at* http://www.wwd.com/retail-news/specialty-stores/trovata-forever-21-copying-case-set-for-trial-2101514.

Although Trovata lost a handful of motions along the way, it eventually made it to trial on the trade dress claim, only to have the judge declare a mistrial. (A second trial never took place.) *See* Rachel Brown, *Trovata, Forever 21 Return to Square One*, WOMEN'S WEAR DAILY (May 29, 2009), *available at* http://www.wwd.com/fashion-blogs/trovata_forever_21_return_to_s-09-05. A jury of eight had been prepared to side with Trovata, but for a single juror, Stephen Sharp, who told *Women's Wear Daily* that he had blocked the win because "design elements in Trovata garments were not widely known and, therefore, any similar merchandise in Forever 21 stores did not confuse the public about the brand." *Id.*[19]

[19] While Mr. Sharp's reasoning was partly on point, it bears repeating that the operative question trademark/trade dress infringement cases is not whether the public *was* confused—though "actual confusion" is indeed one of the *Polaroid* factors—but rather whether a *likelihood* of confusion exists by reason of defendant's conduct, products, or services.

Mr. Sharp's statement about the lack of public recognition of Trovata's designs illustrates one major reason for the zealous advocacy behind legislation that would accord copyright-like protection to unique fashion designs. *See Innovative Design Protection and Piracy Prevention Act* discussed *supra.* For most small-scale designers, the "secondary meaning" hurdle, compounded with evidentiary burdens imposed by the fact-intensive "likelihood of confusion" test, effectively make trademark law useless as a tool to prevent the unauthorized duplication of one's designs (as opposed to one's brand name, where trademark law tends to be quite effective.) In addition to these daunting obstacles, the expansion of the "aesthetic functionality" bar possibly portended by *Louboutin v. Yves Saint Laurent* may further foreclose trademark-related remedies for design knockoffs.

Once one adds the cost of litigation to the difficulties just discussed, trade dress suits based on unauthorized reproduction of fashion designs can start to seem like a very poor investment. If one can find a copyright "hook," invoking one of the exceptions to the "useful article" bar discussed above, that will often be a preferable way to launch a legal assault on a knockoff artist.

Still, despite significant financial and doctrinal challenges, plaintiffs continue to bring trade dress lawsuits, especially in the realm of footwear, where a particular design is likely to stay relevant for more seasons than a typical article of apparel. *See* Michelle Tay, *Copycat Lawsuits on the Rise*, FOOTWEAR NEWS, (July 25, 2011), *available at* http://www.wwd.com/footwear-news/business/ copycat-lawsuits-on-the-rise-3732660. In some of these cases, the plaintiff may genuinely believe that he has a decent chance of winning on the merits (on occasion, he may be right); sometimes, a trade dress plaintiff may be gambling that a weak case will settle before the court reaches any dispositive questions of law or fact. For some, the case may simply be a matter of principle.

Limitations on Trademark Registration, Protection, and Enforceability

As in copyright law, there are several restrictions on trademark protection; further, even when a trademark is valid and protectable, its owner cannot always *enforce* that trademark against a particular defendant.

Bars to Registration and Enforcement

Bars to registration and enforcement of trademarks come in two flavors: partial and absolute. In general, a partial bar can be surmounted with evidence of secondary meaning, while an absolute bar—as the name suggests—simply renders a purported trademark invalid. Absolute bars may *always* be raised as a defense in an infringement action, while only some partial bars may be so raised, depending on the circumstances. Many of these bars may also be used as an offensive tool to cancel a trademark registration, or obtain a declaratory judgment that a purported trademark is unenforceable.

Perhaps most important partial bar to trademark registration and enforceability is *mere descriptiveness*, addressed above. Another partial bar, the *primarily a surname* bar, was briefly discussed. Two absolute bars have also been discussed: *genericism* and *functionality*.

Additional bars to registration and potentially enforcement include the following:

- a trademark consists of immoral or scandalous matter
- a trademark disparages people, institutions, national symbols
- a trademark consists of the flag or coat of arms of the US, any American state or municipality, or of any foreign nation
- a trademark consists of a name, portrait, or signature of a living individual, except by his or her written consent
- a trademark consists of the name, signature, or portrait of a deceased President of the United States during the lifetime of his widow, except by the widow's consent
- a trademark is likely to be confused with an existing mark, *with the caveat* that if conditions and limitations will eliminate the likelihood of confusion, concurrent registrations may be issued
- a trademark is deceptively misdescriptive of the goods or services with which it will be affiliated
- a trademark is primarily geographically descriptive of the goods or services with which it will be affiliated
- A trademark is primarily geographically misdescriptive of the goods or services with which it will be affiliated

15 U.S.C. § 1052. Additional bars to enforcement include, but are by no means limited to, statutory and nominative "fair use" (which differ from the similarly named doctrine in copyright law), parody (which is typically treated as one component of the "likelihood of confusion" inquiry rather than a separate defense), acquiescence and laches. Some of these bars are partial, and some are absolute; further, in some instances, a bar that began as partial may become absolute. Unfortunately, a discussion of each bar is not possible in the context of an introduction to intellectual property; however, these doctrines are not specific to fashion, and other reference guides address each rule in detail.

Territoriality

- Legal Landscape

  One common misconception about trademark rights is that one automatically accrues rights abroad, when, in fact, intellectual property rights—trademarks, copyrights, and patents alike—are *territorial* in nature. Territorial rights apply, as the name suggests, only within the borders of the territory (most often, the country) where they arise or are obtained. Thus, foreign trademark owners sometimes find, to their dismay, that when they attempt to expand into the United States, they are prevented from doing so by a preexisting US rights-holder. Conversely, American trademark owners sometimes run into obstacles when they seek to expand their rights abroad.

  As one would expect, most of the relevant case law available to US lawyers involves foreign corporations attempting to enter the US market and running into "senior users" of the mark here. Cases involving US companies entering foreign markets would likely be adjudicated in the courts of those countries, which would typically apply their own body of trademark law. Difficulties in this area can sometimes be mitigated or avoided altogether through prudent and proper use of the international registration systems discussed below (or even obtaining "local registrations" in countries where one plans to expand.)

Although case law on the international expansion of US countries is difficult to obtain and summarize, for the reasons just mentioned, decisions involving the reverse scenario—foreign companies entering the US market for the first time—are available and illuminating. One recent, illustrative case from the fashion world is *Aktieselskabet AF 21. November 2001 v. Fame Jeans*, 525 F.3d 8 (D.C. Cir. 2008).

In *Fame Jeans*, Danish corporation Bestseller had been selling Jack & Jones jeans since 1990, but did not expand into North American until 2003. When it attempted to do so, it ran into a major obstacle in the form of Fame Jeans' prior registration of the Jack & Jones mark. The dispute worked its way up through the USPTO to the Court of Appeals for the District of Columbia, where the presiding panel required Bestseller to show that it had used the Jack & Jones mark before the date of Fame's application. Bestseller tried to show use in the form of sales, but the court rejected its theory on the following basis:

> Bestseller's allegations fall short of showing a sale, whether in the United States or to an American abroad, as the beginning of a continuous commercial exploitation of the Jack & Jones mark in the United States; but they do give fair notice of a claim to analogous use. While Bestseller clearly sells millions of dollars worth of Jack & Jones branded clothing elsewhere in the world, it fails to allege any sales in the United States or to Americans. The closest Bestseller comes is saying this clothing 'has been available to US consumers through Bestseller's foreign customers and stores as well as through re-sales on eBay.com.' This allegation does not imply any American sales at all, much less continuous commercial sales.

Id. at 20 (internal citations omitted.) On the other hand, the court found that Bestseller had alleged just enough research and marketing activity in the US to give rise to a potential claim of "use in commerce" pre-dating Fame's trademark application. Separately, the court found that Bestseller had eked out a potential claim that Fame's trademark application was made without "a *bona fide* intent to use the mark," which, if successfully proven on remand, would render its registration invalid.

By contrast, the Fourth Circuit Court of Appeals has deemed mere marketing activity insufficient to confer trademark rights on a foreign company. In *International Bancorp v. Société des Bains de Mer et due Cercle des Étrangers à Monaco*, 329 F.3d 359 (4th Cir. 2003), the court ruled that "a mark's protection may not be based on 'mere advertising.'" Yet all was not lost for the Monte Carlo Casino. The majority opinion continued:

> Because SBM [the foreign company] presented no record evidence that [it] did anything other than advertise the 'Casino de Monte Carlo' mark [in the United States], if its case rested on this alone, the plaintiff companies would have the better of the argument. . . . [However,] the record contain[s] evidence that US citizens went to and gambled at the casino. This . . . makes unavoidable the legal conclusion that foreign trade was present here, and that as such, so also was 'commerce' under the Lanham Act.

Id. at 363. It is important to note that foreign companies should be cautious in relying on *International Bancorp*, as other circuits have rejected its reasoning.

The territoriality issue has been further complicated by the so-called "famous marks" doctrine, which, in essence, holds that if a foreign mark is famous enough, that fame can serve as a sort of substitute for actual use in the United States. However, the "famous marks" doctrine has been recognized *as a matter of federal law* only in the Ninth Circuit. The Second Circuit conclusively rejected the "famous marks" doctrine as a matter of federal law fairly recently, in *ITC Ltd. v. Punchgini Inc.*, 482 F.3d 135 (2d Cir.

2007). However, the Second Circuit did "certify" two questions about the continued validity of the "famous marks" doctrine under New York law to the New York Court of Appeals, whose answer was rather vague. *See ITC Ltd. v. Punchgini Inc.*, 9 N.Y.3d 467 (2007). The party that lost before the Second Circuit appealed, but the Supreme Court declined to resolve the split that had resulted from the Second and Ninth Circuits' diverging views. *See* 128 S.Ct. 288 (Oct. 1, 2007).

In short, the federal appellate courts have not conclusively resolved the question of what "use" is required of a foreign corporation in order to establish trademark priority over a US company who would otherwise be a "senior user" of a contested mark.

- Brand Protection Abroad

Because of territorial limitations on trademark protection, it is essential that a company be proactive in ensuring that its brands are protected abroad. There are multiple mechanisms for obtaining such protection.

  - Local Registration

    It is possible that some foreign countries will recognize trademark rights under their own laws based solely on an American entity's commercial interactions with their citizens. However, like common-law trademark rights in the United States, those rights will be inherently uncertain, and will presumably be subordinate to the rights of those who hold trademark registrations in the countries at issue.

    Thus, one mechanism of ensuring protection of one's trademark—and by extension, one's brand and corporate existence—is to file *local registrations* in each of the countries in a company's target market. This process, while time-consuming and expensive, will in many instances provide the maximum protection available to US trademark owners who wish to expand their businesses abroad. The reason this method can be so difficult and cost-prohibitive is that few US attorneys will be able to obtain local registrations for a company in every foreign country of interest; virtually any American firm retained for this type of work will need to coordinate with "local counsel" in each country, which increases the logistical difficulties and cost of obtaining trademark protection abroad.

- The Madrid System (WIPO)

  The Madrid Agreement Concerning the International Registration of Marks (also known as the Madrid System or the Madrid Protocol) is administered by the World Intellectual Property Organization (WIPO), a specialized agency of the United Nations. 85 of WIPO's 184 member states participate in the Madrid System, including many countries of major economic importance. *See Madrid Agreement Concerning the International Registration of Marks* at 16-18 (Status on July 15, 2011), *available at* http://www.wipo.int/export/sites/www/treaties/en/documents/pdf/madrid_marks.pdf.

  Under the Madrid System, a trademark owner may extend either a registration *or* application from one member jurisdiction to any or all remaining member countries. *See generally* Madrid System for the International Registration of Marks, http://www.wipo.int/madrid/en/ (last visited Aug. 8, 2011). The cost to pursue such expansion varies depending on the number and identity of the countries one wishes to expand into. However, WIPO provides a useful tool, the International Application Similar, which enables interested parties to estimate the cost of expanding into target countries. International Application Similar, http://www.wipo.int/madrid/en/madrid_simulator/.

  While it will typically be less expensive to utilize the Madrid Protocol system than to obtain local registrations in a number of different countries, this approach suffers from the drawback that a successful "central attack" on the application or registration in its home country will invalidate protection in all other Madrid Protocol countries.

- The Community Trade Mark (OHIM)

  A *Community Trade Mark* (CTM) is a useful and relatively inexpensive tool to obtain trademark protection throughout the European Union (EU). Administered by the Office for Harmonization in the Internal Market, based in Alicante, Spain, the CTM system allows one to obtain trademark protection throughout the EU—including any countries that may later be added to the EU—via one registration process. OHIM, *What is a Community trade mark (CTM)?*, http://oami.europa.eu/ows/rw/pages/CTM/communityTradeMark/communityTradeMark.en.do (last visited Aug. 8, 2011). Applications may be filed either directly with OHIM in Alicante, or via any national intellectual property office of a member state. OHIM, *Getting a Community trade mark*, http://oami.europa.eu/ows/rw/pages/CTM/protection/theCTM.en.do (last visited Aug. 8, 2011). With application fees starting at 900 Euros, the CTM process is an extremely cost-effective way to obtain protection for one's mark in dozens of countries. OHIM, *Fees and payments*, http://oami.europa.eu/ows/rw/pages/CTM/feesPayment/feesPayment.en.do (last visited Aug. 8, 2011). Further, a Community Trade Mark can be used as the anchor registration for a Madrid Protocol application. OHIM, *Extending a CTM outside the EU*, http://oami.europa.eu/ows/rw/pages/CTM/communityTradeMark/extending.en.do (last visited Aug. 8, 2011).

  The primary drawback of this system is that it covers only the European Union, and not Asian countries (which, as of this writing, are of particular concern for fashion brand owners.) But make no mistake: trademark infringement is alive and well in the EU, especially in Eastern Europe. As a result, a CTM can be very valuable.

The Importance of Controlling One's Trademark

A central tenet of trademark law is that one must maintain control over the use of her mark; if she fails to do so, the mark no longer serves as a reliable indicator of source or quality. Thus, the courts have recognized a number of doctrines (including "assignments in gross," "naked licensing," "non-use/abandonment," and unauthorized third-party use) that seek to ensure the policy objectives of trademark law are achieved. These rules are especially important to keep in mind in the fashion industry of the twenty-first century, where brand-holders often manufacture nothing at all in their own facilities, where even trademark owners that handle some manufacturing themselves outsource the production of specialized categories of goods with which they have little expertise, and where a brand's entire business in another country may be operated by a local licensee. In light of these realities, it is crucial that brand owners keep the following principles in mind at all times.

Trademark protection is valid, and thus enforceable, only to the extent that a mark does, in fact, serve as an indicator of source or quality. Thus, one when acquires a mark, one must use that mark in connection with similar goods of similar quality in order to keep the priority date of the previous owner. This is known as the "assignment in gross" rule, whose rationale is that "[u]se of the mark by the assignee in connection with a different goodwill and different product would result in a fraud on the purchasing public who reasonably assume that the mark signifies the same thing, whether used by one person or another." *Marshak v. Green*, 746 F.2d 927, 929 (2d Cir. 1984). If one purchases a mark and promptly begins using it in connection with completely new goods or services, his priority date will be that of the *new* use, rather than (as he likely wants) the date of the assignor's first use in commerce.

Of even greater importance to the current, licensing-mad fashion industry is the doctrine of "naked licensing," which (with certain narrow exceptions) imposes drastic consequences on a trademark owner who fails to monitor and control the quality of his licensee's goods or services. As the Seventh Circuit explained in *Gorenstein Enterprises Inc. v. Quality Care-USA Inc.*, 874 F.2d 431, 435 (7th Cir. 1989): "The owner of a trademark has a duty to ensure the consistency of the trademarked good or service. If he does not fulfill this duty, he forfeits the trademark." In other words, a trademark owner's failure to exercise quality control over the products sold by the licensee under his brand name can have dire consequences for his own intellectual property. The *Gorenstein* court explained the rationale for the seemingly draconian "naked licensing" rule: "The purpose of a trademark . . . is to identify a good or service to the consumer, and identity implies consistency and a correlative duty to make sure that the good or service really is of consistent quality, i.e., really is the same good or service." *Id.* Thus, it is imperative to hire qualified trademark counsel to draft licensing agreements with adequate quality control provisions, and to exercise the rights reserved under those provisions in the manner specified by counsel.

Yet, from the perspective of trademark owners, there is a positive flipside to naked licensing: "years of precedent make it very clear that proper use of a mark by a trademark owner's licensee or related company constitutes 'use' of that mark attributable to the trademark owner." *Quality Candy Shoppes/Buddy Squirrel of Wisconsin Inc. v. Grande Foods*, 90 U.S.P.Q.2d 1393 (T.T.A.B. 2007). In other words, one may base a claim of priority in a mark in connection with goods produced only by a licensee, provided the licensee's activities were properly monitored and controlled at all times.

The doctrines of non-use, abandonment, and unauthorized third-party use are ideologically related. First, these largely self-explanatory doctrines seek to ensure that the pool of available marks is not depleted by nominal "owners" of marks who wish to simply stockpile brand names, either for some abstract future use or simply for the purpose of extracting money from supposed "infringers." Second, these doctrines (like the rules on assignment in gross and naked licensing) attempt to facilitate reliance on source-designation by punishing trademark owners for failing to use (non-use, abandonment) or police (unauthorized third-party use) their marks. Recall the reasoning behind the Ninth Circuit's ruling for the defendant in the Princess Diana memorabilia case, *Cairns v. Franklin Mint*, 292 F.3d 1139, 1149-50 (9th Cir. 2002): "Between 1981 and 1997, many products, including some that were largely indistinguishable from Franklin Mint products, bore the name and likeness of Princess Diana, who neither endorsed nor objected to any of these products. Consumers, therefore, had no reason to believe Franklin Mint's Diana-related products were endorsed by the Princess." As this passage illustrates, the greater the number of simultaneous users of a mark, the less likely consumers are to associate the mark with one particular source. At some point, a mark may become so widespread as to lose its source-designating power altogether. Among other responsibilities, it is corporate trademark counsel's job to ensure that this does not happen, which accounts for the (sometimes overzealous) cease-and-desist letters emanating from the legal departments of major fashion brands. To be sure, it is important to police *improper*, unauthorized uses of one's mark; however, it should go without saying that one must do so without making frivolous legal claims.

Special Considerations in Trademark Law

Secondary Liability for Trademark Infringement

As in the copyright context, courts have recognized different types of "secondary liability" for those who knowingly facilitate or benefit from trademark infringement. Unfortunately, there is less guidance on the standards of liability for secondary trademark infringement, as "limited case law leaves the law of contributory trademark infringement ill-defined." *Tiffany (NJ) Inc. v. eBay Inc.*, 600 F. 3d 93, 105 (2d Cir. 2010.) Making matters worse, the Digital Millennium Copyright Act, as its name suggests, does not apply to trademark infringement, so the contours of any "safe harbors" from secondary liability for trademark infringement cannot be found in a convenient, centralized statute.

Instead, intermediaries like search engines, auction sites, and Internet Service Providers must stay abreast of case law developments to know what precautions (and affirmative remedial actions) they must take to avoid potential liable. Brands must likewise stay current on the relevant case law in order to understand avoid making frivolous threats against third parties that they would like to hold secondarily liable for trademark infringement.

The conflict between the interests of brand owners and those of Internet intermediaries is not only playing out in the courts, but in the legislative arena as well. The "PROTECT IP" Act (short for "Preventing Real Online Threats to Economic Creativity and Theft of Intellectual Property"), pending in Congress as of this writing, aims to combat trademark infringement and other intellectual property infringement by having

Internet Service Providers filter out user requests for websites found to be engaged in illegal conduct. As one might expect, fashion brands are largely in favor of the legislation, while companies like Google remain staunchly opposed, vowing to fight the law even in the event it passes. It remains to be seen how legislatures and courts will allocate the burden of policing trademark infringement, but it will undoubtedly take years to arrive at an acceptable compromise.

A Word About Trademark Dilution

Most of the previous discussion has focused on trademark *infringement*, which requires that a plaintiff show a likelihood of confusion as to source, sponsorship, affiliation, etc. Trademark *dilution*, first developed by the courts but now codified in the Lanham Act and various state statutes, requires no such showing. Only "famous" marks, as determined using the factors listed in 15 U.S.C. § 1125(c)(2)(A), receive protection from dilution under federal law (state law does not always impose a "fame" requirement.) Once this threshold requirement is met, the critical inquiry is *not* "likelihood of confusion," but rather whether a third party's use of a substantially similar mark is likely to weaken the public's association between the famous mark and its source. This determination is, rather unhelpfully, to be guided by "all relevant factors," including the six factors listed in 15 U.S.C. § 1125(c)(2)(A):

i. The degree of similarity between the mark or trade name and the famous mark.
ii. The degree of inherent or acquired distinctiveness of the famous mark.
iii. The extent to which the owner of the famous mark is engaging in substantially exclusive use of the mark.
iv. The degree of recognition of the famous mark.
v. Whether the user of the mark or trade name intended to create an association with the famous mark.
vi. Any actual association between the mark or trade name and the famous mark.

As these factors illustrates, the dilution inquiry has much in common with concepts previously encountered in this chapter, and does overlap to some degree with the *Polaroid* test. At the risk of oversimplifying, the primary purpose of the dilution cause of action is to eliminate "likelihood of confusion" as a prerequisite for liability under the Lanham Act, so that one may not produce with immunity "Gucci" tires, "Prada" dishwashing liquid, or other goods so far removed from the core business of a famous brand that the public would likely understand that the "real" company is uninvolved.

A Word About Trademark Counterfeiting

Trademark *counterfeiting* is, in essence, the most serious form of trademark infringement. While all trademark counterfeiting will qualify as infringement, not all infringement will constitute counterfeiting.

To prevail on a counterfeiting claim, a plaintiff must prove to the court that the defendant used "a spurious mark which is identical with, or substantially indistinguishable from [plaintiff's] registered mark." *See* 15 U.S.C. § 1127. Note that this is a far more precise standard than the rather amorphous *Polaroid* "likelihood of confusion" test. Indeed, where a plaintiff can making the requisite "spurious mark" showing, the *Polaroid* factors need not be considered at all. Instead, "[t]o determine whether confusion is likely to arise, a court need only determine that the items at issue are counterfeit and that Defendant distributed, offered for sale, and sold the items." *Gucci Am. Inc. v. Duty Free Apparel Ltd.*, 286 F. Supp. 2d 284, 287 (S.D.N.Y. 2003).

From a fashion company's perspective, a cause of action for trademark counterfeiting, as opposed to mere infringement, has several benefits: 1) depending on the circumstances, the applicable legal standard may be easier to meet, 2) heightened damages, 3) *ex parte* seizure of counterfeit goods, and 4) the existence of potentially severe criminal penalties.

Indeed, growing awareness of the problem of counterfeiting was one factor in the 2006 passage of the "Stop Counterfeiting in Manufactured Goods Act," which amended 18 U.S.C. § 2320 to criminally prohibit not only trafficking in counterfeit *goods*, but also in in labels and packaging to which counterfeit marks are knowingly applied. Under the SCMGA, a plaintiff is entitled to the forfeiture and destruction of counterfeit goods, and to the seizure of assets derived from counterfeiting.

In short, where one can make the necessary evidentiary showings, anti-counterfeiting laws can be a very powerful tool against knockoffs of the most egregious variety.

A Word About Cybersquatting

All of the standard tools of trademark law are available to the brand owner whose mark has been infringed or diluted via a third party's domain name. But there is also a specialized statute to deal with this situation: the federal Anti-Cyber-Squatting Consumer Protection Act, 15 U.S.C. § 1125(d). Only those with a "bad faith intent to profit from [a] mark" are considered cyber squatters under the federal statute (state statutes may differ); Section 1125(d) prescribes no fewer than *nine* factors that federal courts should consider when deciding whether a defendant acted with the requisite bad faith. In general, however, when a defendant registered the contested domain first and has some legitimate or at least conceivable use for it; the domain name is not closely related or identical to a *famous* company, brand, or individual; and the first registrant never tried to extort the party who now wants the domain name; an ACPA claim will likely prove to be an uphill battle. It may often be less expensive to simply "pay off" the cybersquatter than to embark on the long, uncertain path of litigation.

Other Types of Intellectual Property

The remaining types of intellectual property are creatures of state law; as such, they vary from one locale to another, and some causes of action may not exist at all in a given state. With that said, this section provides a brief introduction to some of the state-law, IP-like causes of action that arise most frequently.

The Right of Publicity

Something of a cousin to trademark law, the so-called "right of publicity"—sometimes called the "right of privacy"—is a state-law cause of action that, broadly stated, protects against the unauthorized commercial use of one's likeness, name, or identity. As explained above, trademark law is often useful for this purpose as well. But the right of publicity complements trademark protection nicely, in part because it requires no showing of likelihood of confusion. Thus, although few would be confused about whether "Princess Diana plungers" were, in fact, endorsed by the late Princess's estate, the right of publicity would prevent such usage of her name.

The right of publicity is either a creature of state common law or state statute, like New York's Civil Rights Law § 50. New York's law is fairly representative in its general prohibition of the use, "for advertising purposes, or for the purposes of trade [of] the name, portrait, or picture of any living person without having first obtained the written consent of such person[.]" New York law is atypical, however, in its failure to recognize a *post-mortem* right of publicity. Given space constraints, little can be said about the right of publicity here beyond the fact that states vary in the scope of prohibited uses, in the individuals eligible to exercise the right, and in the defenses to otherwise actionable uses.

Note that, as with trademark law, the First Amendment provides a sort of ceiling on the right of publicity; whether or not expressly listed among statutory defenses, critical and/or newsworthy uses of people's names and images will generally be immune from right of publicity claims.

Unfair Competition

"Unfair competition" law is a broad and somewhat amorphous cause of action developed at common law, which has long served as a catchall for conduct that is intuitively wrongful, but might not meet the requirements for liability under one statute or another. Unfair competition comes in at least two varieties: "misappropriation" and "misrepresentation." *Madison Square Garden Corp. v. Universal Pictures Co.*, 7 N.Y.S.2d 845, 853 (1st Dep't 1938). In *ITC Ltd. v. Punchgini Inc.*, 9 N.Y.3d 467, 478 (2007), the New York Court of Appeals observed that the cause of action for unfair competition has "flourished in a variety of factual settings" and that the general "trend of the law . . . has been to extend the scope of the doctrine of unfair competition, whose basic principle is that commercial unfairness should be restrained whenever it appears that there has been a misappropriation, for the advantage of one person, of a property right belonging to another."

Based on the spirit of unfair competition, one might think it prove useful in the context of fashion design knockoffs—and indeed, plaintiffs have repeatedly advanced this theory, with occasional success. More often, however, the federal courts have rejected unfair competition claims based on federal preemption. (A survey of the state courts' application of the preemption doctrine to unfair competition claims is beyond the scope of this chapter.)

Theft of Idea

One exception to the general principle embodied in copyright law's "idea/expression dichotomy," discussed above, is the so-called "theft of idea" claim, recognized in some states but not others. Where recognized, this claim is usually characterized as one for breach of implied contract—namely, "I'll share my idea with you, with the mutual understanding that if you use it, I will be compensated." Theft of idea claims come up in the television and movie industries more often than in fashion, so it may come as no surprise that the body of law on this cause of action is most well-established in California, where "theft of idea" is known as a "*Desny* claim."

With that said, one could theoretically bring a theft of idea claim based on a pitch—even, potentially, an unsolicited one—for a fashion line, a design for a particular garment, a fashion house's advertising campaign, or any number of other fashion-related endeavors. One way to avoid such claims is to institute a strict "no pitch" policy; alternatively, one could have all those who come to pitch ideas to a fashion house sign a waiver of rights. (Most large entertainment companies opt for one of these two policies.) In the event a fashion company is sued for theft of idea, it will sometimes be able to dispose of the claim on federal preemption grounds. Once again, the state courts' rulings on preemption are beyond the scope of this chapter; however, on the federal front, there is currently a split between the Ninth Circuit, which has recently reaffirmed that "theft of idea" claims are not preempted where properly framed as breach of contract actions, and the Second Circuit, where such claims have—at least by the district court—consistently been deemed preempted by the US Copyright Act. *See* Robert W. Clarida & Robert J. Bernstein, *New York and California Courts Split on Preemption of Idea Claims*, NEW YORK LAW JOURNAL (Jul. 15, 2011), *available at* http://www.law.com/jsp/nylj/PubArticleNY.jsp?hubtype=practiceDetail &id=1202501070033&slreturn=1&hbxlogin=1.

Conclusion

While one could never provide exhaustive coverage of the many categories of intellectual property protection in a single chapter—indeed, multi-volume treatises have been dedicated to each type of protection described above—this introduction has outlined the major uses, advantages, and limitations of the most common forms of IP. Regardless of one's role in the fashion world, it is crucial to have an understanding of these legal tools, both to protect one's brand and creative output, and in order not infringe on the rights of others.

Key Takeaways

- While copyright protection is typically granted to the creator of original works authorship fixed in a tangible form, it is often unavailable to the designers and manufacturers of apparel and accessories, who find themselves stymied by the statutory "useful article" bar to protection. It is imperative that a fashion lawyer understand both this general obstacle *and* the exceptions to the general rule. Further, lawyers should stay current on legislative developments in this area: the "bill to watch" at the time of this writing is the Innovative Design Protection and Piracy Prevention Act.
- Ensure that your design clients are aware of the existence of so-called "copyright trolls," *i.e.*, entities that purchase copyrights solely for the purpose of suing (or at least squeezing settlement dollars) out of unknowing infringers. Your design clients should be cautious when purchasing their fabric, buying only from reliable sources and ensuring that they are protected by operative law, contracts, and/or insurance.
- When a client asks "how to keep people from stealing her idea," copyright law typically cannot provide a helpful answer, as it protects only the particular expression of an idea and not the idea itself. However, determining where an idea ends and expression begins can be difficult to pinpoint, such that idea/expression disputes have reached divergent outcomes in the courts.
- Utility and design patents are powerful tools to ward off and/or seek recourse against infringers. Because these types of protection

are available for useful articles, they may be available in areas of fashion where copyright protection is not. However, the expense and time required to procure patent protection may make it unrealistic for designs that have a short "shelf life." Segments of the fashion industry that use similar techniques and designs year after year, like the accessory, footwear, and undergarment markets, tend to find patent protection to be a more viable avenue to protect their intellectual property. In appropriate circumstances, trade secret protection might be available under state law where patent protection is impractical or undesirable because of its public disclosure requirements.

- Trademarks are central to "fashion law," in light of the frequent unavailability of copyright protection for apparel and the difficulty of procuring patent registrations. At its core, trademark law is about protecting the integrity of source designation and affiliation.
- This integrity of source designation is preserved through the judicially created "likelihood of confusion test," often referred to as the *Polaroid* factors. However, because the test has so many prongs, it can be expensive to produce evidence in support of each factor (whether one is on the plaintiff's or defendant's side.) Consumer surveys alone are often cost-prohibitive for small designers. Further, when one is, in essence, attempting to vindicate the theft of a design (as opposed to a pure misrepresentation of source), designers of all but the most famous products may find it difficult to marshal the *Polaroid* factors in favor of the claimed "trade dress" protection. Where possible, it is advantageous to characterize trade dress as "product packaging" rather than "product design," as the Supreme Court has ruled that only the former is capable of "inherent distinctiveness" (whereas the latter always requires "secondary meaning" to obtain trade dress protection.)
- The law governing trademark protection in colors in the fashion industry is currently in flux; attorneys advising fashion clients should keep a close eye on developments in this area. Apart from color, attorneys should understand what makes a mark "weak" versus "strong" and be able to advise clients accordingly. Selecting a suitable mark at the outset can avoid serious problems later on. The quirks surrounding trademark rights in proper names are especially important for fashion lawyers to understand.

- In the trademark arena, controlling the use of one's mark is of the utmost importance. This means, first, that one must police the unauthorized use of the mark (and confusingly similar variations on it) by third parties, and second, that trademark owners must always negotiate for and exercise quality control rights, in order to avoid losing their trademark protection altogether.
- Remember that copyright, patent, and trademark protection are all *territorial* in nature—that is, they accrue, or are obtained, on a country-by-country basis. With that said, there are tools to extend IP protection to multiple foreign countries at once, including the "Madrid System" and the OHIM "Community Trade Mark" protocols, which are especially important for extending trademark (i.e., brand) protection abroad.
- In each area of intellectual property protection, "secondary liability" is a risk for those who intentionally (or recklessly, or sometimes even inadvertently) facilitate the primary infringer. The tests vary among copyright, patent, and trademark law; they are rapidly evolving in the Internet era, and must be closely tracked—especially by those who advise distributors and similar entities.
- The "right of publicity"/"right of privacy," arising under state law, protects against the unauthorized commercial use of one's image, likeness, or identity, and can complement trademark protection or provide an alternative avenue of recourse where trademark protection is unavailable. Fashion companies must be cognizant of this right when, for example, engaging in the creation of ad campaigns or using proper names for product lines.
- Other state-law theories of intellectual property protection, including "unfair competition" and "theft of idea," can be used offensively when federal IP protection is unlikely to achieve the desired result. Conversely, fashion companies may find themselves on the receiving end of lawsuits for such claims. Either way, it is important to keep in mind the risk of a court ruling that such claims are "preempted" by federal copyright or patent law. (Preemption by federal trademark law is almost never a concern.)

Charles E. Colman is the founder of Charles Colman Law PLLC (http://charlescolmanlaw.com), where he litigates intellectual property disputes and otherwise counsels clients in creative fields like fashion, music, film, and visual art. Mr. Colman graduated from Yale College with a BA in linguistics (cum laude, Distinction in Major) and received his JD from Columbia Law School (James Kent Scholar, Harlan Fiske Stone Scholar.) At Columbia, he served as an articles editor for the Columbia Journal of Law & the Arts *and provided research assistance to leading copyright scholar Professor Jane Ginsburg. Immediately after law school, Mr. Colman worked as a litigation associate at Patterson Belknap Webb & Tyler LLP.*

In addition to representing clients, Mr. Colman serves as co-vice chair of the American Bar Association's Special Committee on Copyrights and New Technologies, and as Co-Chair of the ABA's Fashion Design Legislation Subcommittee. He was recently appointed a lecturer in fashion law at Parsons, the New School for Design. Mr. Colman also blogs about legal issues in fashion at http://lawoffashion.com and contributes a regular column on fashion law to Styleite.com.

Acknowledgment: *I would like to thank Robert Sanchez (Fordham Law School, JD expected, 2014) for research assistance toward the completion of this chapter.*

The Tools for Protecting Fashion Law Clients

Darrell G. Mottley

Shareholder

Banner & Witcoff Ltd.

ASPATORE

Introduction: Fashion Design Piracy Driven by Advances in Technology

Fashion is one of the world's most important creative industries. The fashion sector is multicultural and multifaceted in the global marketplace and, in the women's fashions industry alone, it is a multibillion-dollar business annually. Consumer knowledge of specific designers has increased dramatically. More designers are bringing fashion to the masses by designing lines specifically for discount or departments stores. In addition, news blogs, Twitter, and social media now cover the fashion industry as part of their national news coverage, focusing on the ever-changing world of creative designer expressions.

The job of the intellectual property lawyer is to protect creative fashion designs and the speed of technological change has made that job more challenging. I approach fashion law from the perspective of where the client sells its products globally and I tailor intellectual property protection for the enforcement and market protection of the client's designs. Global changes in the speed of information technology, such as iPads connected to the Internet, and the location of manufacturing to take advantage of cheap labor, cause multifaceted issues for creative fashion designers.

The Effect of Technology

With global use of online social media sites, the ease of receiving fashion images has been increased. Digital images or videos can be easily streamed to factories to reverse-engineer creative designs. For example, many people may remember seeing the famous January 2009 presidential inauguration gown worn by Michelle Obama and designed by new designer Jason Wu. Within days of the gown's unveiling, inexpensive copies were on sale to the public before the designer could get the line in to the retail stores.

IP in the Fashion World

Intellectual property rights are an essential business tool to protect fashion design business. The question of legal protection for fashion design includes the chief proposition of intellectual property: the balance between protecting the twin goals of promoting new creative fashion works and creating new business, on the one hand, and on the other hand, promoting the twin goals of allowing existing fashions to be available to consumers and making the creative works available for use by subsequent designers.

Notwithstanding the trifecta of intellectual property options—copyrights, patents, and trademarks—this chapter will focus on the competitive advantage of using design patents to protect fashion designs. A good place to start is to discuss some of the issues with copyright and trademark law in the application to fashion law.

Making Use of Copyright Protection

Copyright protection for fashion design has been difficult to obtain and is very limited, mainly due to copyright rulings that clothing designs are utilitarian or functional. In *Fashion Originators Guild v. FTC,* 114 F.2d 80, 84 (2d Cir.1940) (L.Hand, J.), *aff'd,* 312 U.S. 457, 61 S.Ct. 703, 85 L.Ed. 949 (1941), dresses were determined to be merely useful articles not covered by the Copyright Act. In other words, clothing design is a useful article because its function is to cover or enclose the human body of the wearer. However, many clothing designs and accessories have ornamental, artistic value that probably should be entitled to copyright protection because they are more of an artistic expression rather than solely utilitarian.

The Separability Test

To be entitled to copyright protection, the standard for originality is low. Most clothing designs would pass this standard. While useful articles, analyzed as a whole, are not eligible for copyright protection, the individual design elements comprising a useful article may, when viewed separately, meet the Copyright Act's requirements. The difficult hurdle for copyright protection of clothing designs as useful articles is passing the so-called "separability" test. The separability test permits copyright protection only if, and to the extent that, the design incorporates graphic, pictorial, or sculptural features that are conceptually or physically separable from the utilitarian aspects of the article.

In one well-known decision, *Mazer v. Stein*, 347 U.S. 201, 74 S.Ct. 460, 98 L.Ed. 630 (1954), the US Supreme Court found that a lamp base shaped like a human figure was protectable as a sculptural work. In *Kieselstein-Cord v. Accessories by Pearl Inc.*, 632 F.2d 989 (2d Cir.1980), another case concerning fashion design accessories, the court found that artwork as part of an ornate belt buckle was protectable under copyright law. This was because the buckle design was conceptually separable from the useful belt function. That is, the design did not enhance the belt's ability to hold up a person's pants garment. Rather, the buckle design could be properly viewed as a sculptural work with independent aesthetic value, and not as an integral element of a belt's functionality. In another fashion case, such as *Poe v. Missing Persons,* 745 F.2d 1238 (9th Cir.1984), the court found likely copyrightable an ornate swimsuit design on the basis that it was more of a soft sculpture, rather than a solely utilitarian article of clothing. The swimsuit was characterized as a three dimensional work of art of flexible clear-vinyl and covered rock media. Federal copyright protection is desirable because rights in copyright would start from the creation of the physical clothing and last for the life of the designer plus seventy years.

Recent Congressional Efforts for Fashion Design

In 2010, the Innovative Design Protection and Piracy Prevention Act (S.3728) was introduced in the 111th Congress. This proposed legislation extended copyright protection to new fashion designs that are unique and a non-trivial variation over the prior art. The Copyright Act Title 17, section 1301 *et al.* would be amended to include a limited number of fashion designs classes. Items that would be protected under this bill include clothing, handbags, duffle bags, tote bags, belts, and eyeglass frames. Protection would be automatic for new fashion items when first made public and no copyright registration or examination of rights would be required. This legislation would provide a three-year term of protection for a fashion design. The proposed legislation excludes protection for fashion designs embodied in a useful article made public by the designer more than three years before the date upon which protection of the design is asserted.

In late 2010, the Senate Judiciary Committee cleared the way for the Innovative Design Protection and Piracy Prevention Act (IDPPPA), sending the bill to the full Senate to be voted on. But, the bill was not voted on by the full Senate. Recently, as of July 2011 the Innovation Design

Protection and Piracy Prevention Act, also known as H.R. 2511, was introduced in the House of Representatives. I attended the House Judiciary committee hearing after the reintroduction of bill. The committee appeared concerned about a potential increase in litigation that may come from extending limited copyright protection of these fashion items. It appears that more work may need to be done in Congress to extend statutory copyright protection to fashion items.

Virtual Fashion Goods

One interesting development in fashion law is the intersection of real-world fashion and virtual goods used in online gaming and virtual worlds. Virtual world environments often include imaginary characters or avatars participating in fictional events, activities, and transactions. There are both educational and entertainment benefits in creating new and challenging ways to relate virtual world environments with real-world experiences.

A virtual good is generally a pictorial representation of a real-world object or graphical object bought and sold in a simulated online computer environment. Players in online games "buy" virtual goods to "dress" their computer avatars, for example. A popular online environment is the Second Life virtual world Internet hosted environment. One interesting way to employ copyright law in the virtual fashion world is to file copyright applications to the pictorial representation of fashion design directed to the virtual selling environment. For example, a company known as DE Designs Inc. operates a virtual clothing store in the Second Life environment and has at least one copyright registration to their virtual clothing (e.g. Copyright Reg. No. VA0001627372).

The Value of Trademark Protection

Trademark rights in the fashion design industry have considerable value from both a business and an enforcement perspective. The owner of the mark can possibly extend the term of the trademark indefinitely as long as the mark is in continuous use in commerce.

To be eligible for trademark rights, the mark must be capable of functioning as a source identifier, such as the fashion designer name or business, and cannot be confusingly similar to existing marks. There are two categories of trademarks that can provide protection against fashion design piracy: marks used on or in conjunction with the product, such as the name or logo of the product or manufacturer, and product configuration marks.

While state common law rights may be possible, federal registration is desirable for name or logo marks or product configuration marks. Trademark rights in the name or the logo design can be acquired for various classes of goods, such as men's or women's shirts, pants, or footwear, for example.

Intent-to-Use Trademarks

One recommended strategy for new designers is to use the feature that the federal trademark law allows for intent-to-use trademarks. In this way, the new designer can still obtain trademark rights for a name or logo before selling one product in the marketplace. Under intent-to-use trademark rights, the designer must have a bona fide intention to use the name or logo in commerce. In other words, in the short term, they plan to use the name or logo to sell their fashion garments in the United States or in between the United States and other countries. After the designer obtains the intent-to-use right, the US Patent and Trademark Office (USPTO) allows extendable time periods for the designer to perfect the rights by filing a specimen that shows the mark on the actual goods or packaging or displays associated with the actual products at the point of sale. But the extension period must be justified every six months and lasts no longer than three years from allowance of the mark.

Secondary Meaning and Distinctiveness

For product configuration designs, a three-dimensional product can be protected under federal trademark law. For a fashion design article to be protectable as a trademark, it must have acquired so-called "secondary meaning," which serves to identify the product with its manufacturer or commercial source. In general, there must be evidence that suggests that consumers viewing the fashion design can associate it to a commercial source. *See generally*, *Wal-Mart Stores Inc. v. Samara Brothers Inc.*, 529 U.S. 205, 120 S.Ct. 1339, 146 L.Ed.2d 182 (2000). This type three-dimensional protection for the entire garment is difficult to obtain.

In essence, the owner of the design needs to show that the design has acquired distinctiveness. Distinctiveness is acquired by substantially exclusive and continuous use of the mark in commerce; the primary significance of the product configuration in the minds of the consumers is its commercial source, not the product. This type of protection can be useful for iconic products of established fashion lines. Nevertheless, much work needs to done to show there is consumer association of the garment to the source.

When navigating in fashion issues, trademark law will not prevent the design of a new garment from being copied until it has acquired distinctiveness. For the new or established designer, if pirates are allowed to copy a design early on, then trademark law cannot protect the design because acquired distinctiveness requires that the design be uniquely associated with a single source. It takes a significant amount of media investment to create the unique association in consumer minds. Social media might be able to change the return on investment, if product design goes viral in the online space. One recommended strategy to protect the fashion product is to obtain a design patent to prevent similar designs from entering the market parallel to the marketing of the products to acquire the distinctiveness necessary for trademark rights.

Preventing Piracy

Use of the trademarked name or logo by pirates in the fashion industry can be stopped under trademark law. To enforce and police the marketplace from counterfeit products, the test for trademark infringement is whether there is a likelihood of confusion as to the source, sponsorship, affiliation, or endorsement of a product.

As an alternative right, there are antidilution provisions of trademark law that prohibit blurring or tarnishing the distinctiveness of a mark if that mark has become famous. Antidilution provisions can provide protection under some circumstances regardless of whether there is any likelihood of confusion as to the source of the product. This may be another way to prevent fashion design piracy where the trademark is being improperly used by others in a way that could tarnish its distinctiveness.

Using Design Patents

Design patents have been recognized as important tools for companies that invest in product development. In 2007, the USPTO issued just over 24,000 design patents, an increase of 15 percent from the 20,965 design patents issued in 2006. US design patent protection is available for new, original, and ornamental designs for articles of manufacture.

Unlike utility patents, design patents are directed to the aesthetic appearance of an article of manufacture. Design patents are essential tools in protecting against clone and simulation-type products made by third parties. In essence, a design patent protects the ornamental design. With respect to fashion products, design patents can be used to protect a wide range of products, including jewelry, footwear, handbags, watches, and dresses as well as headwear.

A Tool for Combating Piracy

A design patent can be effectively used to combat fashion design piracy. The fashion design owner has to timely file a design patent application within a year from a first publication, public disclosure, or offer for sale, or design patent protection will not be available. Of course, it is highly recommended that a designer seek design patent protection as soon as possible, and not wait until public disclosure. The commercial realities of the marketplace and time period for design review in the USPTO dictate seeking speedy protection to have effective enforcement. Furthermore, to be entitled to the design patent, the design must be new and nonobvious when compared to prior designs, and the design must not be primarily functional. Additionally, a design patent has an enforceable term of fourteen years and will not afford protection past its term.

From the fashion lawyer perspective, design patent law allows the claiming of important aspects of the fashion design. This is can be done by using portion claiming practice. In this practice, ornamental features or combination of features sought for protection are shown in solid lines, while the unclaimed subject matter may be shown in broken lines for the purpose of illustrating the environment in which the article embodying the design is used. In this practice, the design claimed is clearly shown in the drawings and unimportant features (unclaimed subject matter) are shown differently by using broken lines and non-shaded areas. In a sense, this allows the features for protection to be deliberately separated out from the rest of the fashion garment. An example of practice is shown in the design patent figures in Appendix O. Important features of the fashion design may be a variation of colors or shades of colors. Design patent coverage is flexible to cover colors or different contrasts as well.

Enforcement of Design Patents

In the infringement context for design patents, the "ordinary observer" test set forth in the US Supreme Court precedent in *Gorham Co., v. White,* 81 U.S. 511 (1871) considered whether the patented design and the accused product at issue were substantially the same to the extent that an ordinary observer is induced to purchase the accused product supposing it to be the patented design. In evaluating resemblance, the US Supreme Court counseled that it is not necessary that every aspect of the designs be identical.

In an important recent design patent case, the US Court of Appeals for the Federal Circuit issued an *en banc* decision in *Egyptian Goddess v. Swisa,* 543 F.3d 665 (Fed. Cir. 2008). In this decision, the Federal Circuit ruled that the so-called point of novelty test, noted by the court in *Litton Systems Inc., v. Whirlpool Corp.,* 728 F.2d 1423, 1444 (Fed. Cir. 1984), was no longer a second and freestanding requirement for proof of design patent infringement.

Applying the Ordinary Observer Test

In relying on *Gorham,* the Federal Circuit counseled that the ordinary observer test is the proper inquiry for analysis as to whether the accused design has appropriated the claimed design as a whole. The court noted that the prior art gives the hypothetical ordinary observer a frame of reference from which to view the distinctions between the accused product and patented design.

The court provided some guidance to district court judges and litigants on how to apply the ordinary observer test in the context of the prior art in the infringement analysis. In one case, if the accused design has copied a particular feature of the claimed design that departs conspicuously from the prior art, the accused design is naturally more likely to be regarded as deceptively similar to the claimed design, and thus infringing.

In another point of guidance, the court indicated that, for claimed designs including a combination of old elements that provide a patentable overall appearance, the hypothetical ordinary observer will attach importance to differences between the claimed design and the prior art depending on the overall effect of those differences on the design. In this regard, the court stated that if the accused design includes a combination of old features that creates an appearance deceptively similar to the patented design, even to an observer familiar with similar prior art designs, a finding of infringement would be justified. Otherwise, infringement would not be found.

Proving Infringement

If an accused infringer elects to rely on comparison of prior art as part of its defense against the claim of infringement, then the burden of production of that prior art is on the accused infringer. Regardless of whether the accused infringer elects to present prior art it considers pertinent to this comparison, the ultimate burden of proof to demonstrate infringement by a preponderance remains with the patentee.

Hence, once a design patent is in hand, the patent holder, in this case the fashion designer, can prevent others from producing designs whose appearance is the same or substantially the same as the patented design, as judged from the perspective of an ordinary observer. In this regard, design patent enforcement could be implemented at trade shows with temporary restraining orders through the appropriate federal district court.

The International Trade Commission May Become in Vogue

Recently, fashion design owners have been utilizing the United States International Trade Commission (ITC) to protect their designs against fashion design piracy and fashion pirates. The ITC has been a desired adjudicative agency for patent and trademark owners seeking to stop infringing foreign products from being imported to or sold in the United States. Today's competitive business environment makes the ITC more important in the fashion industry. The ITC is well equipped to handle patent and trademark disputes and has the governmental power to enforce the exclusion of infringing products into the US from any source on the global. In this regard with respect to design patents, the ITC can order the US Customs and Border Protection under the Department of Homeland Security to exclude products at the US border that infringe upon valid US design patents.

ITC design patent investigations are effective for design-driven fashion clients to prevent the sale or importation of infringing products in the United States. ITC design patent investigations are procedurally similar to utility patent investigations and offer the substantive remedies. The ITC can order US parties to the investigation to cease infringing activities in the United States, thus inhibiting their ability to sell fashion products from existing inventories in the United States. The ITC handles design patent disputes more quickly and generally at less cost than district court patent litigation.

The Crocs Case

One recent interesting case dealing with fashion design in the ITC concerns the Crocs brand footwear. Crocs Inc. (Crocs) owns a design patent, D517,789 (included as Appendix N), covering its famous foam footwear with a design claim depicted by seven views. Crocs filed a 19 U.S.C. § 337 complaint with the ITC alleging infringement of its design patent by a number of companies. After the ITC ruled against Crocs finding non-infringement of their design patent, Crocs appealed the decision to the US Court of Appeals for the Federal Circuit. The Federal Circuit in *Crocs v. ITC*, 598 F.3d 1294 (Fed. Cir. 2010), reversed the ITC decision and ruled infringement of the Crocs design patent by applying principles of the new test in the *Egyptian Goddess* decision.

What is important for fashion designers in the enforcement of the design patent is that the minor differences between the patented design and the accused infringing product should not overtake the analysis for infringement. The proper comparison requires a side-by-side view of the drawings of the patented design and the accused product. Using the side-by-side comparison method, the court in the Crocs case concluded the accused infringing shoes appear nearly identical to the patented design by the ordinary observer (i.e. consumer).

The court further added that if the claimed design and the accused designs were arrayed in matching colors and mixed up randomly, the court was not confident that an ordinary observer could properly restore them to their original order without careful and prolonged effort. Hence, when design patents are viewed as a whole, it may be more difficult for design pirates to avoid infringement with minor changes to a deceptively similar product. In the future, more and more fashion houses and designers will look to the ITC when considering how to protect their creative design and maximize the value of their intellectual property.

Conclusion

While combating fashion design piracy is challenging, the United States intellectual property laws can be employed to protect fashion designs from design-driven companies and designers. In most cases, high-value fashion designs need a blend of copyright, trademark, and design patent protection to combat piracy. The client and attorneys will need to determine the best routes for intellectual property protection consistent with the client's business objectives. Copyright legislation for fashion design is still being debated in Congress and we can expect the debate to continue. While many believe fashion design is becoming more of an art form, copyright protection is very limited and rarely granted under the existing copyright law.

Key Takeaways

- Encourage your new fashion designers client to use the intent-to-use trademarks for name or logos. Your clients can obtain rights in trademark for a name or logo before selling one product in the marketplace. But the extension period to perfect the mark is limited to only three years.
- Trademark law does not prevent a new three-dimensional design from being copied until it has acquired distinctiveness. If pirates copy a design early on, then trademark law cannot protect the design because acquired distinctiveness requires that the design be uniquely associated with a single source.
- Use design patents as tools in protecting against clone and simulation-type products made by third parties. Unlike utility

patents, design patents are directed to the aesthetic appearance of an article of manufacture.

- You can use a design patent to combat fashion design piracy, but the fashion design owner should file quickly to obtain protection.
- Use ITC design patent investigations as an effective alternative to prevent the sale or importation of infringing products. The ITC can order customs to exclude products at the border and it can enforce exclusion of infringing products. Plus, the ITC generally adjudicates design patent disputes more quickly and at less cost than district court litigation.

Related Resources

- Digital IP protection blog, http://www.patentarcade.com/
- Fashion blog, http://fashioncloture.blogspot.com/
- Fashion blog, http://www.counterfeitchic.com/

Darrell G. Mottley is shareholder of the intellectual property law firm of Banner & Witcoff Ltd. focusing on patent, trademark, and copyright cases, including opinions, licensing, and litigation. Mr. Mottley represents clients in the fashion industry from sportswear and footwear to accessories and handbags. He blends combinations of design patent, utility patent, trademark, and copyright intellectual property tools for creative fashion-driven design clients. Mr. Mottley's intellectual property practice also includes complex technologies in a variety of fields such as telecommunications, internet-related technology, business methods, computer-gaming, medical devices, semiconductors, mechanical technologies, and electro-mechanical technologies. He is also president of the District of Columbia Bar of Washington, D.C. for the 2011-2012 term.

Mr. Mottley earned his law degree, with honors, from The George Washington University in 2000; his Masters of Business Administration in 1994, and his BS in engineering in 1987 from Virginia Tech, where he was Phi Kappa Phi. He is admitted to practice before the US Patent and Trademark Office and courts in the District of Columbia, Virginia, New Jersey, and the Federal and Fourth Circuits.

Acknowledgment: *I would like to thank Elizabeth A. Almeter, an associate at Banner & Witcoff Ltd., for helping in the research and editing of this chapter.*

Succeeding in Fashion Law: A Mix of Good Fortune, Hard Work, and Skill

Steven R. Gursky

Partner and Head, Intellectual Property Department

Olshan Grundman Frome

Rosenzweig & Wolosky LLP

ASPATORE

Introduction: Style Changes, but the Basics Remain the Same

I have been an attorney representing clients in the fashion business for more than twenty-three years. At its root, fashion law is business law, but it does have its unique aspects. Like other businesses, a fashion business needs someone to form the appropriate entity or entities, establish the trademarks, account for the interrelationship of the wholesale and retail business, opine on advertising, and consider many of the operational needs. There is also a real estate component to fashion law, perhaps most uniquely, the high profile retail locations. While in some respects retail leasing for fashion companies may not be all that much different than a lease for a candy store, among other unique aspects, fashion law considers adjacencies, which are the other fashion retailers that are in the immediate area, whether on Madison Avenue in New York City, Rodeo Drive, or your local retail mall.

I was drawn into this work by opportunity. I was a kid who grew up in Brooklyn, New York and was not the product of a suburban environment who grew up wearing branded products. My career was not driven by a burning desire to enter the fashion industry, although many who have now come to work with me grew up very aware of fashion and branding. Attorneys come to me all the time because they want to combine their interest in fashion with their desire to be a lawyer. For me, there was an opportunity in the late 1980s to represent Tommy Hilfiger when it was a very small company. The expertise I developed representing that company made it possible for me to meet other people who asked if I would be their attorney. Fashion became a great interest of mine as a result. Being an attorney was a lifelong dream, and adding fashion to it was a bonus.

A unique aspect of fashion law is the ability for the attorney to become known as the designer clients become better known. Fashion designers are celebrities, so if are involved in a big licensing deal your name might be mentioned. The same will occur for a real estate deal because people care about what fashion designers do. The fact that I have been involved in a considerable amount of trademark protection and anti-counterfeiting matters, such as large criminal seizures and litigations, including a number of successful suits against Wal-Mart, for high profile companies many of these activities were picked up by the press. In legal matters related to designers, both the designer and their successful attorneys get attention.

The Mania for Licensing in Fashion

The opportunity for a designer to grow his or her empire through licensing is greater and more prevalent than ever. Ralph Lauren is the leader in the expanse of licensing opportunities for fashion companies and for designers. Designers going into eyewear or fragrances were common for a relatively long time, but for a designer to take his product into paint and home products is a huge trend. Years ago, you had Pierre Cardin and Yves Saint Laurent, but that was related to apparel.

In recent years, there has been a proliferation of companies that license most or all of their products for production and sale by others. In the past, companies made the things that they could make and licensed the things that they could not make. For example, a company would license fragrance because they lacked the unique knowledge of how to do bottling distribution, or eyewear because it required a unique technology. Today, companies are more likely to license the things that they could make, but recognize two things:

1. someone else who does it every day might be able to make it better than me, and
2. the revenues I derive from licensing without the risk of maintaining inventories is enough without having to keep all of the profits for myself.

This makes licensing a growing area in fashion law because you have many companies that are totally licensed. They do not even have a house product. They manufacture nothing.

Common Challenges with Licensing and Compliance

Distribution licensing continues to be a very efficient business model for designers. They do not have to invest in inventory; they can focus on products for which they have a technical proficiency. Of course, the party that is granting the licensing rights has some serious concerns. They must keep control over use of trademarks, product approval, and human rights compliance. For many years, my clients have required a human rights component is written into their licenses.

Not only must the licensor review the product bearing its trademark for quality, but the designer also has the ability to get his or her thoughts into products made by others in a cohesive manner. Over the years, there have been products and lines that others and I have referred to as "rent a brands." These are companies that permit others to put their name on anything just because they can generate revenues and collect money. Conversely, the designer whose business is built for the long haul looks into the future and realizes the license is just a step towards a successful future. A fashion company needs to have a cohesive line. To that end, they require license provisions give them the discretion to determine the quality of the products and the design. They also retain the ability to change their lines from season to season and keep the brand alive. Many licensors have learned the hard way that collecting the most royalties is not necessarily the best license deal. More often, the quality of the product, the quality of the licensee, and the retail contacts are the most important things.

As importantly, a designer must be sure that there is a match between the licensees' abilities and nature of the designer's product so they not only have experience in making footwear, but also that the footwear will be marked at the price points which complement the brand. If the product is a high-end product, a designer must be sure that the licensee's sales team has quality contacts with high-end department stores instead of mass buyers. The product and licensing people need to think long term, and need to understand what "blowing out the market" means. Sales protections should be built into the license agreement, which discourages the licensee from maximizing sales in one year that they cannot replicate in the next. Designers have learned is that a licensee which oversells the marketplace and does not have good sell-through, meaning the product sells through in a normal term of retail seasons, ends up with a brand that does not have longevity and that retailers that bought the product do not want to buy for next season. A discounted brand in better stores is not what the retailers want and is, therefore, not what the designers should want.

Asserting Performance Standards with Licensees

A hot button issue with licensees is their desire to avoid aggressive minimum sales and minimum royalty requirements, but those measurements are critical for the fashion designer. With the ability to exclusive licensing rights to only one licensee for each product or product category, licensors must have tools to ensure that such rights are being fully exploited by the selected licensees. As licensees prefer not to have their feet held to the fire, there is often a negotiation to determine the appropriate sales and royalty levels. In addition to sales and royalty levels, consideration must be given to advertising levels to establish an appropriate level of promotion. During a difficult economy, licensees will resist requests for aggressive minimums, but those financial assurances are sometimes the best way that we have of assuring that the licensee will be pressing ahead instead of being distracted by another brand or opportunity.

Beyond the economic protections provided in a license agreement, a well-drawn license agreement will provide protections that are essential under US law. Such minimal protections afford the designer/licensor the ability to review how the trademark is used. The absence of such protection can result in what is referred to as a "naked license," which can result in the designers losing their right to the exclusive use of their trademarks. It is therefore essential to have a professionally prepared license agreement that will not jeopardize the designer's trademark rights.

Technology is Driving Rapid Knockoffs

The impact of fashion on the law is expanding. There is a law in front of Congress that has been sponsored by Senator Charles Schumer (R-NY) to protect designs and the silhouettes of garments.

For as long as anyone can remember, although an intricate fabric design could be protected, the silhouette of a design—even the most unique and creative—was deemed to be part of function and therefore not protected. One of the reasons for the change is the change in the production timeline for a new line of seasonal clothing. Historically, you could show the spring line nine months before the same would appear in the stores of sale, take orders from the show, and then start shipping it to the stores the next year and all was good. It was not until the clothes got into the marketplace that someone would take swipes at you and trying to knock off those creative designs. Today, photographs are taken at runway shows and the knockoff people actually make it to market before the actual product because of the ability of computers to retrofit designs. This has created much more angst among designers than ever existed before; designers were never happy about it, but today a runway designer will see his designs being knocked off with cheaper copies within days. This has changed the face of runway fashion. It used to be a more difficult and time consuming process to copy a design. And, back then, if you came out with your fall line it would not be until after that season's products were in the stores that you would find a knock-off company stealing your work. Designers had become accustomed to the limited head start they had on the market. Now with the expedited pace of the knock-offs, designers find that the creative impact is taken out of their creations and their statement in the market diminished because what they are selling is no longer new or novel. The fact that people are able to buy an inferior product that is lower quality takes a lot of energy out of the fashion community.

The detractors from the protection proposed in Senator Schumer's bill think it will only make lawyers rich. The proposed law contains provisions to ensure that the designer has actually created something novel and unique. The fact it, there are many ideas in fashion that are a spin or play on something else. The concept is to afford protection to silhouettes of garments that are so creative that they are entitled to protection even for a three-year period to give the designer a head start on the market and prevent them from being immediately knocked off.

It does appear that the proposed law has much support and will, in one form or another, be passed. Having said that, it is not entirely clear how it will play out in enforcement. While there are many who think that lawyers just want to sit back and create more litigation, as I am generally on the side of the designers and the property owners, I believe that this will provide enforcement advantages for property owners. Clearly, if the law is passed, it is going to take some time to reach the appropriate level of enforcement.

The Registration Process

Like any new law, which causes a flurry of activity at the beginning and a more normal flow thereafter, there will be a lot of litigation or review of the potential for litigation and at some point, it will level off as people get more comfortable with what they can and cannot protect on an ongoing basis. It will require discretion on the part of the plaintiff's attorneys in picking the right cases instead of just cases, and lawyers will have to use their good sense to know when something is sufficiently creative to be protected. The Copyright Office will have a challenging task determining which designers are worthy of copyright protection.

Trademarks and copyrights follow very different paths to registration. When a trademark is submitted, the intended trademark holder generally has performed a search to see if the mark is available. The Trademark Office does a review of the existing state of the filings as well. The trademark examiners will decide if the proposed mark is either too similar to what exists already or it is not. Others have an opposition period to refute the fact that the design is original.

The Registration Process in the Copyright Office

In the copyright office, the review that is done is to see if the design is sufficiently creative. Unlike the trademark examiner, the copyright examiner will not look to see what other similar copyrights have already been registered or are in the public domain. Therefore, it is possible after a copyright is registered that there will be litigation to determine if the copyright infringes on someone else' copyright.

If the law is passed, it is going to be an interesting and very active time. It is likely to take a significant amount of time for this process to wash through until the system results in design copyrights that are, in fact, the result of unique creative activity worthy of protection for even three years. There has been a lot of effort in getting the law passed, and I think the proliferation of copies and knockoffs and counterfeits will result in the law being passed. The interesting part of it is going to be in the enforcement of it, which will not be black and white.

Ethical Issues Associated with the New Business Environment

If the new copyright law is passed, the ability to exercise discretion in how you enforce trademarks and copyrights will be an important quality. Less-scrupulous individuals who think that this new law is an opportunity to start a number of lawsuits will actually learn that they, and their clients, will end up far worse than they would have been otherwise. Filing suit for its own sake, and charging a client a fee, does not work because clients tire of lawsuits that are not well thought out.

The Economy's Impact on the Fashion Industry and Law

The economic climate has resulted in more brands with multiple distribution channels to capture consumers who are more careful in their spending. There are more designers coming up at the lower levels or designers moving down a notch. This is a business trend that has an impact on lawyers as it changes the provisions in license agreements relating to the permitted levels of distribution and approvals of distribution. Under this economy, a licensor cannot allow itself to be locked into the historical channels of distribution only, so flexibility at the discretion of the licensor will be a key.

The Direct Television Marketing Phenomenon

The growth over the years of not only Internet sales but direct television marketing has created new issues in the law and in the fashion business. An issue that needs to be addressed is how distribution developments affect what you need to be covered in license agreements. How do you protect territorial boundaries when the premise for the boundaries was brick-and-mortar business? Traditionally, a licensor could give one licensee the United States and another Canada, or even divide the United States into different regions by area or state. When the prevalent sales methods are HSN, QVC, or the Internet, there is greater cross-jurisdictional ability to make sales. New issues have emerged relative to how you control sales from jurisdiction to jurisdiction. When you license someone from Europe, do you say that they have an exclusive to Europe, excluding direct response television sales or Internet sales that are to be granted to another?

The Challenge of Internet Counterfeiting

While imitation has been said to be the "sincerest form of flattery," counterfeiting, and the new challenges of the Internet, continue to vex designers. The Internet has presented fashion companies with a productive and legitimate way to market their products, but it also opens the door to those who engage in the sale of counterfeit products. When the sale of counterfeit products occurs from a "bricks and mortar" store location, identifying the responsible parties is easier, but on the Internet, it is more difficult to root out the party who is behind the counterfeiting. Worse still, there are parties on the Internet who use misleading domain names and make their money by getting you to click on an ad. This distracts consumers from the legitimate designer, especially when they put a competitor's key word in the search.

Conclusion

For young attorneys, fashion law can be an interesting and attractive field, but, there are relatively limited opportunities in this area of law, young lawyers are well-advised to learn the basics of business law if they want to be a fashion lawyer. It is also helpful to build a strong base of intellectual property law and contract law. Learning the craft of being a good business lawyer, may provide the opportunity to represent clients that are in the fashion business. When that occurs, the attorney may be able to marry their considerable business skills with those clients and provide an entry point into the area of fashion law.

Key Takeaways

- Match the licensee's abilities and resources to your product so that it is able to sell your product at the price point you expect.
- Build protections into the license agreement that discourage licensees from maximizing sales in one year that they cannot replicate in the next. Someone who oversells the marketplace and does not have good sell-through, meaning the product sells through in a normal term of retail seasons, ends up with a brand that does not have longevity.

- Establish minimum levels for sales, royalty, and advertising levels so that there is an appropriate level of promotion from the licensee. These financial assurances are the best way to ensure that your licensee does not get distracted by another brand.
- Resist the urge to "lock into" being a fashion law specialist from Day One. It is a very narrow field, and it is far more important to focus on building a solid base of business law knowledge.

Steven R. Gursky is a partner with Olshan Grundman Frome Rosenzweig & Wolosky LLP in New York, where he is the head of the firm's Intellectual Property Department. His practice concentration includes contract negotiation, mergers and acquisitions, intellectual property prosecution and protection, real estate, and general corporate practice. His varied experience, ranging from small and midsize business transactions to multijurisdictional, complex transactions for public corporations, provides clients with a unique combination of seasoned business and legal experience.

Mr. Gursky has also developed an expertise in the area of trademark protection, with a particular niche in anti-counterfeiting efforts in the apparel industry and other industries. He is recognized as an expert by the media in this area. He has been repeatedly named to the New York Super Lawyers *list since 2007.*

Mr. Gursky presently serves as a member on the Board of Directors of the Martin Luther King Jr. National Memorial Project Foundation Inc., an organization whose vision was to erect a memorial in Washington, D.C., commemorating Dr. King's life and work, which opened to the public on August 22, 2011. Mr. Gursky received the Alpha Phi Alpha fraternity's Medal of Honor, the highest honor bestowed on a non-member.

Examining the Agreements of Fashion Law

Charles Klein

Partner

Davidoff Malito & Hutcher LLP

ASPATORE

Introduction

I have practiced law since 1977, and had a wide variety of legal experiences. Earlier in my career, I worked at a major Wall Street law firm as a litigator. A partner in that firm came into my office one day and asked if I would like to become general counsel of the Sergio Valente jeans company. In 1983, Sergio was a very large company and a pioneer of the designer jeans business. I agreed to the change, moved to Seventh Avenue, and never looked back.

For four years, I handled virtually all of Sergio's legal matters, from license agreements, factoring agreements, forming companies, pursuing jeans counterfeiters, drafting shareholders agreements and employment agreements, keeping the company out of litigation and handling everyday legal matters that came across my desk. I also helped the company outfit the Chinese national basketball team in Sergio jeans. I made the connection between fashion and entertainment, early on. After seeing an unknown entertainer at a small club in the Hamptons, I tried to convince the company to use her for Sergio commercials. The company did not give the idea much consideration—I was only a lawyer and what did I know about promoting the sale of jeans. That singer was Madonna. But Madonna went on to superstardom. Years later, the fashion/entertainment connection would become a compelling one.

After four years at Sergio, I returned to private practice. In addition to practicing law, I founded an organization called The Fashion Roundtable. The organization held panel discussions on business issues of interest to the fashion industry. I also wrote and published *Fashion and the Law*, a lively newsletter that dealt with legal issues of import to the fashion industry. Around 2001, I started The Fashion Service Network (www.fashion servicenetwork.com), today an organization of twenty-five of the leading service providers to the fashion industry. The network is a one-stop shop for services and opportunities for the fashion industry. I have also lectured widely on fashion legal issues and taught business law at LIM College (the Laboratory Institute of Merchandising) to young people interested in going into the management side of the fashion business.

An important part of my fashion practice has focused on domestic and international license agreements. This is often where the action is for a fashion lawyer. It is also fun. That representation has included representing a leading national luxury department store retailer and famous Seventh Avenue designers in both domestic and international license agreements, including deals with large Japanese trading companies. I've also represented very well-known urban brands in license agreements and promotional and sports related agreements. I have litigated successfully on behalf of brand owners to collect royalties from non-paying licensees. Many brand owners think they have to settle cheaply when going after non-paying licensees. Provided the licensee has the money to pay the judgment, this need not be true. We were successful in getting summary judgments against non-paying licensees despite their raising bogus defenses aimed at cloaking their unwillingness to pay royalties.

When I tell a lay person that I am a lawyer representing fashion clients, they often ask me "do fashion companies get sued a lot?" I explain that most of my work involves contracts. This chapter will discuss four kinds of contracts a fashion lawyer often comes across: trademark license agreements, license agency agreements, factoring agreements and sales representative agreements.

Understanding Trademark License Agreements

Every new fashion company eagerly anticipates the day when it can license its trademark and reap the rewards of the time, creativity and money it has invested in its brand. The discussion below will focus on both the business and legal issues to be considered when entering into a license agreement, from the perspectives of both the brand owner granting the license (the "licensor") and the company receiving the license (the "licensee").

Performing Effective Due Diligence is Often the Key to a Successful License.

Before entering into a license agreement, both parties must do their business homework.

<u>Licensor Diligence</u>

The first issue of concern is the ability of the licensee to pay the royalties. Accordingly, the licensor must review the licensee's financials. Those financial statements may also raise questions about the licensee's financial ability to produce and deliver timely the licensed products, which are, of course, key concerns. The licensor must also confirm that the licensee is experienced in the product categories and distribution channels to be licensed. A company may be a fine maker and seller of apparel to Wal-Mart or Kmart. However, a licensor may not wish to grant that company a license to sell products to Macy's and Bloomingdales. Of paramount importance is whether the licensee can offer well-designed, well-made products. The licensor should also consider whether the prospective licensee is doing business with competitive brands. The licensor may have to accept some competition from its licensee, but does not want its licensed products to be left out in the cold as the licensee's third or fourth option.

Understanding the Licensor's DNA

It is essential that the licensor and licensee share a similar brand vision. If the licensee does not understand the licensor's brand and its "DNA," the license is not going to work. I always tell a brand owner it is better to have no license than a bad one. Brand extensions are great but a bad license can damage the brand and the licensor's core business.

Due Diligence by Licensees: Know What You Are "Buying"

A prospective licensee must review the licensor's trademark rights—does it own the trademark in the territory in the subject product category? It is also important to understand if the brand is one of longstanding success or a likely short-term flash in the pan. It is critically important for the licensee to speak to retailers before entering into a license agreement. The brand owner may discourage that search—it may feel that the licensee is "fishing" and not serious about entering into an agreement. However, at the end of the day, this investigation is critical—the subject brand may be a compelling one but retailers in the subject distribution channels may not want the brand in the licensee's particular product category. If the brand will not open up the key retail "doors," the prospective licensee should not proceed.

The licensee also needs to know, after factoring in the royalty to be paid and the mandated advertising expenditures, whether it can make a reasonable profit. The licensee must also feel synergy with the brand owner, both from branding and human standpoints. The licensee should confirm that the licensor is reasonable—in a licensing arrangement, like any other partnership or marriage, there are always going to be "issues" that arise. The licensee should speak to other licensees of the brand to learn if the licensor is reasonable or difficult.

The Term Sheet and Controlling the Document

When the parties have decided to proceed, a term sheet should be prepared before going to an agreement. It helps to ensure that both parties are on the same page literally and figuratively about the terms of the business deal. Some clients think it is better and cheaper to let the other side draft the agreement. However, the licensor should always draft the license agreement and "control" the document. If the licensor is a celebrity or sports business, and is not accustomed to drafting license agreements, a savvy licensee may succeed in convincing the licensor that it should draft the agreement (and then use a more licensee-friendly form). I confess to having done that.

The Grant: Exclusive versus Non-Exclusive

In the grant of the license, the first issue of concern is whether the license is to be exclusive or non-exclusive. If it is a non-exclusive license, the licensor can license other companies to sell the same kinds of products under the same trademark in the same territory. This is not often the case in the fashion industry, where exclusive licenses predominate. Some fashion brand owners, however, find ways to water down exclusivity. They grant an exclusive license for a particular trademark but then slice and dice up their brand into several similar trademarks offered to different distribution channels. When the licensor does that, the licensee needs to be concerned about the impact that a similar brand in a lower distribution channel might have on its business. Some of my clients' license deals went south precisely because we could not ensure that there would be no competition in its distribution channel from a licensee with another sliced up, diced up version of the same brand. Some license agreements give the licensee an exclusive only for particular distribution channels, leaving the licensor free to license the very same mark to a lower channel—such a "downstairs" licensee could really kill the business for the licensee in the higher channel.

The Term

In a fashion industry license, the typical term runs for three years and six months, with an eighteen month first contract year that affords the licensee a six-month start-up period for the development of the product. When I represent a licensee, I always insist on at least one three-year renewal term, especially when it is building a new product category for the brand. A licensee does not want to find itself doing a good job only to be ousted from the license after the initial term by some larger company offering more money to the licensor. If a licensee is unsure of whether its product will succeed with the brand it may want to sign on for a shorter than three-year term in order to minimize its risk on the minimum royalties. However, a term of less than two years does not show real seriousness on the part of the licensee: a licensor should not agree to a one year term as a "look see" to learn if the brand will work in the licensed category. A licensor client of mine chose to license a trademark to be used in connection with a line of novel products. The licensee, a large company, sought to have a one-year initial term. We insisted on a two-year term which served our licensor client well after the licensee walked away from the license after overselling the market and delivering poor quality goods. Our client licensee nevertheless was able to collect royalties for the second year.

Reservation of Rights

Every license agreement should provide that all rights not expressly granted to the licensee in the agreement are reserved to the licensor.

Territory: Licensee Experience Makes a Difference

The licensor must confirm that the perspective licensee has experience and connections in the licensed territory. For US companies, fashion licenses sometimes include Canada in addition to the United States as part of the licensed territory. The licensor needs to know before it includes Canada whether the licensee has substantial retail connections in Canada or is simply just trying to glom additional territory. If a licensor is uncertain about the licensee's ability to do business in the entire territory, especially in a multi-country territory, the agreement can require that the licensee hit minimum annual levels of sales in each country to maintain the license for the country.

Trademark Costs

A question often arises in a worldwide agreement (typical in the fragrance industry) as to which party should bear the trademark costs for international trademarks. The licensee will argue that since the licensor owns the trademark, it should pay all these costs. On the other hand, the licensor may reasonably question why it should pay trademark costs for a country with little sales potential. A reasonable compromise is for the licensee to bear the costs for countries in questionable marketplaces, but with the licensee to be reimbursed for such expenditures in the form of a royalty credit for sales made in the subject country. Such a clause will cause a licensee to think long and hard about whether it will really do business in a country for which it insists on a trademark registration.

The Licensed Products

The defining of "licensed products" is a true art. Both the licensor and licensee need to make sure that the licensee is given enough product categories to maximize business. However, the licensor must be careful not to license a product category that could be more profitably exploited as a stand-alone license by another licensee. Licensees often try to gobble up as many product categories as they can regardless of whether they have sales connections or experience in those categories. The licensor, accordingly, must ensure that the licensee has manufacturing experience and sales contacts in the product categories to be licensed. A "use it or lose it" provision can be drafted to permit the licensor to delete a product category for which a specified sales target is not satisfied. The "licensed products" definition must also be clearly drafted so as to minimize disputes about what products are included. To minimize the likelihood of inter-licensee disputes over whether particular products are covered by a particular license agreement, the license agreement should give the licensor the right to resolve any such dispute between licensees. However, the licensee should make sure that any such resolution is in accord with the intent of the license agreement. The licensor should not be able to unilaterally amend the agreement through the dispute resolution process.

Authorized Distribution Channels

One of the key components of any license agreement is the specified "authorized distribution channels." The licensee needs to know that it can sell its products in sufficiently broad distribution channels to permit it to pay the minimum royalties discussed below, and to capitalize fully on the licensed trademark. The licensor needs to provide for appropriate channels to maintain brand integrity. Sales in inappropriately low channels could kill the brand entirely. The licensor must make crystal clear the channels in which the licensed products can be sold: Often a list of permitted retail customers is attached as an exhibit to the Agreement. The licensee might also wish to bargain for the right to take the channels "down" if the licensor moves the core product to a lower distribution channel than is presently authorized in the license agreement. Some licensors will preclude Internet sales by its licensees—seeking to have all Internet sales go through the licensor's brand website. In such event, the licensor will usually obligate the licensee to sell licensed products to the licensor at favorable prices, but on a royalty-free basis. In any event, the licensee must be permitted to sell to the Internet sites of its brick and mortar retail customers.

Looking at Royalties

<u>The Key Types of Royalties</u>

There are two types of royalties payable to licensors: percentage royalties and minimum royalties. The former are a percentage of "net sales" that are paid on the invoice price of the goods shipped, less permitted deductions. In fashion licenses, the royalty rates vary from 5 percent of net sales at the low end to 10 percent at the high end, with strong brands in higher distribution channels commanding the highest rates. This royalty is payable on the "net sales," not on the sales proceeds actually received, as the uninitiated licensee might expect. The net sales definition often draws much attention during the negotiation process. That definition typically permits deductions for returns and customary trade allowances and discounts, such as markdown allowances and gross margin allowances. The licensor usually seeks to cap these deductions at no more than ten percent of net sales during the contract year.

The minimum royalty must be paid regardless of actual sales. Typically, there is a payment of minimum royalties required on the signing of the Agreement of anywhere from twenty-five to fifty percent of the first year's minimum royalties, followed by equal quarterly payments. The minimum royalties are typically payable on the first day of the quarter, while the percentage royalties are typically paid within thirty days after the end of the quarter. A key issue is how and when the minimum and percentage royalties are to be credited against each other. The eyes of the lawyers and their clients often glaze over this boring but financially meaningful provision. The licensee should not be paying more than the greater of the minimum royalties or the percentage royalties in any contract year. The licensee wants this crediting to occur on a rolling, cumulative basis, so that at any point in time it has paid the greater of the minimum or percentage royalties, but no more than such amount. Some licensors will not permit crediting until the end of the contract year. If such is the case, the licensee will often overpay total royalties during the course of the year and must catch up at year-end in the form of a credit or reimbursement. In fashion licenses, it is customary that if the licensee has paid more than the minimum royalties owed in any contract year (but no more than total royalties due), the licensee cannot carry those excess amounts forward as a credit against the minimum royalties payable to the next contract year. Each contract year starts anew.

Minimum Royalty Increases

Often, there are bump-ups of the minimum royalties from year to year. The licensee must do its homework to ensure that those increases are reasonable one. Some prospective licensees are so anxious to obtain a license for a brand they covet that they do not focus on the increases in minimum obligations, only to find out later that they cannot do the business necessary to pay the minimums.

Minimum Sales: The License Should Not Be "Parked"

Many brand owners include in the license a provision that includes minimum sales. Some licensees question the reason for minimum sales; if they are paying the minimum royalties, that should be enough, they argue. Minimum sales are required, however, because the licensor does not want the licensee to "park" the license. It wants the licensee to sell the licensed products in volumes that will help extend the brand, and give further momentum to the core product sold by the licensor. The licensor typically receives the right to terminate the license if those minimum sales are not hit. The agreement should, from a licensee perspective, require that notice to be sent within sixty days after the end of the contract year. There may be negotiation about whether the licensor will be able to receive accelerated minimum royalties on termination for failure to hit minimum sales. The licensee can argue that it should not be required to pay liquidated damages if it was a "good citizen" but could not hit the sale minimums. The licensor, facing a year-long search for a new licensee, however, may want the current licensee to make good on some of those royalties that it will lose during that period.

Limiting Off-Price Sales

Licensors seek to include an annual cap on the percentage of sales that are sold, either at a specified price below the wholesale list price or to permitted discounters. The licensor does not want to learn that the bulk of the licensee's sales are going to discounters with obvious deleterious brand impact. In today's environment, it is not uncommon to provide for a cap on off price sales as high as thirty percent of total net sales in (in the past 20 percent was customary). Sometimes a licensor does not wish to terminate the license if the off-price sales exceed the cap, but instead wishes to have the right to impose increased royalties on sales in excess of the cap in the form of a double or triple royalty rate. (This clause can also be used for sales outside authorized distribution channels or sales of unapproved products.) The licensor should also make sure that special "make up" lines may not be sold to discounters early in the season.

The Approval Process

Product approval is a key aspect of any license agreement. Without such approval process a "naked license" will result, which will dilute the value of the trademark. The approval process must include approvals on quality and design. Typically, the approval process includes several steps, the approval of the designs themselves in the form of drawings or CADs, the approval of pre-production samples and finally approval of top of production items that come out of the first factory run. There is often some tussling over whether sole discretion or reasonable discretion standards will apply to the licensor's approval. Most good fashion brands are going to insist on sole total discretion approvals, especially relating to designs. The licensor can justifiably argue that it is not a matter of "reasonableness" as to whether a design is right for the brand. Often, the licensee wants a "deemed approval" provision to be included in the approval section: if the licensor does not reject an item submitted for approval within a specified period of time, e.g., ten days, it is deemed approved by the licensor. Many large brand owners reject deemed approvals. I think they are misguided. They are being paid in part to give or reject approvals. A compromise solution is to provide for a deemed approval if the licensor fails to act within a short window after a second notice for approval is given.

The Rigors of Records and Audits

A licensor clearly want to ensure that the licensee is complying with the agreement, especially its payment obligations. License agreements customarily include a provision that requires a licensee to keep accurate and complete records. The records should be available to the licensor for inspection for two to six years after the agreement expires. Audit provisions should allow for inspection and copying of a very wide range of documents. Those records must include manufacturing records so that the licensor can compare what was manufactured to what was sold. Typically, if an audit discloses an understatement of anywhere from three to five percent, the licensee must pay the (reasonable) audit costs incurred by the licensor. This incentivizes the licensee to keep good books and records. The licensee must ensure that there is a cap on how many audits are going to be performed. Unless there is good reason shown, the licensor should not be permitted to audit more than once per year. Some audit clauses unfairly give the licensor a right to terminate the agreement if there is an understatement of net sales of more than a specified percentage (e.g., 5 to 10 percent). That draconian remedy should only apply where the licensee was engaged in fraud.

Brand Building and Advertising

A key aspect of building a brand is spending money on advertising. Some brand owners curiously do not fully appreciate the role advertising plays in their brand's success. Especially in the jeans business, brands can be built on advertising. Obligated licensee advertising can take the form of licensee contributions to the licensor or licensee expenditures, or a combination of both. These contributions/expenditures can range from one to three percent of net sales (but as much as 35 percent in fragrance deals). Mirroring the royalty obligations, there are often minimum as well as percentage obligations on the advertising contributions and/or expenditures. The brand owner usually prefers to receive advertising fees to maintain control over the use of the funds. However, the licensee may well prefer to spend the money itself in a way that is better targeted to its products. Stronger brand owners usually resist advertising expenditures in lieu of contributions. On occasion, a compromise occurs. If there is a three percent of net sales overall advertising obligation, two percent can be paid to the brand owner and one percent spent by the licensee. Some licensees try to count trade show expenditures, such as booth rental or construction as "advertising expenditures," where they are being permitted to spend advertising monies. A licensor should reject that position. Often, the brand owner seeks to exclude co-op advertising from permitted advertising expenditures. Some licensors, however, will compromise and permit a percentage of co-op advertising to count. Successful brands that take part in large trade shows may want to obligate their licensee to take part in the trade show and to bear pro rata expenses of the show. The licensee should get a copy of third party bills to confirm that it is not getting overbilled for its share of trade show expenses.

Insurance Coverage and Indemnities

License agreements typically obligate the licensee to carry a minimum amount of product liability insurance. Licensors should not accept less than $3 million insurance of coverage. The policy must name the licensor as an additional insured, with a certificate of insurance to be provided to the licensor within thirty days after execution of the agreement.

Indemnity provisions are key aspects of license agreements. Each party should defend and indemnify the other for third party claims arising from its breach of the Agreement. The licensor should also be indemnified for all third party claims relating to all acts taken by the licensee relating to the agreement except for infringement claims discussed below. The licensor should defend and indemnify the licensee for claims that the licensee's use of the licensed trademark strictly in accordance with the agreement infringed the rights of a third party. The licensee wants to be indemnified for all such claims, whether arising on a trademark basis, a contract basis or otherwise, and whether or not the claim was meritorious. Licensors may try to limit indemnifiable claims to meritorious, trademark-based claims that result in the rendering of a judgment against the licensee. Some licensors seek to limit their indemnity exposure to the amount of royalties they receive. I would never accept that cap as a licensee.

The Licensee's Manufacturers

Two manufacturer-related subjects are often highly charged:

a. the licensor's approval of manufacturers and
b. the liability of the licensee for its manufacturer's misdeeds.

During the past fifteen years, it has become especially important for the licensor to ensure that its licensees are not using manufacturers that employ child labor. The licensor should have the right to approve the licensee's proposed manufacturers. There may be negotiation about whether the approval standard is to be a "reasonable" or "sole discretion" standard.

Some licensees may wish the names of their manufacturers to be held in confidence, which can prove to be a point of contention. I handled an agreement for a large apparel company licensee that was seeking to license iconic cartoon characters. My client was known for getting terrific prices from its manufacturers. For this company, keeping the identity of its manufacturers confidential, even from the licensor, was viewed as critical. As a result, a point that usually takes about five minutes to negotiate got embroiled in many long discussions and meetings.

Brand owners typically require factory owners to sign a code of conduct and/or agreements by which they agree to comply with law and with the policies of the brand owner. Those agreements should prohibit the manufacturer from selling products bearing the trademark to anyone other than the licensee (some manufacturers will sell products out their back door to other customers).

Whether or not a licensee should be held responsible for the misdeeds of its manufacturers is a very thorny issue. Large brand owners want to hold the licensee responsible for all acts of their manufacturers. The licensee, conversely, will seek to avoid responsibility arguing that it cannot control the actions of its manufacturers. A compromise position would impose liability on the licensee for a manufacturer's acts only if it does not terminate the manufacturer promptly after learning of the manufacturer's misdeeds.

Default and Termination

The termination provision is often a highly negotiated one. The licensor wants to know that it can expeditiously get rid of a bad apple licensee that is breaching the agreement. On the other hand, the licensee does not want to get terminated for minor breaches, without the right of cure. There are typically two kinds of breaches set forth in the default provision of most fashion license agreements: curable and non-curable defaults. A sophisticated licensor will include a long list of curable and non–curable defaults. Curable defaults typically include, among other breaches, monetary defaults, the failure to indemnify the licensor, the failure to provide sales reports and the failure to maintain insurance. Non-curable defaults typically include selling licensed products outside the territory, selling unapproved products, and selling outside the authorized distribution channels. Licensees often try to relax the absoluteness of the non-curable defaults in order to require that the subject breach involve more than a specified number of units. Some license agreements provide that any non-curable breach gives rise to an event of default entitling the licensor to terminate the license agreement. The licensee should always insist on the deletion of such clause. If the clause remains, the agreement could be terminated for the most minor of breaches with serious repercussions for the licensee: Termination means that the licensee will not only lose its license but also that it will typically be required to pay liquidated damages and often lose its sell-off rights that would otherwise be afforded.

Some licensees seek to obtain a termination right for licensor breaches. Most licensors will resist such a clause. However, where permitted, it should, from a licensor perspective, be limited to breaches of exclusivity and indemnity obligations. State common law will, in any event, usually permit a licensee to terminate the agreement if the licensor's breach of the agreement thwarted the purpose of the agreement.

Liquidated damages in the form of accelerated minimum royalties are typically payable on termination by the licensor. This clause should make clear that the liquidated damages are not a "penalty." The licensee needs to make it clear that the liquidated damages are the licensor's exclusive remedy for the early termination of the agreement (but not for the breach that gave rise to the termination). The amount of liquidated damages that accelerate post-termination advertising fees is typically the subject of negotiation, especially in a weak economy that is often a buyer's (licensee's) market. The acceleration of all remaining minimum royalties and advertising fees, as liquidated damages is sometimes reduced to the minimums payable for twelve to eighteen months following termination.

Sell-Off

A licensee is typically afforded a period of from ninety to 180 days to sell off its inventory of the licensed products after the expiration of the Agreement. The licensee needs to make sure that such sell-off right includes work in process and goods in transit, not only its inventory of licensed products. The licensor, however, does not wish the licensee to make inordinate amounts of products at the end of the license and then "dump" large amounts of goods during the sell-off period. To prevent such dumping, the license agreement may preclude manufacturing during the last four months of the term or set up a standard limiting manufacturing in the last contract year to that of the prior contract year.

Much negotiation revolves around whether a terminated licensee may sell off goods on the same basis as if the agreement expired. Major brand owners typically bar the terminated licensee from selling off goods. A reasonable compromise is to preclude the terminated licensee from selling off goods only if the basis for termination was a serious one, e.g., non-payment, failure to indemnify or failure to maintain insurance, thus permitting a sell-off in the unlikely event that termination occurred due to a more minor event of default. In any sell-off period, the licensee must obviously still comply with all terms and conditions of the contract.

The licensor is customarily given the right to purchase the licensee's remaining inventory before sell-off begins. The licensee should make sure that:

a. such purchase rights excludes licensed products for which it possess binding orders and
b. the purchase price is based on the landed duty paid cost of the goods and not an ambiguous price payable by the licensee on "market value" or "cost".

In order to provide a seamless transition after expiration of the license, the agreement should permit a new licensee to obtain orders and make goods during the last six months of the term only for products to be shipped after the term.

Boilerplate for Miscellaneous Provisions

The miscellaneous or boilerplate provisions are quite important. The licensor must insist that the forum be in the state and county where it is located, and that the law of the licensor's state shall apply. Some licensors prefer to be in an arbitration, others in court. When I represent a licensor, I want to be in court and have easier access to an injunctive relief if I need stop a terminated licensee from selling product. As a licensor, I also want to be before a judge who is more likely to look at the four corners of the contract than an arbitrator who may seek to cut the proverbial baby in half. When representing a licensor, I always include a loser pays the winner's legal fees provision. I want the licensee to know that they will be paying my legal fees as well as their own. They will not be able to factor in what they think my client will spend on legal fees if they offer a settlement. My client_that licensed a novel product line sued a licensee that was a much bigger company for the minimum royalties payable in the final contract year. Our client probably could not have afforded to litigate the case to trial. However, since the licensee knew it was going to lose at trial and pay two sets of lawyers, it settled the case very favorably for our client.

Common Licensing Errors by Lawyers and Clients

1. Clients err in using lawyers in licensing transactions who are inexperienced in the field. Experienced licensing lawyers know where the bodies are buried in these agreements. Using an inexperienced practitioner in this field—even if he or she is otherwise a fine lawyer—is often the first and biggest mistake that clients make.
2. Some licensees sign on for a five-year term, which gives them a sense of certainty, but can lock them into onerous minimum obligations. Instead, the licensee should obtain a three-year initial term with a six month start-up and a three year renewal option.
3. Parties often put too much reliance on their lawyer in the process, and fail to do their own homework about the other party, or the deal itself. Before signing the agreement, the licensee must be confident that the brand will work in the licensed product category. A license agreement should not be based on wishful thinking, but on hard analysis that will help forecast whether the agreement is going to work for the party.
4. Some brand owners do not believe enough in their own brand and make short run decisions. This is a clear mistake.

License Agency Agreements: Brief But Tricky

Licensing agents play a significant role in the licensing world. They help brand owners obtain licenses for product categories. They also help prospective licensees find brands they can license to open up new distribution channels and/or retail doors. Some larger licensing agencies may also manage the brand and even handle the legal work for the brand owner (though this is an obvious conflict—since the agent's lawyer is anxious to get deals closed so as to enable agency fees to be received by its client, it may not be as objective as it should concerning problems with the prospective deal).

License agency agreements in the fashion industry are often for one year. As with the licenses themselves, the agency agreements are either exclusive or non-exclusive. In exclusive contracts, the agent is paid regardless of whether it brought the deal—and all licensee candidates must be referred to the agent. Some agents will only work on an exclusive basis—they do not want to be in competition with the licensor itself or other agents. Other agents, especially in this tough economic climate, are willing to work on a non-exclusive basis. Agents doing that must carefully draft the agreement to avoid being ripped off. The non-exclusive agent does not want to disclose the name of the prospective licensee or brand without a contractual procedure in place which insures that it will get paid if a deal is done.

The agency agreement (from a company perspective) must carefully limit the territory and assignment. The company typically does not wish to give the agent worldwide rights or the rights as to all company brands.

The agreement should provide that the agent will be paid if a license agreement gets signed not only during the term but during a "tail period" of from four months to a year after the term ends. The company should make sure that the tail provision requires reasonable agent progress on the license during the term itself for the agent to take advantage of the tail period.

Agents that find licensees for brand owners typically are paid a percentage of the royalties received by the brand owner on the qualifying agreement. Those fees can range from fifteen percent to thirty percent of royalties received. The company paying an agent to find a brand will typically pay one to two percent of its net sales made under qualifying license agreements.

The company should resist the company being the collection agent in the license agreement. The company should receive its royalties. At most, the company should agree to the agent's fees (not all royalties) being paid by the licensee pursuant to the license agreement.

The duration of fee payment is often a subject of negotiation. The agent's form agreement typically provides for the fee to be paid over the life of the license agreement, including all renewals and amendments. The company may seek to reduce the period of time to just the initial term and/or to have the percentage rate decline over time.

The agent should receive a copy of each license agreement and copies of all sales and royalty reports received by the brand owner or sent by the company when the client is the licensee. The agent should also insist on audit rights and a loser pays the winner's legal fees provision.

Understanding Factoring Agreements

Factoring continues to play a significant role in the financing of fashion companies. A factor lends against the accounts receivables of its client. The receivable is assigned to the factor upon the shipment and invoicing of the subject goods. Upon the creation of the receivable, the factor advances a percentage (from 60 percent to 90 percent) of the receivable. The remainder is credited to the customer's account on receipt of payment. If product is shipped to a credit-approved retail customer, within the amounts credit approved by the factor for that customer, and the retailer fails to pay the invoiced amount solely due to the its inability to pay, the factor will, after the passage of a specified period of time, pay the client the unpaid amount due on the invoice.

For good reason, this segment of this chapter is much briefer than the first discussion about license agreements. License agreements are the subject of much negotiation. Negotiations over factoring agreements are typically much more limited.

Having said that, there are issues that are often negotiated. The fashion company should not sign on to a more than a one-year term—it needs to maintain flexibility over its financial arrangements. Factors often seek to impose minimum factoring fees. If the factor does not receive the minimum fee its client must make up the difference. Especially where the company to be factored is a small one, an annual minimum fee may well be reasonable. A larger factor wants to know that it will receive at least the minimum sum; without that minimum obligation, the deal may not be worthwhile for the factor. However, factors sometime seek to impose minimum monthly or quarterly fee amounts. These minimums should be resisted by the fashion company—in a seasonal business in which certain months or even quarters may have limited invoices to be factored, these periodic minimums could cause the client to pay fee amounts substantially above the annual minimum amount.

The fashion company should also seek to minimize the "collection days," or the period of time the factor will apply to credit the client's account for a payment even if the payment was already received.

Similarly, the fashion company should seek to minimize the period of non-payment that must occur before the factor will pay the client on the credit approved order of the insolvent retailer.

Savvy companies will also seek to cap the cost and frequency of "field visits" by the factor in monitoring its client's business.

Typically, factoring agreements are replete with fee and expense reimbursements to be made by the client. The client should require that such fees and expenses be "reasonable."

Sales Representative Agreements

Often, a new company will retain an independent, multi-line showroom to handle its sales: the new company may not be able to afford its own sales person and/or lack the retail contacts to properly launch its brand at retail. Multi-line showrooms have established relationships with retailers and can present the product of the new company in the most favorable light. Before retaining a sales representative, however, the company should try to learn of the sales representative's knowledge of the company's market and experience with the particular products. The company should also learn if the sales representative represents any of the company's competitors.

Some sales reps try to get a two year agreement and often try to require the company to pay a fee at the end of the term if the agreement is not renewed.. A fashion company does, however, not want to retain a representative for more than one year and should resist any buy-out clause.

Sales commissions are paid on the invoice price of goods shipped, not on orders. However, the sales reps often seek to impose a commission on a minimum of a percentage of orders obtained, e.g., 85 percent of orders, regardless of shipment. The company must ensure that such orders are both approved by the company and its factor to be counted in the equation. The company should make sure that the sales rep takes good care of its sample line while in the sale rep's possession and that it will promptly return the samples at the agreement's end. Some sales reps seek to retain the samples until its commissions are fully paid. The company should resist that.

It is very common for fashion companies to retain West Coast and East Coast reps.

A common area of concern is how to deal with sales coming from outside of the territory of the sales rep. Sales may come into the California showroom from a buyer in New York, or conversely sales could hit the New York office from a buyer based in California. Often, those commissions are divided up between the two reps.

Conclusion

Although the growing importance of on-line business is obviously changing the business of fashion, agreements of the kind discussed in this chapter will continue to provide the contractual backbones of the industry. Lawyers practicing in this field must, to be effective, understand both the business and legal aspects of the subject transaction. In so doing, they should encourage their clients to approach the transaction in a thoughtful manner that will consider both short term and long term pitfalls and opportunities.

Charles Klein is a partner and the head of the fashion practice at Davidoff Malito & Hutcher LLP, a mid-town Manhattan general practice law firm. Charles Klein has, for more than twenty-five years, worked with clients ranging from start-ups to major brand owners in the fashion, home, and accessory industries, handling a wide variety of commercial matters, including domestic and international license and distribution agreements, factoring agreements, sales representation agreements, and mergers and acquisitions.

Mr. Klein was the founding president of both The Fashion Roundtable and The Fashion Service Network and is the editor/publisher of Fashion & The Law. *Mr. Klein's articles about fashion legal issues have appeared in* MR Magazine, License! *magazine and* The Fashion Mannuscript. *He has also lectured widely on licensing matters before the New York State Society of CPAs, Fashion Group International, and the Accessories Council.*

When Licensing and Branding Meet

Douglas Hand

Partner

Hand Baldachin & Amburgey LLP

ASPATORE

Introduction

The issues involved in licensing and branding are interrelated. Licensing enables a brand with an established trademark to leverage the value of that trademark by expanding geographic territories and product lines to cover regions and product offerings. In my practice, I typically represent licensors; what follows is an evaluation of licensing and compliance in fashion law from a perspective that takes into account the needs and wishes of most licensors.

Licensing Motivation and General Terms

The typical license for a fashion industry company in clothing involves an extension into complementary products, such as accessories, jewelry, eyewear, and fragrance, with possible later extensions into other product lines, such as cosmetics, linens, tabletop decor, and furniture. Kenneth Cole, Vera Wang, and Martha Stewart are good examples of companies that actually produce few categories of products but have a significant brand presence across product categories through licensing. A representative geographic license covers an expansion into another territory, such as Southeast Asia, or country, such as China, where the licensee typically has an established production and distribution network.

Many major brands, such as like Calvin Klein, Tommy Hilfiger, and Ralph Lauren, have expanded globally through geographic licensing. When the licensee is up to the task and the licensor is committed to the project, the business around the new product or territory is established more quickly and at a lower overall cost than the licensor would be able to achieve by entering into the product category or region directly.

Royalties

Licenses almost uniformly have a sales-based royalty payment from licensee to licensor with net sales, a term that I have seen defined in many ways. Guaranteed minimum sales or guaranteed minimum royalties are a plus for the licensor and can typically be had unless leverage is disparate. It is important for the client to keep notes on early conversations the client has had with the licensee when the licensee is trying to "sell" the brand on the license, as these conversations often tread into what kinds of sales volumes the licensee expects to be able to achieve and can form the basis for minimums in the contract.

In drafting a licensing agreement, an attorney should push for there to be, as a consequence of a licensee not achieving minimum sales levels, the right to terminate the license by the licensor instead of a payment of the royalty shortfall. Most brands want their licensed products to be marketed well and sold to happy customers who may buy other branded products. Allowing a cure through a shortfall payment allows the licensee to do a bad job and still maintain the license simply by writing a check.

Marketing Minimum

A marketing minimum or commitment may also be included, which may involve a contribution of cash to the brand's overall sales campaign. From the licensee's perspective, this is a further cost but at least one that goes to a business expense of the licensor, which should support revenues for the licensee.

License Terms and Renewals

License terms vary, but for most products and geographic regions, a three to five year term is common. Renewal periods, which are usually another two to three years and generally occur not once, but twice, are almost always asked for by the licensee and, depending upon the licensee's leverage, renewals may be granted.

The justification for renewals is that more time than the initial term is needed to fully recoup the investment to start the brand in a new category or region. This justification goes away, of course, if the licensee is taking over a product category or region in which another licensee has already laid this ground work by virtue of an earlier license. If there are some sales criteria provided in order for the license to be renewed, that is clearly better for the licensee.

In lieu of a unilateral right to renew being in the purview of the licensee, rights of first refusal and rights of first negotiation are sometimes granted. It is important to make sure these rights take place in advance of the end of the license so that the licensor will have an opportunity to move the license to a new licensee, should that become necessary, without any seasonal break in the product offering. It is also important to note that the initial annual period of the term is longer than one year because of the investment of time during the start-up phase of the license. Three to six months (in addition to an annual period) is representative but I have seen even longer periods.

A Proper Licensing Fit

Lawyers advising potential licensors need to be mindful of the aesthetic and overall philosophy of their clients before taking the time and expense of negotiating a license agreement. This is not just an issue of personal fit but also a relevant business concern, since in the eyes of consumers the licensor and licensee are a single company.

For instance, if a loyal consumer of a high-end women's wear brand ends up purchasing a pair of branded sunglasses that do not echo the design sensibilities of the clothes, there is confusion about the brand and what it represents. This is bad enough, but much worse is if the sunglasses are poorly manufactured and break and cannot be returned, even after an unpleasant tussle on the phone with a sales representative. Then all brand goodwill with that customer, and perhaps others within the customer's orbit, is lost.

Uncomfortable Conversations

While aesthetic and philosophy issues could theoretically be fleshed out during term sheet negotiations, this is rarely the case (for a sample term sheet see Appendix Q). Term sheets do not delve into such issues, so this is an area where an attorney needs to force the client to have possibly uncomfortable conversations with the potential licensor to make sure they agree with respect to not only design sensibilities and product quality, but also price-point, marketing and public relations, labor issues, and sustainability and environmental concerns.

Using a Licensing Agent

For an attorney, these conversations can present a difficult client-management problem, which can be rendered more or less difficult if there is a licensing agent involved. If the agent is a good one, seeking to match licensors to licensees for the long-term benefit of both, the attorney has an advocate to elicit the hard questions. If, however, the agent is more interested in a commission than a good fit, it complicates matters. Since many licenses are for three to five years with renewals that can be in the control of the license, a good fit is essential.

In cases of a smaller licensor where the head designer is the point person, if there is a counterpart at the licensee with whom the designer has bonded or whom the designer trusts, consider negotiating certain key provisions, such as a reasonable approval right over that person's successor or, ideally, a termination right if that person leaves.

Cultural Differences

Cultural differences are also important to note and should be pointed out to a client at the beginning of the licensing process. While most lawyers doing international licensing transactions are familiar with cultural differences present within Japanese, Chinese, Korean, Italian, French, Brazilian, and other licensors and are able to navigate these differences in negotiations to get a transaction closed, there might be misunderstandings based on language barriers and cultural dissimilarities between licensee and licensor as the deal rolls forward.

Design Approval Procedures

An important element to ensure fit is maintained is the degree of design approvals and the procedures for these approvals. Approval procedures can be detailed; there is a common perception that as long as the licensor has the final approval and no deemed approval is permitted, then the brand can be assured that nothing will go into production that the brand is not comfortable with. Unfortunately, that is not always the case. A licensee is rarely willing to allow the designer brand to hold up the process of production to the point where the licensee might actually miss a season. Missing a season is usually not good for the licensor and its business, either.

Design approval usually calls for some degree of sophistication and detail in the approval process. The understanding of the licensor's and licensee's lawyers of design process, production schedules, shipping, and wholesale practice is imperative. In a seasonal collection, there is a calendar that should be adhered to and built into the agreement so that licensor approvals throughout various stages of the process are clear.

Phases in Design Approval

Typically in such an agreement there would be a design approval (approval of the actual written or sketched design of the product), an initial sample approval (a sample of the product manufactured in a single run from the design), a final sample approval, and perhaps a first assembly-run approval (an approval of the first product to come off the production line).

From the licensor's perspective, "sole and absolute discretion" in rendering the approval is the goal while the licensee will argue for a "commercially reasonable" standard and further seek to have approval "deemed" to have occurred if the licensor does not proffer a specific approval or rejection. Deemed approval negotiation can be a bloody sport, a tortured mechanism in which the licensor has a period to render the approval after the design or sample is submitted with confirmed delivery. If that time period elapses, the licensee must send another notice giving the licensor another, shorter, time period to comply. The licensee cannot have its production come to a grinding halt because the licensor or designer is unavailable or incapable.

Approvals also cover all uses of the trademark, not just on the product itself, but also the product's packaging, wrapping, hangtags, labels, displays, and signage.

With a smaller licensor, where the head designer is the point person, do not lose sight of the potential investment of time, which means time spent away from the licensor's core business. For design or sample approvals, make sure the designs or samples are sent to the designer wherever the designer is.

Ensuring Quality and Integrity

Related to approvals are the elements of quality control and approved manufacturers. The licensor's right to approve designs and samples is meaningless if the quality demonstrated in the samples is not maintained throughout production.

The Right to Inspect

It is typical to insert a right by the licensor to inspect, upon request, items on the sales floor or on the production line or the manufacturing plants themselves. This right can extend beyond the products to the raw materials, such as cloth, leather, thread, and buttons, as well as the packaging and marketing elements so that the licensor can assure itself that the negotiated quality standards are being adhered to.

Labor Conditions

Labor conditions are both an ethical and a potential liability concern for the licensor; in my practice I ask for a representation from the licensee that it does not engage in conduct in violation of any labor law or practice and does not discriminate on the basis of race, national origin, religion, sex, age, disability, or sexual orientation. A covenant regarding illegal restraints on trade activities is also good to have from the licensee with respect to the manufacturers it uses. Note, however, that any obligation to ensure that the manufacturer, rather than the licensee itself, lives up to a standard may be hard for the licensee to bear.

Approved Manufacturers

A license often contains a list of approved manufacturers. To the extent that the client is not familiar with the list of manufacturers, the lawyer's experience in this area can provide useful insights. The licensee should also have the right to inspect, preferably at the licensor's expense, materials in the manufacturing process as well as general working conditions. For instance, if a client has represented that its products are eco-friendly, sustainable, "green," or cradle-to-cradle, such as Loomstate or Bodkin, or are produced with a positive social impact on the areas in which they are produced, such as TOM's Shoes and Common Threadz, then these inspection rights are paramount, as are strong covenants that the licensee will produce and use production facilities that are consistent with the client's mission statement.

Sales Channels

The retail customers that a licensor is permitted to sell to can be a hotly negotiated area, but the negotiation is usually among the principals rather than the lawyers. Generally, a brand will already have established retail channels it deals with and is comfortable with, channels that consumers have come to recognize as "carrying" the brand. These channels are, most important from the perspective of the brand, divisible based on price point. Preferably, the licensee is targeting the same or similar retail channels, perhaps in a different geographic region.

Consistent Presentation

The licensee is tasked with requiring all retail channels to present the product in a certain way. Often this is within a specifically fixtured in-store environment that is consistent with the brand's broader brand campaign. A licensee usually consults with the licensor on the look and feel of the sales environment and may provide marketing materials that it uses across product categories to fill out the space.

Downmarket versus Upmarket

While a licensor will rarely object to a proposed license to sell in upmarket channels, rarely is the licensee interested in that type of arrangement. Downmarket channels, where price points are lower but volume is significantly higher, are where many licensees want to sell products bearing the licensed mark, and therein lay one of the significant tensions between the parties.

Because the licensee's interest in the brand is shorter in term, the licensee often has little problem with diminishing the brand in the eyes of more affluent consumers to gain revenue. The license should contain a list of authorized retailers and have significant consequences, such as termination, if the licensee sells to unauthorized retailers.

Further Restrictions

There also need to be restrictions against giveaways, tie-ins, diversions, and potentially direct sales. Online sales, while traditionally restricted as well, have shifted a bit with the advent of more bespoke online retail environments, such as La Garconne, Gilt, Moda Operandi, and Net-A-Porter.

If sell-through rates through authorized channels are good, there are usually no issues. If, however, product goes unsold, either at wholesale or at retail, and is sent back to the licensee as a "charge-back," the licensee does not want to be left holding or destroying manufactured product and will seek to sell through closeout retailers and outlets.

<u>Closeouts</u>

Permitted closeout retailers are usually set forth in the license. If the licensor also has its own outlet stores, those retail locations can be used as well; a first option for the licensor to purchase closeouts, preferably at a greater discount, is important in this context. Caps on these types of closeout sales are important. If the market is flooded with the brand's products at sales prices, the brand equity can become greatly reduced. A percentage of 10 percent to 20 percent of actual net sales or the sales minimum is preferred. If that cap is breached, the licensor should have a right to terminate.

The provisions of the license governing closeout sales usually also cover the manner in which substandard product (seconds) may be sold off as well. However, it is usually preferable from the licensor's perspective if seconds can be repurposed or otherwise destroyed rather than sold at all. In such a provision, it is important to adhere to any environmental sensibilities or mission statements of the brand. Repurposing seconds, which includes removing all trademarks, and donating them to needy constituencies is not a costless endeavor, but has been used in several licenses to give clients a solution that both keeps any taint off their products and is consistent with their business principles.

Personal Services Provisions

It is not unusual for a licensee in a related product category or secondary line to have specified design services that are to be performed by the licensor's design team or head designer. If so, then a separate design fee may be appropriate to compensate the designer for the services. This fee can be paid directly to the individual, and usually is, or to the operating company of the brand as a "loan out," which, from the perspective of investors in the brand, may be more appropriate.

The licensor, not the licensee, should maintain the intellectual property created by the designer. Occasionally, licensees push this point but the downside risk for the licensor is that the licensor's designer may create a product that becomes intimately associated with the brand and can actually be sold without the trademark and yet still trade off the brand's goodwill.

Promotional Appearances

Promotional appearances by a designer are common and expected and can take on hallmarks of talent agreements. So if your client has particular travel, lodging, or dietary requirements, they should be included. Also consider whether bringing other members of the design team, a PR rep and/or a personal assistant is appropriate. If so, the costs of bringing along these people should be borne by the licensee.

Photo shoots, store visits, and speaking engagements may be included in the promotional services, but it is well to make sure the designer is comfortable taking on these duties.

It is important to make sure appearances are limited and only take place in accordance with the client's schedule, in particular if the designer is also integral to other elements of the licensee's business, which is not uncommon for smaller brands. In this regard, the licensee may expect the designer to sign the license individually, as well as the licensor, or the designer and licensor may have a separate design services agreement.

If the designer is the "face" of the brand on some level, a morality clause should be expected. I always tie that provision to some actual calculable diminution of value, such as a drop in sales levels, rather than to offending the community or public ridicule.

Structural Issues in Forming a Business Enterprise

In forming a business enterprise, there are elements specific to fashion companies that require attention: capturing any intellectual property (IP) contributed to the business upon its formation or created by it during its operations, the protection of IP assets, organizational flexibility, and insulation from different business liabilities.

In the specific context of licensing, the location of the trademark and the commitment for the designer, or "face" of the brand, are clearly important. The license must be signed by the trademark-holding entity or an entity with an appropriate license from the trademark-holding company. The license or design services agreement must be signed by the designer or the entity that holds the designer's employment agreement.

Crossing Business Endeavors

Fashion companies can span a few separate business endeavors. Traditionally, most fashion companies have wholesale accounts with major retailers, but many also have their own retail operations, which can be online or brick-and-mortar stores or both. Other companies also take on separate consulting jobs that may or may not involve a licensing of the trademark or the designer's name. Some have licensing as a model for a majority of their business. Others still have other components of their business, such as showroom operations or PR services. Each of these businesses require contracts for raw materials, products, services, employees, real estate, and other areas, and each of these other counterparties is a potential litigant, along with any customers or other entities these businesses deal with, in the event of a dispute.

Protecting Liabilities

Given this reality, it makes sense to attempt to insulate the liabilities of each of the distinct businesses, within a reasonable entity structural tree. For example, it would not be unusual for a business to have four separate entities: one top holding company; another company for production, which is the production and the wholesale business; a retail company, which may be both online retail and brick-and-mortar or a separate entity for each; and an IP holding company (see Appendix R for a sample structural chart).

Joint Ventures and Collaborations

On the topic of structural issues, the traditional licensing model is not the only arrangement that can be used to extend the brand into different product categories or geographic areas with a third party.

Joint Ventures

Joint ventures typically involve the formation of a special purpose vehicle (the JV), jointly owned by the licensor and a third party (the joint venture partner), which would have been the licensee in a traditional licensing context. Here, the JV is the licensee. The partner and the licensor split the JV's profits after covering the costs of its operations. There may be little or no royalty payment made to the licensor.

This arrangement reduces the downside risk of the third party that would have been the licensee in a traditional licensing context in that its cost outlay may be paid back before any payments are made to the licensor. In fact, the licensor, as an owner of the special purpose vehicle, may be required to partially fund its operations. The upside for the licensor is sharing a greater amount of the revenues than would be garnered in the mix of royalties, design fee, and marketing spend in a traditional license.

Collaborations

Collaborations or co-branding deals have increased in popularity and typically involve two brands putting their respective trademarks on a product within one or both of their respective product categories (see Appendix S for a list of collaboration discussion points). Fashion companies can co-brand with one another: Stella McCartney for Adidas, Richard Chai for Original Penguin by Munsingwear; or Florsheim by Duckie Brown; or with retailers: Karl Lagerfeld for Macy's, Lanvin for

H&M; or Rodarte for Target; or with companies completely outside the sphere of fashion: Nike-Apple; Lexus-Coach; Adidas-Porsche.

Collaborative or co-branding arrangements can expand the customer base of both brands by exposing core customers of each brand to the other. In addition, offering a product that responds to some apparent need of the customer can increase the perceived value of the brand. Often these arrangements can cover special or limited edition lines that appear at a retailer, such as a specialty store or retailer of private-label apparel, for a single season, as in the Target GO! and Uniqlo collaborations. While the limited term of these agreements mitigates risk and the parties are typically driven to speed the documentation process because of the seeming simplicity of the deal, IP protections are still essential in the agreement and should be built out in much the same way they would be for a longer-term traditional license.

Structurally, the license in a collaboration or co-branding deal is granted in one of two ways: the holder of one trademark, X, licenses it to the owner of another, Y, and the owner of Y produces and markets the XY brand; or the holder of trademark X and the holder of trademark Y each license their respective trademarks to a newly formed special purpose vehicle, which manufactures and markets the XY brand.

The former structure has the trappings of a traditional license, in which the holder of trademark X takes on the role of licensor and the holder of trademark Y takes on the role of licensee. The latter structure is a joint venture structure, as detailed above, but in this case with two separate licenses, which can make the arrangement more of a pure 50/50 joint venture and therefore easier to negotiate. In either case, it is important that each party acknowledge the other party's ownership of their existing trademark as well as ensure that the other party does not have rights to take the co-brand into product categories that would create confusion with the existing product offering.

The co-branding agreement should set forth, with some specificity, the physical placement of the two trademarks in conjunction with one another on the product itself as well as on marketing and PR materials.

An area that can get theoretically complicated is how to deal with any new trademark that might arise out of the combination of the two co-branded trademarks. Assuming both parties have disclaimed any ownership rights in the trademark of one another and have entered into a negative covenant not to file for registration of the joint mark anywhere in the world, there is rarely a trademark created by the combination of the two that would be permitted registration.

However, if elements separate and apart from the literal trademarks X and Y are used, such as a graphic element that links the two visually, the ownership of that element or a disclaimer of all potential rights to ownership of that element should be addressed in the co-branding agreement. In some cases, one brand may want to do further co-branding deals with other parties and use such a unifying element in future co-branded products. If that is the case, that brand should negotiate for clear residual rights or rights concurrent with the agreement if there are other products the brand seeks to co-brand with in different product categories, to ownership over that element and seek to obtain a trademark registration for it.

Termination of Agreements

When considering the termination rights under a collaboration or co-branding agreement, transformative changes in one of the parties should be considered. If one of the parties goes out of business, there should be a termination right on behalf of the other party. But what if the party not going out of business wants to continue using the co-branded trademark? This should be considered and continued usage or some wind-down period introduced. A termination right may also hold true in a merger with or an acquisition by a third party.

- In a licensing agreement, there should be a right to terminate the license by the licensor instead of a payment of the royalty shortfall. Allowing a cure through a shortfall payment allows the licensee to do a bad job and still maintain the license simply by writing a check.
- Lawyers need to be mindful of the esthetic and overall philosophy of their clients when negotiating a license agreement; in the eyes of consumers, the licensor and licensee are a single company.

- Because design approval calls for some degree of sophistication and detail in the approval process, the ability of the licensor's and licensee's lawyers to understand the design process, production schedules, shipping, and wholesale practice is imperative.
- The licensor's right to approve designs and samples is meaningless if the quality demonstrated in the samples is not maintained throughout production. Quality control includes the right to inspect and approve of manufacturing facilities.

Conclusion

The issues involved in licensing and branding are interconnected as licensing enables a brand to expand both geographically and in terms of its product offerings. The negotiation of the licensing agreement should therefore take into account the business realities of the licensor as well as the branding goals. An understanding of the business cycles in the fashion industry as well as the brand's station in the minds of retailers and customers is therefore vital. Throughout the negotiation process, ensuring IP protection (both from a pure legal enforcement perspective but also from a more nuanced brand positioning perspective) is going to be maintained is critical.

There are different legal structures that lead to the same result of a branded product offering being made available by a party other than the licensor. Joint ventures and collaborations are increasingly common and in some cases represent an obviously preferred structure to the traditional long-form license in the context of limited capsule collections.

Key Takeaways

- Be mindful of the esthetic and overall viewpoint of the potential licensor before taking the time and expense of negotiating a license agreement. Do the licensor and licensee "fit" from a business and philosophical perspective?
- Design approvals in the license usually calls for a degree of detail. The understanding of the licensor's and licensee's lawyers of design process, production schedules, shipping, and wholesale practice is imperative.

- What retail customers that a licensor is permitted to sell to, is a conversation the principals should have at an early stage and in an honest way. Letting the lawyers bat this issue back and forth can be a wasteful use of time.
- Design services and promotional appearances by a designer are common and can require the preparation and negotiation of separate agreements with the individual designer in addition to the license agreement.
- In landscape of deals, joint ventures and collaborations are increasingly seen and present some structural differences that the practitioner should keep in mind.

Douglas Hand is a partner with Hand Baldachin & Amburgey LLP. He began his legal career in the New York and Paris offices of Sherman & Sterling, working on public and private M&A transactions. Mr. Hand has represented fashion and lifestyle companies of all sizes throughout his career. His firm, Hand Baldachin & Amburgey, focuses on transactional matters for businesses where intellectual property is a core asset and includes many notable fashion houses among its clients.

As a member of the Business Advisory Council of the Council of Fashion Designers of America (CFDA), as well as the CFDA's Fashion Incubator Program, he is an active participant in the industry, serving on speaking panels and advising member fashion companies. Mr. Hand has also been asked to serve on the advisory board of the Fashion Law Institute of Fordham Law School, the world's first fashion law center, which instructs on intellectual property, business and finance, international trade, and government regulation in the fashion industry.

Dedication: *To my clients. I consider their fulfillment the best measure of my success.*

Working with Clients in the Fashion Industry: IP Tips and Trends

Ann K. Ford

Partner and Chair,

Trademark, Copyright and Media Practice

DLA Piper LLP (US)

ASPATORE

Introduction

As a trademark and copyright practitioner, I have always had a love of words and what they convey. But I also have an avid interest in design and fashion—this includes reading about the industry and its players, closely following fashion advertising and trends, and, of course, being a consumer. Therefore, what we are discussing—fashion law—takes on a highly personal and enjoyable aspect for me. To be able to work with colleagues and clients who share that enthusiasm makes it even more exciting. My career has always been centered around the branding of products and services in many different kinds of industries. However, the fashion industry, because it is so externalized and so visible to consumers, is a particularly interesting industry to pursue. During my career, I have worked for many apparel companies and emerging start-up companies, a number of which that have gone on to become very well-known. It is always interesting to help these clients develop and protect their original brands and designs. This helps my clients fulfill their artistic and commercial objectives and, in turn, helps my team and I protect brands and designs from a legal standpoint. That's the fun of working with a fashion company on the ground floor in particular—the ability to see an idea reach fruition and ultimately being able to wear the clothes, shoes or accessories, sold under the brand.

An Overview of Fashion Law

I would define fashion law as an area of the law that focuses on the full panoply of needs that clients in the fashion industry regularly face, which includes trademark, copyright, patent, and trade secret issues, transactional and licensing matters, export/import, regulatory issues, employment and labor issues, and others. These areas have always been of concern to clients in the fashion industry; however, it has not been until fairly recently that it has come into its own as a specialized area of the law. Of course, counterfeiting issues have been at the forefront of the industry intensely for the past two-plus decades, but the finer, more complex points of fashion law have been a more recent development. Generally, fashion law has been viewed as encompassing a combination of artistic, commercial, and legal elements. Today, fashion law is a central part of the industry. Interestingly, several law schools now have programs dedicated specifically to fashion law. I focus my role as a fashion law practitioner on protection of the client's investment and its concepts through intellectual property (IP) law concepts, primarily trademark, trade dress, copyright, trade secret, and patent. These intellectual property concepts are the best ways in which to seek to protect creative designs for clothing and accessories and their branding, as well as the methods for how they are sold. The design, marketing, selling, branding, and "look and feel" of apparel and related goods, and how these goods are positioned in the marketplace, are all critically important components of our clients' businesses that routinely fall under the realm of fashion law.

Some Core Tools of Protection for Fashion Industry Clients

Some fashion industry players create goods so significant that these goods immediately become a brand unto themselves. For example, the haute couture types are the true innovators, such as Chanel and Hermes. Their creations become part and parcel of their brands, and certain aspects of what they create must be strongly protected from a legal perspective in order to realize and maintain the brand's value in business. Of course, the brand itself must also be protected. Thus, there are generally three buckets of IP protection that members of the fashion industry can avail themselves of—most notably under trademark/trade dress protection, copyright protection, and patent protection.

Trademark/Trade Dress Protection

In brief, a trademark is any word, name, symbol, device, or combination thereof used by an entity in commerce to identify and distinguish its goods from those sold or provided by others, and to indicate the source of the goods. Trademarks are associated with the goods of a particular business and serve to identify and distinguish those goods from those of a competitor. Common trademarks include company and product or service names, logos, and can be encompassed in design elements, as demonstrated below. Trademarks are important because they often represent one of the most valuable assets of a business. A trademark, particularly in the realm of a high fashion brand, has tremendous monetary value associated with it. A trademark symbolizes the goodwill created by a business in association with a particular good or service. In sum, trademarks indicate to the consuming public where the goods emanate from (i.e., the *source* of the goods).

Trademarks not only serve to differentiate competitors to support commerce, but also serve to protect the consumers. Consumers want to know what they are getting, that is, that the brand is the brand they think they are buying, and the quality associated with that brand is intact. It is not just the markings, logos, and names, but also the aspects of the designs that can be considered as source identifiers. For example, you know a Hermes bag because of the unique clasp, which makes that single piece of hardware a strong identifier for the brand. Thus, the designer, as well as the consumer, can have a strong status protection because of that single detail on a Hermes bag.

Further, trade dress encompasses the total image, meaning the distinctive look and feel or overall commercial impression created by a product or its packaging. Specifically, trade dress may include features such as shape, size, color, texture, graphics, or even particular sales techniques. For example, a company's website, the overall design of a shoe, or the distinctive style of a retail outlet.

Hot Trademark Issue: The Red Soles Case

One of the hottest fashion law issues today is the red soles controversy. Christian Louboutin, famed French fashion designer, recently sued Yves Saint Laurent (YSL) for allegedly infringing his claimed trademark—the infamous red-lacquered bottoms of Louboutin's high fashion footwear. Louboutin sought $1 million in damages for alleged trademark infringement and counterfeiting. Louboutin has been selling his fancy footwear with the alluring red bottoms, which cost anywhere from $450 to $3,500 a pair, apparently since 1992. Louboutin claims that YSL has been selling women's shoes with red outsoles, costing about $600 to $800 a pair, that are nearly identical to his women's shoes in the same upscale department stores, such as Saks Fifth Avenue, Barneys, and Bergdorf Goodman.

Under US trademark law, color can be protected and registered if it is not "functional," "ornamental," or "decorative" and if has "acquired distinctiveness" for the relevant goods and services (color itself cannot be deemed "inherently distinctive"). For example, a color would be considered functional if it is essential to the use or purpose of the article or affects the cost or quality of the article (e.g., the color black for outboard boat motors or the color yellow or orange for safety signs). Furthermore, a color would be considered ornamental or decorative if competitors use the same or similar color for their products (e.g. floral pattern design of morning glories and leaves for tableware are merely decorative). Therefore, color can only acquire distinctiveness upon a showing of exclusive and continuous trademark use in commerce for more than five years and concrete evidence that the color is perceived as a mark for the relevant goods or services by consumers.

In this case, the United States Patent and Trademark Office found that Louboutin's red-lacquered soles acquired the requisite distinctiveness for trademark protection and granted a registration covering "women's high fashion designer footwear." However, the US District Court for the Southern District of New York denied Louboutin's request for a preliminary injunction against YSL, finding that the color red served primarily "ornamental and aesthetic functions vital to robust competition" as opposed to a valid and protectable trademark brand. Louboutin has since appealed this court's decision before the US Court of Appeals for the Second Circuit.

The Red Soles case has generated a significant amount of controversy with strong arguments on both sides of the issue. Thus, while it appears that a significant amount of investment went into the red soles on the part of the brand owner to create a source identifier, and consumers did come to see the red soles as emanating from Louboutin, there is a rather large camp of those who believe that no one should be able to monopolize a color or an arguably ornamental feature as a trademark. The red sole has given rise to the issue of color depletion, which is related to the argument that one can only have so many colors to use in its wares. For the up-and-coming companies and those that do not want to be fettered by first entrants, you can understand where there might be a little bit of tension in the industry and in the courts. Thus, these shoes have certainly triggered much discussion in the industry regarding all kinds of apparel innovation.

Copyright: The Murk in Fashion Trends

Copyright law protects works of "original authorship." Specifically, copyright law protects the "expression of ideas," not the "ideas" themselves. In the fashion world, "expression" that has been protected includes unique fabric designs, and original ornamental features of jewelry, watches, belts, and handbags. Copyright rights are created upon the creation of the work itself. In the United States, copyright exists immediately upon the physical creation of the work. Priority of creation, substantial similarity, and whether there is access to the prior design are the core elements of a copyright infringement claim. However, when one looks into the copyright bucket of IP protection, things get a little murkier with respect to fashion designs themselves.

If you were to look at every well-known fashion magazine this month, you will see common trends of "what's hot" throughout the fashion industry reflected on the glossy spreads. While a particularly unique design might stand out, you will also see that there is a dominant color every season—royal blue or cranberry, for example—or certain cuts or features, such as pencil skirts or pleats. No one can claim exclusivity in these sorts of designs and features, not only because they are "ideas," but also because trends rise and fall so quickly in the fashion industry that making a claim is practically irrelevant.

Simply put, clients must understand that there is no blanket copyright protection for fashion design in general in the United States at this time. This concept can be extremely frustrating for clients, so we are often called upon to seek alternative avenues for them to protect and enforce their rights.

Hot Copyright Issue: Possible US Copyright Protection for Fashion Design

Notably, because there are no iron-clad guidelines governing copyright law in the context of fashion design, such as those that you would find for software, books, art work, there is a tradition within the industry of borrowing or building upon trends and other marketplace concepts. However, that could change over time. For example, at the time of this printing, there is legislation pending on Capitol Hill that aims to strike a balance between copyright protection and innovation from borrowing.

In 2010, New York Senator Charles E. Schumer introduced legislation that could provide copyright protection for fashion designs. In December 2010, the Senate Judiciary Committee passed the Innovative Design Protection and Piracy Prevention Act, or Senate Bill S. 3728 (IDPPPA). However, because the full Senate never voted on it before the end of its session, the bill had to be reintroduced this year. In its latest iteration, currently H.R. 2511, the House of Representatives Subcommittee on Intellectual Property, Competition and the Internet held a hearing on the bill on July 15, 2011. On October 12, 2011, the United States Chamber of Commerce released a letter in support of the IDPPPA.

The IDPPPA takes a narrow approach to applying copyright law in the context of fashion. First, IDPPPA will provide a three-year term of protection to new and original fashion designs commencing from the time the item is displayed publicly. Second, it will protect only "unique" designs that are truly distinguishable. Third, it will only cover designs created after its enactment, leaving earlier designs in the public domain.

Infringement claims will be reserved for "substantially *identical*" copies, which means "an article of apparel which is so similar in appearance as to likely be mistaken for the protected designs, and contains only those differences in construction or designing which are merely trivial." This "substantially identical" standard is more stringent than previously proposed legislation which maintained Trademark Law's "substantially similar" standard. As such, a plaintiff will have the burden of proof on these elements, and the legislation directs courts to consider a "totality of the circumstances" in determining whether a claim for infringement has been adequately pleaded.

If the IDPPPA becomes law, fashion designs will automatically be protected upon fixation, as with all copyrights' holders in the United States, so that designers do not have to register designs with the US Copyright Office. This aspect of the IDPPPA is particularly noteworthy because most federal circuits require copyright registration as a prerequisite to filing suit. To discourage frivolous lawsuits, IDPPPA sets out strict "originality" guidelines that a plaintiff must establish before raising a claim. These guidelines include the following three elements:

1. The plaintiff must prove its design had not existed previously; that it is wholly original. The plaintiff must prove it is "a unique, distinguishable, non-trivial and non-utilitarian variation over prior designs";
2. The plaintiff must prove a defendant's design is substantially identical; and
3. The plaintiff must prove that the defendant had the opportunity to have seen the design before it was released for public distribution.

If a dispute does arise, a defendant will be required to show that the design in question was created separately and independently from the protected design or that it was copied from a design already in the public domain. Under the IDPPPA, damages are limited.

As is common with legislation, there remain subjective issues with the IDPPPA. Fashion styles are constantly evolving and inspired by the art of past designers. Thus, under this new law, it will likely be hard to argue that a new design had not existed previously and that it is wholly original. Also, only an article that is "unique, distinguishable, non-trivial and non-utilitarian variation over prior designs for similar types of articles," qualifies as a fashion design. Although fashion is highly artistic, it is unclear how a court will decide what is truly non-trivial and non-utilitarian.

Fair use proponents—individuals and organizations alike—have opposed the IDPPPA, arguing that such protection could stifle fashion innovation: fashion design, they argue, has thus far evolved effectively without copyright protection: as taste-makers introduce new concepts, which are imitated and sold cheaper, industry leaders are driven to remain distinctive and innovative. Others in the industry have chosen not go on the record to oppose, but may do so behind the scenes—or simply hope that the legislation stalls out. Whether this legislation goes forward or not, we can be sure that legislation governing fashion protection under copyright law will continue to be introduced.

Patent Protection: Functionality Meets the Law

Patent law generally seeks to protect the functionality of an item (utility patent), as well as certain non-functional design elements (design patent). Thus, because there are certain functional elements, for example, that one cannot product under trade dress, protection may be provided under patent law. Utility patent protection is particularly important for goods such as shoes, footwear, sports bras, and other items that have some purpose or functionality. As such, utility patents usually cannot be used to protect fashion designs, such as jewelry or accessories, unless the design includes some type of mechanical improvement.

A design patent protects novel aesthetic elements of an article of manufacture (e.g., the ornamental aspects of jewelry, watches, belts, hats, handbags, rings, etc.). These designs must be new and sufficiently different from all prior designs. For example, Louis Vuitton Malletier owns a design patent for the "ornamental design for a handbag" and Tag Heuer owns a design patent for the "ornamental design for a watch."

The Balance Between Protection and Innovation

Certain fashion law concepts have, on the one hand, made it easier for emerging companies to jump into the market, but, on the other, it has become a bit of a free-for-all, especially for companies that are leaders in fashion and spend a lot of time developing and seeking to protect their fashion brands and concepts. In other words, there is a fine balance between protection and innovation. For example, if a client wants to jump in on a trend line too close to a competitor, we will tell them it is not a good idea, particularly if they are peer companies. A big part of the calculation for the clients we work with is not whether our arguments would win in the Supreme Court, even if one knows that the other side ultimately cannot protect a certain aspect of the product, but whether it makes sense to get caught up in a lawsuit for twelve months or much longer.

A lawsuit is an expensive undertaking even if the client wins in the end. It diverts the client's attention away from what it should be focusing on—creating and selling excellent products. Of course, we want the client to preserve its place on the trend line, and we will give them the likelihood of what is going to happen and then they make their own business decision. That is the defensive approach. On the offensive side, certain clients are known for a certain kind of a cut of clothing or other signature features, such as a certain cut or type of waistband, a particular fabric, etc. These clients also have extremely valuable brand names. We help them focus on the signature aspects that are valuable and protectable. If they can draw a line in the sand, and they decide to aggressively protect their unique characteristics, then that is a very productive use of resources.

However, if there is some ubiquitous design that appears in a variety of brands, there is no point in getting distracted with that type of situation. The client may spend a lot of time chasing a company and will probably lose in the end—not to mention losing its focus on creating innovative clothing. It takes companies a long time to understand that they cannot protect everything, but instead should focus on the aspects of their product that the customer sees as intimately related to the brand. That is why the identity and protection of the brand is so important: specifically the use of brand names and logos and other protectable elements, as well as those signature concepts that act as source identifiers—these are the concrete elements that must be aggressively protected without distraction.

The Economy and Fashion

The economy has forced those in the fashion industry to be very cognizant of the resources it spends on lawyers, and to keep the resources in the business. As such, moving the business forward is of paramount concern. Nevertheless, brand owners cannot sit idly by while other parties erode their brands or cause confusion in the market place. The economic environment has, therefore, exerted contrary and conflicting pressures on the fashion industry. You can see it in the amount of money, time, and effort certain fashion companies will spend to demonstrate to the world that their creations are proprietary to them. Many designers are creating their own affordable options and selling them through giant "big box" retailers. Others are going out in September or October right after the school season but before the Christmas season. The notion of selling high-end merchandise from a known designer at affordable prices is working well in this economic environment, especially for consumers of more modest means. Other designers are fighting back with their own modestly priced versions of their high-end products that they can sell legitimately. They are creating a second-tier market for themselves.

The Pressure for Trendy but Affordable Clothing

There is a huge desire in the marketplace for affordable, contemporary, and trendy clothes. Several companies and retail shops are focused on fashion directed to young adults and adolescents. They borrow heavily from higher-priced apparel makers and designers and offer it at a much lower price point. The legitimized third-tier retailers that cater to the youth market and sell at a much lower price point borrow heavily from designers on behalf of consumers seeking an affordable option are adding to the complexity. This is not back-room or back-alley counterfeiting, but a bona fide retail operation that is "borrowing" from the trend. Occasionally, the "affordable" retailer will stray from the trend line and take substantial elements from the couture or higher-end brand that devalue or otherwise threaten the higher-bend brand—and this must be stopped. The explosive growth of social media to create and sustain excitement for brands and fashion fuels this, because it keeps the pressure on to create yet another affordable and trendy line. Retailers and fashion designers reach out to their fan base and customer base 365 days a year, rather than in advertisements in the September issues of fall fashion magazines. The trend will continue—fashion buzz is going to be generated online and interactively.

Working with Fashion Clients on IP Issues

When I meet a client who has not done a lot of work in the IP area, there are extra steps that I take to ensure that they understand the entire process. Then there are clients who are sophisticated: they have in-house counsel and have a solid understanding of how to protect their designs. I converse with them in a kind of code and simply execute on previously agreed-upon strategy. However, emerging companies usually need me to walk them through what they can and cannot protect, the limits of such protection, and where the fine line is between borrowing trends and infringing. We talk about the buckets of IP protection and how they relate to what the client wants to protect. We also talk about a budget for legal protection. Even the biggest and most profitable luxury brand clients have budgets and they are fairly aggressive about keeping IP and fashion law work within a budget.

Setting Strategic Priorities for IP Protection

Setting strategic priorities for protection of a client's IP can help to protect its budget. With counsel's advice, the client must decide how to protect the different aspects of its IP, such as design elements, fabric patterns, logos, brand names, functional items, or design items that can be protected under patent law. The client must also consider how to secure rights from the people it works with, but who are not employees. This is particularly important because under copyright and trademark law, what employees create belongs to the company, but what independent contractors create, absent an affirmative assignment, usually belongs to the independent contractor. You would be surprised how many otherwise sophisticated companies design a retail store and unwittingly hand over all of the rights to their interior designers or architects. Similarly, many companies allow their graphic designers to own their logos outright, or enable their web designers to claim ownership of their websites. Companies in the fashion industry often farm out many pieces of their products. Therefore, it is critical that they implement procedures to ensure that all IP, no matter who is actually creating it, is owned by the company itself.

Similarly, trade secrets must be actively protected. This is a concept that is used in general employment law. The client may own certain IP, for example, that only employees and certain people on the inside know about. Anyone who sees that information must sign a confidentiality agreement and the company must undertake measures to keep that information confidential.

Helping the Client Decide What to Protect

One of the first steps to discuss with the client is deciding what IP can and should be protected. I discuss this with the client, but I also make sure to undertake an independent determination of existing key IP assets—including trademarks (brands and logos) and signature protectable items, for example. We also discuss proposed brands and signature items that may be on the drawing board. I want to know everything I can about these items, including how and when products will be advertised to the public and the extent and scope of the proposed use so that we have all of the necessary rights locked down prior to any launch. After we determine the IP that we want to protect, we will put it in the appropriate IP buckets of protection and develop a budget for each. This makes it possible to prioritize where to apply the resources. For example, if an item is going to be a flash for a single season, it is usually not worth protecting. However, designs, fabrics, and logos that are going to be with the company for a while, and perhaps expanded upon and branded across different product lines, must be protected.

Another factor involves international protection that does not break the budget. Fashion designers and other companies are aggravated by the fact that they start a design in one jurisdiction and then, as it becomes popular in other jurisdictions, they find themselves being precluded from exploiting that brand because another party or company has been to the United States and likes that brand. They take the design and run to a first-to-file trademark jurisdiction. There are ways to handle this, but it is very expensive and difficult. It is important to think strategically across product lines as well as jurisdictions. If the company is expanding, they may have dismissed one territory because of budget, but if they find a joint venture partner or a market opens up, that may accelerate protection. Beginning with protection in a few key jurisdictions and then bumping it up is usually a good strategy.

Tracking Progress with Clients

In order to be of the most help to my fashion industry clients, I meet with many of them on a quarterly basis to track our progress with respect to the IP protection strategy. I record the key points of these conversations in a notebook so that there is a record that keeps us all on track. The first meeting sets the tone in terms of expectations, and I make sure to be diligent about staying in contact with the client. It is reasonable to expect that the client will get busy with creating and marketing products. Therefore, if we do not hear from the client, we contact them so that we are up-to-date on their new product developments. While we would like to do all the thinking about legal implications of a client's work, we cannot do that effectively without regular input—it is a partnership with them.

Conclusion: Old and New Concepts Meet in Fashion Law

Protecting IP related to fashion is a two-way street of aggressively protecting what the client has, while at the same time, recognizing those design elements that have been borrowed from the past or those that are currently hot and available to all. Fashion industry clients need to be educated about the availability of IP protection as related to every aspect of their business. Therefore, one has to go through every element of what is being created and have the client think about different patterns of protection for each aspect of what is being created, whether it is a latch, a clasp on clothing, a repetitive design, or the cut of a sports bra. When the client begins to look at his product in this way, it becomes clear that the company is creating something that is of value and proprietary to the company. I am a firm believer in ensuring that companies focus on their brand identity so that people will know who they are. The key is to protect the expression of its ideas and consider the flow of the marketplace.

Key Takeaways

- Conduct a comprehensive analysis of the client's IP, including existing in-market items and clothing that is on the drawing board, and the manner in which it advertises to the public.
- Ensure that your client acquires affirmative assignments for all of the work done by third-party contractors. This includes work on logo designs, retail design, web design, and other creative elements. This is particularly important because what employees create belongs to the company, but the ownership of work done by independent contractors could belong to the independent contractor.
- Assist the client with determining which items will be sustainable and unique items, and which are likely to be brief "hits" in the market. The former are worth the expense and effort to protect, the latter may not be.
- Keep on top of the client's development via its websites and the media, particularly the trade press.
- Remind your client that the ongoing protection of its designs is a team effort. The client will be caught up in the business of creating and marketing fashion, and may believe that you can read its mind and anticipate its need. You must ensure that the client understands that it must keep you apprised of new developments so you can stay ahead of the curve.
- Consider each unique item of protection in the context of the best way to protect it. The buckets of IP protection (copyright, patent, or trademark) that are available to protect fashion innovations have very specific applications. One item may have protection for multiple components, and some may not be protectable at all.

Related Resources

- *Christian Louboutin S.A. v. Yves Saint Laurent America Inc.*, Case No. 11-CIV-2381-VM (S.D.N.Y. Apr. 7, 2011).
- Piracy Prohibition Act (IDPPPA), H.R. 2511, 112th Cong. § 2(b)(3)(B) (2011).
- Remarks Blog, *available at* Remarksblog.com.
- *Law a la Mode*, DLA Piper's Fashion Law Newsletter, *available at* http://www.dlapiper.com/global/sitesearch/?qu=law+a+la+mode&re=&p=1.

Ann K. Ford is a partner with DLA Piper LLP (US) and is the chair of the firm's Trademark, Copyright, and Media Practice. She practices in the area of US and international trademark and copyright law, including the emerging law governing the use and protection of intellectual property on the Internet. She is a member of the firm's Executive Committee as well as its firm-wide Policy Committee.

Ms. Ford advises clients with respect to business and transactional aspects of intellectual property, as well as litigation and pre-litigation protective measures. She works with clients to acquire, develop, and exploit intellectual property assets, and she has specific experience in restructuring intellectual property assets for tax planning and developing joint venture arrangements to support co-branding efforts. She has extensive experience in working with both mature and emerging companies on developing and strengthening brands in a wide variety of industries. She utilizes her background in communications and media law to counsel clients on the specialized and unique issues faced by those industries. She advises clients on the use of other intellectual property and conducts compliance programs for businesses on their use of copyrighted material. She also protects clients' intellectual property through the courts, agencies, and uniform dispute resolution procedures.

Chambers and Partners recognizes Ms. Ford as one of America's leading lawyers for intellectual property, describing her as "renowned," and has reported that her clients value her "practical and realistic advice" and say she "combines expertise with commercial business judgment" and that she "always keeps the client's business goals in mind." In 2009, the Washington Business Journal *named her to its list of "Top Washington Lawyers" in the intellectual property category. She has been recognized by Legal 500, which praised her for being "pragmatic, not afraid to voice an opinion, but with a great sense of humor." She has also been listed in* An International Who's Who of Trademark Lawyers, *the* Guide to the World's Leading Trade Mark Practitioners, *the* Guide to the World's Leading Women in Business Law, *and* Who's Who Legal: The International Who's Who of Business Lawyers. *She has been selected by the* Legal Times *as one of the leading intellectual property lawyers in the Washington, D.C. area. In 2007 and again in 2009,* Washingtonian *magazine listed her among Washington's top lawyers. She has been named a Washington, D.C. "Super Lawyer." In 2011,* Arrive *magazine, the official publication of Amtrak and Acela Express, named her to its list of "Top Women Lawyers in the Northeast."*

Ms. Ford is an active member of the International Trademark Association's Information Resources Committee's Online Reference Subcommittee. She has also served on the project team for the International Trademark Association's Trademarks in Cyberspace program on the use of trademarks on the Internet. She has been a featured speaker on intellectual property issues to organizations such as the International Trademark Association, the American Society of Picture Professionals, Washington Area Lawyers for the Arts, and the District of Columbia Bar's Arts, Entertainment, and Sports Law Section. She has authored various scholarly works on the subject of intellectual property law, as well as articles on trademark and copyright law for general trade publications. In 2011, she was appointed vice chair of the D.C. Bar's Pro Bono Committee. She earned her BA from Georgetown University and her JD from the Duke University School of Law.

Acknowledgment: *I am grateful to my right-hand, Tom Zutic, whose humor and insight get me through each day so positively, and who helped me crystallize my thoughts in this chapter. I would also like to acknowledge my strong team of IP lawyers and staff, both past and present, most particularly Radiance Walters, Debbie Rosenbaum, and David Kramer, who assisted with the research and materials in this article, and Suzanne Abell, my assistant, who provides a steady hand.*

Dedication: *I dedicate this chapter to my later mother Vera and my sister Rosemary, whose sense of style and fashion influenced me in untold ways.*

APPENDICES

APPENDIX A

H.R. 2511

112th CONGRESS
1st Session

To amend title 17, United States Code, to extend protection to fashion design, and for other purposes.

IN THE HOUSE OF REPRESENTATIVES

July 13, 2011

Mr. GOODLATTE (for himself, Mr. NADLER, Mr. SENSENBRENNER, Mrs. MALONEY, Ms. LINDA T. SANCHEZ of California, Mr. COBLE, Mr. SCHIFF, Ms. JACKSON LEE of Texas, Ms. WATERS, Mr. ISSA, and Mr. RANGEL) introduced the following bill; which was referred to the Committee on the Judiciary

---

A BILL

To amend title 17, United States Code, to extend protection to fashion design, and for other purposes.

Be it enacted by the Senate and House of Representatives of the United States of America in Congress assembled,

SECTION 1. SHORT TITLE.

This Act may be cited as the 'Innovative Design Protection and Piracy Prevention Act'.

SEC. 2. AMENDMENTS TO TITLE 17, UNITED STATES CODE.

(a) DESIGNS PROTECTED- Section 1301 of title 17, United States Code, is amended—

(1) in subsection (a), by adding at the end the following:

'(4) FASHION DESIGN- A fashion design is subject to protection under this chapter.';

(2) in subsection (b)—

(A) in paragraph (2), by inserting ', or an article of apparel,' after 'plug or mold'; and

(B) by adding at the end the following:

'(7) A 'fashion design'—

'(A) is the appearance as a whole of an article of apparel, including its ornamentation; and

'(B) includes original elements of the article of apparel or the original arrangement or placement of original or non-original elements as incorporated in the overall appearance of the article of apparel that—

'(i) are the result of a designer's own creative endeavor; and

'(ii) provide a unique, distinguishable, non-trivial and non-utilitarian variation over prior designs for similar types of articles.

'(8) The term 'design' includes fashion design, except to the extent expressly limited to the design of a vessel.

'(9) The term 'apparel' means—

'(A) an article of men's, women's, or children's clothing, including undergarments, outerwear, gloves, footwear, and headgear;
'(B) handbags, purses, wallets, tote bags, and belts; and
'(C) eyeglass frames.

'(10) In the case of a fashion design, the term 'substantially identical' means an article of apparel which is so similar in appearance as to be likely to be mistaken for the protected design, and contains only those differences in construction or design which are merely trivial.'; and
(3) by adding at the end the following:

'(c) RULE OF CONSTRUCTION- In the case of a fashion design under this chapter, those differences or variations which are considered non-trivial for the purposes of establishing that a design is subject to protection under subsection (b)(7) shall be considered non-trivial for the purposes of establishing that a defendant's design is not substantially identical under subsection (b)(10) and section 1309(e).'.

(b) DESIGNS NOT SUBJECT TO PROTECTION- Section 1302(5) of title 17, United States Code, is amended—

(1) by striking '(5)' and inserting '(5)(A) in the case of a design of a vessel hull,';
(2) by striking the period and inserting '; or'; and
(3) by adding at the end the following:

'(B) in the case of a fashion design, embodied in a useful article that was made public by the designer or owner in the United States or a foreign country before the date of enactment of this chapter or more than 3 years before the date upon which protection of the design is asserted under this chapter.'.

(c) REVISIONS, ADAPTATIONS, AND REARRANGEMENTS- Section 1303 of title 17, United States Code, is amended by adding at the end the following: 'The presence or absence of a particular color or colors or of a pictorial or graphic work imprinted on fabric shall not be considered in determining the protection of a fashion design under section 1301 or 1302 or in determining infringement under section 1309.'.
(d) TERM OF PROTECTION- Section 1305(a) of title 17, United States Code, is amended to read as follows:

> '(a) In General- Subject to subsection (b), the protection provided under this chapter—
>
> > '(1) for a design of a vessel hull, shall continue for a term of 10 years beginning on the date of the commencement of protection under section 1304; and
> > '(2) for a fashion design, shall continue for a term of 3 years beginning on the date of the commencement of protection under section 1304.'.

(e) INFRINGEMENT- Section 1309 of title 17, United States Code, is amended—

> (1) in subsection (c)—
>
> > (A) by inserting 'offer for sale, advertise,' after 'sell,'; and
> > (B) by inserting 'either actual or reasonably inferred from the totality of the circumstances,' after 'created without knowledge';
>
> (2) by amending subsection (e) to read as follows:
>
> > '(e) INFRINGING ARTICLE DEFINED-
> >
> > > '(1) IN GENERAL- As used in this section, an 'infringing article' is any article the design of which has been copied from a design protected under this chapter, or from an image thereof, without the consent of the owner of the protected design.

An infringing article is not an illustration or picture of a protected design in an advertisement, book, periodical, newspaper, photograph, broadcast, motion picture, or similar medium.

'(2) VESSEL HULL DESIGN- In the case of a design of a vessel hull, a design shall not be deemed to have been copied from a protected design if it is original and not substantially similar in appearance to a protected design.

'(3) FASHION DESIGN- In the case of a fashion design, a design shall not be deemed to have been copied from a protected design if that design—

'(A) is not substantially identical in overall visual appearance to and as to the original elements of a protected design; or

'(B) is the result of independent creation.'; and

(3) by adding at the end the following:

'(h) HOME SEWING EXCEPTION-

'(1) IN GENERAL- It is not an infringement of the exclusive rights of a design owner for a person to produce a single copy of a protected design for personal use or for the use of an immediate family member, if that copy is not offered for sale or use in trade during the period of protection.

'(2) RULE OF CONSTRUCTION- Nothing in this subsection shall be construed to permit the publication or distribution of instructions or patterns for the copying of a protected design.'.

(f) APPLICATION FOR REGISTRATION- Section 1310(a) of title 17, United States Code, is amended—

(1) by striking 'Protection under this chapter' and inserting 'In the case of a design of a vessel hull, protection under this chapter'; and

(2) by adding 'Registration shall not apply to fashion designs.' after 'first made public.'.

(g) REMEDY FOR INFRINGEMENT- Section 1321 of title 17, United States Code, is amended—

(1) by striking subsection (a) and inserting the following:

'(a) IN GENERAL-

'(1) VESSEL HULL- In the case of a vessel hull, the owner of a design is entitled, after issuance of a certificate of registration of the design under this chapter, to institute an action for any infringement of the design.
'(2) FASHION DESIGN- In the case of a fashion design, the owner of a design is entitled to institute an action for any infringement of the design after the design is made public under the terms of section 1310(b) of this chapter.'; and

(2) by adding at the end the following:

'(e) PLEADING REQUIREMENT FOR FASHION DESIGNS-

'(1) IN GENERAL- In the case of a fashion design, a claimant in an action for infringement shall plead with particularity facts establishing that—

'(A) the design of the claimant is a fashion design within the meaning of section

1301(a)(7) of this title and thus entitled to protection under this chapter;
'(B) the design of the defendant infringes upon the protected design as described under section 1309(e); and
'(C) the protected design or an image thereof was available in such location or locations, in such a manner, and for such duration that it can be reasonably inferred from the totality of the surrounding facts and circumstances that the defendant saw or otherwise had knowledge of the protected design.

'(2) CONSIDERATIONS- In considering whether a claim for infringement has been adequately pleaded, the court shall consider the totality of the circumstances.'.

(h) PENALTY FOR FALSE REPRESENTATION- Section 1327 of title 17, United States Code, is amended--

(1) by inserting 'or for purposes of obtaining recovery based on a claim of infringement under this chapter' after 'registration of a design under this chapter';
(2) by striking '$500' and inserting '$5,000'; and
(3) by striking '$1,000' and inserting '$10,000'.

(i) NONAPPLICABILITY OF ENFORCEMENT BY TREASURY AND POSTAL SERVICE- Section 1328 of title 17, United States Code, is amended—

(1) in subsection (a), in the first sentence, by striking 'The Secretary' and inserting 'In the case of designs of vessel hulls protected under this chapter, the Secretary';
(2) in subsection (b), in the first sentence, by striking 'Articles' and inserting 'In the case of designs of vessel hulls protected under this chapter, articles'; and
(3) by adding at the end the following:

'(c) NONAPPLICABILITY- This section shall not apply to fashion designs protected under this chapter.'.

(j) COMMON LAW AND OTHER RIGHTS UNAFFECTED- Section 1330 of title 17, United States Code, is amended--

(1) in paragraph (1), by striking 'or' after the semicolon;
(2) in paragraph (2), by striking the period and inserting '; or'; and
(3) by adding at the end the following:
'(3) any rights that may exist under provisions of this title other than this chapter.'.

SEC. 3. EFFECTIVE DATE.

This Act and the amendments made by this Act shall take effect on the date of enactment of this Act.

Courtesy of Susan Scafidi, Fashion Law Institute at Fordham University School of Law

APPENDIX B

WRITTEN STATEMENT ON H.R. 5055, "THE DESIGN PIRACY PROHIBITION ACT"

July 27, 2006

Susan Scafidi
Associate Professor of Law & Adjunct Professor of History, SMU
Visiting Professor, Fordham Law School

presented to the
Subcommittee on Courts, the Internet, and Intellectual Property
U.S. House of Representatives

Chairman Smith, Representative Berman, and members of the Subcommittee, thank you for this opportunity to address the issue of intellectual property (IP) protection and fashion design.

Introduction and Executive Summary

Historically, American law has ignored the fashion industry. While trademark law protects designer logos and patent law occasionally applies to innovative design elements, the Copyright Office has held that clothing design in general is not subject to protection. As a result of this legal and cultural choice, the United States has been a safe haven for design piracy. Creative fashion designers over the past century have been forced to rely instead on social norms and makeshift means of defending themselves against copyists.

Today, global changes in both the speed of information transfer and the locus of clothing and textile production have resulted in increased pressure on creative designers at all levels, from haute couture to mass market. Digital photographs from a runway show in New York or a red carpet in Los Angeles can be uploaded to the internet within minutes, the images viewed at a factory in China, and copies offered for sale online within days – months before the designer is able to deliver the original garments to stores. Similarly, e-commerce is both an opportunity and a danger for designers, who must battle knockoff artists with ready access to detailed photographs and descriptions of their works. Young designers who have not yet achieved significant trademark recognition, and must instead rely on the unique quality of their designs to generate sales, are particularly vulnerable to such theft.

Despite America's role in promoting the international harmonization of intellectual property protection, the U.S. has not joined other nations in addressing the issue of design piracy and its effects on the fashion industry. The U.S.T.R. has repeatedly targeted the rising global trade in counterfeit trademarked goods, including apparel, but copies of a garment rather than its label remain beyond the reach of American law. H.R. 5055 is a measured response to the modern problem of fashion design piracy, narrowly tailored to address the industry's need for short-term protection of unique designs while preserving the development of seasonal trends and styles.

I. Historical Lack of Protection and Changed Circumstances

The lack of protection for fashion design under U.S. law is an anomaly among mature industries that involve creative expression. This exclusion of fashion from the realm of copyright was not inevitable, but was instead the result of deliberate policy choices. Examining the historical and cultural reasons for the differential treatment of fashion design is thus important to understanding the changed circumstances that indicate a greater need for some form of protection today.

A. Theory and Reality: The Historical IP/Fashion Divide

1. *Fashion design is part of the logical subject matter of copyright.*

While in the early days of U.S. copyright only books and maps were eligible for registration, the scope of protection has since increased to include painting, sculpture, textile patterns, and even jewelry design – but not clothing.

Why has clothing been excluded from protection? The problem lies in a reductionistic view of fashion as solely utilitarian. Current U.S. law understands clothing only in terms of its usefulness as a means of covering the body, regardless of how original it might be. Surface decoration aside, the plainest T-shirt and the most fanciful item of apparel receive exactly the same treatment under copyright law. In fact, a T-shirt with a simple drawing on the front would receive *more* protection than an elaborate ball gown that is the product of dozens of preliminary sketches, hours of fittings, and days of detailed stitching and adjustment before it is finally complete. The legal fiction that even the most conceptual clothing design is merely functional prevents the protection of original designs.

Fashion, however, is not just about covering the body – it is about creative expression, which is exactly what copyright is supposed to protect. Historians and other scholars make an important distinction between clothing and fashion. "Clothing" is a general term for "articles of dress that cover the body," while "fashion" is a form of creative expression.[1] In other words, a garment may be just another item of clothing – like that plain T-shirt – or it may be the tangible expression of a new idea, the core subject matter of copyright.

Copyright law, of course, has a mechanism for dealing with creations that are both functional and expressive, although it has not been consistently applied to fashion designs. It is conceivable – and perhaps inevitable in the absence of specifically tailored legislation – that a court could invoke the doctrine of "conceptual separability" to distinguish between the artistic elements of a new fashion design and its basic function of covering the human body. Recent judicial treatment of a Halloween costume design follows essentially this course, noting that elements of a costume like a head or tail are at least in theory separable from the main body of the garment and thus potentially subject to copyright protection.[2] It would require only a small step to find that the uniquely sculptural shape of Charles James' famous 1953 "four-leaf clover gown" or Zac Posen's 2006 umbrella-sleeve blouse are conceptually independent of the human forms beneath them and thus copyrightable. Visual artists, too, have blurred the distinction between art and fashion by designing unique works of art in the shape of clothing.[3]

---

[1] Joanne B. Eicher, *Clothing, Costume and Dress* in 1 ENCYCLOPEDIA CLOTHING AND FASHION 270 (2005);Valerie Steele, *Fashion*, in 2 ENCYCLOPEDIA OF CLOTHING AND FASHION 12 (2005).

[2] Chosun Int'l., Inc. v. Chrisha Creations, Ltd., 413 F.3d 324 (2d Cir. 2005).

[3] *See, e.g.*, Poe v. Missing Persons, 745 F.2d 1238 (2d Cir. 1984).

In short, fashion design is a creative medium that is not driven solely by utility or function. If it were, we could all simply wear our clothes until they fell apart or no longer fit. Instead, the range of new clothing designs available each season to cover the relatively unchanging human body – and the production of specific, recognizable copies – demonstrates that designers are engaged in the creation of original works.

From the perspective of theoretical consistency, then, the relationship between copyright law and fashion design is ripe for change. However, relying on the courts to take this step would be a lengthy and uncertain process, one that might ultimately require a Supreme Court decision to sort through conflicting precedents. The judiciary, moreover, does not have the authority to tailor intellectual property law to the specific needs of the fashion industry and the public, as would H.R. 5055 (discussed further in Section IV infra), but can only apply existing law. The most efficient and reflective way to secure copyright protection for the creators of fashion designs would be an act of Congress.

2. *U.S. law does not support the economic development of the fashion industry.*

Despite the importance of creative fashion design to the global economy, and to many local economies within the United States, it still operates without the benefits of modern intellectual property protection.

In historical terms, the pattern of industrial development in the U.S. and more recent emerging economies often commences with a period of initial piracy, during which a new industry takes root by means of copying. This results in the rapid accumulation of both capital and expertise. Eventually the country develops its own creative sector in the industry, which in turn leads to enactment of intellectual property protection to further promote its growth. This was the pattern followed in the music and publishing industries, in which the U.S. was once a notorious pirate nation but is now a promoter of IP enforcement.

In the case of the American fashion industry, however, the usual pattern of unrestrained copying followed by steadily increasing legal protection is not present. This situation has led to multiple inefficiencies in the development of the U.S. fashion industry. In the legal realm alone, creative designers have borne the costs of a decades-long effort to craft protection equivalent to copyright from other areas of IP law, particularly by pressing the boundaries of trademark, trade dress and patent law. While each of these areas of intellectual property law offers protection to some aspects of fashion design, most notably logos used as design elements and famous designs that have developed sufficient secondary meaning to qualify for trade dress protection, the majority of original clothing designs remain unprotected. Even design patents, which can in theory protect the ornamental features of an otherwise functional object, are seldom useful in a seasonal medium like fashion. The result is a legal pastiche that is confusing, expensive to apply, and ultimately unable to protect the core creativity of fashion design.

Current U.S. IP law thus supports copyists at the expense of original designers, a choice inconsistent with America's position in fields of industry like software, publishing, music, and film. The most severe damage from this legal vacuum falls upon emerging designers, who every day lose orders – and potentially their businesses – because copyists exploit the loophole in American law. While established designers and large corporations with widely recognized trademarks can better afford to absorb the losses caused by rampant plagiarism in the U.S. market, very few small businesses can compete with those who steal their intellectual capital. In fashion, America is still a pirate nation; the future direction of the industry will be directly influenced by the absence or presence of intellectual property protection.

B. Cultural Explanations and Changed Circumstances

The differential treatment of fashion relative to other creative industries with extensive legal protection is the result of specific cultural perceptions and historical circumstances, many of which have now changed. While it is beyond the scope of this testimony to address the entire cultural history of the fashion industry, several recent developments are particularly important to understanding why a change in the law is appropriate at this time.

1. *Fashion design is now recognized as a form of creative expression.*

The origins of copyright law date back to the Enlightenment era, a period that also articulated the Western distinction between art and craft. As copyright developed and extended to include various forms of literary and artistic works, it continued to maintain the division between legally protected, high status "fine art" and mere "decorative arts" or handicrafts. The design and manufacture of clothing, which for most families was a household task, did not rise to the level of creative expression in the eyes of the law.

Even after fashion design became increasingly professionalized during the nineteenth century, with the development of both haute couture and ready-to-wear sectors, the U.S. failed to recognize its creative status. Contributing to this low valuation was fashion's association with women rather than men, a shift influenced by the Industrial Revolution. By the end of the nineteenth century, American sociologist Thorstein Veblen famously linked fashion with "conspicuous consumption," concluding that the role of the female was "to consume for the [male] head of the household; and her apparel is contrived with this object in view."[4] Both the feminizing of fashion and the intellectual attention to consumption rather than production prevented the legal recognition of fashion as a serious creative industry.

Modern attitudes toward fashion design as a creative medium, however, have changed dramatically. Institutions from the Smithsonian to Sotheby's take fashion seriously, and organizations like the National Arts Club and the Cooper-Hewitt National Design Museum have recently added fashion designers to their annual categories of honorees. Even a Pulitzer Prize for criticism was awarded for the first time this year to a fashion writer, Robin Givhan of the *Washington Post*. It is inconsistent with this cultural shift for copyright law to deny fashion's role as an artistic form.

2. *Creative design now exists at all price levels.*

For most of the history of the fashion industry, a small group of elite, Parisian fashion designers dictated seasonal trends, and the rest of the world

[4] Thorstein Veblen, THE THEORY OF THE LEISURE CLASS 132 (1899; Random House 2001 ed.)

followed as best they could. The privileged few were measured for couture originals, the relatively affluent bought licensed copies, and the majority settled for inexpensive knockoffs or sewed their own garments at home.

With the recent democratization of style, creative design originates from many sources and at all price levels. Fashion is now as likely to flow up from the streets as down from the haute couture, and reasonable prices are no guarantee against copyists. Some of the most aggressively copied designs are popularly priced; consider this summer's popular Crocs "Beach" style shoe at $29.99 and its battle with copies sold for as little as $10.00.

In addition, within the past few years high-end designers have shown an increasing desire to reach a wider audience and to collaborate with mass-market producers. Fashion houses are seeking to experiment with new ideas in their runway collections, then to provide customers with affordable versions in their diffusion lines, and finally to adapt the looks for a broad range of consumer needs and budgets. This trickle promises to become a flood, as Isaac Mizrahi's designs for Target are joined by Chanel designer Karl Lagerfeld's line for H&M, Mark Eisen's sportswear for Wal-Mart, and many others.

As a result of these changes, it is no longer necessary for the general public to turn to knockoffs in order to purchase fashionable apparel, as it might have been in past decades. Some creative work is simply affordable; in addition, creators of more expensive designs are now finding ways to enter the mass market as well. A change in copyright law to incorporate fashion would facilitate designers' ability to disseminate their own new ideas throughout the market, much the way copyright law allows book publishers to first release hardcover copies and then, if the book is successful, to print paperbacks.

3. <u>The internet era calls for new strategies to protect creativity</u>.

Creative fashion designers in earlier periods fought copyists by relying on strategic measures like speed and secrecy, the social norms of the industry, and perhaps patterns of consumer behavior. In the absence of copyright protection under U.S. law, these extralegal mechanisms were an important part of the fashion business.

Today, however, the same speed and accuracy of information transfer that affects the music and film industries is also having an impact on fashion. Would-be copyists no longer have to smuggle sketch artists into fashion shows and send the results to clients along with descriptions of color and fabrication. Instead, high-quality digital photos of a runway look can be uploaded to the internet and sent to copyists anywhere in the world even before the show is finished, and knockoffs can be offered for sale within days – long before the original garments are scheduled to appear in stores. Fifty years ago, design houses may have been able to impose somewhat successful embargoes on the press; now, such efforts are futile.

Similarly, the claim that knockoffs enhance demand for ever-newer luxury goods among status-seeking consumers, an economic argument dating back to at least 1928,[5] fails to take into account the modern speed of production. Once upon a time it may have been that the adoption of a new luxury item by affluent trendsetters was imitated first by wealthy consumers, then by the middle class, and then in form of knockoffs by everyone else, at which point the fashion-forward would abandon the item and demand the next new thing – which producers were happy to provide. Today, however, this "fashion cycle" scenario is rendered obsolete by the fact that poor quality knockoffs can be manufactured and distributed even more quickly than the originals, leaving creative designers little opportunity to recover their investment before the item is already out of style. Even if the fashion cycle were ever sufficient to support the design industry, that is no longer the case.

As in other areas of creative production, the digital age should provoke a reexamination of the legal protection available to fashion design.

4. *The future of American fashion is in creativity, not low-cost copying.*

Textile and clothing manufacturing have historically played an important role in the American economy, driving the Industrial Revolution and supporting thousands of jobs. With the increased harmonization of global markets and the January 1, 2005, dismantling of import quotas in this sector, however, it has become apparent that the U.S. can no longer

[5] *See* Paul H. Nystrom, ECONOMICS OF FASHION 18-54 (1928).

compete with China and other centers of low-cost production on price alone. No matter how inexpensively the U.S. can produce knockoffs, other countries can manufacture much cheaper versions.

Instead, the future of the U.S. economy will rest on the ability to develop and protect creative industries, including fashion design. America leads the world in industries like music, film, and computer software, but our history as a pirate nation in the field of fashion has limited our influence in this area. Creative fashion design is a relatively young industry in the U.S., albeit one in which there is growing interest among students choosing their careers. If this industry is to reach its full potential, now is the time to consider the impact of government policies, including intellectual property law.

II. <u>Effects of Design Piracy</u>

The lack of copyright protection for fashion design negatively affects both individual designers whose expressions are copied and the intellectual property system as a whole. As a law professor with a website dedicated to IP and fashion, I frequently receive messages from young designers whose work has been stolen or who hope to prevent the copying of their designs. It is with regret that I must repeatedly explain that while that law can protect designers' trademarks against counterfeiters, in the U.S. the actual designs are fair game for copyists.

A. Impact on Designers

Creativity is an intrinsic part of human nature, not a byproduct of the intellectual property system. Poets would continue to write, musicians to sing, and fashion designers to sew even if all copyright protection were eliminated tomorrow. While the concept of intellectual property is only a few hundred years old, archaeologists have recently discovered 100,000-year-old shell necklaces, which they interpret as the first evidence of human symbolic thinking.

The goal of the IP system, however, is not merely to ensure that authors put pen to paper or needle and thread to fabric, but to encourage and reward individuals so that they can continue to develop their ideas and skills in a productive manner. In other words, intellectual property law ideally serves as a tool for harnessing and directing creativity. For this reason, the Constitution empowers Congress "[t]o promote the progress of science and useful arts." It is this "progress" over time that is hindered by the lack of legal protection for fashion design.

Young designers attempting to establish themselves are particularly vulnerable to the lack of copyright protection for fashion design, since their names and logos are not yet recognizable to a broad range of consumers. These aspiring creators cannot simply rely on reputation or trademark protection to make up for the absence of copyright. Instead, they struggle each season to promote their work and attract customers before their designs are copied by established competitors.

Over the past century successive waves of American designers have entered the industry, but few fashion houses have endured long enough to leave a lasting impression comparable to the influence of French fashion. While it is difficult to quantify or even identify designers who give up their businesses, particularly for reasons of piracy, there is strong anecdotal evidence that design piracy is harmful to the U.S. fashion industry. Consider just two representative examples, one a historical snapshot from an early attempt to develop American fashion and the other from this year.

In 1938 Elizabeth Hawes wrote a best-selling critique of the fashion industry entitled *Fashion is Spinach.*[6] In it, she chronicled her start working for a French copy house, the only job in the fashion industry available to a young expatriate American in the 1920s; her return to New York to design her own line; and her ultimate disillusionment with the tyranny of mass production and the ubiquity of poor quality knockoffs that undercut her own designs. She ultimately closed her business in 1940, but not before leaving a record of the perils of the industry for a creative designer.

From a legal perspective, little has changed in almost seventy years. Handbag designer Jennifer Baum Lagdameo co-founded the label Ananas approximately three years ago. A young wife and mother working from home, Jennifer has been successful in promoting her handbags, which retail

[6] Elizabeth Hawes, FASHION IS SPINACH (1938).

between $200 and $400. Earlier this year, however, she received a telephone call canceling a wholesale order. When she inquired as to the reason for the cancellation, she learned that the buyer had found virtually identical copies of her bags at a lower price. Shortly thereafter, Jennifer discovered a post on an internet message board by a potential customer who had admired one of her bags at a major department store. Before buying the customer looked online and found a cheap, line-for-line copy of the Ananas bag in lower quality materials, which she not only bought but recommended to others, further affecting sales of the original. While Ananas continues to produce handbags at present, this loss of both wholesale and retail sales is a significant blow to a small business.

Copying is rampant in the fashion industry, as knockoff artists remain free to skip the time-consuming and expensive process of developing and marketing new products and simply target creative designers' most successful models. The race to the bottom in terms of price and quality is one that experimental designers cannot win. Nearly every designer or even design student seems to have a story about the prevalence of copying, a situation that makes the difficult odds of success in the fashion industry even longer.

B. Design Piracy and Counterfeiting

Not only does the legal copying of fashion designs harm their creators, it also provides manufacturers with a mechanism for circumventing the current campaign against counterfeit trademarks. If U.S. Customs stops a shipping container with fake trademarked apparel or accessories at the border, it can impound and destroy those items. If, however, the same items are shipped without labels, they are generally free to enter the country – at which point the distributor can attach counterfeit labels or decorative logos with less chance of detection by law enforcement. I have personally witnessed the application of such counterfeit logos to otherwise legal knockoffs at the point of sale; after the consumer chooses a knockoff item, the seller simply glues on a label corresponding to the copied design. The continued exclusion of fashion designs from copyright protection thus undermines federal policy with respect to trademarks by perpetuating a loophole in the intellectual property law system.

III. Comparative IP Regimes and Fashion Design

While the U.S. has deliberately denied copyright protection to the fashion industry over the past century, other nations have incorporated fashion into their intellectual property systems – and have consequently developed more mature and influential design industries.

France in particular has treated fashion design as the equivalent of other works of the mind for purposes of intellectual property protection. French laws protecting textiles and fashion design date back in their earliest form to the *ancien régime*; these laws were subsequently updated and clarified in the early twentieth century. As a result, Parisian fashion designers have been able over the course of their careers to develop and protect signature design repertoires, which even after the departure of the founding designers can serve as a form of brand DNA for their design houses. The formal recognition of fashion design as an art form has thus helped maintain the preeminence of the French fashion industry and augmented the lasting creative influence of both native designers and those who have chosen to work in France.

The association between strong intellectual property protection and a successful creative industry has not been lost on other countries that sought to support their domestic design industries. As long ago as 1840 a British textile manufacturer wrote, "France has reaped the advantage of her system; and the soundness of her view, and the correctness of her means, are fully proved by the results, which have placed her, as regards industrial art, at the head of all the nations of Europe, in taste, elegance, and refinement."[7]

While modern French law still offers the most extensive protection to fashion design, Japan, India, and many other countries have incorporated both registered and unregistered design protection into their domestic laws. In addition, E.U. law has since 2002 provided for both three years of unregistered design protection and up to 25 years of registered design protection, measured in five-year terms.

---

[7] James Thomson, *quoted in* J. Emerson Tennent, A Treatise on the Copyright of Designs for Printed Fabrics (1841).

The global legal trend toward fashion design protection has rendered the U.S. an outlier among nations that actively support intellectual property protection, a position that is both politically inconsistent and contrary to the economic health of the domestic fashion industry. Congress should take these factors into account when considering a reasonable level of legal protection for fashion design.

IV. The Role of H.R. 5055

When analyzed in light of the goals of the intellectual property law system, current challenges to the U.S. fashion industry, and international legal developments, H.R. 5055 is a carefully crafted legal remedy to the inequities resulting from the exclusion of fashion design from copyright law. The bill is narrowly tailored to achieve a balance between protection of innovative designs and the preservation of the extensive public domain of fashion as an inspiration for future creativity. Perhaps most importantly, it is a forward-looking measure that lays the groundwork for the future development of a robust, creative American fashion industry.

The fashion industry's decision not to seek full copyright protection, but instead to request only a limited three-year term, is particularly appropriate to the seasonal nature of the industry. This period will allow designers time to develop their ideas in consultation with influential editors and buyers prior to displaying the work to the general public, followed by a year of exclusive sales as part of the designer's experimental signature line, and another year to develop diffusion lines or other mass-market sales. While many legal scholars have aptly criticized the full term of copyright protection as excessive when viewed solely in light of an incentive-based rationale, a three-year term chosen after careful analysis of the relevant industry is exactly the sort of scheme that "low protectionist" activists have endorsed for copyright as a whole. Such a short term of protection will simultaneously encourage designers to facilitate affordable access to cutting-edge design and contribute to the ongoing enrichment of the public domain.

The choice to amend the Copyright Act, rather than to modify the design patent system or devise a sui generis scheme involving prior review, is also well suited to the needs of the fashion industry. The bill appropriately recognizes that the short lifespan of new fashions is inconsistent with burdensome legal formalities. Indeed, I would suggest that unregistered protection would be even more consistent with the U.S. copyright system, existing European design protection, and the needs of the industry, particularly inexperienced designers. Nevertheless, the establishment of registered design protection is an improvement over the current state of the law.

The language of H.R. 5055, particularly if amended to clarify that only "closely and substantially similar" copies will be considered to infringe upon registered designs, is likewise well crafted to both promote innovation and preserve the development of trends. As with other forms of literary and artistic work, copyright law is clearly capable of protecting specific expressions while allowing trends and styles to form. From a legal perspective, a fashion trend is much like a genre of literature. Granting copyright to a John Grisham novel does not halt the publication of many similar legal thrillers, nor does the protection of Dan Brown's *DaVinci Code* prevent a spate of novels involving Mary Magdalene or the Knights Templar from appearing in bookstores. When an author writes a bestseller, imitators of his or her style tend to follow – but they are not permitted to plagiarize the original. Copyright in this sense is merely a legal framework that supports an existing social norm; neither reputable authors nor creative fashion designers engage in literal copying of one another.

The level of generality at which fashion trends exist, moreover, is far too broad to be affected by the proposed bill. To paraphrase next month's *Vogue* magazine, currently on the newsstand, red will still be the new black following the passage of H.R. 5055. In the same way, common trends such as wide neckties in the 1970s or casual Fridays in the late 1990s were not dependent on the presence or absence of design protection, nor would such nonspecific ideas ever be subject to intellectual property protection.

In addition to the protective benefits of H.R. 5055, the legislation may have a beneficial effect on creativity in the industry as a whole. Former copy houses, no longer able to legally replicate other designers' work, will be forced to innovate or at least transform their work so that it no longer substantially resembles the original products. This in turn can be expected to lead to more jobs for design professionals and more reasonably priced choices for consumers.

At present, the bulk of design-related litigation tends to invoke federal trademark and trade dress as well as state unfair competition claims in order to mimic the protections that would be offered by H.R. 5055, with limited success. To the extent that fact-based disputes regarding copying continue to arise, the new legislation will permit parties to engage in more straightforward, simpler litigation. Not only will this avoid the unnecessary distortion of trademark and trade dress law, but it will also clarify the parameters of what constitutes protected design. As in other creative industries governed by intellectual property law, an equilibrium will arise and manufacturers will find it in their best interests to offer retailers innovative rather than infringing work.

H.R. 5055 promises to remedy a historical and theoretical imbalance in the copyright system and to offer protection to the many young American designers whose work is currently vulnerable to knockoff artists. For these reasons, I encourage you to seriously consider this reform.

Courtesy of Susan Scafidi, Fashion Law Institute at Fordham University School of Law

APPENDIX C

TRADEMARK LICENSE AGREEMENT

Non-Royalty / Very Basic

AGREEMENT made this ____ day of ____________, ____ between ____________________, a _________ [insert state of incorporation] corporation having its principal place of business at ________________________ (Licensor) and ____________, a ______________ [insert state of incorporation] corporation having its principal place of business at __________________________ (Licensee).

WITNESSETH:

WHEREAS, Licensor is the owner of the WAY COOL trademark for ________________ and of Registration No. ________________ for that trademark in the United States Patent and Trademark Office;

WHEREAS, Licensee desires to acquire and Licensor is willing to grant to Licensee a license to use the WAY COOL trademark on ___________________ ("the Licensed Goods") on the following terms and conditions;

NOW, THEREFORE, in consideration of the mutual premises and covenants contained herein, the parties hereto agree as follows:

1. Grant of Rights

Licensor hereby grants to Licensee, subject to the following terms and conditions, a royalty free, nonexclusive license to use the WAY COOL trademark within the United States on the Licensed Goods.

2. Term

This Agreement shall commence on the date of its execution by the parties hereto and shall continue until terminated pursuant to the provisions herein.

3. Quality Control

Licensee agrees that all Licensed Goods sold under the WAY COOL trademark shall be of a quality equal to or higher than the products it presently sells under any other trademark. To ensure that Licensee maintains such quality standards, Licensee shall, prior to the effective date of this Agreement and on or about January 1 and June 30 of each calendar year during which this Agreement is in effect, send a sample to Licensor of each Licensed Good then being sold under the WAY COOL trademark, along with its packaging and any advertising or promotional materials therefor. Licensor shall have the right at any time and from time to time to inspect, at Licensee's premises, any products on or in connection with which Licensee uses the WAY COOL trademark.

4. Designation of Trademark

Other than the Licensee corporate name and the Licensee trademark, no other trademark or trade name of any kind shall appear on the Licensed Goods or any packaging therefor, manufactured, offered for sale, sold, advertised or distributed pursuant to this Agreement. Licensee agrees to use such trademark notice or legends as Licensor shall request on all Licensed Goods and packaging.

5. Ownership of the Trademark

Licensee acknowledges that Licensor is the owner of all right, title and interest in and to the WAY COOL trademark, including without limitation trademark Registration No. 1,234,567, and that Licensee's use of the WAY COOL trademark creates in Licensee no rights in said mark and that all use of the WAY COOL trademark by Licensee inures to the benefit of Licensor. Licensee shall not challenge or, directly or indirectly, assert any right, title or interest in or to the WAY COOL trademark or any application for registration or registration thereof. At the request of Licensor, Licensee shall execute and deliver all documents which Licensor deems necessary or appropriate to maintain any registration Licensor has or may obtain of the WAY COOL trademark, or to facilitate the making or granting of an application for registration of said mark.

6. Enforcement

Licensee agrees to inform Licensor promptly in writing of (a) any infringement or instance of unfair competition of which Licensee may become aware involving the WAY COOL trademark, (b) any challenge to Licensee's use of the WAY COOL trademark, and (c) any claim of which Licensee may become aware by any person to any right in the WAY COOL trademark, in which case Licensor shall have the sole discretion to take such action as it deems appropriate. Licensee shall assist and cooperate with Licensor by, among other things, furnishing such documentary relating to Licensee's use of the WAY COOL trademark as Licensor may request.

7. Compliance with Laws

Licensee shall comply with all governmental laws, regulations, decrees and their equivalent pertaining to the manufacturing, offering for sale, sale, advertising and distribution of the Licensed Goods pursuant to this Agreement.

8. Indemnification

Licensee agrees to indemnify Licensor and hold it harmless against all actions, claims, costs, damages or expenses which may be brought against or made against or incurred by Licensor as a result of or in any way connected with any acts, whether of omission or commission, that may be committed by Licensee or any of its servants, agents or employees in connection with Licensee's performance under this Agreement or in connection with Licensee's manufacturing, sale, offering for sale, advertising or distribution of the Licensed Goods under the WAY COOL trademark.

9. Termination

This Agreement and all rights granted herein shall terminate upon written notice from Licensor to Licensee in the event that:

a) Licensee breaches any of the provisions of this Agreement and fails to cure such breach within _______ (__) days after receiving written notice of such breach from Licensor;

b) Licensee discontinues the manufacture and sale of Licensed Goods bearing the WAY COOL trademark for any period of ____ (__) consecutive months after the commencement of the term of this Agreement;
c) Licensor decides to terminate this Agreement for any reason not included in paragraphs 9(a) or (b), in which case Licensor shall provide Licensee with written notice of such decision ____ (__) months prior to termination.

Upon termination of this Agreement pursuant to this paragraph, all rights and privileges of Licensee hereunder shall terminate, and Licensee shall not thereafter make any use whatsoever of the WAY COOL trademark or any colorable imitation thereof.

10. Assignment and Sublicensee

Licensee shall not assign or transfer the license that is the subject of this Agreement without the prior written consent of Licensor. Licensor may assign this Agreement or any rights under their Agreement without the consent of Licensee.

11. Modification; Waiver

1.1 No change, amendment or modification of any provision of this Agreement shall be valid unless set forth in a written instrument signed by both parties.

1.2 Any failure by either party to enforce any provision of this Agreement shall not constitute a waiver of such party's rights therein.

12. Governing Law

This Agreement shall be governed by and construed under the laws of the State of ___ without regard to its conflicts of laws provisions. The exclusive forum for any actions arising out of or relating to this Agreement shall be the appropriate state or federal court sitting in the County of ____, State of ______.

13. Notice

Any notice, communication, approval or disapproval and request therefor required or permitted to be sent under this Agreement shall be duly made and shall be valid and effective only if in writing and sent by registered or certified mail, return receipt requested, postage prepaid:

a) if to Licensor:

b) if to Licensee:

14. Binding Effect

This Agreement is binding upon the parties, their successors and assigns.

IN WITNESS WHEREOF, the parties hereto have executed this Agreement as of the date first above written.

LICENSOR	**LICENSEE**
By:________________________	By: ________________________
Name:______________________	Name:______________________
Title:_______________________	Title:_______________________

Courtesy of Monica B. Richman, SNR Denton

APPENDIX D

CHECKLIST FOR CONDUCTING BASIC TRADEMARK SEARCHES

☐ **1. Search for the exact mark**

If the mark is composed of two or more words, search for the exact mark as one word and as two words or a continuous string of words. For example, if the mark is PRIME PARTNERS, run an exact search for PRIME PARTNERS and PRIMEPARTNERS.

☐ **2. Search for any marks incorporating the mark**

If the mark is ZEND, you also should search for *ZEND* to cover all marks incorporating ZEND. If the mark is PRIME PARTNERS, search *prime* *partner* and *primepartner*. If a mark is composed of two or more words that are not very common, it may be necessary to search each word separately, within narrower class(es).

☐ **3. Search for phonetic equivalents**

Search for any marks containing the phonetic equivalent of the mark. For example, if the mark is PHARMACARE, run a search for FARMACARE (PH = F) as well. Similarly, if the mark is PEGS, run a search for PEGZ (S = Z).

☐ **4. Search for other logical variations of the mark**

If the mark contains a word in plural form, remember to search for the word in singular form, and *vice versa*. For example, if the mark is SWINGERS, also run a search for SWINGER. If the mark is GREAT AMERICAN SALT & PEPPER SHAKER, search for marks that incorporate the word AMERICA, not just marks that incorporate the word AMERICAN.

☐ **5. Class(es) of Goods and Services**

Begin your search in all classes and then narrow the search down to relevant classes of goods and services as needed. If there are numerous records even in the narrowed class(es), consider a "hit list" from which full records can be selected.

☐ **6. Spelling**

Double-check mark and search logic to ensure that you correctly spelled all search terms.

☐ **7. International Considerations**

Make sure the search includes all jurisdictions of definite and potential interest.

Courtesy of Monica B. Richman, SNR Denton

APPENDIX E

LICENSE POINTS FOR CONSIDERATION

1. Mark: Include the mark(s) you are licensing and get licensee acknowledgement that all rights to the marks are yours

2. Design/pattern: Attach the patterns relating to the license, if possible, if not created yet then at least include the number of patterns/designs obligated under the license. Also, need to address who owns the Designs/patterns and how Licensor (and Licensee) can use besides this one deal, if appropriate. If pattern is an "exclusive," is it exclusive for the product category or "exclusive" such that Licensor cannot use the pattern except with this one licensee?

3. Grant of License: What are you giving in the license? Be very specific.
   Example: "Licensor hereby grants to License a license to use the Licensed Mark and the Design exclusively on fine quality dinnerware."

4. Reservation of License: What are you not giving in the license?
   Example: "Licensor hereby reserves all rights not explicitly granted by this license."

5. Territory: What countries? Do you want conditions, such as, "territory will include Canada and Mexico so long as licensee sells at least $100,000 of the Licensed Product in each country per Annual Year"?

6. Term: How many years? On what conditions will the license renew, if any? For a new licensee, you may want to start with limited product for a limited term with the right to renew if both parties like the way the license is working.

7. Collection: How will the designs/patterns be created? Who pays for the artistic work? What is the quality control for the product? What is the approval process for the Licensed Products?

8. Business Plan/Marketing/Advertising: How does the licensee plan to promote and advertise the Licensed Product(s)? What about showroom visibility? Catalog/website visibility? Personal appearances – how many, who pays? Is there a commitment to the Licensor's brand? Is there a business plan to show development of the brand? Will an employee of licensee be dedicated to your brand? Who? How many employees? Will your brand get enough attention?

9. Royalty: Is there a minimum royalty? Minimum sales requirement? What is the royalty rate? What happens if licensee fails to achieve necessary minimums?

10. Termination: What constitutes default? What are the possible remedies for certain defaults? How will you address inventory at time of termination?

11. Expiration: License expires when it runs its course. What happens to inventory in this scenario?

12. Discounts and Promotional Pieces: If you want to buy the Licensed Products what is your discounted price? How many promotional items of the Licensed Products do you receive annually?

13. Trade Channels: Where do you want the Licensed Products advertised, marketed and sold? Licensor must have prior approval over retail outlets, for example, Kmart or Bergdorf Goodman?

14. Internet: Subcategory of "trade channels" and "advertising/marketing." Do you want a licensee to be able to register a "brand" domain name? Do you want licensee to advertise over the Internet or to sell over the Internet? If so, need to control manner of both.

15. Manufacturing: Where does licensee manufacture? How are the facilities? Do they meet sufficient standards so as not to have human rights issues? Can you inspect the facilities?

16. Standard Clauses such as

    a. Payments: How payment occurs and how often (get a definition of "net sales" that is favorable)
    b. Statements and Reports
    c. Books & Records, Audits
    d. Confidentiality (depends on facts)
    e. Non-Compete (depends on facts)
    f. Indemnification (goes both ways, but for Licensor it is narrowly defined to indemnify for trademark claims and copyright claims, but only if you are the designer of the pattern; licensee has much broader product indemnification)
    g. Insurance (for licensee)
    h. Representations & Warranties (generally stronger for licensee, as it will be manufacturing the Licensed Product)
    i. Choice of law for contract
    j. Jurisdiction for dispute on contract and if you want arbitration clause
    k. Assignability – Under what circumstances can licensee assign license?
    l. Product development calendar and approval rights – Should be carefully negotiated and all details and timing including in contract

Other points not in the license but important to consider before doing the deal:

- Financials: How stable is proposed licensee? Can proposed licensee afford to do the Licensed Products in the way envisioned by Licensor? Does licensee have the money to finance the business?
- Distribution: What is the proposed licensee's distribution network? Is it what you have in mind? Is it strong enough?
- Reputation: What is the proposed licensee's reputation in the business? Does it have other licensees? How are they treated? Do people like working with this company?
- Guarantor: Do you want a guaranty? If so, for payment and/or performance?

Courtesy of Monica B. Richman, SNR Denton

APPENDIX F

MAIN POINTS FOR TRADEMARK LICENSES FOR FASHION DESIGNS

One of the most common and important contracts in fashion is the license agreement for the use of trademarks in categories into which the licensor wants to expand its business. There was a time when the trademark for a brand for shoes appeared on shoes, boots, sandals and slippers and no more. Today, in the luxury sector, but also for sports brands and many others, having a complete line of goods in many categories is a far more common strategy. Due to that cross-category expansion, a typical major fashion company, even one that operates its own factories, does not attempt to design and manufacture all the goods that bear its marks. It relies instead on the talents of third-party contractors who "get" the story of the brand and can translate it into licensed goods such as (to name a few categories that specialty companies handle under license from fashion houses) eyeglass and sunglass frames, swimwear, footwear and home accessories. Although no one form or model fits all purposes, the following is a bullet point outline of key terms to consider when constructing a license agreement. In deals of this kind, lawyers tend to focus on the representations, warranties, indemnities and choice of law, and the business people concentrate more on the grant of rights and the financial terms. Which part of the agreement is in fact the most important? It is likely the one that, by its ambiguity, poor terms or total absence, generates needless and expensive litigation. Since the identity of that clause is never revealed to the party injured by it until the injury is sustained, as with all important contracts, time and attention should be given to negotiating and drafting a license agreement that works right from the start.

Grant of Rights

- Licensor grants licensee the exclusive right and license to use the licensed marks in connection with the manufacture, sale, distribution, advertisement, marketing and promotion of the licensed products.
- The licensed products will only be sold through the named channels of trade, such as (for example) better specialty stores, department stores and online retailers.

- State the territory, which can be regional, worldwide or something in between.
- State whether, how and when licensee must obtain licensor's approval of retail accounts. Consider a mechanism for later withdrawal of approval, especially for luxury brands, in the event that a particular retail account changes in a way that is inconsistent with the reputation, quality control standards or public image of the licensed marks.
- Add any other limitations, such whether licensee agrees not to sell the licensed products to distributors (because doing so can make control over presentation to the consumer more difficult).
- Depending on the nature of the licensed products, licensee may dispose of irregular or damaged merchandise from which the licensed mark has been completely removed (and that do not include any other proprietary rights of licensor, such as a protected design) through its normal channels or other specified channels, such as outlet stores. Option—if removal would destroy or damage the merchandise, the licensed products may be sold with the marks undisturbed as long as the goods are clearly marked as "seconds" and remain of a quality consistent with the standards of the licensor.
- Licensee will refresh its collection of licensed products during each designated period of the term by adding a specified number of new original and distinct styles or designs each specified type of apparel. Optional—licensee reports at the end of each design period, indicating quantities produced of each SKU.
- Loss of rights or reduction of rights to non-exclusivity, as to the entire agreement or designated licensed product or product categories, if licensee fails to produce and distribute a minimum number of new SKUs or to hit other targets. For example, if licensee is required to expand the licensed brand into A, B, C and D categories by Y date, and fails to do so as to any of them, it loses the affected categories.
- Licensor receives the opportunity to purchase reasonable quantities of licensed products for retail sale to consumers and for marketing, promotional, and sales incentive purposes. Those licensed products will be available to the licensor throughout the contract term and

the sell-off period at licensee's lowest then-applicable wholesale price.

- An example of an exception to the exclusive grant for situations in which Licensor itself maintains a significant retail presence: licensor and its designees shall have the right to sell products that compete with, or are substantially similar to, the licensed products solely in its owned, operated or franchised retail stores and outlets, through any dedicated website and catalogues.[8] An option is the reverse of that: licensor commits to buy a certain quantity of licensed products for sale in its own venues.

Licensed Marks

- Licensor will not grant or sanction any other party to use any mark identical with, or substantially similar to, the licensed marks in a manner that conflicts with the rights granted to licensee.
- Licensee will not have any right, title or interest in the marks. All goodwill developed in the marks by licensee inures to the benefit of licensor.
- Licensee may not file any application for any mark similar to any licensed marks or, in some agreements, any marks of licensor.
- In all events, licensor can only license its marks to licensee under its own quality-control standards. It may supply a style guide, designate a quality-control representative, or take a lighter approach such as receiving and reviewing regular submissions of what licensee is doing, whether in the design phase, as samples or actual production models. Whatever the method, licensor should be able to demonstrate that it maintains quality control over the use of its marks.

Approval of Designs and Licensed Products

- State whether licensor will or may supply licensee with designs or cooperation in the creation of designs and at which party's expense.

[8] That would be used when, for example, licensor has its own sources for products that are exclusive to its boutiques.

- All designs, of whatever origin, will be used only for the licensed products during the term.
- State if licensor must give reasons for any disapproval of the use of a design, if licensee has the right to resubmit any disapproved item following modification, and whether silence by licensor as to any submission constitutes its acceptance or rejection. That is usually possible if approval occurs during the design or sample stage—less likely if during the actual manufacturing stage.
- State any specific aspects of product development over which Licensee has approval rights, such as licensed product specifications, materials, product testing and other matters.
- State which party will own the designs and whether and to what extent the other party may continue to make use of the designs following the end of the term.

Term and termination.

- The term provision gives the duration, states if the license automatically renews unless terminated, when that must happen and if there are any specific procedures for renewal.
- As in many other commercial contracts, a provision states what constitutes a breach or default for cause, if it may be cured and by when, and how the other party may terminate the agreement if there is no satisfactory cure. Unique to license agreements: state what happens to licensed products not yet sold and to those that are returned or returnable to licensee.

Manufacturers

- State if licensee has the right to make arrangements to subcontract the manufacture of the licensed products. Licensor may want approval rights over sources.
- Licensee must monitor and maintain its manufacturer's compliance with licensor's standards for the licensed products, as well as compliance with consumer product safety laws, child labor laws and other applicable laws and regulations.

- The subcontractor typically may not sell or distribute products to anyone other than licensee.
- Frequently, unless licensor agrees, licensee does not have the right to sublicense any of the rights granted under the agreement; the right is limited to the subcontracting of manufacture.

Production, Consumer Advertising and Marketing Support

- Outline any Licensee requirements for promotion of the licensed products.
- Specify any requirements for a marketing budget, whether by fixed amounts or a formula.
- Specify any licensee payments to licensor for marketing support (or include those in the financial provisions).
- State whether and how licensee will submit to licensor a written production, sales, marketing and advertising plan for any contractual period and the method of approval, if required.
- State whether co-branding is permitted (with licensee's brands or those of others), any restrictions on it and the approval process.
- State whether licensor designates the advertising agency (usually because it is licensor's own agency) and for what forms of advertising.
- State whether and to what extent licensor has the right to approve individual media vehicles for licensee advertising.

Premium Sales, Endorsements and Events

- State whether and under what circumstances licensee may sell or give away units of licensed products to promote the products, services or business of itself or any individual or entity.
- State whether there are to be any permitted endorsements, such as celebrity endorsements, and how those are to be handled as by the parties.
- State whether and how licensor and licensee shall govern operations concerning licensee participation at trade shows or sponsored events or its participation in connection with any trade shows at which licensor is an exhibitor or any events (such as

sporting events) for which licensor is a sponsor. Describe here or in the financial provisions any division of financial responsibility between the parties for any such participation (or include that in any marketing support commitment).

Financial Provisions

- Guaranteed minimum royalties: the amount to be paid each year by licensee to licensor, regardless of sales volume. The guaranteed minimum, whether paid in advance, in installments or otherwise, is credited against actual royalties owed.
- Earned royalties: licensee will pay licensor a stated percentage of the total net sales of all products. The guaranteed minimum royalty will be credited against the royalty amounts payable in connection with licensed products sold during the relevant period. Define whether and to what extent any part of the guaranteed minimum royalty can be carried forward as a credit from one contract period to another and what circumstances would make that permissible.
- The calculation of net sales (or net receipts, net proceeds—however it is characterized) should be carefully expressed. The gross amount is typically all sales during a stated period. Deductions from that, to determine a net figure for payment of royalties, can include sales taxes, VAT and duties, shipping and customs-clearance charges, returns (or a reserve for returns), promotional goods, damaged goods, goods sold to licensor and bad debts.
- When royalties are paid: quarterly, monthly or otherwise. Note: much may depend on licensee's own deals with its retail accounts, particularly whether and to what extent it accepts returns.
- If royalty rates vary by outlet, be specific. It is often useful to be sure that the various types of outlets are clearly defined. For example, if there is a lower royalty for licensed products sold to "discount stores," define the type of retailer that qualifies as a discount store.
- State whether royalty payments for products sold to any party affiliated with, or related to, licensee, will be computed based on

licensee's regular wholesale price and not on the net sale price.[9] Also state whether royalty rates will vary by retailer, such as a lower percentage for outlet and mass-merchant stores.

Royalty Statements and Sales Reports

- Licensee will supply licensor with periodic statements of sales of the licensed products sold. Each statement must be delivered to licensor within a stated period following the close of the applicable statement period.
- Each report should contain enough information for the licensor to know enough about what is happening with its brand without having to ask too many questions. Typically included will be the price at which the licensed products have been sold, by SKU, and the net sales volume of each during the reporting period. List other details as needed to help understand the figure paid. Depending on the deal, that can include sales by retailer or retailer category, returns, a breakout concerning discounted sales, and expenses for advertising and marketing support expenditures.
- An audit clause permits licensor or perhaps an independent CPA firm hired by licensor the right to audit royalty payments and related compliance issues on due notice. An audit may occur once every stated period of time, and no reporting period can be audited more than once. If the audit discloses any error in the audited period, appropriate adjustments must be promptly paid to licensor. If any such error is made in favor of licensee in excess of a stated percentage of what was owed, licensee will also pay licensor for the cost of the audit.

Other Provisions

- As in all important agreements, add representations, warranties, indemnities, notice, a confidentiality provision and "boilerplate" provisions, as applicable.

[9] That would typically apply if a licensee affiliate does foreign distribution or has its own retail venues.

- If particular creative or business people working for licensee are crucial, add a key person clause.
- Conversely, licensees sometimes want a clause that prevents the licensor from hiring away key talent during the term and for a period of time following its conclusion.
- Licensee is given a specified a period of time, following conclusion of the term, to sell off leftover licensed products. Following the sell-off period, remaining licensed products would be destroyed, donated to charity or otherwise disposed of in a way that would likely not interfere with the activities in the licenses categories of licensor or its new licensee.

Courtesy of Alan Behr, Alston & Bird LLP

APPENDIX G

SAMPLE LICENSE PROVISIONS

Sample "Net Wholesale Sales" Definition

"Net Wholesale Sales" shall be defined as the gross invoiced sales price, net of any sales taxes ("Gross Wholesale Sales"), less trade discounts, returns, allowances, markdowns and charge-backs which would normally be treated as deductions from gross sales according to Generally Accepted Accounting Principles in the United Sates. The combined total of trade discounts, returns, allowances, markdowns and charge-backs in a Year shall not exceed ([ ]%) percent of the Gross Wholesale Sales of the Articles during such Year. No other deduction whatsoever shall be permitted. Any deduction claimed by Licensee must be verifiable and actual. If any amount payable to Licensor is subject to any non-US tax, charge or duty, Licensee shall furnish to Licensor official proof of such payment, including official proof of receipt of Licensee's payment from the government entity imposing such tax, charge or duty.

Sample Advertising Provision

During each year of this Agreement, Licensee shall expend for the advertising of Licensed Products, which advertising may consist of cooperative advertising, an amount that is not less than the "Annual Advertising Obligation", as hereinafter defined, for such year. Licensor and Licensee shall consult with each other regarding the creation, production and placement of all advertising of Licensed Products, but all final decisions with respect thereto shall be made by Licensor in its sole discretion. The "Annual Advertising Obligation" for each year during the term hereof shall be ([ ]%) of the aggregate net sales price of Licensed Products sold during such year. Licensee shall deliver to Licensor within sixty (60) days after the end of each year hereof an accounting statement in respect of amounts expended by Licensee on advertising for the prior year. Each such accounting statement shall be signed, and certified as correct, by a duly authorized officer of License. Prior to each year hereof, Licensee shall submit Licensee's advertising budget for the upcoming year, based on the aggregate net sales price of Licensed Products during the year then ending and on sales projected for the upcoming year. The Annual Advertising Obligation for such upcoming year will initially be calculated and expended based upon such budget. If in any year during the term hereof an amount less than the Annual Advertising Obligation is expended on advertising for any reason whatsoever, the entire amount not expended shall be added to the Annual Advertising Obligation for the following year.

Sample Accounting Provision

1. Licensee shall at all times keep an accurate account of all operations within the scope of this Agreement and shall render a full statement of such operations in writing to Licensor. Such statements shall account separately for each different product category and shall include all aggregate gross sales, trade discounts, merchandise returns, sales of miscuts and damaged merchandise and net sales price of all sales for the previous month. Such statements shall be in sufficient detail to be audited from the books of Licensee. Once annually, which may be in connection with the regular annual audit of Licensee's books, Licensee shall furnish an annual statement of the aggregate gross sales, trade discounts, merchandise returns and net sales price of all Licensed Products made or sold by Licensee certified by Licensee's independent accountant. Each monthly financial statement furnished by Licensee shall be certified by the chief financial officer or controller of Licensee.
2. Licensor and its duly authorized representatives, on reasonable notice, shall have the right, no more than once in each year during regular business hours, for the duration of the term of this Agreement and for three (3) years thereafter, to examine the books of account and records and all other documents, materials and inventory in the possession or under the control of Licensee and its successors with respect to the subject matter of this Agreement. All such books of account, records and documents shall be maintained and kept available by Licensee for at least the duration of this Agreement and for three (3) years thereafter. Licensor shall have free and full access thereto in the manner set forth above and shall have the right to make copies and/or extracts therefrom. If as a result of any examination of Licensee's books and records it is

shown that Licensee's payments to Licensor hereunder with respect to any twelve (12) month period were less than or greater than the amount which should have been paid to Licensor by an amount equal to [__]% of the amount which should have been paid during such twelve (12) month period, Licensee will, in addition to reimbursement of any underpayment, with interest from the date on which each payment was due at the rate of [ ], promptly reimburse Licensor for the cost of such examination.

Sample Currency Exchange Provision

In the event Licensee's sales of Articles are in the currency of a foreign territory, Net Wholesale Sales of such Articles shall be reported to Licensor in U.S. Dollars using the Average Exchange (as hereinafter defined) for each month the report relates to. The percentage royalty payable thereon shall be calculated in the U.S. Dollar equivalent of the Average Exchange Rate, for the reporting period, and paid in accordance with the provisions of this Agreement. For purposes of this Agreement, "Average Exchange Rate" for any period of time with respect to any currency other than U.S. Dollars means the average of the daily average price for each day during such period of time at which the U.S. Dollar could have been purchased with such other currency, on the rates reported for such date(s) by the Wall Street Journal.

Sample Key Person Provision

The Company shall cause Designer to render her services in a professional manner consistent with the intent of this Agreement and to use her reasonable good faith efforts to participate in the promotion and imaging of the Licensed Products including, without limitation, through television, social media and print advertising, in-store videos, appearances and other media presentations or programs and shall use reasonable and appropriate opportunities, in her reasonable discretion, to promote the Licensed Products and the sale thereof including, without limitation, interviews, editorials, press conferences, press releases , social media and television appearances. In light of the considerable demands on Designer's schedule, the Company and Licensee shall cooperate in good faith to schedule the dates, times, places and manner in which Designer shall fulfill her obligations under this Section as far in advance, and in the most convenient manner, possible. Subject to the final sentence of this Section, the Company shall cause Designer to be available to render services under this Section consistent with past practices, but in no event for more than [ ] days annually, inclusive of travel time. Licensee shall pay all costs and expenses in connection with such services including, without limitation, costs of first class air travel (or private plane) and lodging. Any expenses in excess of $[ ] shall be first submitted to Licensee for approval. No failure by the Company to comply with the terms of this provision by reason of the death, disability or incapacity of Designer shall be considered a breach of this Agreement.

Courtesy of Lois Herzeca, Gibson, Dunn & Crutcher LLP

APPENDIX H

INCORPORATION QUESTIONNAIRE

____

Enter Desired Name Of Corporation, Above

INSTRUCTIONS:

A. Items 1, 2, 3, 4, 5 and 6 will appear on the Statement of Information which becomes part of the public record of the California Secretary of State.
B. The addresses required in Items 2, 3, 5 and 6 must be street addresses and not post office boxes. The addresses required in Items 5 and 6 can be either home or business addresses.
C. With respect to Items 4 and 5, the California Corporations Code states that the minimum number of directors shall not be less than three; provided, however, if there is only one shareholder, the number of directors may be one or more. Likewise, if there are two shareholders, there may be two or more directors.
D. A California corporation must have a President, Secretary and a Chief Financial Officer (as well as any other officers it chooses). Any number of offices may be held by the same person; however, it is usually preferable for the offices of President and Secretary to be held by different persons. See Item 6.
E. Items 7, 8, 9, and 10 will appear on the Form SS-4 Application for Federal Employer Identification Number.

PLEASE COMPLETE:

1. General type of business (e.g., software developer, consultant, retail store):

2. Street address:

    a. Of principal executive office:

        Phone:
        Fax:

b. Of principal business office in California if different from 2a:

c. Mailing address if different from 2a:

3. Agent for service of process and address:

4. Authorized Number of Directors (See Instruction C):

5. Names of all Directors:

6. Names of all Officers (See Instruction D):

President:
Vice President:
Secretary:
Chief Financial Officer (Treasurer):
Other:

7. President's Social Security Number:

8. First date wages will be paid:

9. Highest number of employees expected in the next twelve months:

10. Date of Fiscal Year End:

11. Date of Annual Meeting (e.g., First Tuesday in April):

12. Authorized Number and Class of Shares of Stock:

13. Proposed Shareholder(s)[1]:

[1] If any of the proposed shareholders have a trust, please consult your estate planning professional in connection with whether or not the shares of this corporation should be held by a trust.

NAME(S): NO. OF SHARES:

PRICE PER SHARE: $

14. Does your accountant advise that the corporation elect to be taxed as a small business corporation under Subchapter S of the Internal Revenue Code and California Law?

    a. If the answer is "yes", please provide each shareholder's social security number.

Name Social Security Number

    b. If the answer is "yes", please provide the name of each spouse of the shareholder(s) having a community property interest in the corporation's stock as well as each such spouse's social security number.

Name Social Security Number

(We require this information because each spouse holding a community property interest must also sign a consent to the Subchapter S election.)

15. Please provide a list of the state(s) in which you will transact business:

____

____

Courtesy of Vicki Dallas, Rutan & Tucker LLP

APPENDIX I

CHECKLIST FOR CALIFORNIA LLC FORMATION

INSTRUCTIONS:

The name of the LLC must end with "LLC" or "Limited Liability Company" and may not contain the words "bank", "insurance", "trust", "trustee", "incorporated", "inc.", "corporation", or "corp".

Please contact me to discuss possible answers for items about which you are unsure.

PLEASE COMPLETE:

1. Proposed LLC Names:

   First Choice:
   Second Choice:

2. Latest date on which the LLC is to dissolve (or perpetual):

3. Initial principal place of business:

   a. Street address:
   b. Phone Number: (   )
   c. Facsimile Number: (   )

4. Initial agent for service of process:

   a. Name:
   Street Address:

5. The LLC will be managed by:

   a. [] one manager
   b. [] more than one manager
   c. [] limited liability company member(s)

6. Name(s) and address(es) of manager(s), as applicable:

7. If applicable, the maximum liability manager(s) may incur on behalf of LLC without the approval of the members:
   $

8. Names and titles of officers (Optional):

9. Name, address, amount and type (e.g., cash, property, future services, promissory notes) of capital contribution and number of shares or membership interests for each initial member (attach additional sheets as necessary):

   a. Member 1:

      Name and address:

      Capital Contribution and Number of Shares or Membership Interests:

   b. Member 2:

      Name and address:

      Capital Contribution and Number of Shares or Membership Interests:

   c. Member 3:

      Name and address:

      Capital Contribution and Number of Shares or Membership Interests:

   d. Member 4:

Name and address:

Capital Contribution and Number of Shares or Membership Interests:

10. Total number of shares or membership interests authorized for issuance (optional):

11. Distributions of cash flow shall be:

    [ ] in proportion to capital contributions
    [ ] (%) to each manager and the remainder as follows:
    [ ] other (explain)

12. Timing of distributions:

    [ ] annual
    [ ] by election of a majority of members
    [ ] by election of all members
    [ ] other (explain)

13. Preferred return, if desired: (%)

14. Allocations of profits and losses shall be:

    [ ] pro rata based on percentage of contributions
    [ ] other (explain)

15. Voting rights of members shall be:

    [ ] in proportion to interest in profits
    [ ] other (explain)

16. Date of fiscal year end:

17. Accounting method:

18. Type of business to be conducted:

19. Name, title and social security number of member who will sign the SS-4 Application for Employer Identification Number:

20. First date wages were paid or will be paid:

21. Highest number of employees expected in the next twelve months:

Courtesy of Vicki Dallas, Rutan & Tucker LLP

APPENDIX J

SAMPLE TERMS AND CONDITIONS

1. This Order is an offer by the purchaser/customer listed on this Order ("Buyer") upon the terms below and is subject to acceptance based on, among other things, the Buyer's credit approval, and after acceptance by XYZ, Inc. ("XYZ" or "Seller") shall constitute a valid contract unless cancelled in writing by Buyer 60 days prior to the start ship date, or by the applicable cancellation date, whichever is earlier.
2. Buyer understands that certain styles and/or sizes may be unavailable. Buyer will accept all available styles and sizes.
3. All shipments are made at Buyer's risk and Buyer assumes all shipping costs.. Deliveries against this Order are subject to credit approval by XYZ's credit department or factor at the time of shipment. Terms are F.O.B. Los Angeles and title passes to Buyer upon the earlier of delivery to Buyer or carrier. The acceptance of shipment by a common carrier or licensed public truckman shall constitute delivery.
4. Returns will be accepted for merchandise credit only, and only if there is a manufacturing defect. No returns accepted without XYZ's written permission. All claims for any allowances, deductions, or returns must be made in writing by Buyer within 10 days of receipt of goods listed on this order.
5. **Buyer may not display and/or sell "XYZ" trademarks or other XYZ intellectual property, or any XYZ products, on any website without prior written authorization from XYZ.**
6. **Buyer warrants and represents that it is purchasing the items purchased pursuant to this Order (the "Products") for resale to retail customers only at Buyer's retail store(s), and that it will not sell any of the Products to any other retailer, jobber, distributor, wholesaler or any other entity for resale to third parties without XYZ's written consent. Buyer acknowledges that any violation of paragraphs 5 and 6 of this Agreement will cause irreparable damage to XYZ.**

7. All orders are taken subject to delays or non-delivery caused by any reason beyond XYZ's control, and XYZ will not be liable for any force majeur or other factors beyond its control.
8. If any provision of this order is held to be unlawful, the remaining provisions shall remain in full force and effect.
9. The validity, construction, and performance of the agreement reached pursuant to this Order ("Agreement") is and shall be governed by the laws of the state of California. The forum for the resolution of any dispute related to this Agreement, whether in tort, contract or in equity, shall be the state or federal courts located in Los Angeles, California.
10. This Agreement constitutes the entire agreement between the parties and supercedes all prior negotiations and agreements between the parties concerning its subject matter. Notwithstanding any language to the contrary contained in this Order, if XYZ and Buyer have previously entered into a valid written distribution agreement, and there is a conflict between the terms of this Order and any valid written distribution agreement between XYZ and Buyer, the terms of the valid, written distribution agreement shall control.
11. No waiver, amendment, or modification of this agreement by XYZ shall be effective unless in writing and signed by XYZ. No failure or delay by XYZ in exercising any right, power, or remedy shall operate as a waiver of the right, power or remedy, and no waiver of any term, condition or default of this Agreement by XYZ shall be construed as a waiver of any other term condition or default.
12. This order and Agreement is deemed to be drafted jointly by both Buyer and XYZ. Any uncertainty or ambiguity shall not be construed for or against either party based on attribution of drafting.
13. Buyer and XYZ acknowledge that failure of XYZ to perform to the terms of this Agreement may cause Buyer to incur costs the exact amount of which may be difficult to fix. Nonetheless, under no circumstances shall XYZ be liable for any incidental, consequential or exemplary damages relating to its performance or failure to perform pursuant to this Agreement.

Courtesy of Richard Reinis, Stephtoe & Johnson LLP

APPENDIX K

SAMPLE FACTORING FORM

XYZ, LLC

August 24, 2010

Attention: Accounts Payable Department

Ladies and Gentlemen:

Please be advised that we have entered into a Factoring Agreement with ABC Factoring, Inc. ("ABC") pursuant to which we have sold and assigned to ABC all of our accounts receivable arising and/or created on or after____________, 2011.

Accordingly, all payments on accounts receivable arising from goods sold or services rendered by us to you evidenced by invoices dated on or after ___________, 2011 must be made to **and only to:**

ABC Factoring, Inc.
P.O. Box _________
____

Please be further advised that these instructions may not be changed without the written approval of ABC.

Please advise the appropriate departments of this change.

Very truly yours

XYZ, LLC

By:________________________
Name:
Title:

Courtesy of Richard Reinis, Stephtoe & Johnson LLP

APPENDIX L

INDEPENDENT SALES REPRESENTATIVE FORM AGREEMENT

ABC, INC.

This Agreement is entered into this __ day of ____________, ____ by and between ______________________________ ("Independent Rep") and ABC, INC., a California corporation ("COMPANY").

1. INDEPENDENT REP is hereby appointed by COMPANY to be its exclusive sales representative for the womenswear products of COMPANY sold under the labels __________ and ______________. The territory to be covered by INDEPENDENT REP for this Agreement includes the following states: ____.

2. Each month during the term hereof, COMPANY shall pay INDEPENDENT REP a commission of __% of net sales in the territory made by INDEPENDENT REP, except as specifically set forth below. Sales made by others in the territory of INDEPENDENT REP shall generate a split commission, whereby INDEPENDENT REP shall be paid one half the commission which would have been paid by COMPANY to INDEPENDENT REP had it made such sale. Sales made by INDEPENDENT REP to customers outside the Territory wherein no other sales representative is granted an exclusive territory shall generate full commission. "Net Sales" means the invoiced amount of all sales, less freight, insurance, allowances, discounts and returns ("chargebacks"). Not later than the 25th of the month, COMPANY shall render to INDEPENDENT REP a commission statement summarizing all invoices for sales made in the Territory, including documentation of all chargebacks and adjustments for the month prior. INDEPENDENT REP shall serve written notice on COMPANY of any question or complaint with its

commission statement within sixty days of receipt, or said statement shall be deemed approved by Independent Rep.

3. Sales made by INDEPENDENT REP at prices other than published wholesale prices ("Line Price") shall be approved by COMPANY in advance. INDEPENDENT REP agrees to the following schedule of reduced commission with regard to such sales:

	Discount from Line Price	Commission
A.	13 to 20%	__%
B.	21 to 33%	__%
C.	34 and greater	__%

INDEPENDENT REP shall have no authority to make any off-priced sales. "Off-priced sales" means any sale made by INDEPENDENT REP at a discount greater than 10% of line price. Any discounts or returns must be approved in advance by COMPANY.

4. Commencing on the effective date hereof, COMPANY shall advance INDEPENDENT REP the refundable sum of $_____ per month ("draw"), as an advance payment of commissions due hereunder and to be earned by INDEPENDENT REP as contemplated hereby, and COMPANY shall continue monthly to advance funds, except as provided herein. COMPANY may discontinue payment of the draw at any time upon ten days notice if INDEPENDENT REP has received more advances than commissions earned for two or more consecutive months during the term hereof, measured after the second month of the term. COMPANY shall discontinue draws in the event of any breach hereof by INDEPENDENT REP, in addition to any and all other remedies of COMPANY. Any advance hereunder shall be recoverable by COMPANY and charged first against any commission due and owing to INDEPENDENT REP hereunder. INDEPENDENT REP hereby agrees to refund any advance in excess of commissions due as of the date of termination hereof.

5. COMPANY shall have no liability for any expenses incurred by INDEPENDENT REP during the term hereof, except as specifically provided herein. INDEPENDENT REP shall be personally liable for all expenses incurred in connection with the performance of its services required hereunder, including, but not limited to, travel, entertainment, insurance and taxes. COMPANY shall not withhold any tax or tax deposits from payments made to INDEPENDENT REP hereunder, and INDEPENDENT REP shall hold COMPANY harmless from and against any and all liability to any taxing authority relative to payments made by COMPANY TO INDEPENDENT REP hereunder. INDEPENDENT REP shall further indemnify, defend and hold COMPANY harmless from and against any claim or liability arising from INDEPENDENT REP's negligence or wrongful acts or omissions or from and against any claim or liability arising from a complaint of any employee or agent of INDEPENDENT REP, or in the event that INDEPENDENT REP grants a customer of COMPANY any discount, allowance, or return privilege without the prior written or verifiable (by third parties employed by COMPANY) approval of COMPANY.

6. COMPANY shall sell samples of the products to INDEPENDENT REP at 50% of line price, which sum shall be charged against commissions earned for each season. The charge shall be credited against the payment of commissions hereunder, at the rate of one-third per month for each month of the season during which the samples are used. INDEPENDENT REP may return samples of discontinued products, provided that such samples are in salable condition and provided further that COMPANY, in its sole discretion, approves the return in advance. Any unreturned samples shall be charged to INDEPENDENT REP. INDEPENDENT REP shall not be charged for non-salable samples, such as those which are stamped in accordance with import regulations, or those which are damaged by COMPANY.

7. INDEPENDENT REP shall deliver all purchase orders to COMPANY upon receipt. All purchase orders for products of

COMPANY are the property of COMPANY, which in its sole discretion may accept or reject any order. Approval of purchase orders shall be communicated in writing within twenty-one days of the date when COMPANY or its factor determines to reject any order. Notwithstanding any acceptance of an order by COMPANY, any order rejected by COMPANY'S factor at any time shall be deemed rejected. COMPANY shall have no obligation to pay INDEPENDENT REP for any order not shipped due to conditions beyond COMPANY'S control, including without limitation, war, insurrection, strike, embargo, late delivery by supplier, fire, damaged products, theft, vandalism, and other events normally referred to as force majeur which are beyond COMPANY'S control. COMPANY shall pay commissions to INDEPENDENT REP on not less than 80% of all approved orders, subject to the provisions above stated.

8. In the event INDEPENDENT REP sells products of the COMPANY to customers outside the territory of INDEPENDENT REP, then such sale shall generate a commission at fifty percent of the commission rate which would have been paid if the customer was within the territory of INDEPENDENT REP. In the event that sales are made by any other salesperson working for COMPANY to customers in the territory of INDEPENDENT REP, then COMPANY shall pay INDEPENDENT REP fifty percent of the commission INDEPENDENT REP would have earned had it made such sale. Thereafter, INDEPENDENT REP shall have the obligation and responsibility to work with the customer in its territory and it shall receive full commission for sales made to such customer in its territory.

9. Any sale by INDEPENDENT REP to a buying office, centralized buying service, mail order or catalogue account, which sale is accepted by COMPANY, shall be deemed made in the territory wherein the products are distributed, regardless of the shipping or billing address of the purchaser. From time to time, COMPANY shall have the right on three months' notice to declare an account a House Account. In the event that COMPANY has so notified

INDEPENDENT REP of the declaration of House Account, then three months from receipt of such notice, INDEPENDENT REP shall cease to receive commission for sales made to such House Account, and shall have no further obligation to service such account. As of the date hereof, House Accounts are those identified in Exhibit "A", attached hereto and incorporated by this reference.

10. This Agreement shall commence on the __ day of __________, _______ and continue until terminated by either party. Either party may cancel this agreement by written notice, not less than thirty days prior to the commencement of the next selling season. COMPANY shall pay commissions for all net sales of COMPANY derived from accepted orders made by INDEPENDENT REP, including net sales which are shipped after the effective date of termination. COMPANY shall have the right to establish a ninety (90) day reserve upon the effective date of termination in an amount reasonably estimated as of the date of termination to cover chargebacks not received as of the date of termination. INDEPENDENT REP shall assist COMPANY in any reasonable manner to collect all outstanding receivables from commissionable accounts. This covenant shall survive termination of the Agreement.

11. INDEPENDENT REP shall use its best efforts to promote and solicit maximum sales of COMPANY's products and collection of accounts. INDEPENDENT REP shall attend all regional trade shows in its Territory, as well as not less than two national trade shows per annum. INDEPENDENT REP shall adhere to pricing and other policies established by COMPANY, and INDEPENDENT REP shall not make any representation, warranty or commitment on behalf of COMPANY without first obtaining prior written consent. Notwithstanding any statute to the contrary, nothing herein contained shall be deemed to create any employer-employee relationship between the parties. INDEPENDENT REP hereby represents and warrants that it has obtained and will keep in full force and effect during the term hereof, adequate policies of workmen's compensation insurance to

provide benefits for all persons performing services on behalf of INDEPENDENT REP. INDEPENDENT REP may at all times during the term hereof represent any other manufacturer of non-competitive products.

12. During the term of this Agreement, INDEPENDENT REP shall maintain and service not less than two showrooms, one at ________________, New York City, New York, and a second at ________________, Los Angeles, California. A sign bearing the tradenames and trademarks of COMPANY, approved in advance by COMPANY, shall be prominently displayed in and upon said showrooms so as to maximize exposure of the products of COMPANY. All costs of said showrooms shall be borne by INDEPENDENT REP. INDEPENDENT REP shall not sell products from these showrooms, which products are competitive (as hereafter defined) with the products of COMPANY. "Competitive" is defined to mean apparel of the same type and description as manufactured by COMPANY made from similar fabrications and sold at similar or lower prices, which are offered to the same departments of any customers as INDEPENDENT REP offers the products of COMPANY. In the event that INDEPENDENT REP breaches the provisions hereof, COMPANY shall have the right to demand the INDEPENDENT REP cease representation of the competitive products or representation of COMPANY, in addition to any and all other remedies.

13. INDEPENDENT REP shall attend not less than four annual merchandising events at the premises of COMPANY at INDEPENDENT REP's sole cost and expense. COMPANY shall seek to schedule such events so as not to conflict with market calendars and as far in advance of the meetings as possible. INDEPENDENT REP shall attend and exhibit products of COMPANY at all regional trade shows in the Territory, and reasonably staff and service its selling space, at its sole cost and expense.

14. This Agreement shall be governed by the laws of the State of California. In the event of a dispute arising from the terms of this agreement, the prevailing party in such dispute shall be entitled, in addition to any award, to an award of actual attorney's fees and costs incurred therein. This agreement shall be binding upon and inure to the benefit of the parties hereto. Each provision of this agreement is severable for purposes of determining enforceability hereof, and in the event that any provision is found to be unenforceable, all other provisions shall be unaffected thereby. INDEPENDENT REP shall not assign this agreement to any other party for any reason, without the prior written consent of COMPANY, which may be withheld at the COMPANY's discretion for any reason.

15. Notices of any kind required hereunder shall be delivered in writing and addressed to INDEPENDENT REP and COMPANY at the addresses above listed , or at such other address as either my use as their principal office during the term hereof. All such notices shall be given either by (1) personal delivery, (2) U.S. mail, postage prepaid, or (3) facsimile (provided that such facsimile transmission is confirmed). Notices shall be deemed to have been given when either (1) personally delivered, (2) on the first business day following the date of mailing, or (3) on the date sent by facsimile, as such are applicable.

16. COMPANY shall share with INDEPENDENT REP trade secrets which are proprietary to COMPANY and subject to the Uniform Trade Secrets Act, ________________. INDEPENDENT REP agrees to maintain any and all information derived and obtained from COMPANY in confidence solely and exclusively for the purpose of fulfilling its obligations hereunder, and not to release said information to any third party during the term of the Agreement and for a period of one year after termination.

17. In the event of litigation arising with respect to any of the terms hereof, the parties, each of which acknowledges the right to a trial by jury, agree that it is in their best interest to WAIVE THE RIGHT TO TRIAL BY JURY IN ANY SUCH ACTION BASED

UPON, ARISING FROM, OR IN ANY WAY RELATING TO THIS AGREEMENT.

In witness whereof, the parties have executed this Agreement the date above first written.

ABC, INC. ______________________

by______________________ by__________________

Courtesy of Richard Reinis, Stephtoe & Johnson LLP

APPENDIX M

FACTORING AGREEMENT

Los Angeles, CA, DATE

ABC COMPANY, INC.
123 Main Street
Los Angeles, CA

The following is the Agreement under which we are to act as your sole Factor. Capitalized terms shall have the meanings set forth in Section 14 hereof:

1. SALES AND ASSIGNMENT:

You hereby sell and assign to us, making us absolute owner thereof, of all of your Receivables, and we shall have the right to collect and otherwise deal therewith as the sole and exclusive owner thereof. Upon each sale of your Inventory or rendition by you of services, you shall execute and deliver to us such further and confirmatory assignments of your Receivables as we require, in form and manner satisfactory to us, together with copies of invoices or such equivalent electronic document as we may designate for such use, and all shipping or delivery receipts and such other proof of sale and delivery or performance as we, from time to time, may require. All invoices (and other statements to Customers) evidencing Receivables shall clearly state, in a manner satisfactory to us, that each Receivable has been sold and assigned to and is payable only to us.

2. CREDIT AND APPROVAL:

You will submit to us for our credit approval the principal terms of each and every Order. We may, in our sole discretion, approve all or a portion of an Order, by issuing a Credit Approval. No Credit Approval, including approval based upon shipment against Availability under a Credit Line shall be effective unless (i) the Inventory is shipped or the services rendered, within the time specified therein, or if no time is specified, within thirty (30) days after the date our Credit Approval is issued; (ii) the Customer has accepted delivery of the Inventory or performance of the services; and (iii) a confirmatory assignment of the Receivables(s) which arise as a result of the Order which is the subject of the Credit Approval has been delivered to us, within ten (10) days of the delivery of the goods or the performance of the service. Upon the effectiveness of a Credit Approval, we shall be deemed to have accepted the Credit Risk (but not the risk of non-payment for any other reason) to the extent of the dollar amount specified in the Credit Approval and the Receivable which is the subject thereof shall, to the extent of the amount specified in the Credit approval, be a Credit Approved Receivable. In no event, however, shall we have any Credit Risk on (i) the first $____ owing, at any time, from any Customer, or (ii) any Receivable for freight, samples, or sales not made in the ordinary course of your business. We may, in our sole discretion, withdraw any Credit Approval, or withdraw or adjust any Credit Line, at any time before you deliver the Inventory or render the services.

3. CLIENT RISK RECEIVABLES:

All CR Receivables are with full recourse to you and at your credit risk, but are otherwise subject to the covenants, terms and conditions provided herein with respect to Credit Approved Receivables. We shall have the right to charge back to your account the amount of CR Receivables at any time either before or after their maturity and you agree to pay us upon demand the amount thereof, together with all expenses including collection charges and attorneys' fees incurred by us in attempting to collect or enforce any such payment. In addition, if we, at your request, and in our discretion, file a proof of claim in any insolvency proceeding with respect to a CR Receivable and/or forward a CR Receivable to an attorney or agency for collection, we shall charge your account with (i) the fees and expenses of such attorney or collection agency and (ii) a service charge equal to ______ of any amount collected on the CR Receivable.

4. RETURNED MERCHANDISE/DISPUTES AND CHARGEBACKS:

In the event of a breach of any of the representations or warranties contained herein with respect to a Receivable, or the assertion, with respect to a Receivable, of a Dispute, any such Receivable (whether or not a Credit Approved Receivable) shall thereupon become a CR Receivable. You shall notify us immediately of any Dispute, including, a Customer's return of or desire to return any Inventory purchased from you. We may, but are not obligated, to settle, compromise, adjust or litigate any Dispute, including, a return of the related Inventory upon such terms as we deem advisable. We may, at our option, charge back to you all amounts owing on CR Receivables which are not paid when due. We shall have the right to charge back to you the amount of any payment which we receive with respect to a CR Receivable, if we are subsequently required to disgorge such payment for any reason, including, such payment being deemed a preferential transfer. A chargeback shall not constitute a resale or reassignment to you of the Receivable which is the subject thereof. You agree to indemnify and save us harmless from and against any and all loss, liability, claim, cost and expense of any kind, caused by or arising from any Disputes with or claims of your Customers and/or their representatives, including: (i) any disputes or claims with respect to terms, price, quality or otherwise with respect to Receivables; (ii) any claim for a return of any payments (including alleged preferential transfers with respect to payments on Receivables that were not Credit Approved Receivables at the time the payment was received); and (iii) all collection expenses and attorney's (whether in-house or outside) fees incurred with respect to any of the foregoing.

5. REPRESENTATIONS, WARRANTIES AND COVENANTS:

You represent, warrant and covenant that:

5.1. you are fully authorized to enter into this Agreement and perform hereunder and that you will continue to be so authorized for the duration of this Agreement.

5.2. you are solvent.

5.3. the Receivables are, and shall be, at the time of their creation, bona fide, existing and enforceable obligations of Customers arising out of sales made or services rendered by you, free and clear of all security interests, liens, claims and Disputes whatsoever other than Permitted Liens.

5.4. the Inventory is not subject to any security interest, lien or encumbrance whatsoever, other than Permitted Liens, and you covenant that you shall not permit the Inventory to become so encumbered without our prior written consent.

5.5. with respect to each Receivable as it arises: (i) you will have delivered the Inventory or rendered the services pursuant to the Order; (ii) the Customer will accept the Inventory and/or services without any offset or counterclaim; (iii) no known Dispute will exist in any respect; (iv) you will have preserved, and will continue to preserve, any liens and any other rights available to us by virtue of this Agreement; and (v) the Customer will not be your Affiliate.

5.6. you will within ten days of our request therefor, provide us with copies of invoices and shipping or delivery receipts or such equivalent electronic documents as we may designate or other proof of sale and delivery or performance as we may from time to time require.

5.7. you will not, without providing us with thirty (30) days prior written notice thereof, change your name, your state of organization or your principal place of business.

5.8. you shall cause to be maintained, at the end of each fiscal year, (a) Tangible Net Worth in an amount not less than $_______ and (b) Working Capital of not less than $________.

5.9. you do not transact business under any trade names or tradestyles except as set forth on an Exhibit annexed hereto and with respect to any such tradename or tradestyles you have caused the same to be registered in accordance with the laws applicable to the use of such tradenames or tradestyles.

6. COMMISSIONS:

6.1. For our services hereunder, we shall receive a factoring commission (hereinafter referred to as the "Base Commission") of (i) ___% of the gross invoice amount of each Receivable; plus (ii) on those Receivables due from a Customer (or any Affiliates or subsidiaries of such Customer) listed on the Special Accounts Schedule submitted herewith and/or from time to time hereafter, such percentage of the gross invoice amount thereof as equals the surcharge set forth on the Special Accounts Schedule, to the extent of the amount credit approved. All commissions shall be due and payable and chargeable to your account with us at the date a Receivable arises. The minimum commission payable by you to us on each invoice evidencing a Receivable shall be $______.

6.2. Our charge specified in Section 6.1 hereof is based upon maximum selling terms of __ days, and no more extended terms or additional dating shall be granted by you to any Customer without our prior written approval. If such approval is given by us, then for each additional thirty (30) days or part thereof of such extended terms or additional dating, our charge with respect to the Receivables covered thereby shall be increased by an amount equal to the greater of (x) one quarter of one percent (0.25 of 1%) of the invoice amount of such Receivable; or (y) _____ percent (__%) of the charge specified in Section 6.1 hereof. In addition, we shall charge you a fee of $___ for each instance in which you change the terms of sale of any Receivable after you have submitted to us a confirmatory assignment schedule listing such Receivable.

6.3. The minimum aggregate Base Commission payable under this Agreement shall be $______ for each Contract Year, but not less than $________ per ______, which shall be fully earned by us at the beginning of each Contract Year, and which to the extent of any deficiency (after giving effect to the commissions payable under Section 6.1), shall be chargeable to your account with us on a monthly basis.

7. PURCHASE PRICE; INTEREST RATE, ADVANCES AND RESERVES:

7.1. The purchase price for each Receivable shall be the invoice amount of the Receivable, less (i) returns (whenever made); (ii) selling discounts, credits or deductions of any kind allowed, granted to or taken by the Customer at any time; and (iii) our commission provided for in Section 6 hereof. No discount, credit or allowance with respect to any Receivable shall be granted by you, and no return of Inventory shall be accepted by you without our prior written consent. A discount, credit or allowance may be claimed only by the Customer. All amounts collected against the Receivables shall be credited to your account on the Payment Date.

7.2. In our sole discretion, in accordance with the terms of this Agreement, we will, from time to time at your request, advance to you, sums up to ___% of the aggregate purchase price of Eligible Receivables outstanding at the time any such advance is made less the Reserves, if any (the "Receivable Availability"); plus up to ____% of the lower of cost or market value of Eligible Inventory.

7.3. You will pay to us interest on the daily balance of all monies, paid or otherwise advanced to you or for your account net of all payments received from you or on your behalf. Interest will be calculated daily at a rate per annum equal to the Initial Interest Rate as increased or decreased by one quarter of one percent per annum for each one quarter of one percent per annum increase or decrease that is made in the Prime Rate after the date of this Agreement, any such change to become effective when and as the Prime Rate shall change, provided, that at no time shall the rate of interest payable by you hereunder be less than the Initial Interest Rate. The Initial Interest Rate shall mean ___% per annum (i.e. the Prime Rate on the date hereof plus ___% per annum). Interest will be charged to your account monthly in arrears. We may, in our sole discretion, remit to you, at any time, any amount standing to your credit on our books. Interest, as calculated above, will also be charged to you on all other Obligations, except those specifying a different rate, from the date incurred through the date paid. Upon the occurrence of a Default, and for so long as such Default continues, the Obligations shall, at our option, bear interest at the Default Rate. Interest shall be calculated on the basis of a three-hundred-sixty (360) day year for the actual number of days elapsed. In no event shall any applicable interest rate under this Agreement exceed the maximum rate permitted by applicable law and in the event excess interest is paid, it shall be considered a repayment of principal. You shall pay to us any Obligations upon demand.

8. STATEMENT OF ACCOUNT AND EXPENSES:

8.1. We will render a statement of account monthly to you, and such statement shall be binding upon you, except for specific matters which you contest and of which we are notified in writing to the contrary, within thirty (30) days after the date of such statement.

8.2. You shall pay all reasonable expenses (including attorneys, both in-house and outside, fees) incurred by us in connection with the preparation and execution of this Agreement and any other documents or agreements in connection with or related to this Agreement, and the relationship established in connection herewith and/or the transactions contemplated hereby, including, expenses incurred in connection with the filing of financing statements under the UCC and the making of record searches. We may also charge to your account any fees, costs or other expenses we incur to eliminate or cure any lack of capacity that we may now or hereafter have to maintain an action in the courts of any state to enforce payment or Receivables due from Customers located in such state by reason of your acts or omissions, including your failure to qualify as a foreign entity in such state or any other failure on your part to observe the laws of such state that are applicable to you or your assets. You shall also pay to us such fees as we may charge from time to time for, among other things, wire transfers. In connection with our examinations of your books, records and operations you shall pay all of our out-of-pocket expenses plus for each examiner the Standard Examiner's Rate in effect at the time of any such examination. Upon liquidation of any Collateral, settlement of any Dispute, or enforcement of any Obligation, we may charge to your account all costs and expenses incurred, including, attorneys' (both in-house and outside) fees. No delay or failure on our part in exercising any right, privilege, or option hereunder shall operate as a waiver of such or of any other right, privilege, or option, and no waiver, amendment, or modification of any provision of this Agreement shall be valid, unless in a writing signed by us and then only to the extent therein stated. Should any provision of this Agreement be prohibited by or invalid under applicable law, the validity of the remaining provisions shall not be affected thereby. Unless otherwise specifically provided in this Agreement, any notices, requests, demands or other communications permitted or required to be given under this Agreement shall be in writing and shall be sent by facsimile, hand delivery or by a nationally recognized overnight delivery service, to the addresses and facsimile numbers of the parties set forth below (or to such other address or facsimile number as a party may hereafter designate by a notice to the other that complies with this section) and shall be deemed given (a) in the case of a notice sent by facsimile, when received by the recipient if the sending party receives a confirmation of delivery from its own facsimile machine; and (b) in the case of a notice that is hand delivered or sent by such overnight courier, when delivered (provided that the sending party retains a confirmation of delivery). Any notice which, pursuant to the terms hereof must be sent by you by certified or registered mail shall be deemed given and effective when received by us.

If to us
Factor Name
Factor Address

If to you
ABC Company, Inc.
123 Main Street
Los Angeles, CA

Attn: President

Facsimile: (000) 000-0000

The headings used herein are intended to be for convenience of reference only and shall not define or limit the scope, extent or intent or otherwise affect the meaning of any portion hereof.

9. PAYMENTS:

9.1. All remittances obtained by you against Receivables will be received in trust for us, and you will turn over to us the identical remittances as speedily as possible; provided, however, that nothing herein authorizes you to collect Receivables. You constitute us, or any other entity or person whom we may designate, as your attorney in fact at your own cost and expense to exercise, at any time, all or any of the following powers which, being coupled with an interest, shall be irrevocable until this Agreement has been terminated and you have fully and indefeasibly paid and discharged all Obligations (a) to sign and/or endorse your name on all remittances and all papers, bills of lading, receipts, instruments and documents relating to the Receivables and the transactions between us; (b) to deposit any checks or other remittances received relating to the Receivables regardless of notations or conditions placed thereon by your customers or deductions reflected thereby and to charge the amount of any such deductions to your account; and (c) to sign your name to any and all documents necessary to cure or eliminate any lack of capacity that we may now or hereafter have, by reason of your acts or omissions, to maintain an action in the courts of any state to enforce payment of Receivables due from Customers located in such state and to file such documents with the appropriate public officials or agencies.

9.2. If any payment or recovery is received from or on behalf of a Customer which is a Customer on both Credit Approved Receivables and CR Receivables, any such payment or recovery may be first applied to the Credit Approved Receivables notwithstanding (i) any notation to the contrary on or with respect thereto; (ii) the payment terms thereof; (iii) the due date thereof; or (iv) whether such payments were made in the ordinary course of business or otherwise.

10. SECURITY INTEREST; FINANCING STATEMENTS:

10.1. To secure all of the Obligations, you hereby grant to us a security interest in all of your Accounts, Instruments, Chattel Paper, Documents,

Investment property, General Intangibles, Deposit Accounts, Letter of Credit Rights, property at any time in our possession, and the Reserves (whether or not any of the foregoing are specifically assigned to us), in each case whether currently owned or hereafter acquired by you and whether now existing or hereafter arising (whether before, during the effectiveness of, or after the termination of this Agreement) and wherever located, any security and guarantees therefor, in any goods or property represented thereby, in all of your books and records relating to the foregoing, and any equipment containing such books and records, in all sums of money at any time to your credit with us, all of your present and future claims against us under or in connection with this Agreement and in all Proceeds.

Without in any way limiting the generality of the foregoing, you further sell, and assign to us and grant to us a security interest, in all your right, title and/or interest in the Inventory represented by Receivables as well as Inventory returned by or repossessed from Customers, all of your rights as an unpaid vendor or lienor, all of your rights of stoppage in transit, replevin and reclamation relating thereto, and all of your rights against third parties with respect thereto. You will cooperate with us in exercising any rights with respect to any of the foregoing.

10.2. You authorize us to file financing statements and any and all other documents that may now or hereafter be provided for by the UCC to reflect and/or perfect any security interest now or hereafter granted by you to us in any of your presently owned or hereafter acquired property. In the event that any jurisdiction requires a debtor's signature on such financing statements and/or such other documents, you authorize us to file such financing statements and/or other documents on your behalf as your attorney in fact, which such power being coupled with an interest, shall be irrevocable until this Agreement has been terminated and you have fully and indefeasibly paid and discharged all of the Obligations.

11. BOOKS AND RECORDS/FINANCIAL STATEMENTS:

We and our representatives shall, at all reasonable times, have the right to examine all of your books and records. You agree to prepare and furnish to us within ____ (___) days after the close of each of your fiscal ______, financial statements reviewed and in such form and detail as we may reasonably require. You also agree to have prepared, and to furnish to us within _____ (___) days after the close of each of your fiscal years, financial statements, in accordance with GAAP, which have been reviewed by an independent certified public accountant satisfactory to us.

12. TERM:

This Agreement shall commence on the date hereof, shall continue for one Contract Period and shall automatically renew at the end of each Contract Period for an additional Contract Period. Notwithstanding the foregoing, this Agreement may be terminated (i) by us at any time, on not less than thirty (30) days prior written notice to you; or (ii) by you, effective at the end of a Contract Period provided you give us notice in writing, by registered or certified mail, not less than thirty (30) days, and not more than sixty (60) days prior to the expiration of the then effective Contract Period, of your intention to terminate this Agreement as at the end of such Contract Period; or (iii) by you, at any time, upon your written request to us to terminate this Agreement effective as of the date set forth in such request provided that (x) we in our sole discretion agree to such request and (y) you pay to us an Early Termination Fee upon the effective date of such termination. In the event of a Default, we shall have the right to terminate this Agreement at any time without notice, and you shall owe us an Early Termination Fee calculated as of the date of such termination. The Early Termination Fee shall become automatically due and payable in the event a petition is filed by or against you under any provision of Title 11 of the United States Code. Our rights and the Obligations arising out of transactions having their inception prior to the termination date shall not be affected by any termination or notice thereof. Termination of this Agreement shall not become effective in respect of the liens and security interests granted to us hereunder until you have fully and indefeasibly paid and discharged all Obligations, and until such time, you shall continue to furnish confirmatory assignments and schedules of Receivables to us and deliver and pay over to us all Proceeds in respect thereof. After the giving of any notice of termination hereunder and until the full liquidation of your account and the indefeasible payment in full of all Obligations, you shall not be entitled to receive any equities or payments from us, to the extent we are obligated to make payments to you under this Agreement. From and after the effective date of termination, all amounts charged or chargeable to your account hereunder, and all other Obligations, shall become immediately due and payable without further notice or demand.

13. GOVERNING LAWS/JURY TRIAL WAIVER/JURISDICTION/VENUE AND MISCELLANEOUS PROVISIONS:

This Agreement, and all rights and obligations arising hereunder or under applicable law, shall be governed, interpreted and construed in accordance with the laws of the State of New York. No modification, waiver or discharge of this Agreement shall be binding upon us unless in writing and signed by us. Our failure, at any time, to exercise any right or remedy hereunder, shall not constitute a waiver on our part with respect to such right or remedy, nor shall such failure preclude us from exercising the same or any other right or remedy at any subsequent time. If any taxes are imposed upon us, or if we shall be required to withhold or pay any tax or penalty because of or in connection with any transactions between us under this Agreement, you shall indemnify us and hold us harmless in respect thereof. This Agreement embodies our entire agreement as to the subject matter hereof and supersedes all prior agreements (whether oral or written) as to the subject matter hereof. **TRIAL BY JURY IS HEREBY WAIVED BY EACH OF US IN ANY ACTION, PROCEEDING OR COUNTERCLAIM BROUGHT BY EITHER OF US AGAINST THE OTHER ON ANY MATTERS WHATSOEVER ARISING OUT OF OR IN ANY WAY CONNECTED WITH THIS AGREEMENT OR THE RELATIONSHIP CREATED HEREBY (WHETHER SOUNDING IN TORT OR CONTRACT). YOU HEREBY CONSENT TO THE EXCLUSIVE JURISDICTION OF THE STATE COURTS LOCATED IN THE COUNTY OF NEW YORK, STATE OF NEW YORK, AND OF ANY FEDERAL COURT IN SUCH COUNTY AND STATE, FOR A DETERMINATION OF ANY DISPUTE AS TO ANY SUCH MATTERS. IN CONNECTION THEREWITH, YOU HEREBY WAIVE PERSONAL SERVICE OF ANY SUMMONS, COMPLAINT OR OTHER PROCESS AND AGREE THAT SERVICE THEREOF MAY BE MADE BY REGISTERED OR CERTIFIED MAIL DIRECTED TO YOU AT YOUR ADDRESS SET FORTH ABOVE, OR SUCH OTHER ADDRESS AS SHALL HAVE PREVIOUSLY BEEN COMMUNICATED TO US BY REGISTERED OR CERTIFIED MAIL. WITHIN THIRTY DAYS AFTER SUCH MAILING, YOU SHALL APPEAR OR ANSWER TO SUCH SUMMONS, COMPLAINT OR OTHER PROCESS.**

SHOULD YOU FAIL TO APPEAR OR ANSWER WITHIN SAID THIRTY DAY PERIOD, YOU SHALL BE DEEMED IN DEFAULT AND JUIDGMENT MAY BE ENTERED BY US AGAINST YOU FOR THE AMOUNT AS DEMANDED IN ANY SUMMONS, COMPLAINT OR OTHER PROCESS SO SERVED. In the event we shall retain attorneys for the purpose of enforcing the performance, payment or collection of any of the Obligations, then and in that event you agree to pay the fees of such attorneys, plus any and all expenses and disbursements incurred in connection therewith and/or incidental thereto. Our books and records shall be admissible as prima facie evidence of the status of the account between us. The use of "including" or "include" means "including (or "include"), without limitation." The use of "or" means "and/or" if the context so permits or requires. The term "satisfactory to us" as used herein shall mean "satisfactory to us in our sole and absolute discretion". You will not seek advice or counsel from us or any of our representatives with respect to the management or operation of your business and if you deem such advice or counsel to have been offered, directly or indirectly, you will evaluate it and act or decline to act upon it based upon your own analysis and/or the advice or counsel of your own independent expert(s) or consultant(s). You agree that there is no fiduciary relationship between us or our representatives and you or any other entity, affiliated or controlled by you, and that you will not seek or attempt to establish any such fiduciary relationship. You hereby expressly waive any right to assert, now or in the future, that there was or is a fiduciary relationship between you and us and/or our representatives in any action, proceeding or claim for damages. It is necessary in the ordinary course of business that we exchange information concerning our factored clients with other creditors including, without limitation, exchanging information with the credit departments of other lenders, factors, businesses and trade associations and, in connection with same, you agree that you have authorized such exchange of information and you hereby expressly waive any right to assert a breach of confidentiality arising from such exchange of information. If any provision of this Agreement shall for any reason be held invalid or unenforceable, such invalidity or unenforceability shall not affect any other provisions hereof, and this Agreement shall be construed as if such invalid or unenforceable provision had never been contained herein. This Agreement shall be binding upon and inure to the benefit of each of us and our respective heirs, executors, administrators, successors and assigns, provided, however, that you may not assign this Agreement or your rights hereunder without our prior written consent.

14. DEFINITIONS:

As used in this Agreement, these terms shall have the following meanings which shall be applicable to both the singular and plural forms of such terms.

"**Accounts**" shall have the meaning set forth in Article 9 of the UCC.

"**Affiliate**" of a Person shall mean any entity controlling, controlled by, or under common control with, the Person and the term "controlling" and such variations thereof shall mean ownership of a majority of the voting power of a Person, or the contractual power to control such Person's affairs.

"**Agreement**" shall mean this Factoring Agreement, as amended, modified or supplemented.

"**Availability under a Credit Line**" shall mean the unused amount of a Credit Line.

"**Bank**" shall mean JPMorgan Chase Bank or any successor thereto.

"**Base Commission**" shall have the meaning set forth in Section 6.1 hereof.

"**Business Day**" shall mean a day on which we and major banks in New York City are open for the regular transaction of business.

"**Chattel Paper**" shall have the meaning set forth in Article 9 of the UCC.

"**Collateral**" shall mean any property or rights in property whenever arising which now or hereafter secure any of the Obligations.

"**Contract Period**" shall mean (i) the consecutive _______ month period following the last day of the month in which the Effective Date falls; and (ii) each consecutive _____ month period thereafter.

"**Contract Year**" shall mean the consecutive _____ month period following the last day of the month in which the Effective Date falls and each consecutive _____ month period thereafter.

"**Credit Approval**" shall mean either (i) a notice from us to you, in writing or by such electronic means as may be designated by us, that we have approved all or a portion of an Order; or (ii) Availability under a Credit Line.

"**Credit Approved Receivable**" shall mean a Receivable for which we have assumed the Credit Risk.

"**Credit Line**" shall mean a line of credit, established by us and communicated to you in writing or by such electronic means as may be designated by us to you, granting approval for sales by you or rendition of services by you to a Customer up to a specified aggregate amount.

"**Credit Risk**" shall mean the risk of loss resulting from a Customer's failure to pay a Credit Approved Receivable on the due date solely because of the Customer's financial inability to make such payment.

"**CR Receivable**" shall mean any Receivable which is not a Credit Approved Receivable.

"**Current Assets**" shall mean your cash, Receivables and Inventory provided, however, that such amounts shall not include any amounts for any indebtedness owing by any Affiliate to you.

"**Current Liabilities**" shall mean all amounts which would, in conformity with GAAP, be included under current liabilities or on your balance sheet, as at such date, but in any event including the amounts of (a) all indebtedness payable on demand, or at the option of the Person to whom such indebtedness is owed, not more than twelve (12) months after such date, (b) any payments in respect of any indebtedness (whether installment, serial, maturity, sinking fund payment or otherwise) required to be made not more than twelve (12) months after such date, (c) all reserves in respect of liabilities or indebtedness payable on demand or, at the option of the Person to whom such indebtedness is owed, not more than twelve (12) months after such date, the validity of which is not contested to such date, (d) all accruals for federal or other taxes measured by income payable within twelve (12) months of such date and (e) all outstanding indebtedness to us.

"**Customer**" shall mean any Person obligated on a Receivable.

"**Default**" shall mean the occurrence of any of the following events: (1.1.1.1.) nonpayment when due of any amount payable on any of the Obligations; (1.1.1.2.) failure to perform any agreement or meet any obligation in this Agreement or in any agreement out of which any of the Obligations arose; (1.1.1.3.) breach or failure to continue to be true and accurate in all respects of any covenants, representation, warranty or agreement whenever made by you to us, whether pursuant to this Agreement or otherwise; (1.1.1.4.) default by you in repayment, when due, of any indebtedness now or hereafter owed for monies borrowed from anyone other than us; (1.1.1.5.) any statement, or warranty of yours made orally or in writing or in any other writing in or in connection with this Agreement or statement at any time furnished or made by you to us is untrue in any respect as of the date furnished or made; (1.1.1.6.) suspension of the operation of your business; (1.1.1.7.) any Obligor becomes insolvent or unable to pay debts as they mature, makes an assignment for the benefit of creditors, or a proceeding is instituted by or against any Obligor alleging that such Obligor is insolvent or unable to pay debts as they mature, or a petition under any provision of Title 11 of the United States Code, as amended, is brought by or against any Obligor; (1.1.1.8.) death of any Obligor who was a natural person, or death or withdrawal of any partner of any Obligor which is a partnership, or death or withdrawal of any member or any Obligor which is a limited liability company, or dissolution, merger or consolidation of any Obligor which is a corporation or limited liability company (1.1.1.9.) sale, transfer or exchange, either directly or indirectly, of a controlling stock interest of any Obligor which is a corporation or a controlling membership interest of any Obligor which is a limited liability company; (1.1.1.10.) termination or withdrawal of any guaranty of the Obligations or failure of a Person who has executed such a guaranty, to provide to us, no later than 5 days following the anniversary of the Effective Date in each year, a financial statement, signed by such Person, that is satisfactory to us as to form and that reflects, as of such anniversary of such Effective Date, a net worth (in the case of an individual) or equity (in the case of any other Person) that is not less than 90% of the net worth or equity shown on the last financial statement provided to us by such Person; (1.1.1.11.) appointment of a receiver for any collateral pledged for the Obligations or for any of your property, or the property of any Obligor, in which we have an interest; (1.1.1.12.) the Pension Benefit Guaranty Corporation shall commence proceedings under Section 4042 of the Employee Retirement Income Security Act of 1974 (ERISA) to terminate any of your employee pension benefit plans; (1.1.1.13.) we, in good faith, deem the prospect of your payment or performance of the Obligations to have been impaired; or (1.1.1.14.) we deem ourselves insecure.

"**Default Rate**" shall mean the rate which is ____ percent (___%) per annum in excess of the Overadvance Rate .

"**Deposit Account**" shall have the meaning set forth in Article 9 of the UCC

"Deposit Date" shall mean with respect to a payment of a Receivable from or on behalf of a Customer, (i) in the case of a payment that is received by a banking institution and deposited into our account with it, the date such banking institution makes such deposit into our account; and (ii) in all other cases, the date that the payment is actually received by us; provided, however that, if a payment is deposited into our account by a banking institution or received by us on or after 12:00 noon on any day, the Deposit Date calculated pursuant to clauses (i) and (ii) shall be the following Business Day.

"**Dispute**" shall mean (i) any dispute, claim, offset, defense, counterclaim or any other reason for nonpayment of all or a portion of any Receivable (including, merchandise returns) other than a Customer's financial inability to pay, regardless of whether the same is in an amount greater than, equal to or less than the Receivable concerned, whether bona fide or not, and regardless of whether the same, in part or whole, relates to an unpaid Receivable or any other Receivable; and (ii) an act of God, force majeure, the acts of restraint of public authorities whether domestic or foreign, civil strife, war or currency restrictions or fluctuations resulting in nonpayment of all or any portion of any Receivable.

“**Documents**” shall have the meaning set forth in Article 9 of the UCC.

“**Effective Date**” shall mean the date specified on the upper right portion of the first page of this Agreement.

“**Early Termination Fee**” shall mean the amount that you and we agree will compensate us for the damages we will sustain if this contract is terminated by you prior to the end of a Contract Period or by us due to a Default by you or automatically as the result of the filing by or against you of a petition under any provision of Title 11 of the United States Code. The Early Termination Fee, which you and we have agreed represents a reasonable approximation of the amount of such damages (due to the impossibility of calculating such amount in advance), shall be equal to, whichever is greater, (i) 100% of the average of all fees and charges payable by you to us under Sections 6.1, 6.2, 6.3 and 7.3 of this Agreement each month during the portion of the then current Contract Period that had elapsed prior to the date of such termination or filing of such petition, multiplied by the number of whole or partial calendar months remaining during the unexpired portion of such Contract Period; or (ii) the minimum factoring commission pursuant to Section 6.3 hereof, for the then current Contract Period.

“**Eligible Inventory**” shall mean inventory of finished goods on premises (or in a warehouse) within the continental United States) for which we have obtained such agreements with the lessors of such premises (or the owners or operators of such warehouse) as may be acceptable to us in our sole discretion, valued at the lower of cost or market, free and clear of all customs duty and other liens, charges or claims (with the exception of claims for rent, warehouse or storage charges that are not past due), and in which we have a first and only perfected security interest, and which is acceptable to us in our sole discretion, and at all times shall be acceptable in all respects in our sole discretion. In determining eligibility, we may, but need not, rely on your designations of inventory furnished to us but reliance thereon, from time to time, shall not be deemed to limit our discretionary right to determine and/or revise standards of eligibility at any time. In general, inventory shall not be deemed eligible unless it complies in all respects with the representations, covenants and warranties provided herein and on designations of inventory furnished to us from time to time.

"**Eligible Receivables**" shall mean, at the time of the calculation thereof all Receivables less (i) any Receivables subject to a Dispute, (ii) any CR Receivables, (iii) any Receivables owing from a Customer whose total obligations to you exceed _____ percent (___%) of all Eligible Receivables; and (iv) any Receivables which we in our sole discretion deem not to be Eligible Receivables.

"**GAAP**" shall mean generally accepted accounting principles in the United States of America as in effect from time to time as set forth in the opinions and pronouncements of the Accounting Principles Board and the American Institute of Certified Public Accountants and the statements and pronouncements of the Financial Accounting Standards Board which are applicable to the circumstances as of the date of the determination consistently applied.

"**General Intangibles**" shall have the meaning set forth in Article 9 of the UCC (and shall include tradenames, trademarks, tradestyles, service marks, copyrights and patents and all your rights and claims against us hereunder or otherwise).

"**Guarantor**" shall mean any Person, other than you, liable primarily or secondarily, directly or indirectly, on any of the Obligations.

"**Initial Interest Rate**" shall have the meaning set forth in Section 7.3 hereof.

"**Instruments**" shall have the meaning set forth in Article 9 of the UCC.

"**Inventory**" shall have the meaning set forth in Article 9 of the UCC.

"**Investment Property**" shall have the meaning set forth in Article 9 of the UCC.

"**Letter of Credit Rights**" shall have the meaning set forth in Article 9 of the UCC.

"**Net Amount of Receivables**" shall mean the gross amount of Receivables, less maximum discount, less returns, less credits or allowances of any nature at any time issued, owing, granted or outstanding, and less also our commission as set forth herein.

"**Obligations**" shall mean all obligations, advances, liabilities and indebtedness of you or your Affiliates to us or any of our Affiliates, however evidenced, arising under this Agreement, under any other or supplemental financing provided to you or an Affiliate, or independent hereof or thereof, whether now existing or incurred from time to time hereafter and whether before or after termination hereof, absolute or contingent, joint or several, matured or unmatured, direct or indirect, primary or secondary, liquidated or unliquidated, and whether arising directly or indirectly or acquired from others (whether acquired outright, by assignment, unconditionally or as collateral security from another and including, participations or interest obligations to others), and including, all of our charges, commissions, fees, interest, expenses, costs and attorneys' fees chargeable to you in connection therewith, and all of your obligations to us as an indemnitor pursuant to the terms of this Agreement.

"**Obligor**" shall mean you and each other Person (including, any Guarantor or direct or indirect provider of collateral) primarily or secondarily, directly or indirectly, liable on, or providing collateral for, any of the Obligations.

"**Order**" shall mean any purchase order or equivalent document for the sale by you of goods or the rendition by you of services.

"**Overadvance Rate**" shall mean the rate which is _____ percent (___%) per annum in excess of the Initial Interest Rate as adjusted pursuant to Section 7.3 hereof.

"**Payment Date**" with respect to a Receivable shall mean the date which is ___ Business Days after the Deposit Date thereof.

"**Permitted Lien**" shall mean a lien or security interest to which we have specifically consented in writing, subject to any limitation set forth in such writing.

"**Person**" shall mean any individual, sole proprietorship, partnership, joint venture, trust, non-registered organization, association, corporation, limited liability company, government or any subdivision, agency or political subdivision thereof or any other entity.

"**Prime Rate**" shall mean the rate of interest from time to time publicly announced in New York City by the Bank as its prime rate. The Prime Rate may not be the lowest or best rate charged by the Bank.

"**Proceeds**" shall mean all proceeds (as set forth in Article 9 of the UCC), products, rents and profits of or from any and all of the Collateral and, to the extent not otherwise included in the foregoing; (i) all payments under any insurance, indemnity, warranty or guaranty with respect to any of the collateral, (ii) all payments in connection with any requisition, condemnation, seizure or forfeiture with respect to any of the Collateral, (iii) all claims and rights to recover for any past, present or future infringement or dilution of or injury to any Collateral; and (iv) all other amounts from time to time paid or payable under or with respect to any of the Collateral, including licensing and royalty fees.

"**Receivable Availability**" shall have the meaning set forth in Section 7.2 hereof.

"**Receivables**" shall mean all Accounts, Instruments, Chattel Paper, Documents, Investment Property and General Intangibles arising from your sales of Inventory or performance of services, and the Proceeds thereof, and all Supporting Obligations, whether now existing or hereafter created.

"**Reserves**" shall mean any set asides, reductions or reserves which we may establish, from time to time, in our sole option and in our sole discretion in connection with any financial accommodations which we may make available to you in connection with this Agreement.

"**Special Account Schedule**" shall mean a schedule issued, from time to time, listing thereon surcharge commissions applicable to Receivables owing from the Customers listed thereon.

"**Standard Examiner Rate**" shall mean the per diem rate per examiner established by us from time to time. The Standard Examiner Rate on the date hereof is $____.

"**Supporting Obligations**" shall have the meaning set forth in Article 9 of the UCC.

"**Tangible Net Worth**" shall mean (a) the aggregate amount of all of your assets as may be properly classified as such in accordance with GAAP, excluding such other assets as are properly classified as intangible assets under GAAP, less (b) the aggregate amount of all of your liabilities (excluding liabilities subordinated to us) determined in accordance with GAAP.

"**UCC**" shall mean the Uniform Commercial Code as the same may be in effect (subject to revision, from time to time) in the State of New York.

"**Working Capital**" shall mean the amount, if any, by which Current Assets exceed Current Liabilities.

YOU ACKNOWLEDGE THAT WE HAVE ADVISED YOU TO CONSULT WITH AN ATTORNEY PRIOR TO YOUR EXECUTION OF THIS AGREEMENT.

FACTOR

By:______________________

AGREED:

ABC COMPANY, INC.

By:______________________
Name: ____________________
Title: ____________________

Courtesy of Richard Reinis, Stephtoe & Johnson LLP

APPENDIX N

SAMPLE US DESIGN PATENT, CROCS

US00D517789S

(12) **United States Design Patent** (10) **Patent No.: US D517,789 S**
Seamans (45) **Date of Patent: ** Mar. 28, 2006**

(54) **FOOTWEAR**

(75) Inventor: **Scott Seamans**, Boulder, CO (US)

(73) Assignee: **Crocs, Inc.**, Niwot, CO (US)

(**) Term: **14 Years**

(21) Appl. No.: **29/206,427**

(22) Filed: **May 28, 2004**

Related U.S. Application Data

(63) Continuation-in-part of application No. 10/803,569, filed on Mar. 17, 2004, which is a continuation-in-part of application No. 10/602,416, filed on Jun. 23, 2003, and a continuation-in-part of application No. 10/603,126, filed on Jun. 23, 2003.

(51) **LOC (8) Cl.** **02-99**
(52) **U.S. Cl.** **D2/969**
(58) **Field of Classification Search** D2/903, D2/916–918, 919, 969, 926, 932; 36/4, 8.1, 36/10, 11.5
See application file for complete search history.

(56) **References Cited**

U.S. PATENT DOCUMENTS

1,392,350 A		10/1921	O'Brien	
2,180,924 A		11/1939	Dunbar	
2,470,089 A		5/1949	Booth	
3,407,517 A	*	10/1968	Gessner	36/11.5
3,698,107 A		10/1972	Fukuoka	
4,032,611 A		6/1977	Fukuoka	
4,100,685 A		7/1978	Dassler	
4,408,401 A		10/1983	Seidel et al.	
4,476,600 A		10/1984	Seidel et al.	
4,888,887 A		12/1989	Solow	
4,967,750 A		11/1990	Cherniak	
D350,021 S	*	8/1994	Stein	D2/969
5,369,895 A		12/1994	Hammerschmidt	
5,438,767 A		8/1995	Stein	
5,528,841 A		6/1996	Pozzobon	
5,561,919 A		10/1996	Gill	
D381,794 S		8/1997	Gelli	

(Continued)

FOREIGN PATENT DOCUMENTS

CA	2375957	9/2002
EP	0 802 039 A2	10/1997
EP	0 802 040 A2	10/1997
EP	0 802 041 A2	10/1997
EP	0 884 005 A1	12/1998
GB	2322286	8/1998

OTHER PUBLICATIONS

http://web.archive.org/web/19980420230857/www.birkenstock.com/featprof.htm (3 pages).
Birkenstock®, Spring & Summer 2003 Catalog, Birkenstock Orthopadie GMbh, Germany (82 pages).
Cindy MacDonald, *The Entrepreneurs: they're bilingual, multicultural and talented. Distance and language present no barriers to Quebec plastics processors and mold makers as the province's plastics industry continues to increase its level of exports and welcome new companies*, Canadian Plastics, O'99, v. 57(10), pp. 35–50 (9 pages).
Comfortable Walking, Italian Technology, Oct. 1999, n. 3, p. 168 (abstract, 1 page).

(Continued)

Primary Examiner—Dominc Simone
(74) *Attorney, Agent, or Firm*—Faegre & Benson, LLP

(57) **CLAIM**

The ornamental design for footwear, as shown and described.

DESCRIPTION

FIG. **1** is a front perspective view.
FIG. **2** is a right side view.
FIG. **3** is a left side view.
FIG. **4** is a front view.
FIG. **5** is a rear view.
FIG. **6** is a top view; and.
FIG. **7** is a bottom view.
The broken line showing of the sole and surface treatment of the upper is for illustrative purpose only and forms no part of the claim design.

1 Claim, 4 Drawing Sheets

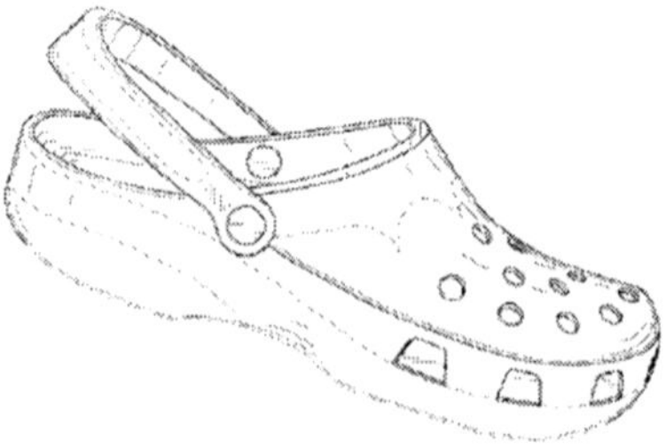

Courtesy of Darrell G. Mottley, Banner & Witcoff Ltd.

APPENDIX O

SAMPLE US DESIGN PATENT, HATFIELD

US00D374551S

United States Patent [19]

Hatfield

[11] **Patent Number: Des. 374,551**

[45] **Date of Patent: *** Oct. 15, 1996**

[54] **PORTON OF A SHOE UPPER**

[75] Inventor: **Tinker L. Hatfield**, Portland, Oreg.

[73] Assignee: **Nike, Inc.**, Beaverton, Oreg.

[*] Notice: The portion of the term of this patent subsequent to Sep. 5, 2009, has been disclaimed.

[**] Term: **14 Years**

[21] Appl. No.: **39,109**

[22] Filed: **May 17, 1995**

Related U.S. Application Data

[62] Division of Ser. No. 32,079, Dec. 2, 1994, Pat. No. Des. 361,885.

[52] **U.S. Cl.** **D2/969**

[58] **Field of Search** D2/969, 970, 902, D2/910, 907, 912; 36/45, 50.1, 83, 84, 113, 114, 132, 89

[56] **References Cited**

U.S. PATENT DOCUMENTS

D. 324,129	2/1992	Hatfield	D2/970
D. 325,287	4/1992	Strauss .	
D. 339,449	9/1993	Hatfield .	
D. 342,148	12/1993	Dahlsten	D2/969
D. 345,246	3/1994	Greene	D2/978
D. 346,272	4/1994	Cessor	D2/970
D. 346,899	5/1994	Hatfield	D2/970
D. 347,109	5/1994	Avar	D2/970
D. 347,317	5/1994	Avar	D2/970
D. 347,519	6/1994	Worthington	D2/970
D. 347,938	6/1994	Smith	D2/970
D. 349,396	8/1994	Hatfield	D2/970
D. 349,807	8/1994	Hatfield et al.	D2/970
D. 351,058	10/1994	Hatfield et al.	D2/969
D. 351,275	10/1994	Hatfield et al.	D2/970
D. 352,389	11/1994	Close et al.	D2/970
D. 354,163	1/1995	Hatfield	D2/970
D. 354,391	1/1995	Hatfield et al.	D2/970
D. 361,885	9/1995	Hatfield	D2/970
D. 364,729	12/1995	Teague	D2/970

OTHER PUBLICATIONS

Nike Spring 1994 Catalog, published Jun. 1993, p. 22.
Nike Fall 1993 Catalog, published Dec. 1992, p. 20.
Nike Spring 1992 Catalog, published May 1991, p. 30.
Nike Fall 1992 Catalog, published Dec. 1991, p. 22.
Nike Fall 1991 Catalog, published Dec. 1990, p. 32.
Nike Fall 1990 Catalog, published Dec. 1989, p. 30.
Nike Spring 1990 Catalog, published Jun. 1989, p. 22.

Primary Examiner—Doris V. Coles
Attorney, Agent, or Firm—Banner & Allegretti, Ltd.

[57] **CLAIM**

The ornamental design for a portion of a shoe upper, as shown and described.

DESCRIPTION

FIG. **1** is a side elevational view of one side of a portion of a shoe upper showing my new design;
FIG. **2** is a side elevational view of the other thereof;
FIG. **3** is a front elevational view thereof;
FIG. **4** is a rear elevational view thereof; and,
FIG. **5** is a top plan view thereof.
The broken line showing the shoe sole and the disclaimed portion of the shoe upper in FIGS. **1**—**5** is for illustrative purposes and forms no part of the claimed design.

1 Claim, 3 Drawing Sheets

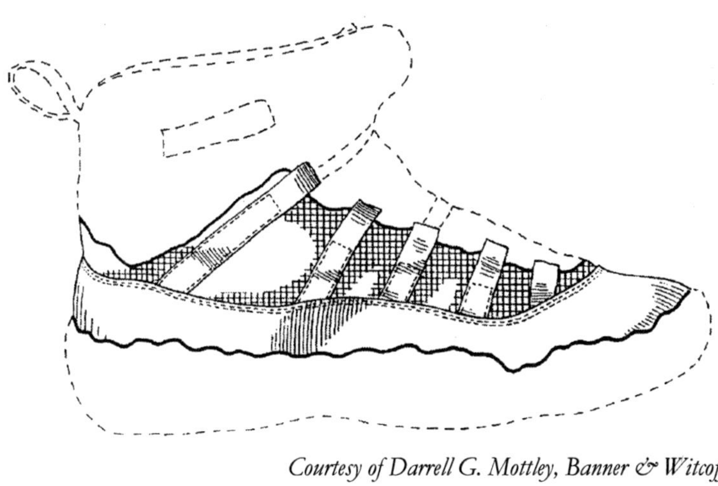

Courtesy of Darrell G. Mottley, Banner & Witcoff Ltd.

APPENDIX P

MODEL TERM SHEET FOR TRADEMARK LICENSING AND DESIGN SERVICES

[__, 201_]

This Term Sheet summarizes the principal terms of a proposed Trademark Licensing Agreement between [__________] ("**Company**") and [__ ______] ("**Licensee**"). The Confidentiality provisions of this Term Sheet shall be binding on both parties. No other legally binding obligations will be created until a definitive agreement is executed and delivered by both parties. This Term Sheet shall be governed in all respects by the laws of the State of New York.

Trademark:	XXX (the "**Trademark**").
Product Categories:	[State the categories of products to which the Trademark may be applied.] (the "**Products**").
Exclusivity:	[Consider whether the use of the trademark will be exclusive for any products or territory.]
Geographic Scope:	[State the territory in which the trademark may be used.]
Trademark License:	Company will grant a license to Licensee to use the Trademark in connection with (i) the manufacture of Products, (ii) marketing the Products in the Territory, and (iii) the distribution and sale of Products in the Territory.

Design Services: Company shall assist Licensee in creating new, exclusive and distinctive Products by: (i) providing input and recommendations on style, quality, fabrications and fit and color for the Products, and (ii) reviewing and approving the manufactured Products.

Sales: The Products will be sold only [at Licensee retail locations and online through Licensee's branded website] OR [to wholesalers and retailers approved by Company].

With the prior approval of Company, on a case-by-case basis as to both the proposed customer and the proposed Products to be included, Licensee may undertake cut-up programs in accordance with industry standards.

Licensee shall clearly and permanently "red line" the label(s) of any Products to be sold as a "second" or "irregular" to so indicate.

Royalty: [__]% of net sales (less returns, discounts). Payable quarterly.

Advances on royalties of $[______] per month.

Bonus/Additional Royalty: Additional royalties of [_]% (i.e., a total of [__]%) will be paid on [net sales in excess of $[______]] [sales of products on the first floor of key retailers as agreed by the parties].

Minimum Sales: $[______] per fiscal quarter.

Design/Services Fee: $[______] payable [quarterly] in advance.

Information Reporting: Licensee shall provide Company with (i) monthly sales updates, and (ii) quarterly statements certified by an officer of Licensee detailing net sales and the calculation of royalties for such quarter.

Audit Rights:	Company shall be permitted to audit Licensee's books. If net sales are understated (i) by 2% or more, Licensee shall pay the cost of the audit, (ii) by 5% or more, Company shall be permitted to terminate the license, and (iii) interest shall be payable on any resulting underpayment of royalties.
Term:	[3] years. [Consider option to renew.]
Sell-Off Period:	Licensee will have the right to sell the inventory to third parties for a period of [60] days after termination or expiry of the definitive agreement, with Company retaining right of first refusal. Company will be entitled to the Products remaining at the conclusion of the sell-off period.
Termination:	For material breaches which are not cured within 15 days after notice is given. By Company if Licensee fails to [achieve the minimum sales targets] OR [produce and market the Products in reasonable commercial quantities for a period of 120 days].
Quality Control:	All Products shall be of a quality and workmanship at least as high as the "top line" of similar products being sold by Licensee at the time of execution of the definitive agreement. Company shall have the right to review and approve (i) proposed designs for Products in the design phase, and (ii) samples of Products and sample collections of Products. Licensee shall forward Product designs and samples showing the representative quality of Product, Product manufacturing, and the intended use of the Trademark to Licensee for approval. In the case of disapproval, the Parties shall work together in good

faith to attempt to modify any such materials so that they are acceptable to Company.

Image Protection: Licensee shall not do anything or suffer anything to be done, whether under or in connection with the Agreement or otherwise, that, directly or indirectly, may reduce or dilute the value of the Trademark or that, directly or indirectly, may disparage or dilute, detract from or reflect adversely upon the reputation, prestige and image of Company, [INDIVIDUAL DESIGNER] or the Trademark.

Marketing Expenditure: Licensee agrees to spend at least $[______] per annum on advertising and promotional support for the Products. Company must approve any and all advertising, packaging, labeling and promotion of the Products or the program, uses of the Trademark or the image of DESIGNER and any other publicly distributed material bearing the Trademark or DESIGNER's image.

Display: Licensee will provide a separate display for Products in a prominent area of each store where Products are sold and on Licensee's website. The design of such display must be approved by Company and such displays and their placement within stores and on the website is subject to periodic compliance checks by Company.

Appearances: Subject to DESIGNER's schedule and reasonable availability, DESIGNER shall assist in promoting and publicizing the Products by attending and participating in a reasonable number of events (i.e. photo shoots, filming of television commercials), not to exceed [___] days, including travel days, per annum. Such promotional appearances shall be held in such place(s) as the parties mutually agree upon. In the event Licensee requests that DESIGNER travel for such appearances, Licensee shall pay for reasonable travel and travel-related expenses incurred by DESIGNER in connection with such meetings.

Business Plan:	Licensee shall, if requested, provide Company with a copy of its business plan regarding exploitation of the Trademark prior to the commencement of each fiscal year of the term.
Intellectual Property Rights:	Company shall retain all rights to the Trademark other than those specifically granted to Licensee in the agreement. [Licensee shall retain rights to the sketches and designs made by Licensee that are used by it in the creation of Products.] [Company shall retain rights to the sketches and designs that it creates for Licensee, but Licensee does not use.] All Products shall bear the Trademark and no items which are substantially similar to the Products shall be sold by Licensee under any trademark or other designation other than the Trademark.
Reps, Warranties, Indemnification:	The definitive agreement will contain customary reps and warranties and indemnification provisions.
Non-Solicit:	Licensee shall not solicit or recruit Licensor employees that have been employed by Licensor within the preceding 12 months.
Governing Law:	The definitive agreement shall be governed by New York law.
Confidentiality:	Neither party will disclose the terms of this Term Sheet to any person other than to its officers, employees, directors, managers and the Company's accountants and attorneys without the written consent of the other party.
Expiration:	This Term Sheet expires 45 days after the date first written above.

IN WITNESS WHEREOF, THIS TERM SHEET HAS BEEN EXECUTED BY THE PARTIES HERETO ON THE DATE FIRST WRITTEN ABOVE.

[LICENSOR]	**[LICENSEE]**
By:________________________________	By:________________________________
__________________	__________________
Name:	Name:
Title:	Title:

Courtesy of Douglas Hand, Hand Baldachin & Amburgey LLP

APPENDIX R

SAMPLE ORGANIZATIONAL CHART

For Closely Held Fashion Company
Engaged in Licensing and Retail Activities

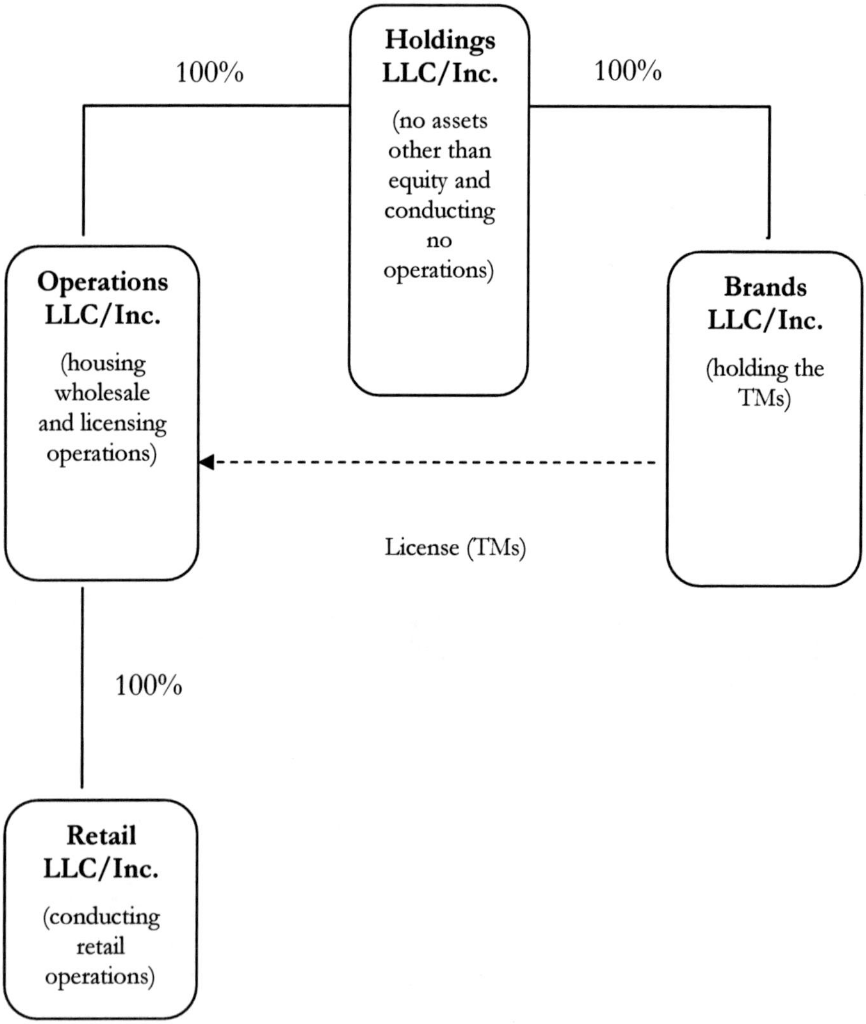

Courtesy of Douglas Hand, Hand Baldachin & Amburgey LLP

APPENDIX R

COLLABORATION DISCUSSION POINTS

1. **Product** Categor(ies)? Creating a new and distinctive line? Exclusivity?
2. **License** of trademark- Any joint use of marks? A new mark? Any affirmative obligation on Licensor (or Designer) to maintain and fight misuses of trademark?
3. **Geographic** scope
4. **Services** rendered? Design, technical direction if requested, Licensor responsible for the cost of merchandise production.
5. **Sales** – only at Licensor retail locations (if so in what environment?) Online? Procedures for close-out sales (redlining).
6. **Royalty**- typical licensing for designer is 4-8% for celebrity is 10%-12% of net sales (less returns, discounts). Advances?
7. **Bonus/Additional Royalty** – above a threshold evincing success
8. **Minimum Sales**– Effectively a minimum royalty as well
9. **Design/Services Fee** – Guaranteed income
10. **Information** reporting- monthly statements on net sales accompany payments. Audit rights.
11. **Term**- 3 years? 5 years?
12. **Termination**- for breaches (failure to reach minimum sales)
13. **Quality control**- fabric requirements, submission of samples before production for Designer approval.
14. **Marketing** expenditure- Advertising and promotional support. PR plan subject to designer signoff. Speed minimum?
15. **Appearances**- How many? Travel? Stipend?

Courtesy of Douglas Hand, Hand Baldachin & Amburgey LLP

APPENDIX S

MELINE FOR INTENT-TO-USE TRADEMARK LICATIONS IN THE UNITED STATES

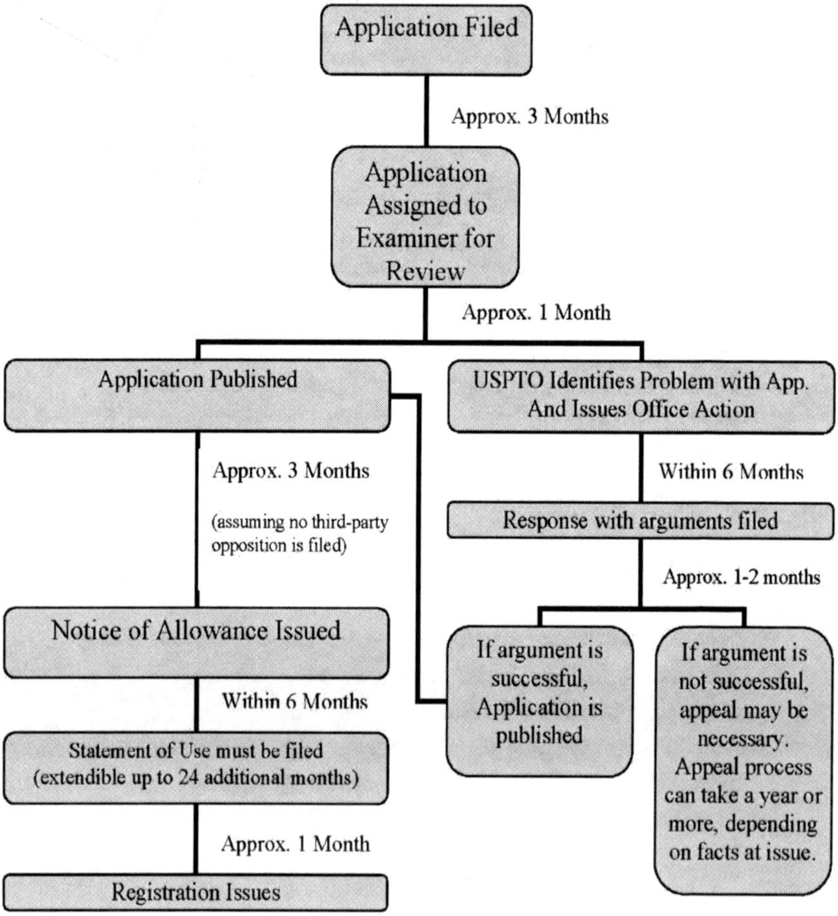

Courtesy of Ann K. Ford, DLA Piper LLP (US)

APPENDIX T

US COPYRIGHT, DESIGN PATENT AND TRADEMARK PROTECTION FOR JEWELRY AND OTHER ACCESSORY DESIGNS

I. Copyright

- Protects designs that are sufficiently creative and artistic.
- Copyrightable works are logos, artwork, or design elements that are stitched, imprinted or embossed onto fabric; and ornamental aspects of jewelry, watches, belts, and handbags.
- Not copyrightable are style, shape, cut, pattern or material of clothing articles and basic utilitarian aspects of jewelry, watches, belts, handbags and other accessories.
- Registration process takes about three months to one year.
- Examples:
    - Reg. No. VA0001111813 for "artwork on handbags, owned by Cappelli Straworld, Inc.
    - Reg. No. VAu000699898 for "belt and buckle collection—Olander Enterprises, Inc.," owned by John N. Olander
    - Reg. No. VA0001664539 for "Marquis Loop Necklace and Earring Set," owned by Rhinestone Jewelry Corporation

II. Design Patent

- Protects the overall aesthetic appearance of a design (i.e., the ornamental design).
    - Designs must be new and sufficiently different from all prior designs.
    - Examples may include ornamental aspects of jewelry, watches, belts, hats, handbags, and rings.

- Registration process takes about one to two years.
- Examples:

  - Patent No. D466,689 for "ornamental design for a handbag," owned by Louis Vuitton Malletier
  - Patent No. D413,815 for "ornamental design for a watch," owned by Tag Heuer

- Utility patents, which protect how an object operates or functions (i.e., functional or utilitarian features), usually cannot be used to protect jewelry or accessory designs unless the design includes some type of mechanical improvement.

III. Trademark

- Protects jewelry or other accessory designs that are inherently distinctive or have acquired secondary meaning in the market (i.e., the design must function as a source identifier).
- Protection extends to the product's name and appearance.
- Registration process takes about one year.
- Examples:

  - Reg. Nos. 3211038 and 3211039 for 3 6 9 12 & Design in Class 14 (watches), owned by Cartier International, N.V.

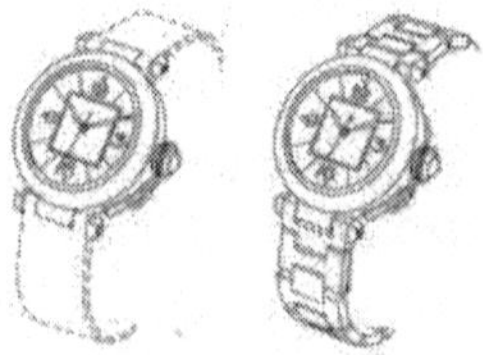

  - Reg. Nos. 3472365 and 3238962 for Design in Classes 18 (wallets, purses, handbags, shoulder bags, clutch bags, and tote bags) and 25

(clothing apparel), owned by Gucci America, Inc.

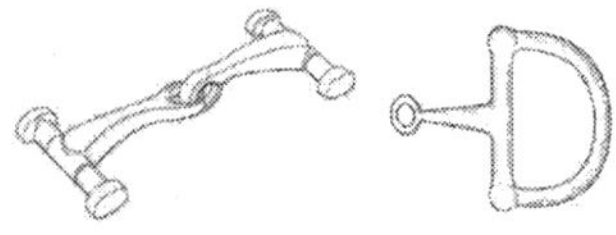

- Reg. No. 3769482 for CC Design in Classes 18 (handbags) and 25 (dresses; gloves; jackets; pants; skirts; tops), owned by Chanel, Inc.

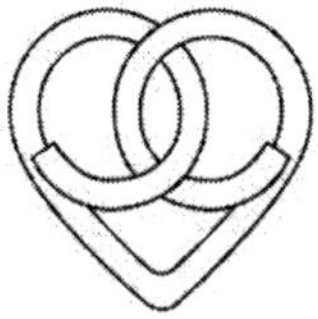

- Reg. No. 3340872 for DAVID YURMAN SIGNATURE HEART COLLECTION in Class 14 (fine jewelry and precious stones), owned by Yurman Studio, Inc.

Please note that copyright, patent and trademark are separate and independent forms of protection. *Yurman v. Studio, Inc. v. Castaneda*, 591 F.Supp. 2d 471 (S.D.N.Y. 2008)(upheld multiple coverage of different aspects of high fashion watch and jewelry designs of Yurman, Cartier, Gucci and Bulgari under the separate laws of design patent, copyright, trademark and trade dress).

Courtesy of Ann K. Ford, DLA Piper LLP (US)

APPENDIX U

IP FLOWCHART

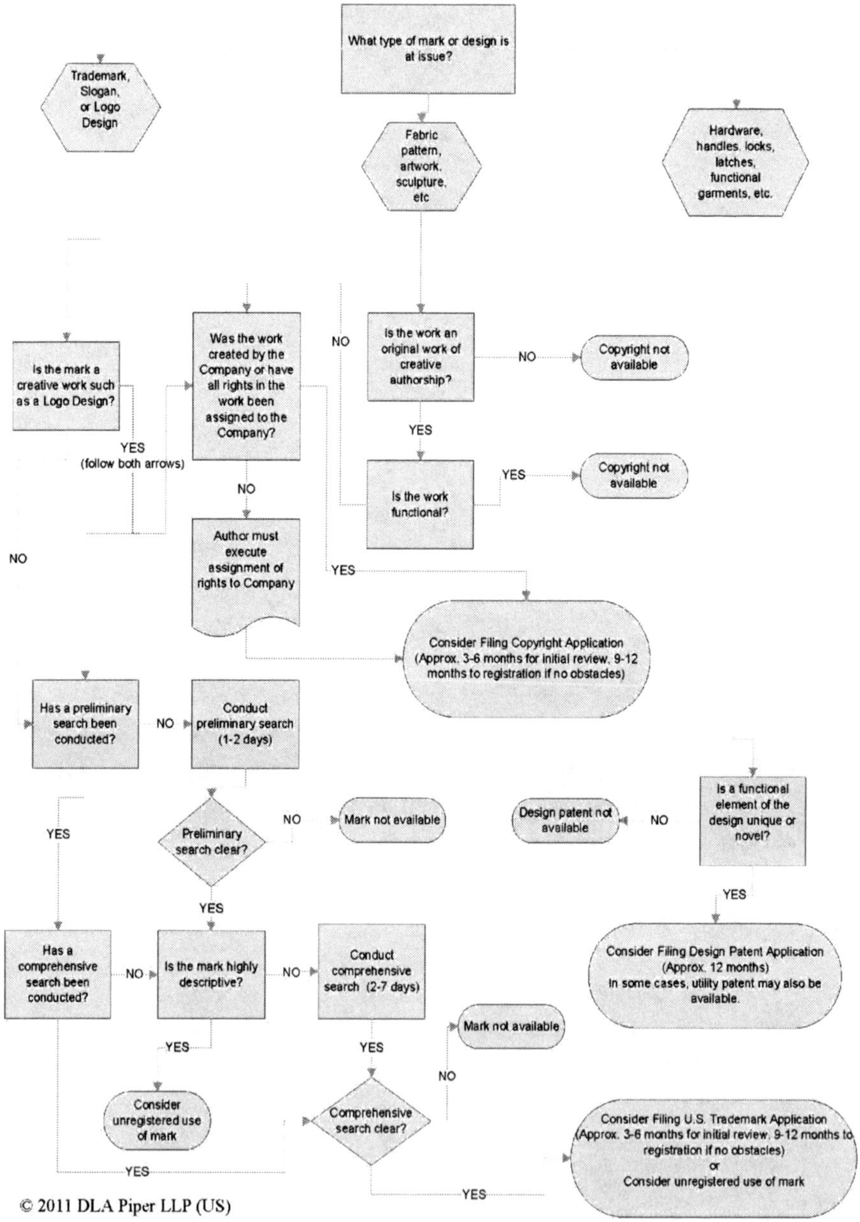

Courtesy of Ann K. Ford, DLA Piper LLP (US)

ASPATORE